D1246894

Philosophical Analysis

PHILOSOPHICAL ANALYSIS

A Collection of Essays

Edited by

MAX BLACK

Essay Index Reprint Series

BOOKS FOR LIBRARIES PRESS
FREEPORT, NEW YORK

Copyright 1950 by Prentice-Hall, Inc.

Reprinted 1971 by arrangement with
Max Black

104
B627p
160741

INTERNATIONAL STANDARD BOOK NUMBER:
0-8369-2214-X

LIBRARY OF CONGRESS CATALOG CARD NUMBER:
78-152158

PRINTED IN THE UNITED STATES OF AMERICA

Preface

These essays are specimens of philosophical analysis, not discussions about the procedures employed; choice of topics and mode of treatment were left to the authors. My hope that they were a good sample of contemporary philosophical activity has been confirmed by their subsequent reception. A much larger collection would have been needed to represent the many philosophers who have made notable contributions to analytical philosophy, but the short bibliography at the end of this volume should serve as a guide to further exploration.

No great importance is attached to the label of "analysis," but it serves well enough to identify philosophers who share a common intellectual heritage and are committed to the clarification of basic philosophical concepts. It has been said that "clarity is not enough," but it will be time enough to worry about that when clarity is generally valued more highly than mystification.

Max Black

Ithaca, N. Y.

Contents

Philosophical Analysis

Introduction

MAX BLACK

Nothing of any value can be said on method except through examples; but now, at the end of our course, we may collect certain general maxims which may possibly be a help in acquiring a philosophical habit of mind and a guide in looking for solutions of philosophical problems.[1]

I

The essays which follow might provide an "ostensive definition" of "philosophical analysis." And if a formal analysis of philosophical analysis is feasible, here, at any rate, are sufficient materials for the exercise. Some readers may be content to enjoy good craftsmanship in regions where logical order and clarity of exposition are hard to achieve, without demanding further dissection in the form of meta-analysis. But others will plead for something more than a parade of instances—some demonstration of an underlying unity of purpose and method in these varied undertakings.

Would it be enough to reply that all the writers are engaged "in criticizing and clarifying notions which are apt to be regarded as fundamental and accepted uncritically"?[2] This is

---

[1] Bertrand Russell, *Our Knowledge of the External World as a Field for Scientific Method in Philosophy* (1914), p. 240.

[2] "The most important part [of the business of philosophy] consists in criticizing and clarifying notions which are apt to be regarded as fundamental and accepted uncritically" (Russell, "Logical Atomism," in *Contempo-*

1

accurate, but not illuminating. For "criticism" and "clarification" are no less equivocal than "analysis"[3] and are as hard to clarify.

It may help to be reminded that many philosophers who might allow themselves to be described as "analysts" have been strongly influenced by the work of Russell, Moore, and Wittgenstein. For while all three have been engaged in "clarification of meaning" they have done so in different and distinctive ways; and the resulting divergences in conceptions of philosophical method have not yet been reconciled. This makes it hard to give any simple account of what is meant today by "philosophical analysis."

Instead of trying, where so many have failed, to analyze analysis, I shall confine myself to some informal comments upon the work of Russell, Moore, and Wittgenstein; these may serve to recall the complexity of the recent historical background and act as a deterrent against treating "Philosophical Analysis" as a "School" having well defined articles of association.

II

Russell's conception of philosophical method (as described in his writings of the period 1910-1924[4]) calls for *the application of scientific method to philosophy.*[5] The intention is to use the empirical data

---

rary British Philosophy; Personal Statements [first series, 1924], p. 379). Cp. C. D. Broad: "Thus there is both need and room for a science which shall try to analyse and define the concepts which are used in daily life and the special sciences" ("Critical and Speculative Philosophy," in *ibid.*, p. 83). And again "The task of Critical Philosophy is to take these proportions which we uncritically assume in science and daily life and to subject them to criticism" (*ibid.*, p. 84).

[3] For some discussions of different senses of "analysis" see M. Black, "Relations between Logical Positivism and the Cambridge School of Analysis," *Erkenntnis* (*Journal of Unified Science*), VIII (1938), 24-35; A. E. Duncan-Jones and A. J. Ayer, "Does Philosophy Analyze Common Sense?" (Symposium), *Arist. Soc. Proc.*, suppl. vol., XVI (1937), 139-176; A. C. Ewing, "Two Kinds of Analysis," *Analysis*, II (1934-5), 60-64; L. S. Stebbing, "The Method of Analysis in Metaphysics," *Arist. Soc. Proc.*, XXXIII (1932-3), 65-94.

[4] Especially in *The Problems of Philosophy, Our Knowledge of the External World,* "The Philosophy of Logical Atomism," and "Logical Atomism." His "Reply to Criticisms," in *The Philosophy of Bertrand Russell* (1944), shows his conception of philosophy to have remained unchanged in essentials.

[5] "Philosophical knowledge . . . does not differ essentially from scientific knowledge; there is no special source of wisdom which is open to philosophy but not to science, and the results obtained by philosophy are not radically different from those obtained by science" (*Problems of Philosophy* [1912], p. 233). At about this time Russell was advocating a "philosophy guided by scientific method" (*Mysticism*

which are the subject matter of the assertions of science and "common sense," and to organize them by procedures of deductive and inductive inference agreeing substantially with those already used in the special sciences. Philosophy, on this view, will not differ from science either in data or modes of argument; but it will be more general in its interests and, above all, *stricter* in reasoning. So although we begin by accepting the assertions of common sense and science as trustworthy *on the whole* (on the common sense ground that they are more likely to be correct than the principles of any known philosophical system[6]), we expect to discover much intermingled error. This must be expelled by "philosophical criticism." In this way philosophy is "stricter" than science or common sense, which are content to *use* what "*passes* for knowledge," without further examination.

The epistemological errors of laymen and scientists are of two kinds: use of unproved "assumptions" and reference to "postulated" or "inferred" entities. Scientific assertions are defective both in evidence and in content: they could not be known to be true unless certain unexamined and even unformulated principles ("assumptions") had been shown to be true; and they refer to unobservables ("postulated" entities) which *could not* be objects of knowledge. Thus the two kinds of error are interdependent.

The chief philosophical method for purifying what merely passes for knowledge is variously called by Russell "methodical" and "systematic doubt."[7] I doubt that a philosopher can doubt at will; and perhaps even Descartes would find systematic doubt, according to Russell's prescriptions, too strenuous a mental exercise. But the intended outcome is clear enough: we are to "doubt" all except the indubitable, i.e., the "primitive certainties" referring entirely to the

---

and Logic and Other Essays [1918], p. 98) and urging the "importance of applying to philosophical problems certain broad principles of method which have been found successful in the study of scientific questions" (*ibid.*). See also Russell, in *Contemporary British Philosophy* (1924), p. 361.

6 "Physics has a much better chance of being true than has the system of this or that philosopher. To set up a philosophy against physics is rash; philosophers who have done so have always ended in disaster" (Russell, "Reply to Criticisms," in *The Philosophy of Bertrand Russell* [1944], p. 700). Cp. Russell, in *Contemporary British Philosophy* (1924), p. 377.

7 "Descartes' 'methodical doubt' . . . is the kind of criticism which we are asserting to be the essence of philosophy" (*Problems of Philosophy*, p. 235). Cp. *ibid.*, p. 28, and *Our Knowledge of the External World*, pp. 242-244.

objects of "direct acquaintance." And the result would be more congenial to Hume[8] than to Descartes.

If this is the intended result of philosophical criticism, the purge is rigorous indeed, and none of the assertions of science and common sense will survive. But reconstruction is to follow upon criticism. Among the "hard data" resisting the corrosive efforts of systematic doubt are "sensibilia" as well as sense-data; and we are said to be acquainted with universals as well as with particulars. Moreover, the resources of mathematical logic are available for the work of reconstruction. *Principia Mathematica* showed that the "postulated" or "inferred" entities of higher mathematics could be replaced by entities *defined* wholly in terms of a primitive basis of logical notions; a similar program is proposed for the entities, such as material objects and minds, whose existence is merely "assumed" in assertions about the external world. The constructive or synthetic task of philosophy is to replace inferences or assumptions by "logical constructions." When the merely postulated entities have been replaced by those contextually defined wholly in terms of "hard data," there will remain all that deserves to be salvaged of the uncritical assertions of scientists and plain men.

Throughout this campaign of criticism and subsequent reconstruction, the philosopher will have been faithful to science (and the crude premonitions of science known as "common sense") in the methods used; for he will have tried to observe, define, and reason just as scientists do, though with more sustained rigour. Philosophy is a kind of stricter general science—science self-critically aware of its presuppositions, and shorn of all that is mere hypothesis, postulation, or speculation.[9]

---

8 We may say of Russell's philosophy what he said of his own *Inquiry*, that it "results from an attempt to combine a general outlook akin to Hume's with the methods that have grown out of modern logic" (*An Inquiry into Meaning and Truth* [1940], p. 6).

9 I have omitted any discussion of what Russell has called "the epistemological problem" (in *The Philosophy of Bertrand Russell*, p. 703)—partly because I am not sure what it is. A fuller account of Russell's methods would pay close attention to his views about language—but for this see M. Black, "Russell's Philosophy of Language" in *ibid.*, pp. 229-255, which contains numerous references. For a most elaborate analysis of "constructions" see Wisdom's "Logical Constructions," *Mind*, XL (1931), 188-216, 460-475; XLI (1932), 441-464; XLII (1933), 43-66, 186-202. For criticism of Russell's principle of reducibility to acquaintance see, for instance, L. S. Stebbing, *Logical Positivism and Analysis* (British Academy, Auunal Philosophical Lecture, 1933) and M. Black, in *The Philosophy of Bertrand Russell*, pp. 229-255.

This is an impressive, even an exciting, program of work—and I have tried to summarize it sympathetically. Its influence has been all the stronger for its roots in previous philosophical history; the generalization of logic, to which Russell himself contributed so much, promised to mitigate the poverty of earlier versions of empiricism; and the method of "logical constructions" might be expected to blunt the edge of Occam's Razor.

Why are these hopes no longer so widely held? Possibly because it now appears that Russell's attempted reduction of philosophy to science was mistaken in principle and not even in accord with his own practice. It is a mistake to regard the practice of "methodical doubt" or the definition of "logical constructions" as any part of the regular concern of a physicist or a mathematician. The "evidence" for the existence of sense-data is quite unlike the evidence for the existence of atoms; and the "grounds" against accepting tables as "genuine constituents" of truths about the world quite other than the mathematician's objections to the use of undefined terms.

That a radical misconstruction of the relations between philosophy and science vitiates Russell's philosophising is shown by the outcome of his work. For in spite of the initial intention to rely upon science *in the main*, the criteria regulating the investigation lead inexorably to wholesale rejection of scientific method and scientific conclusions. Science, according to Russell, is "at war with itself,"[10] and the terms of the armistice require a sacrifice of the principles which led to the fighting. For we find, after all, that science needs unobservables[11] and that scientific inference does rest upon principles which are unprovable.[12] The consistent conclusion would be a radical scepticism indistinguishable from "solipsism of the momentary present." But to some (though not all) of the writers of the essays which follow, Russell's arguments will appear not so much a proof of scepticism as a *reductio*

---

[10] *Inquiry*, p. 15. (The whole paragraph containing this phrase crystallises what is, in my judgment, basically wrong in Russell's approach.)

[11] "An honest recognition of physics demands recognition of unobserved occurrences" (Russell, in *The Philosophy of Bertrand Russell*, p. 701). The earlier part of the paragraph (and the remarks that precede it) shows that Russell here means "unobserv*able*" rather than "unobserv*ed*."

[12] The best that Russell can say at the end of his investigation of the principles of scientific inference is that "they are known in the sense that we generalize in accordance with them when we use experience to persuade us of a universal proposition" (Russell, *Human Knowledge* [1948], p. 526). Is this any better than Hume's reliance upon custom?

ad absurdum of his conception of philosophical method. It may seem to others, as it seems to me, that Russell has systematically, though unwittingly, misused such crucial terms as "doubt," "evidence," and "inference"; that no "philosophical" evidence can be superior to the evidence acceptable in a court of law or in other everyday contexts; and that Russell's pursuit of the indubitable is a jack-o'-lantern hunt for mathematical demonstration of matters of fact.

No doubt these comments will find favour only with those already persuaded by more detailed examination of Russell's writings, and will seem offensively dogmatic to others who still endorse Russell's program. But it seems to me impossible to maintain that Russell has a philosophically *neutral* method. His proposed methods of analysis and criticism rest upon dubious epistemological and metaphysical views, and to accept his program is to be committed to controversial answers to fundamental philosophical questions.

Now the point of an attempt to treat philosophy as science is to avoid being in this position. By adopting scientific method, philosophers are to learn from scientists and mathematicians how to agree; and steady calculation, guaranteed to produce an acceptable answer, is to replace philosophical disputation. If some such hope as this inspired Russell (as it certainly did the Logical Positivists, who learned so much from him) his program was a failure. The merits of his views on philosophical analysis have to be argued on *philosophical* grounds; and to baptise them as "scientific" can only generate confusion. Those who owe most to Russell's work may still be unable to share his conception of method.

III

Some of the authors of the following essays would find in Moore a corrective to Russell. One reason for Moore's great influence upon the younger philosophers may have been the refreshing contrast between his simplicity and clarity and the pretentious technicality of some of his predecessors. After the intoxication of metaphysics, it is good to look upon the world again as a child might—to be told "After all, this *is* a hand. I have a body, so have you, and there are many other people like both of us who can say the same." And again, most characteristically, "How *absurd* it would be to suggest that we don't *know* all this." The "truisms" which Moore reaffirms (for instance, the long list of them in his famous "Defence of Common Sense"[13]) serve the important purpose of reminding us that "common sense" needs *no* defence. If a philosophical assertion about the unreality of space and time is incompatible with the truth of such assertions as "Your body is *at a distance* from mine" and "I had breakfast *yesterday*," it is the philosophical assertion that has to go. It would be ridiculous for a philosopher to tell me that all human bodies are in physical contact, or that nobody *really* ate breakfast yesterday. The "Common Sense view of the world" is, "in certain fundamental features, *wholly* true."[14]

A summary such as this is a poor substitute for the precision and persuasiveness of Moore's own writing. Yet there is a kind of dogmatism in his work which will continue to bother some of his readers. Careful examination of his essays shows again and again that he fails, or rather does not try, to *argue;* on crucial issues, he seems to attack his opponents by vehement affirmation and reiteration.[15] And this has disturbed philosophers who expect philosophical positions to be demonstrable from a priori premises, or their opponents' mistakes to be refutable by strict argument. But Moore can make us see that there is nothing better to do with common-sense truisms than to *assert* them: if an inveterate metaphysician is consistent enough to deny them—to say it is not certain that he sees a hand, or has a body, or ate breakfast yesterday—*argument* is not going to help. A man may be convicted of "abusing ordinary language," but if he glories in the offense, further persuasion is futile. This is a lesson of great importance; if those who learnt it from Moore remain excessively shy of metaphysics, respect for the "Common Sense view of the world" will at least protect them against some kinds of metaphysical extravagance.

---

13 See G. E. Moore, "A Defence of Common Sense," in *Contemporary British Philosophy* (second series, 1925), pp. 193-223. For criticism, see C. A. Campbell, "Common-Sense Propositions and Philosophical Paradoxes," *Arist. Soc. Proc.*, XLV (1944-5), 1-26; M. Lazerowitz, "Moore's Paradox," in *The Philosophy of G. E. Moore* (1942), pp. 371-393; C. A. Mace, "On How We Know That Material Things Exist," in *ibid.*, pp. 283-298; N. Malcolm, "Moore and Ordinary Language," in *ibid.*, pp. 345-368; N. Malcolm, "Defending Common Sense," *Phil. Rev.*, LVIII (1949), 201-220; A. E. Murphy, "Moore's 'Defence of Common Sense'," in *Philosophy of G. E. Moore*, pp. 301-317.

14 Moore, in *Contemporary British Philosophy* (1925), p. 207.

15 "Let us examine the general nature of Moore's refutations. There is an inclination to say that they one and all *beg the question*" (Malcolm, "Moore and Ordinary Language," *Phil. Rev.*, LVIII [1949], p. 348). Almost any of Moore's essays will illustrate the point. See, for instance, p. 305 of his famous "External and Internal Relations," in *Philosophical Studies* (1922).

The notion of "analysis" especially associated with Moore's philosophical practice is another and, I think, more questionable side of his teaching. Moore says "Such an expression as 'The earth has existed for many years past' is the very type of an unambiguous expression, the meaning of which we all understand."[16] And, as explained above, he holds the proposition expressed by the sentence he has mentioned to be wholly and certainly true. Yet though we understand the meaning of the sentence, we do *not* "*know what it means,* in the sense that we are able to *give a correct analysis* of its meaning."[17] The question as to the correct analysis is "a profoundly difficult question, and one to which . . . no one knows the answer."[18] Accordingly, followers of Moore at one time thought of their business as that of answering such "profoundly difficult" questions, by providing *analyses* of the meanings of expressions whose meaning "we all understand." Yet the most intensive discussion of the aims and methods appropriate to *his* kind of philosophical analysis has not made clear what such an analysis would be like.[19] And attention to what Moore says brings formidable difficulties to light.

Consider, for instance, what is said about the proposition, *P,* says, expressed by the words "This is a hand," when uttered in the appropriate circumstances. Moore thinks there are "three, and only three alternative types of answer possible."[20] Let us suppose that three different propositions, A_1, A_2, and A_3, are offered as possible analyses of *P*. Now if one of them is the *correct* analysis of *P,* it must, according to Moore, be identically the same proposition as *P*. So we must have either $P = A_1$, or $P = A_2$, or $P = A_3$ (where "=" means *identically the same as*). Since we know *P* to be certainly true, we must, therefore, know either A_1 or A_2 or A_3 to be certainly true. How is it, then, that Moore can say that none of the possible analyses of *P* "comes anywhere near being certainly true"[21] without at once using this as a conclusive ground for rejecting all of them?

It would seem that since the correct analysis must be identically the

16 Moore, in *Contemporary British Philosophy* (1925), p. 198.
17 *Ibid.*
18 *Ibid.*
19 See, for instance, C. H. Langford, "Moore's Notion of Anaylsis," in *The Philosophy of G. E. Moore*, pp. 321-342, and Moore's rejoinder, "A Reply to My Critics," in *ibid.,* pp. 660-667.
20 Moore, in *Contemporary British Philosophy* (1925), p. 219.
21 *Ibid.*

same as a proposition known to be certainly true, any proposition *not* known to be certainly true must be eliminated as a possible answer: there seems no room for hesitation or doubt. If the expressions used in formulating the proposed analyses were obscure or recondite, the reasons for hesitation might be intelligible: if we cannot identify the proposition offered, we are naturally unable to determine whether it coincides with *P*. And this may indeed be the answer. Perhaps such expressions as "[a sense datum] *is part of* [a surface]" have never been sufficiently explained; so that the difficulty is not that of selecting a well described analysis but rather that of understanding the language in which the "possible analyses" are expressed. Here, in his discussions of the analysis of material-object propositions, Moore no longer uses the language of common sense exclusively and may be a victim of false analogies suggested by the philosophical terminology of sense-data.

In any case, none of Moore's younger successors has been able to *find* analyses of the kind of proposition he considered. Moore himself never claimed to have a formal "method" capable of formulation in explicit maxims of procedure and has, indeed, said very little *about* analysis. To a friendly critic of his procedure who suggests there may be no way of settling doubts about proposed analyses, Moore says "There is certainly something else to do besides going on doubting; and that is to go on thinking about it."[22] But in the absence of further information about the *kind* of thinking which would offer some hope of success, we can hardly expect very much from *this* kind of "analysis."

IV

To omit all reference to Wittgenstein would be cowardice. Yet even more than in the previous sections, a summary account must be inadequate. For one thing, Wittgenstein has said emphatically, and consistently illustrated by his practice, that philosophy is an activity, not a doctrine.[23] When the activity is idiosyncratic and owes its value so much to the living interplay of actual discussion, prosaic description is bound to fall flat. (One might as well try to convey the "look" of a painting by a verbal description.) But I will try to say something,

---

[22] Moore, in *The Philosophy of G. E. Moore*, p. 638.
[23] "Philosophy is not a theory but an activity" (L. Wittgenstein, *Tractatus Logico-Philosophicus* [1922], p. 77).

if not about Wittgenstein, then about what I hope I may have learnt from him.

Consider one of Russell's epistemological questions, "What is the evidence for the existence of the external world?" Russell treats it as if it were a question clearly understood, whose difficulty lay only in finding a correct *answer*. But it might be well to refuse to take the question at face value and to make strenuous efforts to understand clearly what it asks. We might begin by asking for even *one* thing which would count as "evidence"—that is to say, by asking for *instances of application* (not a definition) of the key terms. We do know, of course, what would count as evidence for the propositions *There is an inhabited world outside the Solar System* or *The earth existed before there were any men*—or, indeed, for most of the propositions about matters of fact about which we are sometimes in doubt. But the types of evidence that are relevant differ from case to case, and this is one reason why the question about "evidence" in the philosophical context has no clear sense; it is by no means plain what is to count as evidence for the "existence of the external world." Will showing Russell a hand help—will it supply him with even the slightest reason for saying "the external world exists"? Of course not—and in spite of all that Moore can say! Such a gesture will certainly not allay the sceptic's uneasiness. Would some general principle, deductively entailing the "existence of the external world," be satisfactory? Again, no. For the general principle will have to be deductively stronger than the conclusion inferred from it; and if we were worried by lack of "evidence" for the weaker proposition, how much the more shall we be worried by the stronger principle's lack of support. The fact is that *nothing* in the way of evidence will satisfy a hardened "epistemological sceptic." (To be satisfied, with Hume, by something irrelevant like "custom" or "habit" or "animal faith" is merely a sign of fatigue.)

This is the first step—the realization that metaphysical questions (if they are still to be called "questions") have no answers and that metaphysical assertions have no refutations. It is a cardinal confusion to suppose that the metaphysician is an "extra-cautious scientist"—trying to talk like the physicist, but more carefully and about *everything*. Whatever metaphysics may be, it is not a science of sciences, a more general *theory* of the universe; but neither is a metaphysical system a set of assertions refutable by common sense.

Yet this is not to recommend contempt for metaphysics. Metaphysics is far from being a wilful aberration, and those who think so will be in danger of talking the crudest and most naive metaphysics themselves. (The positivist has a metaphysics, no less than his opponents.)

What is the source of the constant fascination exerted by metaphysics? It is to be found, says Wittgenstein in a characteristically obscure but stimulating remark, in the attraction exercised by a "peculiar mode of expression." There are moods in which nothing but *one* way of describing the world seems right—and metaphysical insight naturally results in a series of *necessary* statements. The solipsist, for instance, feels that a word like "I" or "My" ought to enter into every description of experience; and no other language will seem adequate. This is to be subject to what Wittgenstein calls a "mental cramp." We can try to cure it by making the metaphysician talk even greater "nonsense" than he is at first inclined—for instance by showing that solipsism is a halfway house to the kind of mysticism that does not even try to say "what cannot be said" but is in fact reduced to silence. Or we may try to relax the linguistic paralysis by showing how many, and very different, languages can work just as well as "*the*" language. As we begin to see the endless variety of ways in which words like "I" and "My" are used in colloquial language and the never ending ways in which they *could* be used (in the simple linguistic systems Wittgenstein calls "language games"), the solipsistic temptation begins to lose strength. The trouble in many such cases is "treating language as a calculus"—as though it were subject to determinate and relatively simple rules. But colloquial language is immensely complicated and indefinitely flexible.[24] Metaphysics fossilises the infinitely adaptable metaphors by which the meaning of one segment of language is linked to the meaning of all the others.

One of the most noteworthy of these metaphysical "cramps" is that which leads us to treat all words as names—or, as Wittgenstein puts it, to expect that behind every substantive there must be a substance. This fortifies the search for *what is common* in all cases of "evidence" or "truth" or "meaning" or "justice." But it is at least as important to look for the *differences* among the cases; and instead of a "class concept" we more often expect to find a "family" of cases, related by a spectrum of gradually shifting criteria. In searching for "the general case" we easily commit the mistake of treating philosophy as if it were mathematics; for a mathematician might almost be defined as a man who hates exceptions. Philosophical activity has no more to do with mathematics than it has with science. The exhibition of families

---

[24] *Ibid.*, p. 63.

of criteria, i.e., the subtle variations and interconnections of meaning of related terms, is far removed from the construction of a calculus or the determination of empirical fact.

So Wittgenstein's way of doing philosophy is a radical departure from the procedures of Russell and Moore (and, indeed, of any of his predecessors). Resemblances and affinities can of course be found, especially in the *Tractatus*. Wittgenstein's insistence upon transforming the question "What does X mean?" into the down-to-earth "What would you do to recognize an instance of X?" has been called a "Principle of Verifiability" and has been said to place him in the line of succession of the British empiricists. His respect for colloquial language can be likened to Moore's care for "ordinary usage"; and the linguistic analysis of philosophical expressions (the search for the "hidden grammar") has some similarity to Russell's early critique of language. But his differences from his predecessors are more important than these superficial resemblances.[25] He has introduced an exciting and stimulating way of looking at the old problems; and I think his influence will prove lasting.[26]

V

A man who had to describe "philosophical analysis" might resort to talking about a climate of opinion. The weather, he might say, is congenial to empiricists, naturalists, agnostics; the well acclimatized have

---

[25] For descriptions of Wittgenstein's methods see B. A. Farrell, "An Appraisal of Therapeutic Positivism," *Mind*, LV (1946), 25-48, 133-150; J. Findlay, "Some Reactions to Recent Cambridge Philosophy," *Australasian Jour. Psych. and Phil.*, XVIII (1940), 193-211; XIX (1941), 1-13; S. S. Orr, "Some Reflections on the Cambridge Approach to Philosophy," *Australasian Jour. Psych. Phil.*, IV (1946), 34-76, 120-167; J. T. Wisdom, "Metaphysics and Verification," *Mind* XLVII (1938), 452-498 (and Wisdom's other papers). But none of these is really satisfactory.

[26] Something should be added about the relations of Russell and Wittgenstein to the writers commonly known as "Logical Positivists." In America, at any rate, very little distinction is commonly drawn between those who try to use Wittgenstein's methods and those who regard themselves as working within the tradition of the Vienna Circle and "Scientific Empiricism." There is some excuse for the confusion, since the members of the Vienna Circle were strongly influenced by Russell's essays in method and closely studied Wittgenstein's *Tractatus*. Schlick and Carnap were in sympathy with Russell's conception of philosophy as science. But I have urged that Wittgenstein broke sharply with this conception. Those, like the later Carnap, who are interested in developing formal axiomatic systems are guilty of what Wittgenstein regards as *the* philosophical evil of "treating language like a calculus." Whatever merits this way of doing philosophy may have, it is so utterly alien to Wittgenstein's notions that nothing but confusion can result from the use of the same label.

admired the two *Principia's* and the *Tractatus* and have read a hundred pages of Hume for one of Kant. Here rhetoric is viewed with suspicion and enthusiasm barely tolerated; this is a land of "prose writers, hoping to be understood."[27]

But if the complaint were made, once again, that this evokes a mood, not a method, there might be no better answer than to invite examination of the essays which follow. If a formula or a slogan is wanted, it is easy enough to say that these writers (like Russell, Moore, and Wittgenstein before them) are engaged in *clarification of meaning*. But it will be a poor sort of questioner whom such a phrase will satisfy. One important effect of the men whose work I have been discussing has been to give to "meaning" more flexible and sensitive uses than it has ever had before. The essays in this collection show a lively awareness of the complexities of the relations between thought and language and the subtle ways in which we can stumble into verbal booby traps of our own making; but they also show how it is sometimes possible to free ourselves of such hindrances to clarity. And if those who are best at the work of clarification might feel embarrassed to provide a satisfactory analysis of "analysis," that is perhaps no cause for apology or alarm. For it is a mark of life to resist arbitrary confinement, and "philosophical analysis" is still much alive. The essays themselves must make the claim good.

---

[27] J. M. Keynes, in the preface to *A Treatise on Probability* (1921).

The Problem of
Linguistic Inadequacy[1]

ALICE AMBROSE

In how far is it possible to express the processes of mathematical thinking by means of symbolic languages?"[2] Such a question gives vent to a pervasive distrust, not merely of our mother tongue, but even of artificially contructed languages, which are the best we have as models of clarity. The question "Is any language adequate?" expresses openly the doubt that one often detects in semiconcealment and that quite frequently is answered boldly in the negative. Whitehead, for example, says, "It is merely credulous to accept verbal phrases as adequate statements of propositions."[3] "No verbal statement is the adequate expression of a proposition."[4] Further, "language, in its ordinary usages, penetrates but a short distance into the principles of metaphysics."[5] Philosophers can never hope finally to formulate . . . metaphysical first principles. Weakness of insight and deficiencies of language stand in the way inexorably."[6]

These statements condemn language as being seriously de-

---

[1] Throughout this paper I am much indebted to M. Lazerowitz for discussions I have had with him.

[2] See P. Bernays' review of E. Beth's *Inleidung tot de wijsbegeerte der wiskunde, Jour. Symbolic Logic,* VIII (1944), 145.

[3] *Process and Reality* (1929), p. 17.

[4] *Ibid.,* p. 20.

[5] *Ibid.,* p. 254.

[6] *Ibid.,* p. 6.

fective and as failing to do what it is intended to do. They give rise to the idea that language is like a tailored suit that does not fit. If the comparison is justified, then the duty of philosophers who have led the cry against language is clear: to silence the criticisms by making alterations of such a sort that language will expose what it is designed to express. In this paper I want to maintain that such criticisms are quite unlike ordinary ones, that they are pseudo complaints, which masquerade as genuine. The curious thing about them is that they remain even after each specific vocabulary limitation, each specific clumsy expression, is remedied. Nonphilosophical people on the whole, seem to be satisfied with language; and when they are not they know how to remove their dissatisfaction—as when they become aware of important phenomena for which there are no words or when no words at hand are just the right ones. By contrast, philosophers who find fault with language are *chronically* dissatisfied; and, what is to be noticed, their attempts at linguistic reform always fail of realization. Philosophers appear to have discernment where ordinary sensibilities are blunt. They appear to be genuinely attempting to correct language in accordance with their discernment, and their attempts at reform create the impression that reform is possible. These impressions are, as I shall argue, illusory. For what is in theory corrigible should not always fail of correction. What, then, is the cause of their failure? Why should their complaints be chronic? I think the answer is that these complaints are *theoretically* impossible to silence.

Now, language, particularly ordinary language, has been the object of an extensive catalogue of criticisms, some of them genuine and, as just claimed, some of them not. It is important to distinguish these two sorts of criticism, since outwardly, because of their verbal form, they appear to be the same. I shall call genuine those complaints against language which settle upon deficiencies for which there is at least in theory a remedy, a remedy which removes the dissatisfaction decisively. All of us are acquainted with shortcomings in language which have been satisfactorily corrected. For example, ambiguity. Double meanings are quite usually capable of elimination with the exercise of care. Further explanation removes misunderstanding. Inconsistency is another such fault in language, the theory of types serving as a satisfactory means of eliminating inconsistencies the source of which was at one time unknown. Still others are specific vocabulary inadequacies, vagueness, inexactness of expression.

In the case of each of these latter three features, the remedies are familiar: when we find our vocabulary too restricted to make useful discriminations, we introduce new classifications. At one time the term "insane" was adequate for the purposes of describing the mentally unbalanced. When differing types of mental unbalance were observed, convenience dictated the introduction of new terminology—"schizophrenia," "paranoia," etc.—and with its introduction the cause of dissatisfaction was removed. The same type of remedy suffices in the simple situation in which some new phenomenon is discovered for which a name is needed. Again, we all know what kind of thing satisfies us when we are "groping for the proper words" and feel that the way in which we have expressed ourselves is inexact, does not say precisely what we mean, or describe exactly how we feel. The right words exist in the language and we struggle to make a point clearer or to describe a feeling more carefully by a new choice of words. Again, when we feel that language is vague, as when we find ourselves arguing at odds about religion or democracy, we remedy the situation, and thereupon carry on or dismiss the argument, by agreeing on a definition of terms. This agreement will represent a decision to fix on some feature or features not yet fixed by convention. When terms are vague, the vagueness is not a result of any lack of information about facts. *All* evidence relevant to deciding the application of a term, e.g., "vegetable," is at hand, and the indecision remains. That is, it is not logically possible, by reference to the fixed criteria and the presented facts, to decide either that a term or its opposite is applicable. For this reason the only means of decision will be an arbitrary one. The fruit vendor who argued against his prosecution for selling tomatoes on a Sunday, on the ground that anything containing its own seed is a fruit, was asking that he be acquitted of the charge of selling vegetables by an arbitrary decision to fix on "containing its seeds" as the defining feature of fruit. Any dissatisfaction felt with a decision is then not with language but with how the decision has affected one's fortunes.

Of course dissatisfaction with a decision that is not determined by rules but for which new rules are invented, i.e., which is made arbitrarily, may be turned back upon language. When this happens, the fact that there exists a twilight zone of cases which we cannot classify as either ϕ or non-ϕ is cited as evidence of linguistic inadequacy. It is argued that if the only ways open to us of resolving vagueness are either to add new criteria for the application of a word, or to add new words in place of the old, then language is at fault—and not only ordinary language but artificially constructed languages. Questions which cannot be answered because of vagueness are somewhat of a commonplace in ordinary English; for example, "Is this a plant or an animal?" "Is he in his right mind or not?" "Did he break his promise or not?" But their existence does not indicate shortcomings of ordinary English from which a language of less rambling growth is free. Within the language of mathematics, which by comparison with English is carefully constructed, we come upon similar questions. For example, "Is an existential argument employing noneffective processes to be classified as a proof or not?" Even in a logistic system, where a point is made of stating exactly what constitutes a correct proof, the question whether the use of noneffective processes declasses an argument can arise. The suspicion grows that no matter how carefully a language system is set out, the problem of vagueness will inevitably crop up. Further, supposing with Whitehead that "one source of vagueness is deficiency of language,"[7] the deficiency is of a kind which defies remedy. Penumbral cases spring up afresh with every attempt at elimination. No sooner is a classification effected by the introduction of a third category "perhaps ϕ" in addition to the categories "ϕ" and "non-ϕ" than a new indecision, Hydra-like, arises over the application of "ϕ," "non-ϕ" and "perhaps ϕ." Inasmuch as there are *always* real or imaginary cases which we are unable to classify, there appears to be some justification for the complaint that language is chronically incapable of making sharp distinctions.

Nevertheless, I wish to hold that this is a pseudo-complaint and fundamentally different from those complaints which are silenced by such practical remedies as the introduction of new terminology ("neutrons," "quanta"), a better choice of words for the expression of an idea, or an arbitrary decision to resolve vagueness. There is a series of complaints like this one, "metaphysical" complaints of the kind commonly made by philosophers, which continue to arise despite the remedies that remove the specific dissatisfactions felt at the time, and which remain no matter what philosophic attempts at reform are made. It is with such complaints, which I shall argue are completely nongenuine because they are raised against situations hopelessly, i.e., theoretically, beyond remedy, that we shall concern ourselves.

---

[7] *Essays in Science and Philosophy* (1947), p. 127.

A number of these grievances are connected with the claim that our vocabulary is too limited to express what we wish to express, that there are gaps in language comparable to those left between the relatively few names for colors in the color spectrum. "Language is incomplete and fragmentary, and merely registers a stage in the average advance beyond ape-mentality. But all men enjoy flashes of insight beyond meanings already stabilized in etymology and grammar. Hence the rôle of literature, the rôle of the special sciences, and the rôle of philosophy:—in their various ways engaged in finding linguistic expressions for meanings as yet unexpressed."[8]

The charge of vocabulary deficiency often takes a form which is easily confused with the ordinary dissatisfaction over the limitations or inaccessibility of our own vocabulary. We sometimes complain of "being unable to find the right words," though when we do so we know how to go about effecting a remedy. The philosophic complaint is not at all an expression of frustration over not finding the words which are there for the choosing. The trouble is that *no* words are exactly the right words. They do not exist. Language is accordingly claimed to fall short, to lag behind both experience and conceptual thought. In studying the history of ideas we are asked to remember "the struggle of novel thought with the obtuseness of language."[9] Again, we are told that "content cannot be communicated": language is incapable of conveying the ineffable in experience. No color word, for example, ever conveys the precise color experience, partly because what is unique in individual experience cannot be shared, partly because the specificity of experience always escapes embodiment in general terms, which we of necessity use. In the attempt to describe our experience we are in constant struggle with the coarse medium of expression. The claim that the words we have are deficient in power of expression, especially in expression of quality, suggests that if the gaps in language were filled we should have words capable of doing what the present ones cannot do. The type of grievance just expressed is not, however, to be assuaged by the invention of new terminology. No new word fills the need exactly.

Further, in those cases where a practical dissatisfaction is actually allayed by the introduction of new terms, the fact that new dissatisfactions are possible tempts one to a new and different type of complaint.

---

[8] A. N. Whitehead, *Adventures of Ideas* (1933), p. 291.
[9] *Ibid.*, p. 153.

In practice one sometimes finds that when certain linguistic gaps are filled further gaps are discovered, whence one comes to feel that however many holes may be plugged in the dike there will always be others. For example, suppose that a vague word like "insanity" is replaced in psychiatric usage by a series of words which discriminate between the various types of mental disorder. These words again may need to be replaced by others. Whenever this kind of situation occurs it is natural to complain that the old language, which was felt to be adequate up to the time when new discriminations were needed, was actually inadequate all the while, because its words were neither precise enough nor numerous enough. It is like a meager kit of blunt tools beside a complete kit of precision instruments. The trouble is that there is always the possibility of new and sharper precision instruments with which present instruments would compare unfavorably. One is then tempted to say no tools are really sharp enough since there could be still sharper tools which would be better; nor are there enough of them since a greater number would be more useful. And one is tempted to say a revised and augmented language is unsatisfactory for analogous reasons. It is in the same position with respect to the language of the future as the outmoded language now is with respect to it. It too has gaps and imprecisions; we are merely not aware of them at present.

The existence of rudimentary languages alongside more highly developed ones gives additional force to the suggestion that every language has gaps which in a more highly developed language would be filled in. Looking back on the rudimentary language we attribute to it the lacks which, from our present vantage point, we should feel if we were forced to continue using it. Whenever the merits of the new symbolism are extolled, the rudimentary language suffers by invidious comparison. Thus one philosopher writes: "The development of mathematics . . . shows that with new linguistic means new kinds of facts can be described. In a language possessing, say, five numerals and the word 'many,' even the simple fact that in a field A there are six more sheep than in a field B cannot be stated. The use of an arithmetical calculus permits us to describe relations which simply could not be described without it."[10] Now of course it is quite true that one notation can express facts which another notation cannot. This is a matter of fact. But it can be turned into a matter of complaint, and one, further-

---

[10] K. R. Popper, "Why Are the Calculuses of Logic and Arithmetic Applicable to Reality?" (Symposium), *Arist. Soc. Proc.*, suppl. vol. XX (1943), 58-59.

more, which leads to a complaint forever beyond remedy. It is natural to suppose that the poorer notation suffers from deficiencies that the richer notation makes good, and that such deficiencies existed even before the need for a new symbolism was felt. Now, if a given language which served its purpose for a period of time could at the same time be defective, there seems to be no reason for supposing other languages are not in the same position. Our attitude towards both rudimentary and more highly developed languages should be the same: if the one is defective, why not the other? The only difference between a language with which we are at present satisfied and one with which we are dissatisfied is that we have not yet discovered, in the first case, the inherent inadequacies which may very well exist. Our attitude towards less highly developed languages than our own is infectious: if, unlike a house intended to keep out rain but built without a roof, those languages could be deficient without our knowing it, then we seem to have a ground for dissatisfaction with every language. For all we know, every language may have gaps. And it is a source of dissatisfaction with every language that this doubt must remain. Such a dissatisfaction can never be removed, since so long as a new symbolism is unneeded there is no way of determining whether there are deficiencies or not.

There remains one further criticism, directed against natural languages, which should I think be classified with the "philosophic" complaints just discussed. This is that natural languages are not constructed after the manner of formal systems: they have no rules that determine which sequences of symbols are meaningful sentences and not a sufficient number of rules for deciding in a great many cases whether one proposition is a consequence of others. In a formal system such rules are framed independently of any meanings the symbols may have. By contrast, in our ordinary language the rules of grammar will not decide, without recourse to the meanings of the constituent symbols, whether a given combination makes sense. Nor will formal transformation rules provide a complete list of consequence relations; for many consequence relations, such as that between "This is a horse" and "This is an animal," are not formal. Consequently, logicians often express dissatisfaction with the vernacular because it falls short of the model—of the consciously planned language of a logistic system.

But is this a dissatisfaction which can, at least in theory, be remedied? If we were to adjoin to ordinary language a set of special rules to the effect that "goodness is tastier than 10" does not make sense, etc., and a further set of rules telling us that "*x* is a horse" implies "*x* is an animal," etc., should we in this way achieve the ideal set by the model? There would be no disguising the fact that these rules differ from the usual formation and transformation rules. Disregarding the fact that there would be an astronomical number of them, would we be satisfied with the resultant "system"? Should we have a formal system with formal rules, or a more explicit statement of what we already have—ordinary English, with some of the transformation rules functioning as rules for the use of individual words? Such a statement as " '*x* is a horse' implies '*x* is an animal' " tells us that we may not apply the word "horse" in any case where we cannot apply the word "animal." And if we wish to call this a "formal" rule, then we do so by courtesy only; and no one will be deceived into supposing we have what would ordinarily be called a formal rule. The complaint, then, that natural languages lack precise rules of formation and transformation seems, like the "metaphysical" dissatisfactions canvassed thus far, incapable of being dispelled.

The claim that language is a clumsy vehicle never quite fitted to its task, that it is *intrinsically* unequal to the demands we make of it, has been contrasted as sharply as possible with the uncontested fact that language has certain defects which are difficult to overcome but which conceivably, and often in practice, are overcome. It was necessary to emphasize this distinction because on the surface the claim and the statement of fact look so much alike. Both appear to express regrets about imperfections of language, and the similarity between them is accentuated not merely by the use of exactly the same words in the expression of specific complaints but by a parallel delineation of possibilities of remedy. I have tried to show that the philosophic complaints against language, for all their similarity to ordinary complaints, are the sort which are never stilled.

I shall further try to show that they are pseudo-complaints, counterfeits of the genuine article. They correspond to the genuine complaints like the shadow of a man to the man; they have no substance. Philosophers who deplore the shortcomings of language create the impression that these are remediable by proposing various means of improvement. It must be admitted that it is usually not clear whether they are endeavoring to remove an ordinary dissatisfaction or are only going through the motions. I wish to maintain that if it is a philosophic dissatisfaction which they are attempting to remove, then the appearance that remedial steps are being taken is illusory. Attempts to silence philosophic complaints *must* fail. By analysis of what is demanded in order for each specific inadequacy to be corrected I shall try to show that the ideal of adequacy is not simply in fact impossible of attainment, but that it is logically impossible. What must be done in order to free language from philosophic criticisms cannot conceivably be done. And if this can be shown, it will thereby be established that the criticisms are spurious. No complaints over failures to overcome shortcomings are real complaints if success is ruled out by logic.

I shall first give an account of various philosophic attempts to correct language. Each attempt is foredoomed to failure, although each has the appearance of being a genuine attempt to overcome a genuine shortcoming. Consider first the attack made by philosophers on vagueness. At least two methods have been proposed for its elimination or diminution. One is the construction of ideal language systems; another is analysis. The first, of which the main proponents are the logical empiricists and certain logicians, creates a new symbolism, not to fill out the gaps in ordinary language, but to provide a model by means of which the reform of common syntax could be accomplished.[11] The second, of which Professor G. E. Moore is the primary exponent, aims at clarification of concepts; and this clarification has been claimed to effect a diminution of vagueness.

It is not entirely clear how the construction of artificial language systems is to contribute to the reform of common syntax, though the following has been offered by way of explanation: "the syntactical property of a particular word-language, such as English . . . is best represented and investigated by comparison with a constructed language which serves as a system of reference."[12] In the work from which this quotation is taken, Carnap did not attempt to establish this thesis, but one would expect syntactical reform to proceed by the elimination of such expressions as violate the rules for the construction of correct sentences. That there will be differences between a language which has "just grown" and the formalized counterpart which replaces it is assured by the fact that "in constructing a syntax and semantics for a natural language, say English, [a point is made of resolving] certain uncertainties, vaguenesses, and inconsistencies, which are found in the

---

11 Y. Bar-Hillel, "Analysis of 'Correct' Language," *Mind*, LV (1946), 339-340.

12 R. Carnap, *The Logical Syntax of Language* (1937), p. 8.

existing (pragmatical) usage. . . ."[13] One would expect comparisons to be effected between the natural language and its formalization. At least it would be expected that similarities and divergences, for example, between the English usages of "implies" and the single usage of this term in the interpreted system, would show up, even though not pointed out.

I think it is doubtful whether the construction of an artificial language with any considerable divergence from ordinary English would induce anyone to reform ordinary language to conform to it. In respect of certain imperfections in a natural language, e.g., ambiguity and inconsistency, it cannot be denied that the model language can serve a useful function. If in ordinary English one had occasion to construct sequences of symbols which according to the theory of types were nonsense, one would doubtless reform one's language. But in respect of vagueness, an exact formal language provides no cure whatever. Its exactness is lost when it is applied to the vernacular. For example, the model makes the term "implies" relatively free from vagueness in the connections in which it functions. But when the term is placed within the vague contexts existing in English, the model turns out to be useless. The formalized language has nothing to offer which is in any way relevant to resolving the vagueness prompting such questions as "Does '*S* has $50,000' imply '*S* is rich'?" In fact, if a linguistic change is effected in such a way as to give an answer, it is the pressure of the practical need for a decision, not the example of a model language, which brings it about.

It is not part of the views of practicing philosophical analysts that language suffers from an *intrinsic* inadequacy. As the work of Moore bears witness, it is unquestioned that language, even ordinary discourse, is always capable of satisfactory emendation. It is usually supposed that analysis yields an expression which is clearer than the original; and if it does this it yields a positive and practical satisfaction, undiluted by the hopeless dissatisfaction residing in philosophic complaints. It is when analysis is claimed at least to diminish vagueness[14] that one wonders whether this means is being used to allay an ordinary or a pseudo dissatisfaction. The latter would appear to be the case from

---

[13] Alonzo Church, "Carnap's *Introduction to Semantics*," *Phil. Rev.*, LII (1943), 298.

[14] I. M. Copilowish, "Border-line Cases, Vagueness, and Ambiguity," *Phil. of Science*, VI (1939), 181-195.

the account given by Copilowish. For although he maintains that "any borderline case may be resolved by means of an analysis and definition of the term,"[15] he at the same time casts doubt on the possibility of fulfilling the promise he holds out. He admits that because the terms of the definiens are vague, the definiens must likewise be vague, so that our hope of diminishing vagueness in the definiendum lies in repeated analysis. However, "we cannot assume an attainable limit to this process, even though we tend towards absolute precision as a limit. . . . [This] is perhaps not even theoretically possible."[16] If it is not even theoretically possible to reach a goal, it is difficult to see what it means to say that we approach it, or even to say that a goal exists. The process of removing vagueness, if conceived as a process of approaching what is not theoretically attainable, is no process of *removing* vagueness. "Removing vagueness," like "approaches the horizon," describes nothing.

It seems to be undisputed that analysis of a general idea (or definition of a general term) has some merit, though it is difficult to say precisely what it is. I do not think it can be the removal of vagueness, or even the diminution of it. If an analysis is correct and if the definiendum is vague, it is hard to see how the definiens could be any less vague. For example, the definition of "animal" as "any member of the group of living beings typically endowed with sensation and voluntary motion" leaves it still undecided in certain cases whether a thing is animal or plant. If an analysis makes the application of a word sharp in cases where it was not sharp before, then it has not merely elicited features already contained in the meaning of the word; it has added something. The criteria for the word's application in these cases have not been analytically derived. They have been added, and analysis has *elicited* nothing. The only thing an analysis would seem capable of doing is to make our *knowledge* of the meanings of words nonvague. But this it could do only if the words were nonvague to begin with. Closer inspection of the foliage of a tree will show the leaves to be sharply outlined instead of blurred, as they seem to be from a distance, only if in fact they have sharp outlines. When the application of a word is genuinely vague, the close inspection we make of it in an analysis will only reveal its vagueness.

The fact that borderline cases still exist in the face of correct analytic

---

15 *Ibid.*, p. 188.
16 *Ibid.*, pp. 187-188.

definitions is evidence that continued analysis will not resolve such cases. In actual practice our means of coming to a decision about a borderline case is not to engage in a series of definitions. We not only do not continue with a series of definitions; we do not even go a few steps. Usually the resolution of borderline cases is effected *arbitrarily,* by settling on some feature of the analysans and ignoring others, or even by allowing some further feature not given in the definition to decide the issue. The decision to classify desmids as motile plants rather than as animals must have been made by virtue of some other feature than those listed in the above definition of "animal." In some cases a question about classification is settled without any appeal to definition. The classification of $\sqrt{2}$ and $\sqrt{-1}$ as numbers was justified once it was proved that every algebraic equation of nth degree has n roots, whence $x^2 = 2$ and $x^2 = -1$ would have to have roots. It might be claimed that this proof showed up analytic properties of roots, and hence of numbers, which were previously unknown. I should say this proof did not demonstrate an analytic connection between numbers and algebraic equations, but that *accepting* it as a proof constituted an extension of the meaning of the term "root," whereupon the meaning of "number" was likewise extended. It would have been awkward to divide algebraic equations into those having roots and those not, and much simpler to say some had rational roots, some real, and some imaginary. After choosing the simpler alternative it again would have produced an awkward asymmetry not to call these new roots numbers. The decision whether the negative numbers were properly to be called numbers was most likely settled in a similar manner, by reference to considerations of symmetry: if numbers can always be arrived at by the process of addition, one does not want to say the process of subtraction yields them only up to the point where zero is reached.

It is significant that continued analysis should be proposed as a means of resolving vagueness when there exists the simple expedient of making a decision. I think with this proposal the resolution of vagueness changes from a practical problem to one of those recalcitrant philosophic problems whose solution we shall always despair of. For the remedy for vagueness is conceived in such a way that the dissatisfaction must remain. Making a correct analysis looks like *finding* some feature which will settle the application of a term. But there is no discovering a feature, say, of being rich which would decide whether a man with $50,000 was rich. To elicit it by analysis would be to find a feature which is not there to be found, inasmuch as the conventional definition of "rich" does not stipulate a minimum sum the possession of which makes one rich. Continued analysis would obviously not help. If it becomes necessary to come to a decision, then the only settlement will be an arbitrary one. For example, if a man were legally bound to give up two-thirds of his earnings when he became rich, and at no point would admit to being rich, a successful suit to compel payment would no doubt involve a court decision that part of the meaning of "being rich" was to have, say, $50,000. And the court's decision would not be an interpretation of what the word already meant but of what the court decreed it was to mean in this case.

It cannot be denied that analysis does sometimes help in making a decision in a dispute. It may elicit a feature which we choose to emphasize as the deciding factor. That is, it may make explicit a feature not explicitly grasped before, which we select as the most important defining criterion. But the analysis does not in any way determine the importance we place on it.

That certain complaints against language are spurious but that they have a deceptive similarity to genuine ones, even in the matter of remedies for their removal, has I think been sufficiently established. I wish now to show the pseudo-character of each complaint, by showing that the improvement of language which would be required to allay the dissatisfaction is logically impossible. In each case we are apparently presented with an ideal which language falls short of. But it turns out that the attainment of that ideal is not possible even in theory; the improvement which seems to be sought is a self-contradictory will-o'-the-wisp, which there is no real chasing, but only the semblance of chasing.

Let us consider first the desire for a more adequate terminology which is expressed in the complaint that we cannot find the right words to say precisely what we mean. Sometimes a psychological blockage prevents our finding the right words, but what prevents the philosopher from finding the right words is that they do not exist. The philosopher's dissatisfaction is that no word in the existing vocabulary is exactly the right word. The obvious remedy would seem to be creation of new words to express what one intends. Whitehead's large-scale manufacture of new terminology looks to be this sort of remedy. He says: "Every science must devise its own instruments. The tool required for philosophy is language. Thus philosophy redesigns language in the same way that, in a physical science, pre-existing appliances are redesigned."[17] What philosophers do indicates that such redesigning of language has a twofold aim. One is to name new phenomena which philosophers claim to have discovered; the other is to enable us to express ideas of which we are aware but which are "verbally unexpressed"[18] and moreover, in the present language, inexpressible.

The invention of symbolism to name new philosophic discoveries has an interesting feature worth remarking on. A new philosophic terminology for this purpose gives the impression of satisfying a linguistic need in a quite straightforward way; and its introduction is therefore not to be classified with attempts at linguistic improvement which are bound to fail. What philosophers do when they introduce such new words as "sense-data," "monads," or "universals" appears to have its model in what scientists do when they become aware of an important phenomenon for which there is no word. One philosopher, for example, characterizes the analysis of "I seemed to see a penny but there was none" as "I sensed a penny-like sense-datum but it was not of a penny" as follows: "The new notation is given in an attempt to reflect more adequately the form of the fact which the original sentence expresses; and it does so because it *names* an element not hitherto named."[19] If philosophers do make empirical discoveries and for convenience give names to the entities discovered, it is quite proper to describe their invention of new terms as a straightforward provision for a linguistic need. What they do is then of the same order as what chemists do when they discover a new element. But the curious feature of their terminological revision is that there is no general agreement among philosophers as to whether it is needed—whether there *is* any new phenomenon named by the new name.[20] Discoveries claimed by philosophers differ in a puzzling way from those claimed by scientists. Disagreements over the existence of the purported facts, which all are in a position to examine, persist despite all "evidence."[21] The question about the introduction of philosophic terms for new discoveries thus

---

[17] *Process and Reality*, p. 16.

[18] A. N. Whitehead, *Modes of Thought* (1938), p. 49.

[19] Helen Smith, in "Symposium: Is There a Problem About Sense-data?" *Arist. Soc. Proc.*, suppl. vol., XV (1936), 84.

[20] See G. A. Paul, *ibid.*, pp. 61-77.

[21] For a study which works out this kind of point in another connection, see M. Lazerowitz, "The Existence of Universals," *Mind*, LV (1946), 1-24.

seems to be, not whether one can fill a linguistic need by this means, but whether there is any need. The case is different with regard to the redesigning of language demanded by philosophers who claim to have no words for the ideas they wish to express.

It is a commonplace that a person who knows one language may find, when he learns another, that what is expressible in his native language is not always exactly expressible in the acquired one; something gets lost in the translation. Such a person is in a very different position from one who asserts, within his language, that no word is the right word for what he wants to say. His complaint suggests that what is needed is an adaptation of language so as to express those meanings which it is now too gross to express. To this end new words are required, since the old ones will not do.

Now, is it logically possible for a new word to be the right word for an idea? How will a new word, which so to speak comes naked, be the right word? To be the right word it must carry exactly the right meaning, whereas being new, it has, to start with, no meaning. It will have to be given its meaning in the way in which the unsatisfactory word was given its meaning: ostensively, by application to phenomena, or verbally, by being correlated with known words. But the new ostensive definition can do no more than the old one did; and if a verbal definition gives the word the *right* meaning, the meaning it *should* have, then there exist expressions in the language which do have exactly the right meaning, in which case there is no real cause for complaint.

But if the old words cannot be the right ones, then neither can the new ones, since they must be explained by the old ones. A tailor cannot hope to satisfy a customer who complains that the old fabric is no good by spinning a new fabric from the old threads. To introduce a new word by means of old ones is of course to do with the old words what was claimed could not be done. Any description of what would make an expression, which we do not as yet have, the proper one to express what we cannot now say would involve our actually having the proper words for expressing what we wish. It would appear, then, that "finding the proper words because the old ones will not do" is but a pretended task. For what must be done is self-contradictory: invent new words to which the meaning we wish them to express is assigned, but to which that meaning cannot be assigned for lack of the right words.

Another closely related complaint, though a somewhat different one, is that language is not capable of expressing the ineffable in experience, that what we experience "words cannot describe." Communication of the concreteness of our experience is impossible, and for a variety of related reasons. One is that its specificity always escapes embodiment in general terms, another that words cannot unlock the door to an individual's private world. Only if language could "embody what it indicates" would our experience be communicable: "The art of literature, vocal or written, is to adjust the language so that it embodies what it indicates."[22] But that such a state of affairs should be achieved is self-contradictory. For what would it be like for the experience indicated by a color word to be incorporated in the language? Apparently the experience itself would be in the position of a word. But in that case the embodiment would function to indicate something beyond itself. It would then not be an embodiment, but a symbol—the original unsatisfactory substitute for the experience. The only meaning we can give to the expressed aim that what the symbol inadequately stands for should be *embodied* in the symbol is that what the symbol stands for should *replace* the symbol. This means that it would take over its *representative* function. But to do so would be self-stultifying; for once what the symbol denotes takes over the role of denoting, the old complaint would reappear. It must reappear, since it is the representative, denoting function of the symbol that is complained against.

If we consider what would happen to a symbol, as contrasted with what it symbolizes, were it to embody what it indicates, we arrive at an equally paradoxical consequence: a symbol embodies what it designates only when it no longer designates. Suppose we require that terms describing experience be made less and less general until finally a point is reached where they carry in themselves what they indicate. At this point one would apparently not have a symbol at all, but the experience. An experience, not a symbol, would now be a constituent of the description, in which case understanding a statement about someone's experience would consist in *having* the experience. This is to say the symbol would incorporate its referent only by no longer referring to something beyond itself. But then it would no longer be a symbol. It turns out that the complaint against language is that a self-contradictory state of affairs does not exist: words do not function both as symbols to indicate a content lying beyond themselves and at the same time carry that content in themselves. This is scarcely a complaint.

[22] A. N. Whitehead, *Essays in Science and Philosophy*, p. 107.

It is sometimes urged that words are no better instruments for the communication of thoughts than they are of subjective experiences: "although the dictionary or the encyclopaedia gives what may be called the official and socially sanctioned meaning of a word, no two people who use the same word have just the same thought in their minds."[23] It is to be supposed from this statement of Russell's that a word is like an ill-fitting garment for the thought which it clothes, since it is used to clothe so many different thoughts. A thought can only make an appearance to us in its verbal clothes, and in accordance with this view we must say there is merely an illusion, created by the repeated use of the same clothes, that the words dress one and the same idea.

But now is it not impossible that a word should have a socially sanctioned meaning and yet that no two people who use the word ever have that meaning in mind? How could one and the same meaning be attached to the word by society and yet no two of its members attach that meaning to it? That a word has such and such a meaning fixed by convention means that it is customarily used in social intercourse to express that meaning, whereas that no two people have the same thought corresponding to the same word entails that no two are giving the word its customary use. From Russell's claim it follows that no two people use the word in the way many people by custom use it, which is absurd. It therefore provides no reason for condemning language as unfitted to communicate thoughts.

It might be supposed that the invention of new symbolism is conclusive evidence of the inadequacy of the language to which it is adjoined, and that one would be justified in condemning such a language even before the need for further symbolism is felt. It is natural to view symbols of the form $a + bi$, for example, as additions made to the existing language of numbers for the purpose of filling in gaps which the language previously had. The situation is the same with rudimentary languages which a highly developed language seems to complete. Thus, the present language of arithmetic, in which we have the possibility of indefinitely writing numerals, seems to complete the language having the numerals from one to five and the word "many." That it is capable of expressing facts (e.g., that $6 > 5$) which the rudimentary language cannot seems properly to be ascribed to the superiority of a complete language over a fragmentary one.

Is this, however, a proper account of the difference between a simple

23 Bertrand Russell, *A History of Western Philosophy* (1945), pp. 50-51.

and a highly developed language? And if it is, must we not be forced to say that for all we know every language is incomplete? A counter-question is in order here: Incomplete with reference to what standard? Unless there exists a wider language of which a given symbolism is a part, we have no standard in relation to which it is incomplete. Further, even the fact that a symbolism L_1 is part of another, L_2, does not necessarily make L_1 incomplete, although it may be inadequate for certain purposes. The language of arithmetic can be said to be part of the language of real numbers; it lacks certain symbols and the rules for their usage. But although arithmetic is *inadequate* for certain purposes, e.g., for solving algebraic equations, it is not an *incomplete* arithmetic. No parts of it are *missing*, as there would be from a symbolism which purported to be our arithmetic but which lacked the operation 4×4. Taken by itself it is the whole language. It is completely unlike a dictionary with missing pages. Any inadequacy which at a given moment a *language* comes to have is not due to incompleteness. The classification "incomplete" (and hence also the classification "complete") is not properly applicable to a language. A symbolism which purports to be a language but which has missing parts can be called incomplete, but a language L_1 does not become incomplete when it becomes a part of L_2, because it does not purport to be L_2. It is a whole even though additions are made to it, since these additions do not supply missing parts. To repine that, for all we know, every language may be incomplete is to indulge in the absurd complaint that a whole language is perhaps not a whole language. Furthermore, it sounds as though a remedy may be needed, whereas there is no completing what is already a whole. We can add to it; but we cannot complete it.

It is natural, when we have the new language and look back at the old one, to read into the old one the inadequacy we should feel were we to continue using it in certain contexts. We assert that the rudimentary language cannot express certain relations among concepts which the more highly developed one can, as though this were a deficiency which is internal to it. Actually we are merely stating the fact that certain symbols, together with the rules for their use, are not part of it. And this is not like saying that certain cards are missing from the deck. It is like saying the deuces play no role in a game which uses a deck without them. This is not a defect. The game played without the deuces is not a deficient game, but a *different* one. Similarly, the game

with "one," . . . "five," "many" is simply a different one from that
with "one," "two," and so on. The adequacy of the rudimentary language to the purposes for which it was constructed is in no way affected
by the fact that the symbols "6," "7," "8," . . . do not occur in it and
that "many" plays a role in certain respects dissimilar to these. A language is in some ways like a map. A map that gives only the rivers
of a certain territory and gives no detail of the mountains will be of no
help to the mountain climber; but it is not thereby shown to have been
inadequate before he needed a map for such a purpose. Similarly, there
was no linguistic inadequacy before the need was felt which prompted
introducing a more useful notation. A symbolism *cannot* be inadequate
so long as it does the work it was designed to do. It cannot be criticized
for not doing more than this. To say a language fails to come up to
certain specifications when it was not constructed according to them
is simply nonsense.[24]

I want now to consider the invidious comparison often made between
our ordinary correct English and the model language of symbolic logic.
The point of the comparison is not merely to cite the advantage, in
fact the necessity, of a consciously planned syntax for a logistic system; it is evidently a criticism that English falls short of an ideal, and
the criticism is made with the intention of reform. There is one general goal which I should suppose would determine the reformation of
ordinary discourse: a reconstruction in the direction of exactness. To
this end I should expect a basis to be laid for it in explicitly stated
formal rules of formation and transformation. At the same time I
should suppose the reformed English would still be expected to do
what English does now—serve our ordinary purposes. Now, is it
logically possible for English to be governed by formal rules and to
do what it does now? In particular, is it logically possible that an
implicative sentence such as " '*x* is red' implies '*x* is colored' " be con-
verted into a formal transformation rule? This sentence states a
typical instance of a nonformal consequence relation which, clearly,
cannot also be formal, as the word "formal" is at present used by
logicians. The terms "formal" and "nonformal" are used just to distinguish relations such as "$p \supset p$" from relations of this kind. If we
were to remodel English by dropping out all nonformal relations we
should be left with a language that would not serve our practical

---

24 For guiding ideas of the last two paragraphs I am indebted to lectures at
Cambridge University by Dr. L. Wittgenstein.

needs. We are quite ready to improve English in the direction of consistency; but it is a logically impossible demand that English be both a formal language and a natural one.

In all the philosophic criticisms made against language we find operative what appears to be a perfectionist ideal. The case is the same with the charge that inexactness in language is responsible for vagueness. Here again, as I want to show, attainment of the ideal situation is logically impossible. Vagueness is a source of complaint only if there is a standard which the existence of this phenomenon shows language to fall short of. Now, the ideal is exactness, an exactness such that we can always discriminate verbally between things having ϕ and those not having it. Given that the thesis of Platonic realism is correct, that beyond language there exists a realm of universals, we seem to be provided with standards of exactness of which language falls short: "The world of [universals] is unchangeable, rigid, exact, delightful to the mathematician, the logician, and the builder of metaphysical systems. . . ."[25] Universals, in contrast with the words by which we designate them, are precise: either ϕ or non-ϕ characterizes a given thing; there seems to be no sense in talking of vague universals. In fact a standard procedure for refuting the thesis that there are universals is to argue that common properties are not exact.[26]

It would appear from this that vagueness resides in our language and precision in what it inexactly designates. In accordance with the demands of logic, a thing must be characterized by either ϕ or non-ϕ. That is, logic declares the exactness of universals by the law of excluded mean: $(x) \cdot \phi x \lor \sim \phi x$. However, when we come to specific instances of the law, e.g., x is a bush or not a bush, we find that the exactness supposedly possessed by the characterizing properties is not reflected in the language by which we designate them. With all information at hand we are unable to say whether a thing has either property. If we try to resolve our indecision by introducing a third category, "perhaps ϕ," we find ourselves without any means of discovering whether what is *perhaps* ϕ is actually ϕ. A new indecision is replaced by the old. We are like a tailor who asks a customer to try on a suit, with the remark "Perhaps this one fits you," but who is never in a position to say more than "Perhaps it fits," even when the cus-

25 Russell, *Problems of Philosophy*, p. 156.
26 See Locke, *Human Understanding*, bk. III, ch. iii, 13.

tomer has it on. No matter how closely he looks he is never able to discover whether what perhaps fits does fit.

This analogy raises the question whether "perhaps ϕ" makes any sense if there is no conceivable means of resolving our uncertainty into ϕ or non-ϕ. In the present situation we do not know what it would be like to come to this sort of decision. And this is to say that neither "perhaps ϕ" nor "actually ϕ" has meaning. The two are correlates, and if it is not logically possible to determine that ϕ applies, then the "perhaps" loses its function. Without the means, even in theory, of being certain that a thing is ϕ, we have no logically possible goal of certainty of which we fall short in saying "perhaps it is ϕ." The view that vagueness resides in language and precision in what it designates suggests that universals are analogous to patterns which the tailor's scissors are too blunt to follow accurately enough to get an exact fit. But the analogy is misleading because the pattern, "actually ϕ," cannot exist if "perhaps ϕ" can never conceivably be supplanted by the definite knowledge that the thing either conforms or not to the pattern.

The demand that words have the precision of the characterizing properties they stand for, with its presupposition that we have in precise universals a standard with which language can be compared, can be shown to be logically unreasonable on somewhat different but related grounds. The assumption motivating the demand is that a word can be vague while the universal it designates is sharp. But is this logically possible? Since the universal is the meaning of the word, the assumption is that a word can have a vague application though its meaning is nonvague. But the application of a word is fixed by its meaning, so that the application could not be less sharp than the meaning.

It might be held that the demand that language be exact would be unobjectionable if it were divorced from reference to the existence of universals. But this is not the case. What would it be like for language to be free from vagueness? Does "having no possible borderline cases" describe a possible situation? I think that it does not and that we have only the pretense of a standard in the demand that words be applicable in such a way as always to set off things having ϕ from those not having it. For it is always theoretically possible to construct cases which we are unable to classify as one or the other. Given any two things one can imagine one slowly merging into the other, and if this is the case, there will always be a point in the transformation at which the application of a word, or its negative, is undecided. If it is always possible in theory that there be such cases, then it is logically impossible that there be none such. So it could be no real condemnation of language to point to the presence of vagueness, just as it is no condemnation of an infinite series that it has no last term.

The Reality of the Past

G. E. M. ANSCOMBE

The first statement of the problem of the reality of the past is in Parmenides. "It is the same thing that can be thought and can be," so "what is not and cannot be" cannot be thought. But the past is not and cannot be; therefore it cannot be thought, and it is a delusion that we have such a concept.

The doubt raised here is not a Cartesian doubt which is meant to be a doubt about facts; the question is not "May not all our apparent information about the past be incorrect?" but "Is not our apparent concept of the past impossible?" Parmenides' remarks suggest the enquiry "How is it that statements about the past have meaning?"

We are not concerned here with any other objects of thought besides particular things, events, circumstances, places, persons, and so on. That is, not with abstractions, generalizations, imaginary things. When I think of my acquaintance *A*, and think that he is in Birmingham, it is he, *A*, the very man himself, and Birmingham, that very place, that I mean, and not some intermediate representation of them. I might try to emphasise this by going and finding and pointing to the man and the city; not that I imagine that I should thereby make clear what it is to mean them, but I should then be exhibiting them themselves, and I want to insist that I meant them as directly as that. It is as if my name for any actual object were a pointer, and by coming to the object I followed up the pointer and exhibited that to which it already pointed, thus bringing out that it was really that and not anything intermediate that was pointed to. And what I now point to is not an *example* of what I mean, as I can point to an example of some generalization that I have made. It *is* what I mean. (This might be used to give a sense—though not Hume's—to Hume's contention that the idea of a thing's existence is none other than the idea of the thing. For in a way this seems absurd. But the thought of an actual thing is not the thought of a possibility with the note of actuality somehow added, or of a possibility to which in fact something actual corresponds.)

The name or thought of something past seems to point to its object in just the same way as the name or thought of any other actual thing; yet how can it, since its object does not exist?

Kant's idea that it is only through the representation of time that the possibility of change is noncontradictory is similar to that of Parmenides. But Parmenides rejects the concept of time as nonsensical precisely because it introduces contradiction. Let us imagine that some-one is taught (1) to say "red" when a red light is switched on before him, "yellow" for a yellow light, and so on; and (2) next to say "red," "yellow," etc., when lights of the appropriate colours *have* been switched on but are now off. Imagine a spectator who finds (2) unin-telligible, since the learner is not corrected for saying "red" when there is no red light, but this is accepted. It is as if the learner were taught first to act according to a certain rule and then to break that rule. The in-compatibility is only removed by our introducing the ideas of the present and the past into our formulation of the rule according to which he is taught to act: "He is taught to say 'is red' when a red light is showing, and 'was red' when a red light not is, but has been, show-ing."—But he was not taught to say "is red" or "was red," but only to say "red," first as described in (1), then as described in (2). But what he does in (2) *contradicts* what he learns in (1) unless we suppose that "red" in (2) really means "was red." There is, of course, no reason to think it impossible that he should behave as is described—one can act quite differently at different times. But then to learn the procedure of (2) is to unlearn the procedure of (1)—and this we do not want to say. We want to say that he learns something in (1) which he applies in (2). But just what he learns in (1)—namely to utter the names of the colours in face of the appropriate lights—is annulled in (2). He does indeed repeat the names of the colours, but he does not apply them as he did. Yet we want to say that he does apply them as he did, namely to the same colours, only now not when they *are* but when they *have been* showing. But what is the explanation of this "have been" which is introduced to explain that the learner is still using, and not mis-using, the names he has learnt? One points to red and says "The explanation is that what *was* showing *was* just the same as this"; nevertheless one tends to concentrate on "the same" and "this" without noticing the problem raised by "was." To bring out this problem, let us imagine that we teach "the same" and "this," and that our learner not only learns the colour names but also learns to say "the same as this" correctly for various colour samples presented to him. Now has he everything he needs in order to say "*was* the same as this," without any *new* training? Or, to put it differently, is it unimaginable that he should have got so far but should be unresponsive to attempts to teach him the procedure of (2): is it not, rather, natural that he should hesitate at (2) as if he were being tempted to do what he will be corrected for? But now suppose that he does respond and uses the colour names as described in (2). The explanation " 'red' in (2) really means 'was red' " or "refers to the red that *was* showing" would only be an explanation for someone who understood "was red" but had failed to see that this was the rule according to which the learner was being taught to act. But we are not concerned here with such a misunderstanding, but rather with what is understood by someone who does understand the explanation. "Red" in (2), or "was red," is a new use of "red," whose outstanding feature is that "red" can be said when there is no red. It is of no use to say to someone philosophically perplexed at this that "red" is said when there has been red. For he is looking for, and cannot find, a difference between there having been red and there not having been red. We say "He is looking in the wrong place, in the present and not in the past." But what is it to look in the right place? He is looking for a justification; for surely "was red" is not said without justification when it is said rightly. But there seems to be no justification unless he finds himself reiterating the very thing he is trying to justify.

It seems possible to show someone what to mean when one wants him to say "red" with meaning, but impossible to show him what to mean by "was red"; for how does one get his attention directed to what he is to speak of? When one has to teach "red" one can at least ensure that the learner's eyes are looking in the right direction; and one would not expect to be able to teach him except on this condition. But if one is trying to teach the use of the past tense, then there is nothing to which one can direct his attention and nothing in him to direct in the hope of directing the attention, as in the other case it was possible to direct the eyes. Yet it seems that a necessary condition of his being able to grasp the meaning of "there was red" *is* his attending to the right thing, i.e., to the past showing of red, and that this can only happen if his mind is looking in the right direction; but how can his mind look in the right direction unless he already has the idea of the past? It might seem enough to *have* directed his attention to the red light, which one now recalls by using the expression "was red." But that he *did* attend to the red light does not mean that he *now* has an experience for which he can learn the expression "was red." Just as the occurrence of a succession of ideas does not provide an adequate explanation of the idea of succession, so the fact of a past experience does not provide an adequate explanation of the idea of the past.

It seems that memory must be the key to the problem; that it is memory that gives one the essential meaning of the past tense; that it is like an eye that can look in the required direction, or like sight that corresponds to visible space. So that if the learner in saying "red" in (2) remembers the red light and means what he remembers, *then* he says it rightly, just as he says "red" rightly in (1) if he sees the red light and means what he sees. I know what it is to remember, and what memory gives is the past. We speak of past times and events that form no part of our memories. But (the suggestion is) a past event is something that could be remembered, and someone who remembered it would really know it as past; others understand it because the grammatical form used in describing it has been given sense for them by their own memories. But is it memory as knowledge or as experience from which I am supposing that I derive the idea of the past? As an experience, apparent does not differ from genuine memory; and an apparent memory may be false, or even if it is true it is not genuine memory unless the person who has it was a witness to what he remembers. This shows that I could not use the idea of memory as knowledge—i.e., memory that is both genuine and true—for an "analysis" of the idea of the past, since my analysis would implicitly include unanalysed references to the past. Still, without intending any such analysis, and without pretending to state any conditions under which memory was knowledge, I may take examples of memory which I insist *are* knowledge.

I think of something that I remember, such as that I had coffee for breakfast, and I want anyone, with whom I am discussing, himself to recall something that he can remember with certainty. (I am not arguing from the *fact* that I had coffee for breakfast, for unless he was with me and can remember it too, I do not expect it to be his example; the point is for him to have the idea of finding an example.) Now I say, "This and similar cases must show you the meaning of the past tense. For are you not certain of them; do you not want to call them knowledge? But you cannot know without understanding what you know. Since, then, you know this, the meaning of the past tense is contained in what you know. Scrutinize what you know and you will see that meaning in it." Suppose that I am thinking of a representation, *B*, of a certain fact, *A*, and that I want to understand the meaning of *B*. I insist that I know *A*, and that I understand *B* by understanding it as the representation of *A*. If I ask how I know *A*, or how I understand what it is for *A* to be the case, I answer that I simply do know it and understand it: and this I cannot explain further. And it is this knowledge and understanding that explains *B*. Further questions are like raising a doubt about *A*, and, as I am certain of *A*, I reject them.

But how can I explain *B* to myself as a representation of *A* unless I have some other representation of *A* which I use in explaining *B*? If I am confronted with *A* itself, I may think I can evade this difficulty somehow. But if I am not and cannot be confronted with *A*, because it it past, then it is futile for me to appeal to *A* as explaining *B;* for I can only appeal to *A* by using a representation, and the question arises anew about this representation, whatever it is. Knowledge of a past fact can only explain the meaning of some representation of that fact to someone who already has some *other* representation of it; i.e., such explanation is trivial and does nothing for us philosophically. Thus the insistence that I *know* something that has happened is philosophically irrelevant; nor do I want to raise a doubt about such knowledge. To insist that I *know* that such has happened is to protest that it *has* happened: if the question is what it means to say that it has happened, one is not helped to answer the question by repeating that it certainly has happened.

It is different if I think that the *experience* of memory is what gives me the idea of the past, and say that memory need be neither genuine nor true in order to contain this idea. Both a false and an apparent memory are of what *seems* to have happened. If I say this, I am holding that memory gives me the form of representation of the past by supplying me with representations which all have this form and that the distinctions of apparent and genuine, and of false and true, are posterior. For a *sense* occurs in a false representation no less than in a true. If, then, I regard my understanding of the meaning of the past tense as got from my memory representations and regard these as the fundamental data for my understanding, then I regard the true and the false indifferently.

Or: I ask myself how I know what the past tense means. And now I say "I remember . . ." thus giving myself an example of a statement about the past, which, I argue, has sense for me by being an expression of a present mental content. I am on secure ground, because what I say is not doubtful even though what I remember did not happen or I was not there. If I base my understanding on this, then it is secure. I cannot be challenged on the ground that I have covertly introduced an unexplained understanding of the past tense into my pretended explanation of what I understand by it: for all I claim to understand is my own act of recollection, and *that* I understand by making it; and I do not claim for it that it is true, or even that it is genuine, memory.

It is natural in attempting to give an account of memory to draw an analogy between memory and perception, by introducing the notion of memory-data, whose place in the theory of memory is made to correspond to that of sense-data in the theory of perception. When we perceive anything, our senses receive certain impressions, and one of the main philosophical questions about perception is whether we should regard these impressions as "data," as the material for judgments of perception. One can ask someone who is perceiving something to concentrate on the sensible appearances of what he is perceiving, or on the impressions that he is receiving, and to describe these. The following example will bring out the doubtfulness of the analogy between memory and perception that is suggested by the idea of memory-data. Suppose that I witness the commission of a crime and that afterwards I say I remember seeing a certain man standing at the scene of the crime. Someone who does not believe that I have told a lie or made a mistake of memory may nevertheless believe that that man was not present. He discovers a waxwork figure which resembles the man, arranges it in the place where I say I saw him, shows it to me, and I say "Yes! That is exactly what I saw," or "Move it a little this way and draw that curtain. Now it is exactly what I saw." I now become convinced that my previous memory judgment was in fact false, and yet even if it was false, it was not a mistake of *memory*. The explanation of this might seem to be that the mistake was made at the time when I witnessed the crime, and was therefore not a mistake of memory. But suppose—as is possible—that at the time I did not think "That is so-and-so," and took no notice of what I saw, but afterwards said "I saw so-and-so." In that case the mistake was not made at the time of seeing but apparently only at the time of remembering; yet it was not a mistake of memory. But *should* I not have thought, at the time, *if* I had taken account of what I saw, "That's so-and-so"? How is it that I can tell what I should have thought? When I say "I should have thought that if I had taken account of it," I am not necessarily denying that explicit consideration on the spot might have made me think something quite different: "I should have thought it" is a way of expressing, rather than of proving, that the mistake was not one of memory. Is it, then, that I remember a state of mind, which was not an articulate thought, but the not-yet-consciously-articulated thought "That is so-and-so"? Then is this what I *really* remember? Yet when I said "I saw so-and-so" I need not have been thinking about what my state of mind was at the time. Or am I to say that what I really remembered was the appearance, which I misinterpreted as the appearance of the man when it was really the appearance of the waxwork? Yet it might be that I did not remember the appearance until I was asked to recall it, or until I was confronted with it again. And when I did remember it, what I had was simply a new memory, which led me to reject the old one. One can ask someone who remembers something to consider just what appearance he saw. But this is not drawing his attention to a memory-datum; it is trying to elicit a new memory—of a sense-datum. If, then, I still wish to use the idea of a memory-datum, I must try to say what it is. In the case that I have described, for example, is it just the memory *that* I saw so-and-so? But it is strange to call this a datum, for the memory is a falsehood, so it should seem to follow that the datum is a hallucination or what is called "a nonveridical appearance"; but these expressions do not seem to apply. The memory is, of course, a judgment; but if we ask whether the judgment expresses the possession of a datum or is less immediate than that, the question does not seem to apply—unless we think of the datum in question as belonging to the original occasion; but this is not what is meant by the idea of a memory-datum. If we look for a datum, then should we ask the rememberer to consider exactly what he is experiencing when he has the memory (as we can ask "Just what impressions are you receiving now when you say you see a chair?")? But he may not be able to produce anything that seems relevant if he has no image, and it is not necessary that he should have an image. It is, of course, possible to speak of memory-data in the sense "remembered data," or to speak of memories as data ("My only data for reconstructing this scene were my father's memories"); but it is a mistake to say that memories are constituted by a particular kind of data together with judgments founded on them. The idea of a datum arises originally in the discussion of philosophical questions about sense perception, where there is a contrast between descriptions of impressions and of objects, both of which are noninferential. There would be a point in speaking of memory-data if there were two sorts of memory judgment, the memory-impression judgment and the description of the remembered things. If one makes the analogy between memory and sensation that I have been discussing, one is led to assume that memory is always accompanied by memory images. For it is difficult to see what a memory-datum could be except a memory image. But in fact it is not necessary that a memory judgment should be accompanied by images.

If we reject the analysis of memory in terms of memory-data, it appears less plausible to think that the idea of the past is derived from memory contents, or that it characterises them, in such a way that it can be "seen in them."

The examples that I need to consider in order to clarify the problem are those in which something is (ostensibly) remembered, but there is no memory image. For example, someone asks me what I had for breakfast, and I say "I had coffee"; he then asks me, "Did you have an image when you said 'I had coffee'?" and I say "No." Yet I (ostensibly) remembered that I had coffee for breakfast. If I consider what took place in me, I say that I had a memory or at least an apparent memory that I had coffee for breakfast; and I can think of no further mental occurrence that is in any way relevant or in which I can say this memory consisted. If I want to maintain that it is the experience of remembering that shows me the meaning of statements about the past, then I ought to be able to maintain that I can see that meaning in the experience of memory that I have in this example. But what I have got is the experience of seeming to know as a witness, without inference and without being told it, the truth of a statement framed in the past tense. I shall therefore be arguing that I understand the past tense because I know what it is to judge that something has happened, noninferentially and as a witness. But the same objection applies to this as applies to the idea that the *knowledge* that something has happened shows one what the past tense means. If the question is "What does it mean to say that such and such happened?" one is not helped to answer it by saying "It *did* happen"; nor is one helped by saying "I have the idea of its having happened, without being told and as a witness." For the question is "What is the idea?" If I could think that a memory judgment was necessarily made in face of a memory-datum distinct from it, I could seek in the datum what would show the sense of the judgment or would supply some foundation for it. Now, however, I am considering an example in which the ostensible memory is made such by being (at least ostensibly) the judgment of a witness about the past. If therefore I say that the experience of memory shows me what the past tense means, this amounts to saying that the experience of seeming to know something about the past as a witness shows me what the past tense means. Thus in appealing to memory I am not appealing to something which I can understand independently of understanding the meaning of the past tense.

I was tempted to use the idea of memory to explain how the learner who named the coloured lights after they had been switched off was able to mean them. If he said "red," etc., *remembering*, then his behaviour was intelligible and intelligent; his use of "red" in (2) was not a misuse; he was applying the colour names to their appropriate objects as he learned to do in (1), only he was now applying them to past, not present objects. But now it appears that I cannot understand what it means to say he said "red" *remembering*, without understanding what it means to say that he meant the past event; hence my explanation is not an explanation but contains within itself the thing that it purported to explain; nor can I think that if I say he remembers I am saying that he has something that *shows* him the meaning of the past tense. I am saying that the learner acted intelligently if his saying "red" in (2) was an expression of knowledge of the past showing of the red light; I am not stating an independently intelligible *condition* on which his utterance would express such knowledge.

I now seem to be brought to the position of saying that *I* know what it is to have (or apparently have) such knowledge, and that it is only if that understanding which *I* have is in the learner that he can mean "red" in (2) as a report of the past showing of the red light. Suppose there to be in me a state of consciousness, an experience, which I call a memory. What makes this a memory of something that has happened? The memory is an idea that such and such happened. I will suppose that the thing I say happened did happen, that I did witness it; and now I have this experience. The experience could surely be the same even though the idea were inaccurate and though I was not a witness. Then what makes my state or act of consciousness a memory *of that thing*? Is it the mere fact that the thing happened and that I witnessed it? In that case, there is nothing in the memory itself that makes it refer to the actual past event. And if so, why should the experience of memory have anything to do with actual past events or show one what it means for something to have happened? If the expression "it happened" is made intelligible by being the expression of a state of consciousness, it cannot be understood as anything but the expression of a state of consciousness. The experience will make one understand what it is to have this state of consciousness. But what has that state to do with *the facts*? If I appeal to the experience of memory to show me what is meant by the past tense, then all I can claim to understand is what it is to have an *idea* which for some reason I call the *idea* of something's having been so: I cannot claim to understand what it is for something to *have* been so. To make this clearer, let me consider something that is taking place before me (or within me) now. Later I shall be able to speak of it. How will what I say be related to the event? How can the attribution of anything to the state of mind I shall *then* be in establish any connexion between my words *then* and this thing that is happening *now*? When I look into the past and wonder how I can mean any past thing by what I say—how my thoughts can reach the past thing—I cannot get at that thing except always by means of representations; so my enquiry how my words represent the actual events may seem an impossible one. How can I conceive an event-in-itself beyond the representations, and so ask for a connexion between the representations and the event-in-itself? But if I consider some present thing (which can, if you like, be a state of mind) and my future ability to speak of it, it is brought out more clearly how difficult it is to make out that anything I may attribute to my future mental state will make what I say refer to *this*. My mental state may have any characteristics I please to imagine; but if it could be imagined to have those characteristics without being veridical it will have no relation to *this* event except that of coming after it, or possibly of being caused by it. And these relations do not seem to be enough to make it a memory of this event.

In general we must fail if we try to explain the sense of statements about the past by means of present memory, consciousness of meaning, quality of images, or anything else of the kind. For either we have left out all reference to the actual past, or we have surreptitiously introduced it into an explanation that proposed to do without it.

When one thinks of the meaning of a statement about the past, one often thinks of saying, "If I (or anyone else) had been there then, we should have seen, heard . . ." and so on. Thus Mr. R. Rhees says that there is not any special difficulty (for a phenomenalist) in explaining what it means to say that material things existed before there were living beings: "If there are difficulties, they apply to the phenomenalist interpretation of *any* statement about what is not immediately observed. . . . The phenomenalist would say you have still to give an account . . . in terms of the observations that could have been made. . . . The question of how or whether human beings could have got into positions to make these observations at these times is not really relevant."[1] The relevant question, however, is not how human beings could have got into positions to make those observations at those times, but how it is that we understand "those times." We proceed as if we had a prepared empty time scheme and the only work to be done were the analysis of what is to be put into the various places of the scheme. If someone tells me the criteria, say, for a person's being dead, I do not ask him for what date these criteria hold good: they are the criteria at any date, or rather date does not come in. The description of the criteria tells us in what circumstances we are to say a thing; we think the actual situation in which the criteria occur supplies us with, so to speak, a sense-giving apparatus for the words. But we use the words although the apparatus is not present, and now when we think of criteria we think of the *possibility* of their application. So we hear it discussed what are the criteria for there being a table before one; and then "There is a table in the next room" is explained by means of such remarks as "If one were to go into the next room one would

---

[1] *Mind*, LVI (1947), 380.

see . . ." and so on. Now suppose a question is raised about the meaning of such hypothetical statements: a great difference can be seen between "if p were to happen, q would happen" and "if p had happened, q would have happened." For in "if p were to happen, q would happen" the antecedent is fulfillable. The meaning of this "if . . . then" can be shown by means of actions or by means of what happens, where the antecedent is fulfillable. One makes a conditional threat and carries it out if the antecedent is fulfilled; one makes a conditional prediction and remarks that one was right if the consequence follows, or that one was wrong if it does not follow; and if the antecedent was not actualised, one does not thereupon claim to be either refuted or confirmed. The sense of the conditional is learnt from such examples. But the sense of the unfulfillable past conditional could not be made clear in any such way; it is difficult to imagine how it could make sense to someone who did not already understand both the fulfillable conditional and the use of words to describe the past—that very past time that is spoken of in the conditional, not some other time that, e.g., falls within his memories. If we have described the criteria for a certain happening by saying what observations justify the statement that it is taking place, then it does follow that if there was such a happening in a certain place and time, some such observations could have been made at that place and time; but this is a mechanical drawing of consequences and is of no use as a combination to discussion of the meaning of statements about the past.

I am at this point tempted to say: A statement about the past cannot possibly have present criteria; it can only have present evidence. For if I think that a statement about the past has present criteria, must I not suppose that it is possible for the past to change; will not a change in the things that serve as criteria involve a change in the truth of the statement for which they are criteria? But nothing that happens now could change what has happened: this would be an absurdity except in a particular kind of case in which the description of an event depends on what happens after it (e.g., Aristotle describes the use of the Greek word which we translate "involuntary" in such a way that an action can come to have been "involuntary" if it produces consequences which the agent regrets).

"The past cannot change." It might be retorted that the past has constantly changed: first one thing has happened, then something quite different. But a denial of this is not what is meant by "The past cannot change." Things have taken a certain course, which perhaps can and perhaps cannot be reversed; some actions can be undone. But it makes sense to wish that they had never been done, and when one says "The past cannot change" one is stating that this wish is unfulfillable. But "a change in the past" is *nonsense,* as can be seen from the fact that if a change occurs we can ask for its date. If the idea of a change in the past made sense, we could ask the question "When was the battle of Hastings in 1066?" and that not in the sense "When in 1066 was the battle of Hastings?" The idea of a change in the past involves the idea of a date's being dated. This could of course be given a sense in a particular context—say of a change in a system of dating. But until one gives it sense in some such way—which does not serve one's purpose—it is nonsensical. This consideration helps to remove the impression that when one says "the past cannot change" one is saying of something *intelligible* that it is an impossibility.

If someone said: "The future cannot change, for if it is true that something is going to happen then it is going to happen"; this would seem perfectly empty. Similarly "If it is true that something has happened, then it has happened" is empty. "But," it may be said, "there is a difference between the past and future which shows what is meant by 'the past cannot change.' If something is going to happen, it is going to happen; but a change does come about precisely when it does happen. When it has happened it is no longer going to happen. Thus the future changes in just that sense in which we say that the past can't change." To say this is to regard the happening of an event as an irreversible change that takes place in it, and fixes its character. These are two different points, which I might represent in the following way. Suppose that I have a set of pictures in a row: those on my left represent the past, and those on my right represent the future, and the row moves constantly to the left. The idea that happening is an irreversible change which takes place in the event could be represented by the fact that once a picture has passed me it cannot be removed from the row, whereas a picture on the right-hand side can be removed. The idea that happening fixes the character of the event could be represented by the fact that the pictures become set as they pass me so that they cannot be altered whereas the pictures to the right are in a fluid state or are as yet mere blanks. This is an exact image of what I have in mind when I speak of the changelessness of the past. In the image the impossibility of removing or altering the left-hand pictures is a fact which could be otherwise. I use the image to represent what

I regard as a fact which could *not* be otherwise. But I have to admit that the force of the idea that I am stating some kind of fact when I say that the past cannot change lies in the inclination I have to draw such an analogy. In the analogy, the impossibility is empirical. I retain the analogy but say that in the original the impossibility is nonempirical. But if I dismiss such analogies, I am unable to say what is left.

This idea of the past as something *there,* to which true statements about the past correspond as a description corresponds to the object that we can compare with it, is what produces the puzzlement of which this paper is a discussion; for now when I wish, as it were, to locate this object I cannot do so. My thought of past things seems like a pointer that points to nothing: and yet to say that the whole conception is a mistake seems to be like denying the reality of the past. This idea, of course, is not what anyone could put forward as an *account* of the meaning of statements about the past. The situation is rather that one has this idea and then tries to justify it, or to find out whether there is any sense in it; whether it contains a point which there is some acceptable way of expressing, or whether it is possible to get rid of it without thinking that one has let go of something essential to an understanding of the past tense.

It is clear that it does not make sense to say that the past has changed. But this does not make it clear that it is equally nonsensical to deny the possibility of a change in the past; it may seem that the idea of a change in the past is nonsensical *because* this changelessness is so absolute a necessity. Nor does it solve the problem to say that the necessity is one of meaning and not of fact, for then the question arises what such a necessity of meaning is: is it that we have an insight into meaning that is expressed in the idea of the changelessness of the past, and is it the business of philosophy to bring about this insight, to distinguish it from recognition of empirical facts, and to leave it at that? How is it that one can, as it were, see a meaning that is no meaning in the idea of the past changing?

Suppose that a child wanted a cake that it had eaten. That it cannot have it again is a mere physical fact. But suppose that it wanted a bang that it had heard, that is, that actual individual bang. (I will disregard the difficulties of making this supposition.) How could it even express such a want? "Make that bang again!" does not express what we want expressed. We can devise a highly artificial[2] method of doing so. We

---

[2] This artificiality makes the problem seem much easier to solve than it actually is.

know how to use proper names. Let us name a particular bang and call it *"A."* Now we are able to express the desire: "I want *A* again." And we say that it is impossible to get what is asked for. If *A* were a cake which had been eaten, the impossibility of getting it again would be of a different kind. One has the idea that this is because of the nature of a bang and the nature of a cake, and that it is this that we see when we see that we cannot have *A* again if *"A"* is the proper name of a bang. It is as if in prescribing that *"A"* should be the proper name of a bang we were directing the attention to something which we see cannot be repeated: this impossibility is a consequence of its nature, not of its physical but of its logical nature. It is a consequence of the physical nature of the cake and the process of digestion together with certain laws of nature that it cannot be got again after it has been eaten. But—and it is important that we want to stress not the analogy but the contrast— it is a consequence of the *logical* nature of the bang that we cannot have it again. Wittgenstein[3] argues that in such examples, while we think we are insisting on the contrast, we are misunderstanding the one case on the analogy of the other: but in fact what we do with the name— i.e., that we do *not* speak of getting *A* again—is a *part* of (not a conse-quence of) its being the proper name of a bang. It goes to characterise the use which makes *"A"* have that meaning. If a bang were made in response to this request and satisfied it, then this would show that *"A"* was not being used as the proper name of a bang. For we could not say that the asker was satisfied because he mistakenly supposed the new bang to be the old one again. What sense could there be in the idea (that we are supposing to exist) of the numerical identity of a bang, if a bang heard now could be identified—even wrongly—with a bang heard before? That *"A"* is the proper name of a bang means that we do not speak of getting *A* again. "Getting *A* again" is an expression similar to ones which have use in other contexts, as when *"A"* is the name of a cake. When we transfer it to this context we do not transfer its use; for to describe its use we should have to describe in what circumstance we should say we had got *A* again, as we could do if *"A"* were the name of a cake. But though we do not transfer its use we think we transfer some meaning and so we think that what is meant is something im-

[3] In this example I have repeated some remarks made by Dr. Wittgenstein in discussion. Everywhere in this paper I have imitated his ideas and methods of dis-cussion. The best that I have written is a weak copy of some features of the original, and its value depends only on my capacity to understand and use Dr. Wittgenstein's work.

possible. We think we cannot imagine getting *A* again because of the essential character of what is denoted by the name. But the real reason is that "getting *A* again" is an expression for which we have yet to invent a use in this context; so far no use for it exists. This doesn't seem enough, however: we think we *could* not give it a use—meaning that we could not give it the use it has in other contexts, the use that the form of expression suggests or reminds us of. We may stop thinking that the request is impossible because it is a request for the impossible and come to think that it is impossible because it could not make sense; i.e., it is a necessary fact that the use of "*A*" as the proper name of a bang excludes the use of the expression "getting *A* again." And this is because we *could* not describe the circumstances in which we should say we had got *A* again. For if we say merely that we *do* not speak of getting *A* again, this will seem arbitrary or accidental; it might be objected that we *could* do what we do not in fact do, unless it is impossible.

Suppose that someone learns to perform the following exercise, with little connexion with anything else he says and does (as might be the case if a child were set to learn dates in the void): he learns to say after his teacher, "The battle of Hastings was in 1066; the battle of Waterloo was in 1815" and so on for a number of battles. Now the word "when" is introduced in this way: the teacher says, "When was the battle of Hastings?" and the learner responds, "1066," and so on for the rest of the battles. This is all that happens; but there is correct and incorrect response, and the learner learns to make only the correct responses. And now if the teacher says, "When was the battle of Hastings in 1066?" the learner has not been taught what to do; what he has been taught to do in response to "when" has not included any response to this question. Suppose that there is nothing that he does spontaneously which is accepted by the teacher. The teacher *could* teach him something to do in response to this new question; but, until he does, the question does not belong to the exercise. This exercise as I have described it has no point. But the *actual* senselessness of "When was the battle of Hastings in 1066?" seems to be like its senselessness in this exercise. In order to give it a sense, one has to invent circumstances, such as a change in the system of dating, in which we are to speak of a date's being dated. The senselessness seems to consist in the fact that we have no use for this combination of words. But it follows from this that the only sense that can be made of the philosophical assertion that the past cannot change is that to speak of a change in the past is to produce an expression for which no use exists and which therefore has *no* sense. For if we could speak of a change in the past, such questions as "When was the battle of Hastings in 1066?" would be applicable. It therefore seems to follow that the *sort* of sense-lessness in such a question is the *sort* of senselessness that there is in speaking of a change in the past. But the senselessness that there is in that question does seem to be like its senselessness in the artificial exercise that I imagined.

If I consider these examples, I am less inclined to say "The past cannot change" as if I were thereby saying something which could be compared with a statement of physical impossibility. It remains true, nevertheless, that an idea of a change in the past retains an apparent meaning which is one of the sources of perplexity. For this appearance of meaning is such that one wishes to say that one can see that it is somehow not a *legitimate* meaning, and because of this one seems to be saying something positive in saying that the past cannot change. This might be expressed by saying that "a change in the past" is an expression that *could* not be given a sense, meaning that the vague sense that one perceives in it could not be embodied in a use—as if one could understand the sense that it could not be given. It is possible that a reason for this can be found in the existence of two usages of the past tense; the unfulfillable past conditional sentence and the wish that the past had been otherwise. I have already remarked that the former cannot be imagined to be intelligible except to someone who already understands the conditional and past indicative, and similar remarks, *mutatis mutandis,* would apply to the latter. One can imagine the existence of a people whose language did not include the expression of a wish that things had been otherwise. It would be possible to formulate the wish in their language by using their expression for wishing and their past tense; yet it might be that to them this sounded incomprehensible, or like mere bad grammar. If such a people existed they would seem to be psychologically different from ourselves. The fact that to us this wish makes sense may help to account for the apparent positiveness of "The past cannot change." But if I ask: "Why does the wish make sense to us?" I can find no answer, except that we do use the past tense in this way in connection with wishing.

I considered "The past cannot change" because I was enquiring into the idea of saying "The criteria for statements about the past must lie in the past." Present criteria for past statements seemed to entail the possibility of a change in the past. The reason for thinking this is that if one states the criteria for saying something one may be claiming, or may seem to be claiming, to give a translation or analysis. It would follow that a change in the things that were the criteria for a statement about the past would entail a change in the truth of the statement. But if one gives up the idea that to give the criteria is to give a translation, then this no longer follows. And it is certain that we do use present criteria for statements about the past, and also that no change would make us say "It used to be the case that Brutus killed Caesar, but since such and such a time it has been the case that Caesar killed Brutus." Yet one can imagine changes which would make present criteria for statements about the past inapplicable: constant conflicting shifts in people's memories, chaotic changes in monuments and documents, and so on. And I want to say: Whatever happened—and such things are conceivable—nothing that happened in the future could make it not *still true* that the things that happened in the past did happen as they happened, even though nobody could know it. But this expression, "still true," shows that I have not properly grasped what is implied by saying that the question "When was the Battle of Hastings in 1066?" is senseless. Someone might reply to us, "Yes, Brutus killed Caesar. But how can you make this have any sense but the one given to it by the use which you have learnt for it? How do you think you add anything to that by saying that it would be 'still true' whatever happened?" Yet this is not to say that something could make it false. Still, something could destroy its sense, make it impossible for it to make sense. One wishes to say that the truth is beyond the reach of any thing which would destroy the use of the sentence. It is as if one saw *through* the use to the fact to which it is related.

It is possible that I am dominated in this discussion by the idea that in making a philosophical enquiry into the meaning of the past tense I must try to show what it is that we know in knowing anything about the past. Or that it must provide a justification of the concept of the past, as opposed to the normal justifications of particular statements about the past. When I discussed the example of the learner being shown coloured lights, I was looking for something that would make what the learner learned to say stand for the past red light. Suppose it should be objected, "You will not find what you are looking for. You have yourself shown that the *kind* of thing you want is an impossibility. To speak of something past is to have the kind of practice that you have made the learner acquire in your example. The example is, of course, artificial, but a description similar in principle, but far more extensive and complicated, would tell you how words are used in speaking of the past: and to use words in this way *is* to speak of the past." Now for many reasons this criticism is extremely persuasive. In particular, the idea of meaning which it indicates is one that resolves the problem presented by the fact that a sense occurs in a false representation no less than in a true one. For this suggests that in an investigation of meaning one ought to attend to the experience of having the idea independently of truth or falsehood; but then one gets into difficulties when one has to relate the idea to the facts. Suppose that one person, *A*, were sitting by another, *B*, who was making reports by telephone to a third, *C*, on events that were taking place before *A* and *B*; *A* is watching and listening, but there are certain words, the meaning of which he does not know, but which he learns on this occasion. (This is shown by the fact that he afterwards uses them correctly.) Now *C* learns the facts; but *A* does not learn the facts, but the sense of the words. Let us suppose that *B* tells lies: *C* is misinformed, but *A* is not misinformed but—if anything—learns a wrong sense for the words. In general, *A* could not learn the right (i.e., the usual) sense of the words except from their being used to make *true* reports. And it is not that *A* sees in what circumstances they *are* true; for he cannot see that a statement is true unless he already knows the sense of the statement. The situation which verifies a remark and that in which the sense of the remark is shown may be identical; and one is strongly inclined to think that in understanding a sense one grasps a fact or an apparent fact. But if one says this, one's problem "What is it to understand this sense?" reappears for the sense of the description of *that* fact or apparent fact.

A particular objection suggests itself to accepting a description of usage as an answer to the enquiry how the past tense has meaning. Namely, that this gives the impression that what I know in knowing some past fact is a usage. Or rather, since I can hardly be said to know this until I have found the description of it, it seems as if this method of investigation professed to discover that all there really was to know when I knew a past fact was that I was using words in a certain way. But this is in fact a mistake about the purpose of the description, which is not to show one what one is really knowing when one knows something about the past. Indeed, if that were supposed to be its function, it must fail; no one could understand, e.g., the description that I gave of the practice of the learner in connexion with the coloured lights, if he did not *already* understand the past tense; for it was used in the description of what the learner did. The purpose of the description is rather to make us stop asking the question "What is it that I really know?" and stop looking for a foundation for the idea of the past. I spoke earlier of the perplexity which arises from the fact that one looks for a *justification* of "red" in stage (2) of the procedure I described, or of "was red," and cannot find what one is looking for. The purpose of answering the question "How does the past tense have meaning?" by giving a description of use is to make one think that this search for a justification is a mistake.

So far I have spoken only of that use of the past tense in which a witness reports what he has witnessed. We also receive and use testimony, tell and hear stories, make deductions and guesses, use unfulfillable past conditional sentences, express wishes about the past, make historical statements and investigations. If we were to describe the usages of words made in these cases, our descriptions would all lack one particular feature. The descriptions would not in these cases include any mention of actual events corresponding to the past-tense sentences or clauses, such as is made in any description of the personal-report use of the past tense. This would not seem to be of any importance except as regards those uses of the past tense which are supposed to be statements of actual fact. But in these cases one has the idea that a philosophical description of what it is to know the facts necessarily tells one *what* one knows in knowing them, i.e., what the facts themselves consist in. If then the description does not bring in the facts themselves, it seems that what our knowledge really consists in must be considered as reduced to what the description does bring in.

Now it is clear that no theory of knowledge can introduce any mention of actual past events—other than those which are remembered —into its description of what it is to know statements about the past. And so far as I can judge, only the account of meaning given by Wittgenstein enables one without begging the question to introduce mention of actual past events into one's account of knowing the past that one *has* witnessed. This is made possible precisely by that feature of his method which is most difficult to accept: namely, that he attacks the effort at justification, the desire to say: "But one says 'was red' because one knows that the light *was* red!" One says "was red" in these circumstances (not: *recognizing* these circumstances) and that *is* what in this case is called knowing the past fact. To say this is *not* to profess to give an analysis of what one really knows. If we proceed to give similar descriptions of usage for statements about the past other than statements of memory and find in these descriptions an answer to the question how those statements have meaning, our descriptions will not include any mention of the actual past events; but as these descriptions will not be analyses or translations we shall not be faced with the difficulty that we have apparently analysed away the actual facts. We shall say, "It is in these circumstances that we speak of knowing such and such; it is this use that gives that statement a sense." One of the aims of this description of usage is to stop one from asking "What do I know?" except as one asks this question in daily life, i.e., unphilosophically; and if one says: "But now it seems to me as if I did not really have any knowledge about the past; all that I can say is that I use words in such and such a way," the reply is that "I have no knowledge about the past" has a sense (e.g., in the mouth of someone who has lost his memory) which is certainly not that according to which one is using it here, and that one has not yet given it a sense as one is now using it.

Basic Propositions

A. J. AYER

Philosophers who concern themselves with the theory of knowledge are apt to be haunted by an ideal of certainty. Seeking a refuge from Descartes' malicious demon, they look for a proposition, or class of propositions, of whose truth they can be absolutely sure. They think that once they have found this basis they can go on to justify at least some of their beliefs, but that without it there can be no defence against scepticism. Unless something is certain, we are told, nothing can be even probable.

The discussion of this problem is now usually confined to the case of empirical propositions. For what is required is certainty about matters of fact, in Hume's sense of the term; and while it is generally agreed that a priori propositions can be certain, it is also held that they do not afford us knowledge about matters of fact. But even the claim that a priori propositions are certain is not without its difficulties. For surely it is possible to doubt them. People do make mistakes in mathematics and in logic; they miscalculate, they draw invalid inferences, they contruct abstract systems which turn out to be self-contradictory. And I suppose that someone who had discovered that he was addicted to such errors might come to doubt the validity of any a priori statement that he made. Admittedly, his only ground for supposing that a particular answer was wrong would be that it failed to tally with some other answer which he took to be right; nevertheless the as-

sumption that he was justified in so taking it would be one that he
could still go on to question. Recognizing that some answers must be
right, he would remain eternally in doubt as to which they were.
"Perhaps" he would say to himself, "the procedures that I am trying
to carry out are not the correct procedures; or, even if they are correct,
perhaps I am not applying them properly in this particular case."

But all that this shows, it may be said, is that we must distinguish
the propositions of mathematics and logic as such from empirical
propositions about the behaviour of persons who do mathematics or
logic. That someone is carrying out the right procedure, or that someone is carrying out a certain procedure rightly, is an empirical proposition which can indeed be doubted. But the result at which he arrives,
the a priori proposition of logic or mathematics itself, is either certainly true or certainly false; it is certainly true, if it is true at all. But
what is meant here by saying of such a proposition that it is certain?
Simply that it is a priori. To say that the proposition is certainly true,
or that it is necessary, or that it is true a priori, is, in this case, just
to say the same thing in three different ways. But what then is the point
of saying that a priori propositions are certain if it is to say no more
than that a priori propositions are a priori? The answer is that people
wish to pass from "*p* is certainly true," in this sense, to "*p* can be known
for certain to be true." They make the tacit assumption that the truth
of an a priori proposition can be "clearly and distinctly perceived." But
if their ground for saying that such a proposition can be known
for certain is simply that it is certain in the sense of being a priori,
then their use of the word "certain" gains them nothing. They are
still saying no more than that an a priori proposition is an a priori
proposition. And if by saying that such propositions can be known for
certain they mean that they sometimes are known for certain, then
their conclusion does not follow from their premiss. For in any case
in which such knowledge is claimed, there is room for the empirical
doubt; perhaps this is not the correct procedure, or perhaps it has not
been applied correctly in this instance. Thus, while there is a sense in
which a priori propositions are unassailable, to explain which would
be to explain what was meant by calling them a priori, there is also
a sense in which they are not. They are not unassailable, inasmuch as
it can always be asked of any "clear and distinct perception," in
Descartes' sense of the term, whether it really is clear and distinct. Of
course, such a question easily becomes futile. If I doubt whether I have

done a sum correctly, what can I do except look up the rules as set out in the textbooks, check my result with those of other people, go over the sum again? And then it remains possible that I have misread the textbooks, that other people are deceiving me, that if I went over the sum yet again I should get a different answer. Now clearly this process can go on for ever, and just for that reason there is no point to it. If nothing is going to satisfy me, then nothing is going to satisfy me. And if nothing counts as satisfying me, then it is necessarily true that I cannot be satisfied. And if it is necessarily true, it is nothing to worry about. The worrying may in fact continue, but at this point the state of doubt has become neurotic. It is never settled because it is not allowed to be.

For the most part, however, philosophers are not troubled in this way about a priori propositions. They are content to say that these propositions are certain, and they do not regard it as an objection to this way of speaking that people often reason incorrectly or that they get their calculations wrong. On the other hand, they are very often troubled about empirical propositions, just because they are not a priori. For, following the same line as before, they argue that since these propositions are not necessary, they are not certain; and that since they are not certain they cannot be known for certain to be true. But, reasoning in this way, they find themselves exposed to the taunts of the G. E. Moore school. "Of course empirical propositions are not certain in the way that a priori propositions are. Of course they can be denied without self-contradiction. If this were not so, they would not be empirical propositions. But it does not follow from this that they cannot properly be said to be certain in any sense at all. It does not follow that they cannot be known for certain to be true. Do you mean to tell me," says Professor Moore, "that you do not know that you are awake and that you are reading this? Do you mean to tell me that I do not know that I have a pen in my hand? How improper it would be, what a misuse of English, to say that it was not certain that I had a sheet of paper in front of me, but only highly probable. How absurd it would be to say, 'Perhaps this is not a pen. I believe that it is but I do not know it.' "

Now clearly Professor Moore and his friends are right. It is good English to use the words "know" and "certain" in the way that they encourage us to use them. If someone wants to know what day of the week it is and, when I tell him it is Monday, asks me whether this is certain, then an answer like "Yes, quite certain; I have just seen it in the newspaper, and anyhow I remember that yesterday was a Sunday" is a correct answer. To answer, "Well, I seem to remember that yesterday was a Sunday, and I believe that this is today's newspaper, and I seem to see 'Monday' written on it; but I may be wrong about the newspaper, and anyhow both memory and perception are fallible. Therefore I cannot be certain that it is Monday but I think it very probable"—to give an answer of this sort would be tiresome, and not only tiresome but misleading. It would be misleading because, in the ordinary way, we say that something is not certain but at best highly probable only in cases where we have some special reason for doubting, some reason which applies particularly to the case in question. Thus, in the example that I have just given, I might be justified in saying that I did not know that it was Monday if my memory was frequently at fault in matters of this kind, or I had glanced at the newspaper only carelessly, or the newspaper could not be relied on to print the right date. But if my reason for saying that it is not certain is merely the general reason that all empirical beliefs are fallible, then it is not consonant with ordinary usage to say that it is only probable. It is correct to say that it is certain. It is correct for me to say that I know.

All the same, this does not take us very far. It is all very well for Moore to prove the existence of external objects by holding up his hands and saying that he knows that they exist;[1] the philosopher who sees this as a problem is unlikely to be satisfied. He will want to say that Moore does not really know that these physical objects exist, that he cannot know it. At the very least he will want to raise the question "How does he know it?" Now it may be argued that this is not a sensible question. But one is not going to stop people from asking it merely by giving them an English lesson, anymore than one is going to make people feel comfortable about induction merely by arguing that it is correct for a schoolmaster to say that he knows the truth of Archimedes' law, that he would be misleading his pupils if he said that he did not know it to be true but only thought it probable. Even if this is so, it is beside the point.

But in that case what is the point? Why are people not satisfied with Moore's sort of answer. Presumably the reason is that they feel that it does not meet the question which they are trying to ask. After all, it

---

[1] *Proof of an External World* (British Academy Annual Philosophical Lecture, 1939).

is to be supposed that the philosopher who says that Moore does not really know, that he cannot really know, what he says he knows is as well acquainted with the English language as Moore. He is not making a philological blunder, nor is he casting doubts upon Moore's honesty. If he says that Moore does not know for certain the truth of such a proposition as "this is a human hand," it is because he thinks that nobody can know for certain that such a proposition is true, that it is not the sort of proposition that can be so known. But this means that he has decided to use the word "know" in an unconventional way. He is making it inapplicable to a set of propositions to which it does apply in ordinary usage. And this, we may assume, is not a mere piece of eccentricity on his part. He has some reason for his procedure. Let us consider what it might be.

I can think of two reasons for taking such a course, both of which are good reasons in the sense that they call attention to valid points of logic. In the first place, it may be suspected that someone who claims to know, without giving any proof, that such and such is the case, is relying on an act of intuition; and then the rejection of the claim proceeds from the denial that any act of intuition can constitute knowledge. The logical point is that from the fact that someone is convinced that a proposition is true it never follows that it is true. That A believes p may be a good reason for accepting p, if A is a reliable person; but it is in no case a conclusive reason. It is never self-contradictory to say both that A believes p and that p is false. It is indeed self-contradictory to say that A knows p and that p is false, but the explanation of this is just that part of what is meant by saying that A knows that p, as opposed to merely believing it, is that p is true. If p turns out to be not true, then it follows that it was not known, though it does not follow that it was not believed. Now one way of bringing out this distinction is to say that knowledge guarantees the truth, or reality, of its object, whereas belief does not; and this can be allowed to pass so long as it is nothing more than a picturesque way of expressing the linguistic fact that it is self-contradictory to speak of knowing something which is not the case, but not self-contradictory to speak of believing what is not the case. But what such formulations are all too often taken to imply is that the property of guaranteeing the truth or reality of its object belongs to knowledge as a special kind of mental activity; from which it is concluded that the truth, or reality, of the supposed "object of knowledge" can be inferred simply from the occurrence of the act of knowing, considered in itself. And this is a serious mistake. For knowledge, in the sense which is here alone in question, is always knowledge that something or other is so. In order that it should be knowledge, it is necessary that the symbols which express what is known should state something true; and whether this is so depends upon the existence or nonexistence of the situation to which the symbols refer. It is not to be decided merely by examining the "state of apprehension" of the knower. My own view is that it is extremely misleading to speak of "acts of knowing" at all.[2] But even if we allow that something is described by this expression, it can never follow from the occurrence of such an act, considered in itself, that anything is known.

Thus, if Moore's ground for saying "I know that this is a human hand" were merely that he apprehended that it was so, it would not be conclusive; and it may be because some people have thought he was maintaining that it was conclusive that they have wished to reject his claim. But, in fact, one's reason for making an assertion like "This is a human hand" is never just that one is convinced of it. It is rather that one is having certain visual or tactual experiences. And this brings us to the second of my reasons why people may be dissatisfied with the "What I know, I know" technique. It is that in the case of propositions like "This is a chair," "This is a human hand," "There is more than one picture in the room"—all of which I should say that I now knew—it is not absurd for someone to ask me "How do you know?" And the answers he will get are "Because I can see it," "Because I can touch it," "Because I have counted them," "Because I remember seeing it," and so on. In short, a proposition like "I know this is a chair" cannot be true unless some propositions of the form "I am seeing . . . ," "I am touching . . . ," "I remember . . ." are true. On the other hand, a proposition of this type can be true in cases where the corresponding proposition at the "I-know-this-is-a-chair" level is false. Next, let us give the name "sense-datum statement" to a description of what is seen, touched, or otherwise perceived, in a sense of words like "see" and "touch" which does not carry the implication that what is so perceived is a physical object. Then, no statement like "This is a chair" can be true unless some sense-datum statement is true; but once again the converse does not hold. And this, I think, explains why some philosophers have wished to deny that any proposition which asserts the presence of a physical object can be known for certain to be true. The point that they are thereby making is that such a proposition does not follow from any one sense-datum statement; it is based upon the fact that somebody is having some sensory experience, but the description of the experience in question does not logically entail it.

This gives us the clue also to what is meant by those who say that propositions about physical objects can never be certain. They are not denying that there is a good and familiar sense of the word "certain" in which it can apply to such propositions, nor that it is good usage to say that one knows them to be true. What they are maintaining is simply that they do not follow from any finite set of sense-datum statements. The suggestion is that however strong the evidence in their favour may be it is never altogether sufficient; it is always consistent with their being false. Now this, indeed, may be disputed.[3] It might be argued that we should in fact take a finite quantity of sensory evidence to be sufficient; and that if subsequent evidence proved unfavourable we should account for it in some other way than by saying that what we took to be a physical object never really was one; we might prefer to distrust our present experience, or to save the appearances by introducing some new physical hypothesis. The difficulty is that there is no established rule to meet such cases. A procedure has to be laid down; and this, I think, is what is being done by those who deny that any proposition about a physical object can be certain. They are expressing a resolve to treat all such propositions as hypotheses, which are liable to revision in the light of further experience.

Now we may or may not agree with this proposal. But even if we reject it in favour of allowing the existence of a physical object to be conclusively established by a finite number of sensory experiences, we shall still have to recognize that no description of any one such experience entails the descriptions of the others. So that, if the test which a proposition has to satisfy in order to be certain is that it should follow from the description of a particular experience, we shall still reach the conclusion that all propositions about physical objects are uncertain. But all that this then comes to is that a proposition about a physical object is something more than a description of some particu-

---

3 Cp. C. Lewy, "On the Relation of Some Empirical Propositions to Their Evidence," *Mind*, LIII (1944), 289, and "Entailment and Empirical Propositions," *Mind*, LV (1946), 74; also A. H. Basson, "The Existence of Material Objects," *Mind*, LV (1946), 308, and my own paper, "Phenomenalism," *Arist. Soc. Proc.*, XLVII (1946-7), 163.

lar experience. To say that it is therefore uncertain is to imply that of all empirical statements only those that refer exclusively to some immediate, present experience are to be regarded as certain. Now this, again, is not an account of ordinary usage. It is a philosopher's recommendation. The question which concerns us is why anyone should wish to make it.

The answer is that "certainty" is reserved for statements of this kind because it is thought that they alone cannot be challenged. If I make a statement of the form "I perceive . . ." or "I know . . ." or "I remember . . . ," the truth of my statement can be questioned. It may turn out that I was having an hallucination, or that what I claimed to know was false, or that my memory was betraying me. But suppose that I am more cautious. Suppose that I merely say "It looks to me . . . ," "I have a feeling that . . . ," "I seem to remember. . . ." How can these statements be challenged? In what way could one set about refuting them? Of course, someone who says "I feel a headache" or "There is a red patch in the centre of my visual field" may be lying. But surely, it is argued, he must know whether he is lying or not. He can deceive others about what he sees or feels. But if his statement refers only to the content of his present experience, how can he possibly be mistaken? How can he even be in doubt as to whether it is true?

Let us look into this. Is it impossible that someone should wonder whether he was in pain? Certainly it would be a queer sort of doubt. Suppose that someone were to tell me "You think you are in pain but you really aren't." What should I understand him to be saying? Perhaps that nothing was wrong with me physically, that it was all my imagination, or, in other words, that the cause of my pain was psychological; and this might very well be true. But it would not follow that I was not feeling pain. To suggest to me that I do not feel it may be a way of making the pain stop; but that is a different matter. It does not alter the fact that when I feel the pain, I feel the pain. This is, indeed, an analytic truth.

But this, it may be objected, is not the point at issue. The question is "What am I feeling?" Might I not think that it was pain when it was really something else? Might I not think that such and such a coloured patch was magenta when it was really scarlet? Might I not think that such and such a note was E sharp when it was really E natural? Surely one can misdescribe one's experience. And if one can misdescribe it, can one ever be certain that one is describing it correctly? Admittedly,

I see what I see, feel what I feel, experience what I experience. That is a tautology. But, so it may be argued, it does not follow that I know what I am seeing, or that I know what I am feeling. For my knowing what I am seeing entails that some set of symbols, which I use to describe what I am seeing, does describe it correctly; and this may not be so.

But what is "misdescribing" in this case? What is the test by which it is determined that the coloured patch which I have called "magenta" is really scarlet. Is it a physical test? In that case I can very well be making a mistake, and a factual mistake. Is it what other people would say? Here again I can easily make a factual mistake. But suppose I intend merely to name what I am seeing. Can I be mistaken then? Plainly the answer is that I can not, if I am only naming. But if that is all that I am doing, then I am not saying anything at all. I can be neither wrong nor right. But directly I go beyond naming and try to describe something, then, it may be argued, I run the risk of being mistaken even about the character of my own immediate experience. For to describe anything is to relate it to something else, not necessarily to anything in the future, or to anything that other people experience, but at least to something that one has oneself experienced in the past. And the attributed relation may not, in fact, obtain.

Now this is a very common view, but I am persuaded that it is mistaken. No doubt, if I have learned to use a sensory predicate correctly in the first place, it will in fact be true that any object to which I properly apply it on any occasion other than the first will resemble some object to which I have properly applied it in the past. But it does not follow that in using the predicate I am making any reference to the past. Many philosophers have thought that it did follow, because they have assumed that an ostensive word was defined in terms of the resemblance of the objects which it denoted to some standard object. Thus, allowing, what is undoubtedly true, that I learned the use of the English word "green" by being shown certain objects which resembled each other in respect of being green, it is suggested that what I now assert when I say, for example, that the blotting paper in front of me is green is that it resembles these objects in the way that they resembled one another. But this suggestion is false; and to see that it is false we have only to reflect that from the statement that this piece of blotting paper is green it cannot be deduced that anything else exists at all. No doubt, what justifies me in calling it green, as opposed, say, to blue, is the fact that it resembles one set of objects rather than another; but this does not mean that in calling it green I am saying that it resembles any other objects. There are two propositions here which we must be careful not to confuse. One is that if *a* and *b* are both green they resemble one another in colour more than either of them resembles in colour anything outside the class of green things; and the other is that if *a* is green there is at least one other thing *b* which it resembles in colour more than it resembles in colour anything outside the class of green things. The first of these two propositions is analytic, it exemplifies the grammar of colour classification; but the second is empirical. That there is such another thing *b* is at best a matter of fact which has to be established independently. It does not follow from the fact that *a* is green.

This shows, incidentally, how little is accomplished by talking about classes in preference to talking about predicates. For suppose that for "*a* is green" we substitute "*a* belongs to the class of green things." Then how is the expression "belongs to the class of green things" to be interpreted? If it is merely a way of saying "is a green thing" there is no point in the substitution. If it is taken as equivalent to "is one of the things that are green," it is a mistranslation, since from the fact that *a* is green it does not follow that there are any other green things. If it is taken as equivalent to "resembles other things in being green," it is again a mistranslation for the same reason as before. There remains the possibility that the class is to be defined by enumeration. But then we have the strange consequence that all ascriptions of class membership become either analytic or self-contradictory: analytic, in our example, if *a* in fact is green, since "*a* is green" will then mean "*a* is either *a* or *b* or *c* or *d* . . . ," where the alternatives comprise the list of green things; and self-contradictory if it is not, since "*a* is green" will then mean "*a* is either *b* or *c* or *d* . . . ," where it is understood that *b, c, d* . . . are other than *a*. Another strange consequence will be that "*a* is green" does not formally contradict "*a* is not green"; for if in fact *a* is not green, then "*a* is not green" will mean "*a* is not either *b* or *c* or *d* . . . ," and if in fact *a* is green, then "*a* is green" will mean "*a* is either *a* or *b* or *c* or *d* . . ."; and these two propositions, so far from being incompatible, are both necessarily true. The explanation of this is that when it is interpreted in this way the meaning of the word "green" varies according to its denotation. So that the result of turning predicates into classes and treating these classes extensionally is that one cannot tell what a sentence means until one knows whether it is true. Now I agree that to know what a sentence means is to know what would make it true. But it would ordinarily be held, and I think with reason, that one could not tell whether it was in fact true unless one already knew what it meant. For otherwise what would it be that one was verifying?

However this may be, the fact remains that the ascription to one member of a class of the predicate by which the class is defined does not imply that the class has any other members. And from this it follows that if I use a sensory predicate to describe what I am now experiencing I need not be making any claim about a situation other than the one before me. Accordingly, no appeal to such other situations can show that I am mistaken. They are not relevant, since my statement makes no reference to them. But then am I saying anything even about this situation? We seem here to have fallen into a dilemma. Either I just name the situation, in which case I am not making any statement about it, and no question of truth or falsehood, knowledge or ignorance, certainty or uncertainty, arises; or I describe it. And how can I describe it except by relating it to something else?

The answer is, I suggest, that I do describe it, not by relating it to anything else, but by indicating that a certain word applies to it in virtue of a meaning rule of the language. I may be in doubt as to its description in the sense that I may hesitate over what word to apply to it, and I may be mistaken about it in the sense that I may describe it incorrectly, the standard of correctness being furnished by my own verbal habits, or by the verbal habits of others who use the same language. Let me try to explain this further.

It would now be generally conceded that a descriptive language, as opposed to a merely formal language, is not sufficiently characterized by its formation and transformation rules. The formation rules prescribe what combinations of signs are to constitute proper sentences of the language; and the transformation rules prescribe what sentences are validly derivable from one another. But if we are to use and understand a language descriptively, we require also rules which correlate certain signs in the language with actual situations; and it is these that I am calling meaning rules. Thus it is a meaning rule of English that anyone who observes something green will be describing it correctly if he says that it is green; or that anyone who feels pain will be describing what he feels correctly if he says that he feels pain. These

examples sound trivial, because the statement of these rules is not informative, except where it is a question of translation from one language into another. The rules are learned ostensively. The verbal
statement of them is normally superfluous. For that reason it may even
be misleading to call them "rules" at all. But, whatever may be called,
unless one knows how to employ them, one does not understand the
language. Thus, I understand the use of a word if I know in what
situations to apply it. For this it is essential that I should be able to
recognize the situations when I come upon them; but in order to effect
this recognition it is not necessary that I should consciously compare
these situations with memories of their predecessors. Neither is it
necessary, as some philosophers have mistakenly supposed, that I
should have a previous image with which the situation is found to
agree. For if I can recognize the image, then I can recognize the situation without the image; and if I cannot recognize the image, then it
does not help me to identify the situation. In either case its presence is
superfluous. Whether I recognize the situation or not is to be decided
by my behaviour; and one of the criteria is my being disposed to use
the appropriate words.

Thus, the sense in which statements like "This is green," "I feel
a headache," "I seem to remember . . ." can be said to be indubitable
is that, when they are understood to refer only to some immediate experience, their truth or falsehood is conclusively determined by a
meaning rule of the language in which they are expressed. To deny
them in the situations to which they refer is to misapply the language.
And it is in this sense also that one can know for certain that they are
true. But it is to be remarked that this is rather a case of knowing how
than of knowing that. If I have an experience, say an experience of
pain, it does not follow that I know what experience I am having. It
is perfectly possible for me to have the experience without knowing
anything at all. My knowing what experience it is is my being able to
identify it as falling under a particular meaning rule. It is therefore
not a matter of my knowing or ignoring some empirical fact but of
my knowing or not knowing how to use my language. I have certain
knowledge in the sense that the truth of what I say is not open to question, on the assumption that I am using my words correctly; but this
is an assumption which remains open to doubt. And here the doubt
is not like the ordinary empirical doubt, which turns upon the accuracy of some extrapolation, but like the logical doubt which we

considered at the outset. It is to be settled by looking up the rules. But this again lets in the empirical doubt as to whether one has actually carried out the correct procedure. I am told that "magenta" is the correct name for this colour, and I find this confirmed by the colour atlas. But perhaps my informant is deceiving me, or perhaps I misheard him, or perhaps this colour atlas is untrustworthy, or perhaps my eyes are playing me false. There are ways in which these suppositions can be tested, but the results of such tests can be questioned in their turn. So that here again the doubt may become neurotic and interminable. In this sense, therefore, nothing need be certain. Only, if nothing is allowed to be certain, the word "certain" ceases to have any use.

It is sometimes made an objection to the choice of sensory predicates as basic that sense experience is private. For it is argued that the fact that I have the sensations that I do is not of any great significance, since I cannot communicate them to anybody else. But the answer to this is that I can and do communicate them, inasmuch as my coming out with such and such a statement on such and such an occasion will count for another person as evidence in favour of the proposition that I am having such and such a sensation, and of any other proposition for which this proposition counts as evidence. His assumption is that I am using the language correctly; and this he can test by his own observations of my behaviour and of my environment. The meaning rules are impersonal in the sense that they do no more than prescribe what words are to be used in what situations. That some other person is in such or such a situation is an empirical hypothesis which I test by making observations, the proper description of which will in its turn depend upon a further meaning rule. The making of an observation is, of course, a private experience. But this is not to say that my description of it cannot be understood by anybody else.

It is, however, to be noted that while it is necessary that a descriptive language should contain meaning rules, it is not necessary that it should contain any sentences which express basic propositions, if a basic proposition is defined as one whose truth or falsehood is conclusively established, in a given situation, by a meaning rule of the language. It might be that the rules were such that every correct description of an empirical situation involved some reference beyond it; and in that case, while the use of the sentence which was dictated by the relevant meaning rule would be justified in the given situation, its truth would not be conclusively established. Suppose, for example, that our language contained no purely sensory predicates, so that the lowest level sentence that one could express in it was a sentence which ascribed some property to a physical object. Such a language could perfectly well be understood and consistently applied. Words like "table" would be introduced, as indeed they normally are introduced, by meaning rules; and understanding these words would again be a matter of knowing in what situations to apply them. The difference would be that from the fact that it was correct to use a given sentence in a given situation it would not follow that what the sentence expressed was true. That the use of the sentence was prescribed in these circumstances by a meaning rule would establish that what the sentence stated was probable but not that it was certain.

Thus, if my reasoning is sound, it is at least misleading to say that unless something is certain nothing can be even probable. What is true is that no proposition can ever be discovered to be even probable unless someone has some experience. But to say that someone has some experience is not, in any ordinary sense, to say that anything is certain. Whether anything is certain or not, in the sense which is here in question, will depend upon the meaning rules of the language; whether they are such as guarantee the truth or falsehood of a given statement in the appropriate situation, or merely justify its use. In neither case, as we have seen, is doubt excluded; but at the point where such doubt becomes perpetual, it ceases to be of any theoretical importance.

The Expression Theory of Art

O. K. BOUWSMA

The expression theory of art is, I suppose, the most commonly held of all theories of art. Yet no statement of it seems to satisfy many of those who expound it. And some of us find all statements of it baffling. I propose in what follows to examine it carefully. In order to do this, I want first of all to state the question which gives rise to the theory and then to follow the lead of that question in providing an answer. I am eager to do this without using the language of the expression theory. I intend then to examine the language of that theory in order to discover whether it may reasonably be interpreted to mean what is stated in my answer. In this way I expect to indicate an important ambiguity in the use of the word "expression," but more emphatically to expose confusions in the use of the word "emotion." This then may explain the bafflement.

I

And now I should like to describe the sort of situation out of which by devious turnings the phrase "expression of emotion" may be conceived to arise.

Imagine then two friends who attend a concert together. They go together untroubled. On the way they talk about two girls, about communism and pie on earth, and about a silly joke they once laughed at and now confess to each other that

71

they never understood. They were indeed untroubled and so they entered the hall. The music begins, the piece ends, the applause intervenes, and the music begins again. Then comes the intermission and time for small talk. Octave, a naive fellow, who loves music, spoke first. "It was lovely, wasn't it? Very sad music, though." Verbo, for that was the other's name, replied: "Yes, it was very sad." But the moment he said this he became uncomfortable. He fidgeted in his seat, looked askance at his friend, but said no more aloud. He blinked, he knitted his brows, and he muttered to himself. "Sad music, indeed! Sad? Sad music?" Then he looked gloomy and shook his head. Just before the conductor returned, he was muttering to himself, "Sad music, crybaby, weeping willows, tear urns, sad grandma, sad, your grandmother!" He was quite upset and horribly confused. Fortunately, about this time the conductor returned and the music began. Verbo was upset but he was a good listener, and he was soon reconciled. Several times he perked up with "There it is again," but music calms, and he listened to the end. The two friends walked home together but their conversation was slow now and troubled. Verbo found no delight in two girls, in pie on earth, or in old jokes. There was a sliver in his happiness. At the corner as he parted with Octave, he looked into the sky, "Twinkling stars, my eye! Sad music, my ear!" and he smiled uncomfortably. He was miserable. And Octave went home, worried about his friend.

So Verbo went home and went to bed. To sleep? No, he couldn't sleep. After four turns on his pillow, he got up, put a record on the phonograph, and hoped. It didn't help. The sentence "Sad, isn't it?" like an imp, sat smiling in the loud-speaker. He shut off the phonograph and paced the floor. He fell asleep, finally, scribbling away at his table, like any other philosopher.

This then is how I should like to consider the use of the phrase "expression of emotion." It may be thought of as arising out of such situations as that I have just described. The use of emotional terms—sad, gay, joyous, calm, restless, hopeful, playful, etc.—in describing music, poems, pictures, etc., is indeed common. So long as such descriptions are accepted and understood in innocence, there will be, of course, no puzzle. But nearly everyone can understand the motives of Verbo's question "How can music be sad?" and of his impulsive "It can't, of course."

Let us now consider two ways in which one may safely escape the expression theory.

Imagine Verbo at his desk, writing. This is what he now writes and this gives him temporary relief. "Every time I hear that music I hear that it's sad. Yet I persist in denying it. I say that it cannot be sad. And now what if I were wrong? If every day I met a frog, and the frog said to me that he was a prince, and that there were crown jewels in his head ('wears yet a precious jewel in his head'), no doubt I should begin by calling him a liar. But the more I'd consider this the more troubled I should be. If I could only believe him, and then treat him like a prince, I'd feel so much better. But perhaps *this* would be more like the case of this music: Suppose I met the frog and every day he said to me, 'I can talk,' and then went on talking and asked me, 'Can I talk?' then what would I do? And that's very much how it is with the music. I hear the music, and there it is again, sad, weeping. It's silly to deny this. See now, how it is? There's a little prince, the soul of a prince, in the frog, and so there's the soul in this music, a princess, perhaps. See then how rude I was denying this princess her weeping. Why shouldn't music have a soul too? Why this prejudice in favor of lungs and livers? And it occurs to me that this is precisely how people have talked about music and poems. Art lives, doesn't it? And how did Milton describe a good book? Didn't Shelley pour out his soul? And isn't there soul and spirit in the music? I remember now that the poet Yeats recommended some such thing. There are spirits; the air is full of them. They haunt music, cry in it. They dance in poems, and laugh. Pan-psychism for the habitation of all delicacies! So this is how it is, and there is neither joke nor puzzle in this sad music. There's a sad soul in it."

And then it was that Verbo fell asleep. His resistance to the music had melted away as soon as he gave up his curious prejudice in favor of animal bodies, as soon as he saw that chords and tones, like rhymes and rhythms, may sigh and shed invisible tears. Tears without tear glands—oh, I know the vulgar habit! But surely tones may weep. Consider now how reasonable all this is. Verbo is suddenly surprised to discover something which he has always known, namely that music is sad. And the discovery startles him. Why? Because in connection with this, he thinks of his sister Sandra (Cassie to all who saw her cry). And he knows what her being sad is like. She sobs, she wipes her eyes, and she tells her troubles. Cassie has a soul, of course. So Cassie is sad and the

music is sad. So the question for Verbo is "How can the music be like
Cassie?" and he gives the answer "Why shouldn't there be a soul of
the music, that flits in and flits out (People die too!) and inhabits a
sonata for a half-hour? Or why shouldn't there be a whole troupe of
them? 'The music is sad' is just like 'Cassie is sad,' after all. And
Octave who was not disturbed was quite right for he must have a kind
of untroubled belief in spirits. He believes in the frog-prince, in the
nymphs in the wood, and in the psyche of the sonnet."

This then is one way of going to sleep. But there is another one, and
it is based upon much the same sort of method. Both accept as the
standard meaning for "The music is sad," the meaning of "Cassie is
sad." We saw how Verbo came to see that the meaning is the same,
and how then it was true in the case of the music. He might however
have decided that the meaning certainly was the same, but that as
applied to the music it simply made no sense at all, or was plainly
false. Souls in sonnets! Don't be silly. There is the story about
Parmenides, well-known to all readers of Dionoges,[1] which will illustrate the sort of thing I have in mind. According to the story,
Parmenides and his finicky friend Zeno once went to a chariot race.
The horses and chariots had been whizzing past and the race had been
quite exciting. During the third round, at one turn a chariot broke an
axle and horse and chariot and rider went through the fence. It was a
marvelous exhibition of motion done to a turn at a turn. Parmenides
was enjoying himself thoroughly. He clutched at the railing and
shouted at the top of his voice, "Go, Buceph! Run!" The race is close.
But at about the seventh round, with Buceph now some part of a
parasang behind, Parmenides began to consider: "Half the distance in
half the time; a quarter of the length of a horse in a quarter of the
pace it takes. . . ." Suddenly, before the race was half over, Parmenides turned to Zeno. "Zeno," he said, "this is impossible." Zeno,
who was ready for his master, retorted, "I quit looking a long time
ago." So they left the chariot race, a little embarrassed at their nonexistence showing as they walked, but they did not once look back to
see how Buceph was doing.

This then is the story about Parmenides. It may be, of course, that
this story is not true; it may be one of Dionoges' little jokes. But our
concern is not with Parmenides. The point is that it illustrates a cer-

---

[1] An author of no repute at all, not to be confused with Diogenes.

tain way of disposing of puzzles. Parmenides has been disciplined to a certain use of such words as "run," "go," "turn," "walk," etc., so that when he is thoughtful and has all his careful wits about him, he never uses those words. He is then fully aware that all forms of motion are impossible. Nevertheless the eyes are cunning tempters. In any case as soon as Parmenides reflects, he buries himself in his tight-fitting vocabulary, and shuts out chariots and horses, and Buceph, as well. "Motion is impossible, so what am I doing here? Less than nothing. N'est pas is not." This disposition of the puzzle is, of course, open only to very strong men. Not many of those people who believe in the impossibility of motion are capable of leaving a horse race, especially when some fleet favorite is only a few heads behind.

Now something like this was a possibility also for Verbo. When, puzzled as he was, asking "How can that be?" he hit upon the happy solution "Why not?" But he might surely have said, stamping his foot, "It can't be." And in order then to avoid the pain of what can't be, he might have sworn off music altogether. No more concerts, no more records! The more radical decision is in such cases most effective. One can imagine Parmenides, for instance, sitting out the race, with his eyes closed, and every minute blinking and squinting, hoping he'd see nothing. So too Verbo might have continued to listen to music, but before every hearing invigorating his resolution never to say that the music was sad. Success in this latter enterprise is not likely to be successful, and for anyone who has already been puzzled it is almost certainly futile.

We have now noticed two ways in which one may attempt to rid oneself of the puzzle concerning "The music is sad," but incidentally we have also noticed the puzzle. The puzzle is identified with the question "How can music be sad?" We have also noticed how easy it is, once having asked the question, to follow it with "Well, it can't." I want now to go on to consider the expression theory in the light of the question "How can it be?" In effect, the expression theory is intended to relieve people who are puzzled by music, etc. They listen and they say that the music is sad. They ask, troubled and shaking their heads, "How can it be?" Then along comes the expression theory. It calms them, saying, "Don't you see that the music expresses sadness and that this is what you mean by its being sad?" The puzzled one may be calmed too, if he isn't careful. In any case, I propose to consider the question "How can it be?" before going on further.

This question "How can it be?" is apparently then not a question primarily about the music. One listens to the music and hears all that there is to hear. And he is sure that it is sad. Nevertheless when he notices this and then returns to the music to identify just what is sad in it, he is baffled. If someone, for instance, had said that there is a certain succession of four notes on the flute, in this music, and he now sought to identify them, he could play the music, and when they came along, he would exclaim, "There they are," and that would be just what he aimed at. Or again if someone had said that a certain passage was very painful, and he explained that he meant by this that when it is heard one feels a stinging at one's finger tips, then again one could play the music and wait for the stinging. Neither is it like the question which leaped out of the surprise of the farmer at the birth of his first two-headed calf. He looked, amazed, and exclaimed, "Well, I'll be switched! How can that be?" He bedded the old cow, Janus, tucked in the calf, and went to consult his book. He did not stand muttering, looking at the calf, as Verbo did listening to the record on the phonograph. He took out his great book, *The Cow,* and read the chapter entitled "Two Heads Are Better than One?" He read statistics and something about the incidence of prenatal collusion and decided to keep an eye on collaborators among his herd. And that was all. When now it comes to "The music is sad," there's no such easy relief. What is there to listen for? What statistics are there?

We have noticed before how Verbo settled his difficulty. He did this, but not by examining the music any further. He simply knew that the music was sad, and supplied the invisible tears, the unheard sobs, the soul of the music. If you had asked him to identify the tears, the unheard sobs, the soul of the music, he could not have done this. He might have tried, of course, and then he would have been baffled too. But the point is that he tries to think of the sadness of the music in the way in which he thinks of Cassie's sadness. Now we may be ready to explain the predicament, the bafflement. It arises from our trying to understand our use of the sentence "The music is sad" in terms of our uses of other sentences very much like this. So Verbo understands in terms of the sentence "Cassie is sad." One can imagine him saying to himself, "I know what sadness is, of course, having Cassie in the house, so that must be how it is with the music." Happily, as in the case of Parmenides, he thought of only one use, and as with a sharp knife he cut the facts to suit the knife. But suppose now that there are several uses of sentences much like "The music is sad"; what then? Is it like this use or this use or this use? And suppose that sometimes it's like this and at other times like this, and sometimes like both. Suppose further that one is only vaguely aware that this is so, and that one's question "How can that be?" is not stated in such a way as to make this possibility explicit, would it then be any wonder that there is bafflement?

Let us admit then that the use of "The music is sad" is baffling, and that without some exploration, the question "How can that be?" cannot be dealt with. Merely listening to the music will not suffice. We must then explore the uses of other sentences which are or may be similar to this, and we may hope that in this process we may see the expression theory emerge. At any rate, we'll understand what we are about.

II

What now are some of these other types of sentences which might be helpful? Well, here are a few that might serve: "Cassie is sad," "Cassie's dog is sad," "Cassie's book is sad," "Cassies face is sad." Perhaps, one or the other of these will do.

Though we have already noticed how Verbo came to use "Cassie is sad," I should like to consider that sentence further. Verbo understood this. When, as he remembered so well, the telephone call came and little Cassie answered—she had been waiting for that call—she was hurt. Her voice had broken as she talked, and he knew that the news had been bad. But he did not think she would take it so hard. And when she turned to him and he asked her what the man had said, at first her chin quivered and she didn't speak. Then she moved towards him and fell into his arms, sobbing: "Poor Felicia, poor Felicia!" He stroked her hair and finally when she was calm, she began to pour out her confidences to him. She loved her cat so; they had been brought up together, had had their milk from the same bottle, and had kept no secrets from each other. And now the veterinary had called to say that she had had another fit. And she burst into tears again. This was some years ago. Cassie is older now.

But this is not the only way in which "Cassie is sad" is used. Verbo had often heard his father and mother remark that it was good that Cassie could cry. They used to quote some grandmother who made a

proverb in the family. It went: "Wet pillows are best." She had made
this up many years ago when some cousin came to sudden grief. This
cousin was just on the verge of planned happiness, when the terrible
news came. (Her picture is the third in the album.) She received the
news in silence and never spoke of it or referred to it as long as she
washed the dishes in her father's house, for, as you may have guessed,
she never married. She never cried either. No one ever heard her
sniffling in the middle of the night. She expressed no regrets. And
she never told cat or mirror anything. Once she asked for a handker-
chief, but she said she had a cold. All the family knew what had happened, of course, and everyone was concerned, but there was nothing
to do. And so she was in many ways changed. She was drooping, she
had no future, and she tried to forget her past. She was not interested.
They all referred to her as their sad cousin, and they hoped that she
would melt. But she didn't. Yet how can Cassie's cousin be sad if she
never cries?

Well, there is a third use of "Cassie is sad." Tonight Cassie, who is
eighteen now, quite a young lady, as the neighbors say, goes up to her
room with her cat, her big book, and a great bowl of popcorn. She
settles into her chair, tells kitty to get down, munches buttery corn,
and reads her book. Before very long she is quite absorbed in what
she reads and feels pretty bad. Her eyes fill with tears and the words on
the page swim in the pool. It's so warm and so sweet and so sad! She
would like to read this aloud, it's so wonderful, but she knows how the
sadness in her throat would break her words in two. She's so sorry;
she's so sad. She raises her eyes, closes them, and revels in a deep-
drawn sigh. She takes up a full hand of popcorn and returns to her
sadness. She reads on and eats no more corn. If she should sob in corn,
she might choke. She does sob once, and quite loud, so that she is
startled by it. She doesn't want to be heard sobbing over her book.
Five minutes later she lays her book aside, and in a playful mood, twits
her cat, pretending she's a little bird. Then, walking like old Mother
Hubbard, she goes to the cupboard to get her poor cat a milk.

Cassie is sad, isn't she? Is she? Now that you consider it, she isn't
really sad, is she? That cozy chair, that deliberate popcorn, that playing
sparrow with her cat, that old Mother Hubbard walk—these are not
the manners of a sad girl. She hasn't lost her appetite. Still one can see
at once how we come to describe her in this way. Those are not phony
tears, and she's as helpless in her sobs and in keeping her voice steady

and clear as she was years ago when her dear cat had that fit. And she can, if you are so curious, show you in the book just what made her feel so sad. So you see it is very much like the case in which Cassie was sad. There's an obvious difference, and a similarity too. And now if you balk at this and don't want to say that Cassie in this situation is sad, your objection is intelligible. On the other hand if Cassie herself laughingly protests, "Oh, yes, I was sad," that will be intelligible too. This then may serve as an illustration of the way in which a puzzle which might become quite serious is fairly easily dealt with. How can Cassie be sad, eating popcorn and playing she's a sparrow?

In order to make this clear, consider Cassie now a grown woman, and an accomplished actress. She now reads that same passage which years ago left her limp as a willow, but her voice is steady and clear, and there are no tears. She understands what she reads and everyone says that she reads it with such feeling—it's so sad!—but there isn't a sign of emotion except for the reading itself, which as I said, goes along smoothly and controlled even to each breath and syllable. So there are no wet eyes, no drunken voice, and not a sob that isn't in the script. So there. Is she sad? I take it not. The spoken words are not enough. Tears, real tears, a voice that breaks against a word, sighs that happen to one, suffered sobs—when the reading occasions these, then you might say that Cassie was sad. Shall we say, however, that the reading is sad? How can that be? Well, you see, don't you?

Let us now attend to a sentence of a different type: "Cassie's dog is sad." Can a dog be sad? Can a dog hope? Can a dog be disappointed? We know, of course, how a Cartesian would answer. He might very well reply with this question, "Can a locomotive be sad?" Generous, he might allow that a locomotive might look sad, and so give you the benefit of a sad look for your dog. But can a dog be sad? Well, our dog can. Once during the summer when Cassie left her for three weeks, you should have seen her. She wouldn't look at the meatiest bone. She'd hang her head and look up at you as woebegone as a cow. And she'd walk as though her four hearts would break. She didn't cry, of course, and there were no confidences except those touching ones that come by way of petting and snuggling and looking into those wailing eyes. In any case our dog acted very much like that sad cousin who couldn't cry. She had plenty of reason, much too much, but she kept her wellings-up down. It's clear in any case what I mean when I say that our dog was sad. You mustn't expect everything from a sad dog.

So we pass to another type of sentence: "Cassie's book is sad." Well, obviously books don't cry. Books do not remember happier days nor look upon hopes snuffed out. Still, books that are sad, must have something to do with sadness, so there must be sadness. We know, of course. Books make people sad. Cassie reads her book and in a few minutes if she's doing well, she's sad. Not really sad, of course, but there are real tears, and one big sob that almost shook the house. It certainly would be misleading to say that it was imaginary sadness, for the sadness of Cassie isn't imagined by anyone, not even by herself. What she reads on the other hand is imaginary. What she reads about never happened. In this respect it's quite different from the case in which she is overwhelmed by the sad news over the telephone. That was not imaginary, and with the tears and sobs there was worry, there was distress. She didn't go twittering about, pretending she was. a little bird five minutes after that happened. So a sad book is a book that makes Cassie, for instance, sad. You ask, "Well, what are you crying about?" And she says, "Booh, you just read this." It's true that that is how you will find out, but you may certainly anticipate too that it will be a story about a little boy who died, a brave little boy who had stood up bravely for his father, about a new love and reconciliation come almost too late, about a parting of friends and tender feelings that will die, and so on. At any rate, if this is what it is like, you won't be surprised. It's a sad book.

There is one further sentence to consider: "Cassie's face is sad." The same sort of thing might be said about her speaking, about her walk, about her eyes, etc. There is once again an obvious way of dealing with this. What makes you say her face is sad? Anyone can tell. See those tear stains and those swollen eyes. And those curved lines, they all turn down. Her face is like all those sad faces in simple drawings where with six strokes of my neighbor's pencil I give you "Sad-Eye, the Sorry Man." The sad face is easily marked by these few unmistakable signs. Pull a sad face, or droop one, and then study it. What have you done? In any case, I am supposing that there is another use of "Cassie's face is sad," where this simplicity is absent. Oh, yes, there may be certain lines, but if you now ask, "And is this all you mean by Cassie's face being sad," the answer may very well be "No." Where then is the sadness? Take a long look and tell me. Cassie, hold still. The sadness is written all over her face, and I can't tell you it's here and not there. The more I look, the more I see it. The sadness in this case is not identified with some gross and simple signs. And you are not likely to find it there in some quick glance. Gaze into that face, leisurely, quietly, gently. It's as though it were composed not of what is sad in all sad faces, but rather of what is sad only in each sad face you've ever known. This sad face is sad but when you try now to tell someone what is sad in it, as you might with the drawing I made, you will have nothing to say. But you may say, "Look, and you will see." It is clear, of course, that when Cassie's face is sad, she need not be sad at all. And certainly when you look as you do, you need not be sad.

We have noticed briefly several types of sentences similar to "The music is sad," and we have seen how in rspect to several of these the same sort of puzzling might arise that arose in respect to "The music is sad." We have also seen how in respect to these more obvious cases this puzzling is relieved. The puzzling is relieved by discerning the similarity between the offending use and some other use or uses. And now I should like to ask whether the puzzle concerning "The music is sad" might not also be relieved in some similar fashion. Is there not a use of some type of sentence, familiar and relatively untroubled, which is like the use of "The music is sad"?

We have these types of sentences now ready at our disposal: There are two uses of "Cassie is sad," in the first of which she is concerned about her cat, and in the second of which she is cozy and tearful, reading her book. We have "Cassie's cousin is sad," in which Cassie's cousin has real cause but no tears, and "Cassie's dog is sad," in which her dog is tearless as her cousin, but with a difference of course. You could scarcely say that Fido restrained his tears. Then there were the uses of "Cassie's face is sad" and "Cassie's reading is sad." And, of course, there is the use of "Cassie's book is sad." I am going to take for granted that these uses are also intelligible. Now then is the use of "The music is sad" similar to any of these?

I suppose that if the question is stated in this way, one might go on by pointing out a similarity between it and each one of these other types of sentences. But what we must discover is enough similarity, enough to relieve the puzzle. So the question is: To which use is the use of "The music is sad" most similar? Certainly not to "Cassie is sad (about her cat)," nor to "Cassie's cousin is sad," nor to "Cassie's dog is sad."

There are two analogies that one may hopefully seize upon. The first is this: "Cassie is sad, reading a book," is very much like "Verbo is sad, listening to music." And this first is also very much like "Cassie is sad, hearing the news over the telephone." And just as the first involves "The book is sad," so the second involves "The music is sad," and the third involves "The news is sad." Now let us consider the first. Reading the book is one thing, and feeling sad is quite another, and when you say that the book is sad, you mean by this something like this: When Cassie reads, she feels sad about what she reads. Her feeling sad refers to her tears, her sobs, etc. So too listening to the music and hearing it is one thing, and feeling sad is another, and when you say that the music is sad, you mean that while Verbo listens to the music, he feels sad. And shall we add that he feels sad about it? This might, if you like, refer to something like his half-tears, sub-sobs, etc.

Suppose now we try to relieve Verbo in this way. We say, "Don't you see? 'This music is sad' is like 'The book is sad.' You understand that. That's very much like 'The news is sad.' " Will that satisfy him? I think that if he is very sharp, it won't. He may say, "I can see how 'The book is sad' is like 'The news is sad.' But when it comes to these you can easily point out the disturbance, the weeping, but the music— that's different. Still there might be something." What now bothers him?

I think what bothers him may be explained in this way. When you say that a book is sad, or a certain passage in a book is sad, you may mean one or other or both of two things. You may mean what has already been defined by the analogy above. But you may also mean something else. The following illustration may exhibit this. Imagine Cassie, then, in her big chair, reading, and this is the passage she reads:

> "I say this in case we become bad," Alyosha went on, "but there's no reason why we should become bad, is there, boys? Let us be, first and above all, kind, then honest, and let us never forget each other! I say that again. I give you my word, for my part, that I'll never forget one of you. Every face looking at me now I shall remember even for thirty years. Just now Kolya said to Kartashov that he did not care to know whether he exists or not. But I cannot forget that Kartashov exists and that he is blushing now as he did when he discovered the founders of Troy, but is looking at me with his jolly, kind, dear little eyes. Boys, my dear boys, let us all be generous and brave like Ilusha, clever, brave and generous like Kolya (though he will be ever so much cleverer when he grows up), and let us all be as modest, as clever and sweet as Kartashov. But why am I talking about those two! You are all dear to me, boys, from this day forth I have a place in my heart for you all, and I beg you to keep a place in your hearts for me! Well, and who has united us in this kind,

good feeling which we shall remember, and intend to remember all our lives? Who, if not Ilusha, the good boy, the dear boy, precious to us forever! Let us never forget him. May his memory live forever in our hearts from this time forth."

Cassie reads this and Cassie cries. Let us call this Cassie's sadness. But is there now any other emotion, any other sadness, present? Well, there may very well be. There may be the Alyosha emotion. Whether that is present however depends upon how the passage in question is read. It may be read in such a way, that though Cassie understands all she reads, and so knows about the Alyosha emotion, yet she will miss it. This will be the case if she cries through the reading of it. If she reads the passage well, controlled, clear, unfalteringly, with feeling, as we say, which does not mean with crying, then the Alyosha emotion will be present. Otherwise only signs of it will be present. Anyone who has tried to read such a passage well, and who has sometimes failed and sometimes succeeded, will understand what I have in mind. Now then we have distinguished the Cassie emotion and the Alyosha emotion. They may be present together, but only. I think, when the Cassie emotion is relatively weak. And so when someone says that the passage in question is sad, then in order to understand we must ask, "Is it sad in the Cassie emotion or is it sad in the Alyosha emotion?"

And now we are prepared again to examine the analogy: "The music is sad" is like "The book is sad," where it is sad with the Alyosha emotion. This now eliminates the messiness of tears. What we mean by Alyosha's emotion involves no tears, just as the sadness of the music involves no tears. And this now may remind us of Cassie reading the passage, cool, collected, reading with feeling. But more to the point it suggests the sentence "Cassie's face is sad." For see, when the music is sad, there are no tears, and when the passage is read, well read, there are no tears. And so when I look into this face and find it sad, there are no tears. The sadness in all these cases may be unmistakable, and yet in none of these is there anything to which I might now draw your attention, and say, "That's how I recognize it as sad." Even in the case of the reading, it isn't the sentences, it isn't the subject, that make it sad. The sadness is in the reading. Like a musical score, it too may be played without feeling. And it isn't now as though you both read and have these feelings. There is nothing but the reading, and the feeling is nothing apart from this. Read the passage with and without feeling, and see that the difference consists in a difference in the reading.

What baffles in these cases is that when you use the word "sadness" and the phrase "with feeling," you are certain to anticipate sadness and feeling in the ordinary sense. But if the sadness is in the sounds you make, reading or playing, and in the face, once you are forewarned you need no longer anticipate anything else. There is sadness which is heard and sadness which is seen.

This then is my result. "The music is sad" is like "The book is sad," where "The book is sad" is like "The face is sad." But "The music is sad" is sometimes also like "The book is sad," where "The book is sad" is like "The news is sad." If exhibiting these analogies is to be helpful, then, of course, this depends on the intelligibility of such sentences as "The book is sad," "The face is sad," "The news is sad," etc.

III

So far I have tried to do two things. I have tried to state the problem to which the expression theory is addressed, and then I have gone on to work at the solution of that problem in the way in which this statement of the problem itself suggests that it be worked out. In doing this I have sought deliberately to avoid the language of the expression theory.

Here then is the phrase to be studied. The expression theory maintains: The music is sad means: The music is the expression of sadness or of a certain sadness. The crucial word is the word "expression." There are now at least two contexts which determine the use of that word, one is the language of emotion, and the other is the language of or about language.

Let us consider first the use of the word "expression" in the language of emotion. In the discussion of the types of sentences above, it will be remembered that Cassie's cousin is sad, but doesn't cry. She does not "express" her emotion. Cassie on the other hand carries on, crying, sobbing, and confiding in everyone. She "expresses" her emotion, and the expression of her emotion is tears, noises, talk. That talk is all about her cat, remember. When she reads her book, she carries on in much the same way. In this latter case, there was some question as to whether there was really any emotion. She was so sad, remember, and ate popcorn. But in terms of what we just now said, whether there is emotion or not, there certainly is "expression" of emotion. These tears are just as wet as other tears, and her sobs are just as wet too. So in both cases there is expression of emotion, and in the first case there is emotion, thick as you please, but in the second case, it's not that thick. It appears then that you might find it quite natural to say that there is expression of emotion but no emotion, much as you might say that there was the thought of an elephant, but no elephant. This may not seem so strange, however, if we reflect that as in the case of Cassie's cousin, there may be emotion, but no or very little expression of emotion.

In order to probe the further roots of the uses of this phrase, it may be useful to notice that the language of emotion is dominantly the language of water. So many of our associations with the word "emotion" are liquid. See then: Emotions well up. Children and young girls bubble over. There are springs of emotion. A sad person is a deep well. Emotions come in waves; they are like the tides; they ebb and flow. There are floods and "seas of passion." Some people gush; some are turbulent. Anger boils. A man blows up like a boiler. Sorrow overwhelms. The dear girl froze. We all know the theory of humors. In any case, it is easy enough, in this way, to think of a human being as like a reservoir and an everflowing pool and stream of emotions. All flow on toward a dam, which may be raised or lowered, and over and through which there is a constant trickle. Behind the dam are many currents, hot, cold, lukewarm, swift, slow, steady, rippling, smooth. And there are many colors. Perhaps we should say that currents are never exhausted and do not altogether trickle away. Emotions, like our thoughts, are funded, ready to be tapped, to be rippled, to be disturbed.

Let us see how the term "expression" fits into this figure. How was it with Cassie's cousin? Well, once there was a clear, smooth-flowing current of affection, and it flowed, trickle, trickle, over the dam in happy anticipation and a chestful of hope's kitchen and linen showers. And suddenly a planet falls, in the form of a letter, into that deep and flowing pool. Commotion follows, waves leap, eddies swirl. The current rushes on to the dam. And what happens? The dam rises. Cassie's cousin resists, bites her lip, intensifies her fist. She keeps the current back. Her grief is impounded. She does not "express" her emotion. And what happens to Cassie, when she felt so bad about the cat? That's easy. Then too there was a disturbance. The current came down, splashed over the dam which did not rise at all, and it flowed away in

a hurly-burly of "Oh! It's awful! My poor kitty!" Cassie let herself go.
She "expressed" her emotion.

The use of the word "expression" in the light of this figure is, I take
it, clear enough. And the use of the word in this way describes a
familiar difference in the way in which good news and bad news may
affect us. And now we may ask, "And is it something like this that
people have in mind when they say that art is the expression of emotion?" Certainly something like this, at least part of the time. Consider
how Wordsworth wrote about poetry: "Poetry is the spontaneous overflow of powerful emotions." Overflow! This suggests the pool and the
dam and the "powerful" current. An emotion, lying quiet, suddenly
gets going and goes over. There is spontaneity, of course. No planet
falls and no cat is sick. The emotion is unprovoked. There is also the
common view that artists are people who are more emotional than
other people. They are temperamental. This once again suggests the
idea that they have particular need of some overflow. Poetry is a little
like blowing off steam. Write poetry or explode!

This isn't all that Wordsworth said about poetry. In the same context he said: "Poetry is emotion recollected in tranquility." Again this
suggests a hiding place of emotion, a place where past heartaches are
stored, and may be taken up again, "recollected." We store ideas. We
also put away emotions. So we have the pool as we had the pool before
in describing Cassie's cousin and Cassie. But now we have something
else, "the spontaneous overflow" and the "recollection in tranquility."

Let us consider this for a moment, again in order to notice the use
of the word "expression." Cassie hears bad news and cries. She "expresses" her emotion. The emotion is aroused and out it flows. What
now happens in the case of the poet? Ostensibly in his case too emotions are aroused, but they do not flow out. Poets do not cry enough.
Emotions are stored up, blocked. Emotions accumulate. And what
happens now? Well, one of two things may happen. Emotions may
quite suddenly leap up like spray, and find a way out, or again a poet
may dip into the pool with his word dipper, and then dip them out.
It's as though the emotions come over the dam in little boats (the
poems) and the little boats may be used over and over again to carry
over new surges. And this too may be described in this way: The poet
"expresses" his emotion. Cassie cries. The real incident is sufficient.
The poet does not cry. The real incident is not sufficient. He's got to
make poems in order to cry. All men must cry. This may seem a bit

fantastic, but this sort of phantasy is common in explaining something as old, for instance, as Aristotle's use of the word "catharsis."

The analogy which we have tried to exhibit now is this one: As Cassie "expresses" her emotion at hearing the news, so the poet or reader "expresses" his emotion at reading the poem. The news and the poem arouse or evoke the respective emotions. Now most people who expound the expression theory are not content with this analogy. They say that Cassie merely vents or discharges her emotion. This is not "expression" of emotion. Cassie merely gets rid of her emotion. And what does the poem do? Perhaps in terms of our figure we may say: It ripples it, blows a gentle wind over it, like a bird skimming the water. At any rate the emotion stays. And so the theory seeks a more suitable analogy and finds it conveniently in the language about language.

I should like first to notice certain distinctions which lead to this shift from the first to the second analogy. In the first place poems and music are quite different from the occasions that make Cassie and Cassie's cousin so sad. Tones on a piano and a faithless lover or a dying cat are not much alike, and this is enough to disturb the analogy. But there is also an unmistakable difference in the use of the word "emotion" in the two cases. An "emotion recollected in tranquility" is, after all, as I suggested before, more like a ripple than like a tempest. It is, accordingly, these distinctions that determine the shift. It may be useful to notice that the general form of the first analogy is retained in the second. For the poem and the music are still conceived as "arousing," as "evoking," the emotion.

The new analogy accordingly is this one: Music "expresses" sadness (art expresses emotion) as sentences "express" ideas. And now, I think, it is easy to see why this analogy should have been seized upon. In the first place so much of art involves symbols, sentences themselves, and representations. There are horses in pictures. It is quite easy then to fall into regarding art as symbolic, that is, as like sentences. And now just as sentences symbolize ideas and serve to evoke them as distinguished from real things, of which ideas are more like shadows, so too music and poems serve to evoke emotions of a peculiar sort, emotions which are like the shadows of real emotions. So this analogy is certainly an improvement. Art is after all an artifice, like sentences, and the emotions involved are related to the real things in much the way that ideas are to real things, faint copies. All this fits in very well with the

idea that art is like a dream, a substitute of real life, a vicarious more
of what you cannot have, a shadowland. And now how does this analogy succeed?
Before answering this question, I should like to notice the use of the
words "evoking" and "arousing." Sentences "evoke" ideas. As one
spieler I know, says: "When I read a sentence, an idea pops into my
head." Pops! This is something like what, according to the analogy, is
meant by sentences "expressing" ideas. I am not interested in criticizing
this at this point. I wish only to clarify ideas. Pop! Consider the
sentence "The elephant ate a jumbo peanut." If at the moment when
you read this sentence you see in your mind's eye a big elephant
nuzzling around a huge peanut, this will illustrate what "evoking" is
like. The sentence evokes; the idea pops. There is the sentence and
there is this unmistakable seeing in your mind's eye. And if this happened, surely you would have got the idea. What I wish to point out is
that it is this view or some similar view of how sentences work, that
underlies this present analogy. They "evoke." But the word "evoke"
has other contexts. It suggests spirits, witchcraft. The spirit of Samuel
appearing at the behest of the witch of Endor is an "evocation."
Spiritualistic mediums "evoke" the living spirits of the dead. And the
point of this association is that the spirits are waiting, in the second
or third canto of Dante's *Comedy*, perhaps, to be called. They are in
storage like our ideas, like our emotions. And the word "arouse" is
like the word "evoke." Whom do you arouse? The sleeper. And so,
sleeping ideas and sleeping emotions lie bedded in that spacious
dormitory—hush!—we call the mind. Waiting to be called! And why
now have I made a point of this? Because this helps to fill out this
analogy by which in particular we are led to use the word "feeling"
or "emotion" in the language of the expression theory. The music
"evokes," "arouses" feelings.

Now then, do poems and music and pictures evoke emotions as
sentences evoke images? I think that they frequently do. Cassie reading
her book may be cited as an instance. This seems to me a very common
type of experience. It happens at the movies, in reading novels, and
even in listening to music. People are moved to tears. If, accordingly
the expression theory were intended merely to describe experience of
this sort, I should say, "Very well." In that case there would be no
particular puzzle, beyond presenting this analogy clearly. But I, at
least, am convinced that this is not all.

The difficulty then does not arise concerning experiences of this sort. The puzzle arises and remains most stubbornly where the sadness is dry-eyed. And here the analogy with language seems, at least, to be of no use. Cassie may read the passage with feeling, but without the flicker of an eyelash. And she may listen to sad music as cool and intent as she is gazing at a butterfly. She might say that it was more like watching, fascinated, the pain in a suffering face, herself quite undistressed. Santayana identifies the experience in this way: "Not until I confound the impressions (the music; the sentences) and suffuse the symbols with the emotions they arouse, and find joy and sweetness in the very words I hear, will the expressiveness constitute a beauty. . . ."[2] I propose now to study this sentence.

Now notice how curious this is. Once more we have the sentences or the music. And these arouse emotions. This describes Cassie reading her book. So we might expect that Cassie would cry and would sob and so on. But this isn't all. Cassie is confused. Actually she is crying but she thinks the words are crying. She wipes her tears off those words. She sighs but the words heave. The sentence of Santayana suggests that she sees the sentences she reads through her tears and now her tears misserve her much as blue moods or dark glasses do. So Cassie looks through sadness and the sentence is tearful. What a pathetic fallacy! From confusion to suffusion! Are there misplaced emotions? Imagine what this would be like where sentences aroused not emotions but a toothache. And now you confused the toothache with the sentence, and before someone prevented you, you sent the sentence to the dentist.

Nevertheless, Santayana has almost certainly identified an experience that is different from that in which Cassie is sad over her book. We find "joy and sweetness in the very words" we hear. Clearly, too, Santayana has been misled by these words "joy and sweetness." For if there is joy and sweetness, where should these be but where they usually are? Where is joy then and where is sweetness? In the human breast, in the heart ("my heart leaps up when I behold"), in the eye. And if you say this, then indeed there must be some illusion. The sentence is like a mirror that catches and holds what is in the heart. And so artful are poets' sentences that the best readers are the best confused. I want now, however, to suggest that indeed joy and sweetness, and sad-

---

2 *Sense of Beauty* (1896), p. 149.

ness too, are in the very words you hear. But in that case, joy and sweetness must be of the sort that can be in sentences. We must, accordingly,
try to figure out what this "joy and sweetness in the very words" is like.
For even though, making a mistake, one imagined they were in the
words, their being there must make some sense. And Santayana too
does not imagine that sentences cry.

Let me return now to the analogy: The music is sad is like: The
sentence expresses an idea. We saw before how the sentence "The elephant ate a jumbo peanut" might be accompanied by an image and
how this was like sentences or music arousing emotions. We want now
to see how we might use the phrase "joy and sweetness in the very
words." Do we have a meaning for "The idea in the very words you
hear." Where is the idea of the elephant eating a jumbo peanut? Suppose we say, "It's in the very words you hear." Have you ever seen, in
your mind's eye, that is, an elephant eating a peanut in the very words
you hear? A sentence is like a circus tent? I do not suppose that anyone
who said that joy and sweetness are in the very words you hear would
be likely to say that this was like the way in which you might also see
an image in the very sentence which you hear—a bald head in the word
"but." I should like in any case to try something different.

I do not intend to abandon the analogy with language yet. Music is
expression of emotion as sentences are expression of ideas. But now
how do sentences express ideas? We have noticed one way in which
sentences do sometimes have meaning. Sentences, however, have been
described in many ways. Sentences are like buzzers, like doorbells, like
electric switches. Sentences are like mirrors, like maps, like pictures;
sentences are like road signs, with arrows pointing the way. And so we
might go on to ask, "Is music like buzzers, like pictures, like road sign
arrows?" I do not however intend to do this. It will be noticed that
the same analogy by which we have been trying to understand music,
art, etc., may serve us also to understand what language is like. The
analogy presupposes that we do know something about music, and so
turning the analogy to this use may be fruitful. It might show us just
how enlightening and how unenlightening the analogy is.

In order to study the analogy between music and the sentence and to
try in this way to find out what the sentence is like, I now intend
to offer a foolish theory. This may throw into clearer relief what
Santayana says. What is understanding a sentence like? Understanding
a sentence is speaking the sentence in a certain way. You can tell,

listening to yourself talk, that you are understanding the sentence, and so can anyone else who hears you speak. Understanding has its rhythm. So the meaning of the sentence consists in a certain reading of the sentence. If, in this case, a sentence is spoken and not understood by someone, there would be only one thing to do, namely, speak the sentence again. Obviously this account will not do for there are other ways of clarifying what we mean. Nevertheless in some cases it may be all that is necessary.

Now notice. If this were what the meaning of a sentence is like, we should see at once what was meant if someone said that the meaning or the idea is in the sentence. For if there is meaning, where could it be but in the sentence, since the sentence is all there is. Of course, it is true that the sentence would have to be spoken and, of course, spoken in some way or other. And with every variation in reading it might then be said to have a different meaning. If anyone asked, "And what does the sentence mean?" expecting you to point to something or to elaborate the matter in gestures or to translate, it would be clear that he quite misunderstood what meaning is like. One might even correct him, saying it is even misleading to say that the meaning is in the sentence, as though it were only a part of the sentence, or tucked away somehow under overlapping syllables. A sentence having meaning in a case like this would be something like a living thing. Here too one might ask, "Where is the life in a squirrel and in a geranium?" Truly the life is the squirrel and is the geranium and is no part of either nor tucked away in some hidden fold or tiny vein. And so it is with the sentence, according to our imaginary theory. We might speak of the sentence as like a living thing.

And now let us see whether we have some corresponding use for "The joy and sweetness are in the very words you hear." People do ask about the meaning of poems and even about the meaning of music. Let us first of all say that the meaning is "the joy and sweetness," and the sadness. And where are these? In the very words you hear, and in the music. And now notice that what was admittedly a foolish theory in respect to sentences is not a foolish theory in respect to poems or music. Do you get the poem? Do you get the music? If you do not, pointing, gestures, translations will not help. (Understanding the words is presupposed.) There will be only one thing to do, namely, read the verses again, play the music once more. And what will the joy and sweetness and the sadness be like? They will be like the life in the living thing, not to be distinguished as some one part of the poem or music and not another part, or as some shadow that follows the sounded words or tones. "In the very words you hear," like the squirrel in fur!

I infer now that the analogy between the "joy and sweetness" in words and the meaning in sentences is misleading and is not likely to be helpful. The meaning of sentences is translatable, but the "meaning" of poems, of music is not. We have seen how this is so. There may, of course, be something in the sounding of all sentences which is analogous to the "joy and sweetness in the very words," but it is not the meaning of those sentences. And now this is an interesting consequence. It makes sense to ask, "What does the sentence express?" It expresses a meaning, of course, and you may have some way of showing what this is, without using the sentence to do so. But now it makes no sense to ask, "What does the poem express?" or "What does the music express?" We may say, if we like, that both are expressive, but we must beware of the analogy with language. And we may prevent the helpless searching in this case, by insisting that they "express" nothing, nothing at all.

And now let us review. My assumption has been that the expression theory is plagued with certain analogies that are not clearly distinguished, and none of which finally is helpful without being misleading. The first analogy is that in terms of which we commonly think of emotions. The second is that in terms of which we think of language, the doorbell view. Besides this there are two different types of experience that arise in connection with art. One of these types may be fairly well described by the analogy with doorbell language. The similarity of our language, however, in respect to both types of experience, conceals the difference between those two types. Santayana's sentence reveals the agony that follows the recognition of this difference in these types of experience and the attempt to employ the language which describes the one to describe the other. The language requires very interesting translation. My conclusion, accordingly, is this: The analogy drawn from language may be useful in describing one type of experience. It is practically useless in describing the other. Since, then, these two analogies dominate the use of the word "expression," I suggest that, for the sake of clarity and charity, they be abandoned in seeking to describe that "expressiveness" which Santayana says constitutes "a beauty."

If we now abandon these analogies, are we also to abandon the use of the word "expression"? Not unless we please to do so. But we do so at our risk, for these analogies are not easily abandoned. We may, however, fortify our use of this word by considerations such as these. We use the word "expressive" to describe faces. And we use "expressive" in much the same way that we use the phrase "has character." A face that is expressive "has character." But when we now say that a face has character, this may remind us that the letters of the alphabet are characters. Let us suppose for a moment that this is related to "He's a character!" I suppose that he's a character and he has a character do not mean quite the same thing. There are antics in he's a character. Try again: The zig-zag line has character and the wavy line has character. Each letter of the alphabet is a character, but also has character. The number tokens, 1 2 3 4 5 6 7 8 9—each has its character. In the same way sounds have character. Let me see whether we can explain this further. You might say that if some dancing master were to arrange a dance for each of the numbers, you might see how a dance for the number one would not do at all for number five. Or again if the numbers were to be dressed in scarfs, again a certain color and a certain flimsy material would do for six but would not suit five at all. Now something of the same sort is true of words, and particularly of some. Words have character. I am tempted to say that all these things have their peculiar feel, but this then must be understood on the analogy with touch. If we, for instance, said that all these things have their peculiar feeling, then once again it might be supposed that in connection with them there is a feeling which is aroused by them.

Let your ears and your eyes, perhaps, too, feel these familiar bits of nonsense:

> Hi diddle diddle!
> Fee! fi, fo, fum!
> Intery, mintery.
> Abra ca da bra.

Each has its character. Each is, in this sense, expressive. But to ask now "What is its character or what does it express?" is to fall into the pit. You may, of course, experiment to exhibit more clearly just what the character, in each case, is. You may, for instance, contrast the leaping, the stomping, the mincing, the shuffle, with what you get if you change the vowels. Try:

Ho! doodle doodle!
Fa, fo, fu, fim!
Untery, muntery.
Ay bray cay day bray.

One might also go on to change consonants in order again to exhibit
character by giving the word new edges and making their sides steeper
or smoothing them down.

I do not intend, in proposing illustrations of this sort, to suggest that
art is nonsense and that its character is simple as these syllables are. A
face, no doubt may bear the impress, the character, of a life's torment
and of its hope and victory. So too words and phrases may come blazing
out of the burning past. In art the world is born afresh, but the travail
of the artist may have had its beginnings in children's play. My only
point is that once the poem is born it has its character as surely as a cry
in the night or intery, mintery. And this character is not something that
follows it around like a clatter in a man's insides when he reads it. The
light of the sun is in the sun, where you see it. So with the character of
the poem. Hear the words and do not imagine that in hearing them you
gulp a jigger to make yourself foam. Rather suppose that the poem is as
hard as marble, ingrained, it may be, with indelible sorrow.

If, accordingly, we now use the sentence "Art is expression," or "Art
is expressive," and the use of this sentence is determined by elucida-
tions such as I have just now set out, then, I think, that our language
may save us from some torture. And this means that we are now prepared to use freely those sentences that the expression theory is commonly inclined to correct. For now, unabashed, we shall say that the
music is sad, and we shall not go on to say that this means that the
music expresses sadness. For the sadness is to the music rather like the
redness to the apple, than it is like the burp to the cider. And above all
we shall not, having heard the music or read the poem, ask, "What
does it express?"

IV

And now it's many words ago since we left Verbo and his friend at
the corner. Verbo was trying to figure out, you remember, how the
music was related to his grandmother. How can music be sad? I suggested then that he was having word trouble, and that it would be
necessary to probe his sentences. And so we probed. And now what
shall we tell Verbo?

Verbo, we will say, the music is sad. And then we will remind him that the geranium is living, and that the sun is light. We will say these things so that he will not look away from the music to discover the sadness of it. Are you looking for the life in the geranium? Are you looking for the light in the sun? As then the life and the light describe the geranium and the sun, so too does sadness describe the music. And then we shall have to go on to tell him about these fearful analogies, and about Santayana's wrestle on the precipice. And about how we cut the ropes! And you may be sure that just as things are going along so well, Verbo will ask, flicking the ashes from his cigarette, "And what about the sadness?"

And now it's time to take the cat out of the bag, for so far all that has been exposed is the bag. The sadness is a quality of what we have already described as the character, the expressive. One piece of music is like and unlike some other pieces of music. These similarities and these differences may be perceived. Now then, we have a class of sad music. But why sad, that is, why use this word? It must be remembered, of course, that the use of this word is not precise. So there may be some pieces of music which are unmistakably sad, and others which shade off in gradations to the point where the question "Is it sad?" is not even asked. Suppose we ask our question "Why sad?" in respect to the unmistakable cases. Then, perhaps, some such answer as this will do. Sad music has some of the characteristics of people who are sad. It will be slow, not tripping: it will be low, not tinkling. People who are sad move more slowly, and when they speak, they speak softly and low. Associations of this sort may, of course, be multiplied indefinitely. And this now is the kitten in whose interest we made so much fuss about the bag. The kitten has, I think, turned out to be a scrawny little creature, not worth much. But the bag was worth it.

The bag was worth it? What I have in mind is that the identification of music as the expressive, as character, is crucial. That the expressive is sad serves now only to tag the music. It is introspective or, in relation to the music, an aside. It's a judgment that intervenes. Music need not be sad, nor joyous, nor anything else. Aestheticians usually account for this by inventing all sorts of emotions without names, an emotion for every piece of music. Besides, bad music, characterless music, the unexpressive, may be sad in quite the same way that good music may be. This is no objection, of course, to such classifications. I am interested only in clarifying the distinction between our uses of these several sentences.

And now that I have come to see what a thicket of tangle-words I've tried to find my way through, it seems to me that I am echoing such words as years ago I read in Croce, but certainly did not then understand. Perhaps if I read Croce again now I shouldn't understand them either. "Beauty is expression."

The Theory of Appearing

RODERICK M. CHISHOLM

Philosophers who have written about perception have usually found it convenient to speak in terms of "appearances," "impressions," "phenomena," "sense-data," and the like. Many now believe, however, that by avoiding this sort of terminology we can eliminate the difficult metaphysical puzzles traditionally associated with our knowledge of the external world. They contend: (1) that we can say all we know about perception without employing this "sense-datum terminology"; (2) that the alternative terminology does not lead us to metaphysics; and, accordingly, (3) that the metaphysical problems which the consideration of perception sometimes seems to involve are really "pseudo problems," arising out of the misuse of language. In the present essay I want to show that, although (1) is true, (2) is false, and hence that (3) remains problematic.

THE SENSE-DATUM PUZZLES

What do the "sense-datum terms" refer to? Unfortunately, these terms are used in a number of different ways and few, if any, who use them succeed in conveying to others what their own particular usages happen to be. We may do well, then, to speak of a hypothetical "sense-datum philosopher" and to state his case as clearly and as fairly as possible.

The sense-datum philosopher apparently believes sense-data are entities having at least these three characteristics: (1) they may be found in any perceptual experience; (2) they are some-how essential to the perception of physical things; and (3) they are, in an important respect, independent of the physical things in the perception of which they are involved. What kind of evidence is there for assuming that such entities exist? The sense-datum philosopher would reason, I think, somewhat as follows:

"The root of the problem lies in the fact that every perceptual experience contains something that can be made to vary independently of any of the physical things being perceived. When, for example, you look at the wallpaper six feet away, you experience a fairly uniform color, but if you were to approach the wall you would find that the color you experience becomes more and more differentiated. The object you are perceiving doesn't change (we may assume), but *something* does. Or, again: if you will look at the top of the coffee table, you will find in your experience something whose geometrical shape you can change merely by walking around the table. From here you experience something diamond-shaped; if you were to stand directly above the table, you would experience something rectangular; and, in moving from here to there, you could, if you chose, note the change occurring in the experienced shapes. (There is nothing esoteric about this variation. If you were to make accurate sketches or photographs of what you see from here and of what you see from there, you would find that the variation also occurs in *them;* the one taken from here will contain a rhomboid, the one from there a rectangle.) Similarly, merely by altering the conditions of observation in an appropriate fashion, you can vary experienced sizes, sounds, smells, and so on.

"In general, we may give the name 'sense-datum' to anything in a perceptual experience which *could* thus be varied independently of the objects being perceived. It is clear (1) that sense-data can be found in any perceptual experience, since one can alter any such experience merely by properly distorting one's perceptual apparatus or otherwise varying the conditions of observation. And (2) sense-data are *essential* to the perception of physical things: for, if the sense-data present in a perceptual experience were somehow removed and replaced by nothing else, one would not be perceiving anything at all; i.e., if everything which is capable of the sort of variation described were removed from the experience, nothing would be left of the experience. Finally, (3) sense-data are independent of the objects of perception in the sense that the sense-data and the objects are capable of the sort of independent variation described."

Once we admit that these entities referred to as "sense-data" are to be found in every perceptual experience, we are confronted with a number of perplexing questions concerning their status. In order to answer these questions, many philosophers have been led to devise intricate accounts both of the nature of the universe and of the nature of man. These questions, which we may call the *sense-datum puzzles,* may be illustrated as follows: *16074*

"Consider the various sense-data which you may experience if you examine this rectangular table top; from this corner you experience one which is diamond shaped; if you were to look straight down from the ceiling you would experience one which is rectangular; and from the roof you would experience one which is smaller than the other two. The sense-data are of different shapes and sizes; hence they cannot be identical with each other; and therefore (presumably) they cannot all be in the same place at once. Perhaps one of them is where the surface of the table is; but, if so, where are the others? Are they somewhere in the space surrounding the table? Perhaps we should say that all of them exist in the mind—or in the brain. But, in this case, what becomes of the table and how can one know anything about it? If all sense-data are thus subjective, the world must be exceedingly barren when no one is observing it. Do the sense-data come into being when we experience them, and, if they do, what kind of creation is that? Perhaps we should deny the principle that distinct things must be in different places at the same time and say that all of those sense-data are right there on the surface of the table. Or perhaps we should say that sense-data, even though some of them seem to be spatially related to each other, don't occupy places at all. . . ."

Something seems to be amiss here. These *are* metaphysical questions; the possible answers are "neutral with respect to experience." Moreover the puzzles seem to be artificial; the question "Where is the diamond-shaped sense-datum?" sounds suspiciously like the notorious pseudo problems concerning the nature of nothingness and the where-abouts of the golden mountain. And, finally, the statement "From the corner of the room the table presents a diamond-shaped sense-datum" seems to be merely a clumsy and misleading way of saying something which could have been expressed without reference to sense-data at all.

The contention to be examined, then, is that by revising the language we escape the puzzles.

THE LANGUAGE OF APPEARING

The fundamental objection to the sense-datum philosopher is that his way of discussing perception is "metaphysically charged" and needlessly so. Obviously there *is* a sense in which every perceptual experience can be made to vary independently of the physical things being perceived. But this phenomenal variability (as it might be called) can be described without referring to any "somethings" other than the physical objects which we perceive.

We don't need to say such things as "From the corner of the room, the table presents a diamond-shaped sense-datum (appearance, impression, sensation . . .)." We could say instead, "From the corner of the room, the table *appears* to be (or seems to be, or looks) diamond-shaped." So, too, with the other stock examples of the sense-datum philosophers: we can say "The stick appears bent; the railroad tracks appear to converge; the oculist's 'A' looks blurry; the train sounds fainter in the distance than it does nearby," and so on. Indeed this is the way we ordinarily *do* speak; no one tells the oculist that his "A" presents a blurry sense-datum. And with this mode of speaking we avoid the curious "somethings" which perplex the sense-datum philosopher.[1] Following Mr. Ayer, we may refer to this alternative mode of speaking as the "language of appearing," contrasting it with our preceding "sense-datum language."

It is important to note that the terms of our "language of appearing" —terms such as "appear," "look," "seem," "sound"—have a number of different senses and that only one of these senses is applicable in the present context. These are often used, not to describe phenomenal variation, but to express inclination-to-believe and to state judgments of probability. If I say "Mr. Dewey appears to have abandoned all hopes of becoming President," I mean something like "On the basis of the available evidence, it is probable that (or I am inclined to believe that)

---

[1] An admirably clear statement of this point of view is to be found in G. A. Paul, "Is There a Problem about Sense-Data?" *Arist. Soc. Proc.*, suppl. vol., XV (1936), 61. For earlier versions see H. A. Prichard, *Kant's Theory of Knowledge* (1909), p. 75 ff., esp. p. 85; P. Coffey, *Epistemology or the Theory of Knowledge* (1917), I, 356-358; II, 167 ff., esp. 177; G. Dawes Hicks, *Critical Realism* (1938), p. 68 ff., esp. p. 78; and F. J. E. Woodbridge, *Nature and Mind* (1937), pp. 400-401.

Mr. Dewey has abandoned his hopes. . . . ." But when, in discussing epistemology or esthetics we employ the language of appearing and say, "The penny appears to be elliptical from this point," we *don't* mean to convey that in all probability the penny *is* elliptical or that we have any inclination to believe that it is. Mr. Broad has stated the essence of the matter:

> Appearance is not merely mistaken *judgment* about physical objects. When I judge that a penny looks elliptical I am not mistakenly ascribing elliptical shape to what is in fact round. Sensible appearances *may* lead me to make a mistaken judgment about physical objects, but they *need* not and so far as we know, commonly do not. My certainty that the penny looks elliptical exists comfortably alongside of my conviction that it is round. But a mistaken judgment that the penny *is* elliptical could not continue to exist after I knew that the penny was really round. The plain fact is then that "looking elliptical to me" stands for a peculiar experience, which, whatever the right analysis of it may be, is not just a mistaken judgment about the shape of the penny.[2]

It is the sense of the term "appear" (or "looks") which Mr. Broad has in mind that is intended by the phrase "language of appearing." The use of this term may be explicated in much the same way in which the sense-datum philosopher explicates the term "sense-datum," i.e., by referring to the possibility of phenomenal variation.

The sense-datum philosopher, of course, will admit that the language of appearing *can* be used in discussing these facts. But he contends that from statements in the language of appearing we can *deduce* statements in the sense-datum language. That is to say, he contends that from statements such as: (*A*) There exists something which appears diamond-shaped, we can deduce statements such as: (*S*) There exists something which *is* diamond-shaped. If he is cautious, he may grant, as Mr. Ayer does, that *S* describes exactly the same state of affairs as does *A*.[3] But he will cite the "somethings" mentioned in statements such as *S* as instances of what he means by "sense-data."

One fundamental question, then, concerns the inference from statements such as *A*, in the language of appearing, to statements such as

---

[2] C. D. Broad, *Scientific Thought* (1923), pp. 236-237. Broad, although he does not advocate the theory of appearing, presents an excellent account of it. Cp. Thomas Reid, *An Inquiry into the Human Mind on Principles of Common Sense* (1764), ch. vi; sec. 3.

[3] Cp. A. J. Ayer, *The Foundations of Empirical Knowledge* (1940), p. 25. Cp. pp. 55, 116-117.

S, in the sense-datum language. We may call this the *sense-datum in-ference.* And we may say that the *sense-datum theory* is the view which countenances this inference, whereas the *theory of appearing* is the view which does not.

Some philosophers who refuse to countenance the sense-datum infer-ence seem to hold that it is *invalid;* others seem to hold merely that it in *inadvisable.*[4] But in either case it is agreed that, in discussing percep-tion, the language of appearing is preferable to the sense-datum lan-guage; that, by making the inference to sense-data, we multiply en-tities beyond necessity; and that, by avoiding the inference, we lose nothing but the metaphysical puzzles.

It is easy to see the *prima-facie* case for the theory of appearing. When we describe perception in terms of sense-datum we seem to have, in ad-dition to the external objects (e.g., the table, the oculist's "A" and the train), *another* set of entities (e.g., the diamond-shaped datum, the blur, and the diminishing sound). And these other entities turn out to be extraordinarily perplexing. But when we speak in terms of appearing we have only the original external objects. Thus we avoid multiplying entities and we avoid the puzzles concerning the status and whereabouts of sense-data.

Moreover, when we describe perception in the language of appearing, without "wandering in the usages of phenomena, sense-data, impres-sions, and their like,"[5] we seem at the outset to preserve the convictions of the naive or nonphilosophical realist. For we can say that, when you look at the table from the corner of the room, it's the real table that you see—the table as it appears under those conditions. And we can say that when you look down the railroad tracks, or at the oculist's "A," or when you listen to the train go off into the distance, it's the real ex-ternal object that you perceive—the object as it appears, in each case, under the conditions of observation. The menu may appear pink to me, with my odd glasses, and white to you; yet each of us is seeing the real menu—I am seeing it under one set of conditions and you are seeing it under another. To say that it appears pink to me and white to you is no more puzzling that to say it is north of me and south of you; in relation to me it's north and appears pink; in relation to you it's south

---

[4] Prichard, Coffey, and Dawes Hicks speak as though they believe the inference to be invalid; Paul seems to feel that it is merely inadvisable. See the works cited above.

[5] A. E. Murphy, *The Use of Reason* (1943), p. 35.

and appears white. No matter how bizarre the conditions may be, if an external object appears to us at all, then clearly it is the external object that we perceive. "To be sure," writes Mr. Murphy, who is one of the most persuasive spokesmen for this way of looking at the matter, "we gain our perceptual information about such objects through such expedients as looking at them, and what we thus see of them is the way they look (appear) under the conditions in which they can be observed. But how else would a human organism see a material object?"[6] There are many philosophers, I suspect, who are content to leave the matter here.

MORE PUZZLES?

The theory of appearing, as we now have it, seems to say that appearing is relational; for instance, that "appearing pink to" designates a relation which obtains between the menu and me when I put on these odd glasses and look. Suppose, now, we ask, "*What* things may be appeared to?" The obvious answer is, of course, that the only things which may be appeared to are human beings and other organisms endowed with the appropriate sort of sense organs and nervous systems. This is certainly a sensible way to deal with the question and it is, I take it, the answer which Mr. Murphy, for instance, would be inclined to give.[7] But let us consider what follows if we answer the question this way.

If appearing is what we have said that it is, the answer would entail that where there aren't any perceiving organisms, nothing is appeared to and hence nothing appears. When no one is looking, roses don't appear red, the menu doesn't appear pink *or* white, and, when no one is listening, the train doesn't sound any fainter when it goes off into the distance. But when we put the matter this way, this particular version of the theory of appearing becomes remarkably similar to the classical sense-datum philosophy known as "psychophysical dualism" (or at least to that version of it defended by Mr. Lovejoy in *The Revolt*

---

[6] A. E. Murphy, in *The Philosophy of G. E. Moore* (1942), p. 312.

[7] Murphy presents a clear statement of this view in "Dewey's Epistemology and Metaphysics," in *The Philosophy of John Dewey* (1939), pp. 219-220. Possibly some who incline toward this version of the theory of appearing might also want to add that cameras, recording machines, and other such devices can be appeared to. The sense-datum philosopher, however, is more likely to be interested in the analogies between these devices and perception.

Against Dualism) and seems to have just about the same merits and limitations. This type of dualism, it will be recalled, is the view which "bifurcates nature" into the world of sense-data and the world of things-in-themselves. In order to see the merits and limitations of the theory of appearing generally, it will be instructive to note the parallel between classical dualism and the version of the theory of appearing to which we seem to have been led.

According to dualism, sense-data come into existence only where there are observers who satisfy the appropriate conditions; hence, in those portions of the universe where there are no observers, or where no one is observing, there are no sense-data. According to this version of the theory of appearing, objects appear only when there are observers who satisfy the appropriate conditions; hence, in those portions of the universe where there are no observers, or where no one is observing, nothing appears.

Are unperceived roses red? According to dualism, they could be said to be red in the sense that they have powers or dispositions to contribute to the production of red sense-data for certain sorts of observers; but no red sense-datum exists out there with the roses. On this version of the theory of appearing, the roses may be said to be red in the sense that they have powers or dispositions to appear red to certain sorts of observer; but they don't appear red when no one is looking. Before anyone looks, the redness of the rose (on either view) exists as a power, possibility, or disposition. The rose is such that, if only a "normal observer" were to come into the garden, it *would* present him with a red sense-datum (or appear red for him). When, finally, he *does* come and look, the disposition of the rose is activated and, on the one view, sense-data are *produced,* and, on the other, the roses *appear.* (Sometimes it is said, on the one view, that sense-data *emerge* and, on the other, that the roses *take on* appearances or relations of appearing.[8])

Do we perceive the real external objects? The dualist may say that we perceive them by means of their effects or "representatives" in us. But they never have such effects or representatives unless they are perceived. On this version of the theory of appearing, we perceive the external objects "the way they appear" under the conditions of observa-

---

8 Murphy speaks of what external objects "take on" when we perceive them (*The Philosophy of John Dewey,* p. 220).

tion. But they never appear that way, or any other way, unless they are perceived.

Does one theory provide us with a more "objective" account of the matter than the other does?[9] According to dualism, it is an *objective* property of the external thing to be able to produce the sense-data it does when the appropriate observers are perceiving it; but the property is *subjectively* dependent in that no sense-data can be produced unless observers are present. On the present version of the theory of appearing, it is an *objective* property of the external thing to be able to appear as it does to observers like us; but the property is *subjectively* dependent in that the object cannot appear in *any* way unless observers are present.

Do our claims to knowledge become more precarious on the one theory than on the other? On each theory we perceive the real external objects. But the dualist must decide how the sense-data which are produced in us by the external things aid us in knowing about the things-in-themselves; for the sense-data come into being when we perceive and disappear when we cease to perceive. On the other view, we must decide how our being appeared to aids us in knowing about the things which thus appear; for they appear that way only when we perceive and when we cease to perceive they no longer appear at all. The dualist sometimes says that our experience of sense-data provides us with a "representative" of other parts of nature; Mr. Murphy says that our being appeared to provides us with a "fair sample" of other parts of nature.[10] To the question "How do we *know* that we have a faithful representative (or a fair sample)?" each theory may provide a similar answer.

Certainly, up to this point, the theories are remarkably similar. The classical objections to the above dualistic theses apply with equal force to our version of the theory of appearing. Whitehead and others are disturbed by the "vacuous actuality" with which unperceived objects seem to be left on the dualistic hypothesis; those who call themselves

---

[9] Murphy sometimes refers to his view as "objective relativism" in order "to stress the fact that the experienced world is *at once* in some of its major features dependent on and conditioned by the special relations in which sentient (and more particularly human) organisms stand to their environment *and also* a direct presentation of that environment itself, or the order of natural events as is is under such conditions" (*ibid.*, p. 219). "Objective relativism" is here in question only to the extent that it may be correctly interpreted as a version of the theory of appearing.

[10] *Ibid.*, p. 220.

"naturalists" are sometimes disturbed by the "miracle" which is alleged to occur when sense-data "emerge"; the skeptic asks about the credentials of "representative"; and so on. The treatment of unperceived objects, on this version of the theory of appearing, is indistinguishable from that of dualism and thus they retain their qualitative vacuity; the "taking on of appearances" is as much (or as little) a "miracle" as is "emergence"; and the "fair sample" has as much (or as little) reliability as the "representative."

At one point, the parallel may seem to be strained, namely, in connection with the question "Do we perceive external objects?" For, in answer to this, the dualist sometimes says that we perceive only sense-data and never external objects. Here, however, we *are* in danger of linguistic confusion. If the statement "We perceive external objects" is understood in its ordinary sense, *neither* theory entails anything that is inconsistent with it. If one wanted to prove that Jones, for instance, doesn't perceive external objects (in the ordinary sense of these words) one would not offer a theory about the status of sense-data; rather, one would try to show that Jones is dead, or asleep, or that his perceptual apparatus is out of order. When the dualist passes from "No sense-data exist in the external world" to "We don't perceive external objects," he may be "corrected" by reference to ordinary usage. Anyone who has doubt on *this* point may be referred to the large body of contemporary literature concerning the relation between philosophical statements and ordinary language.[11]

So far, then, the two theories are pretty much parallel. Each involves further metaphysical questions, however, and here they seem to diverge. The sense-datum philosopher is puzzled about the status of his sense-data in the physical world. He asks whether they are identical with any of the entities treated by physics; the theory of the dualist is that sense-

---

11 Cp. N. Malcolm, "Moore and Ordinary Language," in *The Philosophy of G. E. Moore*, pp. 345-368; M. Lazerowitz, "Moore's Paradox," in *ibid.*, pp. 371-393; O. K. Bouwsma, "Des Cartes' Skepticism of the Senses," *Mind*, LIV (1945), pp. 313-322; M. Black, "Linguistic Method in Philosophy," *Phil. and Phenom. Res.*, VIII (1948), 635-649. Not all dualists, of course, have needed this enlightenment. Thus C. A. Strong, for example, held "that the sense-datum is representative, but that perception by means of the sense-datum is direct. We directly apprehend the real thing, and nothing else; its characters and also its existence" ("Is Perception Direct, or Representative?" *Mind*, XL [1931], 217). Cp. also the scholastic doctrine according to which the external object is *that which* we perceive and the "sensible species" that by *means of which* we perceive it: "Species non est *id quod* cognoscitur, sed *id quo* mens cognoscit rem" (Coffey, *op. cit.*, II, 178).

data are "in the mind" or possibly that they are "the brain seen from its metaphysical insides." The theorist of appearing may ask, similarly, whether his relations of appearing can be identified with anything treated by physics or whether they are something which the universe somehow "takes on" when perceivers come into being. Both philosophers may also be led—I think unfortunately—to make philosophical statements about the nature of physical objects. The dualist talks about "things-in-themselves" and it is easy to imagine the theorist of appearing ensnared in questions such as the following:

"Consider the statement, 'We see the rose as it appears to us.' Does this substantive phrase, 'the rose-as-it-appears-to-us,' designate a special kind of complex? If we are to continue to be sensitive to language, we should prefer to say it doesn't. Instead of saying 'We see the rose as it appears to us' we could say 'We are appeared to by the rose.'[12] This is less felicitous and possibly less pleasing to the professional naive realist; further it brings to clearer focus the problem of the *terms* of our appearing relation. Can we think of even a single respect in which they are distinguishable from the 'things-in-themselves' of the dualist? On the other hand, if we say that our substantive phrase 'the rose-as-it-appears-to-us' *does* designate a special kind of complex we are confronted with puzzles not unlike the original sense-datum puzzles. For example, what is the relation of these complexes to the rose; does the entire rose occur in them or just a part, say the surface; is the rose somehow the totality of the complexes in which it would be commonly said to occur; do these complexes, like the dualist's sense-data, exist outside of space; do they exist only when perceived? And what are the *other* terms of the appearing relation—minds, selves, brains? . . ."

As in the case of the sense-datum puzzles, something seems to be amiss. In general, such philosophical speculations about the nature of matter do not seem altogether happy. *Neither* the sense-datum philosopher nor the theorist of appearing, after all, needs to compete with physics. As we have seen, the two theories have similar consequences with respect to the nature of physical things and to the possibility of knowing them; or perhaps we should say the two theories are similarly *devoid* of such consequences. But some philosophers seem to feel that such theories, in making sense-data or appearing relations depend for their existence upon perceiving organisms, somehow "impoverish" the

---

12 This recalls Aristotle's statement: "The activity of the sensible object and that of the percipient sense is one and the same activity" (*De Anima* II, 425 B 27).

physical world. And these philosophers may be tempted to *extend* physics and talk about the metaphysical insides of matter. Possibly they could be shown that this "impoverishment" is not as serious as they are at first led to believe. In any event, however, the problem is the same whether we choose sense-data or appearing.

But let us see whether we might be better off with some *other* version of the theory of appearing.

<h2 style="text-align:center">STILL MORE PUZZLES</h2>

From the point of view of the antimetaphysician, the other possible versions of the theory of appearing are even less hopeful than the one just considered. We need do little more than mention what the alternatives might be.

According to the version just considered, appearing is "relational" and only sentient organisms may be appeared to. Suppose, now, we deny the latter contention and say instead that *anything* may be appeared to. The redness of the rose may appear to the objects around it (and possibly to itself), and the views from mountain tops need not await the presence of living things in order to appear. This version would certainly meet some of the objections to the previous one. The uninhabited portions of the universe would have more than the "qualitative vacuity" which they possess on dualism and on our former theory; nor would there occur any "emergence" or "taking on" when sentient beings appear on the scene. But now we seem to be saying that the rose may appear red to the stone!

I suspect that by giving the theory of appearing this twist we obtain the key to significant portions of Whitehead's and Alexander's speculations. Perhaps, if we were unable to before, we can now begin to understand Whitehead's doctrine of "prehensions" according to which "all actual things are subjects, each prehending the universe from which it arises."[13] And we now have light on Alexander's thesis that "the cognitive relation" is "the simplest and most universal relation between finite things in the Universe," and that we "may ascribe 'mind' to all things alike, in various degrees."[14] Of course, if we say that the

---

[13] A. N. Whitehead, *Process and Reality* (1929), p. 89.

[14] S. Alexander, "The Basis of Realism," *Proceedings of the British Academy*, VI (1914), 10, 32. Cp. Francis Bacon's *Natural History*: "It is certain that all bodies whatsoever, though they have no sense, yet they have perception . . ." (quoted in

rose may appear red to the stone as well as to sentient organisms, we have to explain what it is that the sense organs and the rest of our perceptual apparatus do for us and why it is that the stone doesn't need such aids. Alexander's answer to this is that, although both the man and the stone bear a *cognitive relation* to the rose, only the man is *conscious of the rose;* Whitehead's answer is similar.[15] If we decide that the table appears to the other furniture in the room, we can ask whether it appears diamond-shaped to one piece and square to another. And so on.

If this version of the appearing seems difficult to accept, we need only turn to the various sense-datum theories in order to find suggestions for further possibilities. Recall, for example, Russell's doctrine that sense-data are constituents of the brain, or Moore's suggestion that possibly sense-data might appear to be different from what they really are. We might try saying that it is a portion of the brain that appears (and we could still say, of course, that we perceive external objects: we perceive them by being appeared to by the brain). Or, if we were really pressed, we could try saying that things might appear to appear in ways in which they don't really appear.

And if none of these possibilities gives us a satisfactory theory of appearing, there are still others. We could try saying that appearing is not relational—e.g., that the rose may appear without appearing red *to* anything. In this way, we avoid the difficulties of our first theory; we don't have the cognitive stones (monads, occasions) of the second; we don't have the complications involved in saying that a brain may appear to its owner or that things may appear to appear in ways other than they really appear. But now we have a theory, which is the analogue of the theory of "unsensed sense-data," and *this* catches us in still further puzzles. Now shall we say that, when no one is around, the menu appears pink *and* white at once? We can no longer add the qualification "pink to one observer, white to another." Does "appearing pink" entail "appearing not white"? How do we answer such questions? Suppose we say that an object cannot appear pink and white at once, or clear and blurry at once, or diamond-shaped and rectangu-

---

Whitehead, *Science and the Modern World* [1925], p. 58). See also Locke's *Essay,* bk. IV, ch. iii, sec. 6.

[15] Whitehead believes, of course, that the relations obtain not between stones and roses but between entities of a more "concrete" sort. Thus the theory of appearing seems to lead back to something like Leibniz's monads and their conscious and unconscious perceptions.

lar. Consider the table in the other room; which way is *it* appearing
now—diamond-shaped or rectangular, large or small, clear or blurry?
How does one decide; how could one ever tell? Or perhaps we should
say that the thing manifests *all* these appearances at once[16]—that at this
moment the oculist's "A" appears clear, appears completely blurry, and
appears in all the intervening ways; that it appears yellow (as the
jaundiced man discovers); that it appears double (as one may discover
by pressing the eye). . . . These, then are *puzzles of appearing* and
they may be multiplied indefinitely.

SENSE-DATA AND APPEARING

Thus there are sense-datum puzzles and there are puzzles of appearing. The presumption may be that there really *is* something genuinely
puzzling about perception and that we must choose, not between metaphysics and enlightenment, but between good and bad metaphysics. In
the meantime, however, is there any ground for choosing between the
sense-datum theory and the theory of appearing?

The two theories differ with respect to the validity of what we have
called the "sense-datum inference." But otherwise they seem to be
pretty nearly parallel. Given a statement in the "sense-datum language," it is an easy matter to transform it into the "language of appearing," and vice versa. Two points can be made at this stage however, which may help us to make a choice.

(1) If we want to keep our metaphysical puzzles down to a minimum
(and this certainly seems to be desirable), we should prefer not to be
left with the evils of *both* sense-data and appearing.[17] Now there is a
significant group of experiences, other than those involved in external
perception, which all of us tend to describe in the manner of the sense-
datum language—namely, those experiences which involve images,
after-images, dreams, hallucinations, and so on. An after-image, for
instance, seems to be an entity of much the same sort as a sense-datum
and it involves similar puzzles ("Is it outside of space; is it in the
brain; does it come into existence when perceived; can it exist unper-

---

[16] This seems to be Coffey's version of the theory of appearing (cp. *op. cit.*, II,
175).

[17] The sense-datum philosopher, although he countenances statements in the
language of appearing, does not have to face the puzzles of appearing in addition
to the sense-datum puzzles. For statements in the language of appearing are to be
"analyzed" into sense-datum statements.

ceived . . . ?"). If we continue to speak of such experiences in this manner, we have *one* good reason for preferring sense-data to appearing: viz., if we choose sense-data we shall have but one curious category; if we choose appearing we shall have two.

It is true that one *could* describe these experiences in the language of appearing. When I imagine a unicorn or a golden mountain, I *could* describe the experience by saying, not that I have an image of such and such a sort, but that something appears in such and such a fashion. This way of putting the matter, however, leads us at once to the peculiar problems which the theory of appearing involves. For, in this language, we speak of *something* which appears. One may now ask, "What is it that appears when I imagine a unicorn?" ("Is it a subsistent entity, or part of the brain, or parts of previously seen physical objects, . . . etc., etc.?") Here, perhaps, the language of appearing seems even more artificial than the language of sense-data. It is significant that no philosopher (as far as I know) has suggested that the language of appearing be applied to experiences other than those involved in external perception.[18]

(2) The objection to the validity of the sense-datum inference has something in common with the so-called "anti-rational" or "anti-intellectual" philosophies of the nineteenth and twentieth centuries. A few years ago, it will be recalled, some philosophers were saying that to "hypostatize" entities which are "finite" is to falsify reality; that these are but aspects of the Whole, to which no finite concept is adequate; and that we are not likely to advance to the Whole wandering through the mazes of tables, chairs, and railroad tracks. And others were making similar charges about the "conceptualization" of a reality which is essentially "fluid." On either objection, statements such as "Here is a table" and "There is a railroad track" are somehow illegitimate. Most of us, however, are prepared to defend the conviction that, although physical objects may never exist in isolation and although their temporal boundaries are somewhat indefinite, they are,

---

18 Mr. Paul, however, makes an interesting proposal. Consider the sort of situation which the sense-datum philosopher might describe as follows: "I was deceived into thinking that I saw a penny; but what I really saw was an elliptical sense-datum which was not 'of' any physical object." Paul suggests that one might do well to describe such a situation in this way: "It only seemed to me as if there was a round penny which looked [appeared] elliptical. I was really not seeing anything at all" (*op. cit.*, p. 68). But, obviously, this kind of formulation, if taken quite literally, would give rise to still another set of problems concerning what is intended by the phrase "It only seemed to me as if. . . ."

all the same, "legitimate" subjects of discourse. Let us compare this with the conviction that there is a diamond-shaped "something" to be seen from here, a blur to be seen in the oculist's shop, and, in the case of the double images, two "somethings" to be seen and counted.[19] Possibly one will say that the entities which these terms purport to designate are "adverbs" of something else, as one may say that the chair is an adverb (aspect, stage) of something else, and there may even be good reason for making such assertions. But when it is objected that we cannot talk about chairs and images and sense-data, the reply must consist, essentially, of a defense of analysis and of our ability to make abstractions. Mr. Lewis has put the point emphatically: "The condemnation of abstractions is the condemnation of thought itself. Nothing that thought can ever comprise is other than some abstraction except the concrete universal; and the concrete universal is a myth."[20] The diamonds and blurs are at least as well off as the tables and chairs.

---

[19] Cp. H. H. Price, *Perception* (1932), p. 63.
[20] C. I. Lewis, *Mind and the World Order* (1929), p. 55.

De Principiis
Non Disputandum . . . ?

On the Meaning and the Limits of Justification

HERBERT FEIGL

Arguments purporting to justify beliefs or evaluations often proceed from specific to more general issues. Opposition and challenge tend to provoke critical reflection; through various dialectical moves higher levels of justification are reached and made explicit. Argument usually terminates with appeals to principles which are considered indisputable, at least by those who invoke them. But, notoriously, initial disagreements cannot always be removed by what is called "rational argument." Frequently enough, initial disagreement can be traced back to disagreement in basic presuppositions. It is a characteristic of those modern cultures which endorse freedom of thought that they countenance divergencies in religious, political, or economic positions. "It is all a matter of one's ultimate presuppositions"—this phrase and its variants indicate that enlightened common sense is aware of the limits of argument and justification. But on the other hand there is also the deep-rooted wish to be *right*, absolutely right, in one's basic outlook. When the disagreement concerns mere gastronomical matters, we are quite willing to reconcile ourselves with the saying, *"De gustibus non est disputandum."* Art critics and aestheticians, however, do not unreservedly extend such tolerance to all issues of aesthetic evaluation. Most people, including the majority

113

of philosophers, are still more reluctant to grant any relativity to the basic standards of moral evaluation. There is, at least in this age of science, almost complete unanimity as regards the criteria by which we judge the claims of ordinary factual knowledge. And perhaps genuine indisputability is attributed to the principles of formal logic. At least the simplest canons of deductive reasoning, as they are exemplified, e.g., in some of the syllogisms or in elementary arithmetic, are quite generally accepted as indispensable presuppositions of any sort of argument.

While there is no intention here to cast doubt upon the particular gradation just sketched, it need not be taken for granted either. What we do wish to clarify is the status of the very principles which in each of these various fields constitute the standards of validity or the bases of justification. The question mark attached to the title of this essay is not only to indicate that I am going to raise more questions that I shall be able to answer, but also to stress the deeply troublesome and controversial character of the main issues of justification.

The present essay aims at the illumination and at least a partial resolution of the following puzzling questions:

(1) What are the meanings of the term "justification" and what are the logical structures of the corresponding procedures of reasoning?

(2) If justification consists in the stating of reasons, and if the fallacies of the petitio principii and of the infinite regress are to be avoided, what are the limits to which justification can legitimately be pursued? By what criteria do we know that we have reached the limits of justification?

(3) What is the nature of the "ultimate presuppositions" which serve as the uppermost principles of justification?

(4) Can disagreement with respect to these principles be settled only by such nonrational procedures as persuasion, indoctrination, propaganda, therapeutic influence, or coercion? Or else, *if* rational argument concerning first principles *is* possible, what are *its* standards of justification?

(5) How is the issue regarding the primacy of "theoretical reason" vs. the primacy of "practical reason" to be resolved?

In order to approach these intriguing questions with any hope for clarification we shall first have to make sure that we understand what we mean by "justification" and what major types of justification are employed in various contexts.

The search for justification, the capacity for critical reflection, are among the marks of the much vaunted rationality of man. He is sometimes able, and often willing, to state the reasons for accepting or repudiating knowledge claims and evaluations. The procedure of justification is here taken to be precisely this stating of reasons. More fully explicated, justification consists in the disclosure (exhibition, demonstration) of a conformity of that which is to be justified (the *justificandum*) with a certain principle or a set of principles which do the justifying (the *justificans*). We justify claims of factual knowledge by means of empirical confirmation. We cite evidence. But the facts that constitute what we call "evidence" have a bearing on our knowledge claim only by virtue of some principles of confirmation (or induction). We justify claims of mathematical truth by proof. But the validity of a proof depends upon conformity with the principles of deduction. We justify moral approvals or condemnations by reference to ethical principles, and so on. Justification as here understood thus invariably involves at least an implicit reference to some standards or norms which serve, in the given context, as principles of justification. When challenged to justify any one of these principles in turn, people are apt to get impatient or "probably blow up right in your face, because you have put your finger on one of [their] absolute presuppositions, and people are apt to be ticklish in their absolute presuppositions."[1] Indeed, if we ask a typical laboratory scientist what justifies him in his unquestioning acceptance of arithmetic or of the principle of empirical induction, he will, at the very best, tell us that he takes these principles for granted and that it is not part of his business to validate or justify them. We are apt to get an analogous answer from, say, a democratically minded statesman engaged in promoting some measure of social reform, if we ask him for a justification of the principle of justice for all. However, all this is psychology. The facts mentioned may be taken as symptoms of the ultimacy of the principles in the given context. A symptom of a distinctly logical character (but not decisive either, as regards logical ultimacy) is the circularities that are apt to arise on this level of argument. Requests for justification, if complied with at all, tend to elicit answers which are more or less disguised forms of question begging.

It is generally recognized that one of the major tasks of philosophical analysis consists in making explicit (i.e., formulating articulately) the

---

[1] R. G. Collingwood, *An Essay on Metaphysics* (1940), p. 31, cf. also p. 44.

more basic justifying principles. It is almost equally well recognized that *giving reasons* for our beliefs is something altogether different from pointing out their causes. He who has not grasped this difference has not even begun to understand what philosophy is all about. For philosophical analysis endeavors to reconstruct (explicate, clarify) the procedures of justification.

The uses of the word "reason" suffer unfortunately from a good deal of ambiguity. Besides naming a capacity of the human mind (part of which may be the ability to state reasons), it is used to designate causes and purposes, as well as grounds of validation. What a rich source of confusion lies in the little phrases "the reason why," "because," and "since"! Aristotle and Schopenhauer and many thinkers between and after have struggled to disentangle these and other meanings of "reason." Kant stated what concerns us here very clearly by distinguishing between the questions *quid facti* and *quid juris*. Husserl, at the beginning of this century, opposed most explicitly the psychologistic confusion of the two questions. But, even like Kant and Husserl, many other philosophers have not been free from serious relapses into the very confusion they had recognized and severely criticized.

The word "justification" shares some of the ambiguities of the word "reason" (as used in phrases like "giving reasons"). As we proceed we shall find it not only indispensable but also highly clarifying to distinguish between justification in the sense of *validation* and justification in the more usual sense of an argument concerning *means* with respect to *ends*. The type of justification which we wish to distinguish from validation may be called "pragmatic" or "instrumental" justification (*justificatio actionis* as contrasted with *justificatio cognitionis*). In what follows we shall take the terminological liberty of using the term "vindication" as a short expression for this second meaning.

Other terms related to "justification" are "criticism" and "appraisal." In their ordinary meanings these terms stand for reflective acts which are directed toward other acts or attitudes, rather than upon the cognitive content of propositions. If it is cognition that is under critical examination it is usually the process of reasoning, or the acceptance or rejection of knowledge claims, rather than the validity of the relevant propositions that is being "criticized." But here again the two meanings are usually so intimately intertwined that it takes a special analytic effort to separate them neatly from one another. The distinctions that we just indicated will be applied presently in the comparative study of four domains of justification; and it will be more systematically elaborated in the concluding part of this essay.

Material for the analysis and rational reconstruction of justification abounds in the countless varieties of argument. A review of the interplay of dogmatic theses, skeptical antitheses and critical syntheses in some of the major domains of argument will help in avoiding the dangers of pale abstraction and sterile formalism that unavoidably impairs discussions of justification in general and *in vacuo.* We are now going to discuss (1) logical, (2) methodological, (3) epistemological, and (4) ethical contexts of justification.

Justification involving appeal to principles of formal logic. Justification or criticism of the processes or the results of reasoning may involve, *inter alia,* questions of meaningfulness, of truth (or of reliability), of consistency, and of formal correctness (or conclusiveness). We shall concentrate on the two last mentioned criteria in the present section.

In appraising the correctness of a deductive argument we confront it with the rules of deductive logic. Conformity with these rules establishes the correctness, violation establishes the incorrectness of our reasoning. In traditional logic we may prove the legitimacy or expose the illegitimacy of some argument by reference to the rules of the syllogism. In the more generalized disciplines of modern logic a much greater wealth of forms and standards becomes available.

A specific deductive argument such as a valid syllogism may then be justified by reference to the well-known rules of the syllogism. And these rules in turn may be justified by reference to definitions and more fundamental principles such as the *dictum de omni et nullo* or (in modern logic) the rules of substitution and inference. Here the logician qua logician usually rests his case. But if he is *philosophically* curious in regard to the justification or justifiability of those basic rules of formal deduction, he will involve himself in peculiar perplexities. If he assumes that the laws of logic are the most general laws of nature, he ascribes a factual content to them that, no matter how thin, would require inductive justification. But inductive justification, while irreducible to deductive justification, presupposes the rules of deductive logic and is therefore impossible without reliance upon them. It may be urged that those most general laws of the universe are known by a priori intuition and, thus being self-evident, are neither in need nor capable of validation. This reply, however, is unacceptable for at least three reasons: The difficulties (Kant's heroic efforts notwithstanding) of accounting for the possibility of synthetic a priori knowledge are notoriously insurmountable. The reference to self-evidence involves us in the confusions of psychologism. Finally, closer analysis reveals a difference of kind (not merely of degree) between the laws of logic and the laws of nature.

The view (espoused by Mill and others) which construes the laws of logic as psychological laws of thought is merely a variant of the just criticized factualistic interpretation. Thought, as a matter of fact, does to *think* a simple self-contradiction, it is only too painfully obvious that not generally conform to the rules of logic. Even if it were impossible even a slight degree of complexity in argument often conceals just such an inconsistency to the thinker who then blithely asserts self-contradictions at least by way of implication.

A more promising view construes the rules of logic as the *norms* of correct reasoning. Leaving the question of the nature and status of rules or norms aside for the moment, we may say that the *rules* of logic in their totality *define what we mean by correct reasoning.* This view presupposes that we possess, at least implicitly, a criterion (or a set of criteria) by which we can tell whether reasoning is correct or incorrect. The formulation of the rules then merely explicates these criteria.

But this position provokes the question: What assures us of the adequacy of our explicandum, i.e., our pre-analytic notion of correct reasoning? The most widely accepted answer here refers us to the analytic character of all implication relations upon which correct deductive inference must be based. Deducibility, logical (or "strict") implication, entailment, or whatever else we may call it can be accounted for by reference to the *meaning* of the terms employed in deductive argument. We are then likely to say that whatever follows from propositions by virtue of the meaning of the terms they contain and by virtue of the meaning the propositions have as structured wholes follows *with necessity.* But how are we to decide what (if anything) follows from a given set of premises or is implied by given meanings unless we utilize the very rules of logic which we were going to justify? The emergence of circularity, here as well as elsewhere, is symptomatic of the fact that we have reached the limits of justification, that we are at least in the neighborhood of what are called "ultimate presuppositions."

More specifically, what is it that makes a presupposition ultimate? One well known reply to this question maintains that any attempt to deny, reject (or replace by alternatives) an ultimate principle involves its reaffirmation. This view appears indeed most plausible in the domain of formal logic; it is much less convincing in other domains of justification. Yet, even in regard to the laws of deductive logic, the argument, if intended as a *validation,* is specious. The denial of the law of noncontradiction leads to contradiction, that is, if we use all terms ("contradiction," "denial," etc.) in their customary sense. This sense is the "customary" one precisely because it conforms with the basic rules of ordinary (two-valued) logic. The argument therefore demonstrates only that a denial (in this sense!) of the laws of logic involves us in inconsistencies. These inconsistencies, however, are such only within the frame of the rules that determine the logic from which we expect to deviate and define the meaning of "denial" by means of which we attempt to deviate.

Let us then examine the widely held claims as to the legitimacy of *alternative logics.* The three-valued systems of Lukasiewicz and Tarski, of Brouwer and Heyting, or the logic for quantum mechanics of von Neumann, etc., are called systems of *logic* not only because they, like the two-valued systems of Aristotle or of Whitehead and Russell, are capable of axiomatic deductive presentation, but also because (and this is much more important) they too provide us with rules of inference. We shall pass over in silence the rather confused claims of the disciples of Hegel, Marx, or Engels—not to mention Korzybski—in favor of a dialectical logic. If there are any tenable insights in these trends of thought, they would have to be first separated from a great deal of outright nonsense or egregious equivocation. Only by the most charitable interpretation can those tenable elements be assimilated to the aforementioned three-valued (or many-valued) systems.

Is it a matter of "arbitrary" decision whether or not to bestow the title of "logic" upon such alternative systems? An adequate discussion of this controversial question would take us too far afield. I can here only sketchily indicate what seems to me to be involved. First there is the question whether "deduction" or "deducibility" as defined in various alternative logics despite vague analogies is not something so radically different from what these terms signify in two-valued logic that the use of these terms without proper qualification is bound to lead to confusion. Secondly, there is the question whether the rules according to which we manipulate the symbols in a three- (or many-) valued calculus must not themselves be applied according to yes-or-no principles which in turn would impose two-valued character upon their metalinguistic formulation. No matter what the structure of a language or of a calculus, if we are to proceed according to constant rules at all, if we are to be able to answer questions, solve problems, etc., in a responsible manner, must we not at some level introduce the *definiteness* which has throughout the ages been regarded as the very essence of the logical? Is not the requirement of unambiguous designation the very root of the regulative principles of semantics? And is not *logic* as we customarily understand it predicated upon adherence to rules of univocal designation? Can communication from person to person, as well as with oneself, dispense with the principles that ensure self-consistency? Are we not continually trying to remove ambiguity and vagueness from our concepts precisely in order to safeguard ourselves against inconsistency?

These questions and their obvious answers seem also to imply a repudiation of a view of logic which has lately gained some currency especially among mathematically oriented philosophers. These thinkers take their cue from the conventionalism of Poincaré and from Duhem's views on scientific method. According to this outlook there is no way of justifying laws or principles in isolation. Only the total set of laws, hypotheses, and principles is capable of test by experience. The principles of logic are simply the ones we are unwilling to surrender or modify, except as the last resort if our total system proves inadequate. The principles of logic are thus considered as in no way sharply distinguishable from those that we ordinarily would call "empirical." The advocates of this view then deny that there is a sharp distinction between the analytic and the synthetic types of propositions, and they deny accordingly also the sharp distinction between the a priori and the a posteriori type of validity. While it is difficult to see how such a position can be maintained wherever analyticity depends upon explicit definitions (as in "All roans are horses"), it may be granted that the distinction between analytic and synthetic propositions within such systems as theoretical physics is more problematic. A given formula may represent an analytic or a synthetic proposition depending upon the context of inquiry. Or, more precisely speaking, it depends upon the specific interpretation (by way of co-ordinating definitions, or semantical designation rules) to which the given formula (or a whole postulate system) is subjected. But the admitted last-ditch-surrender policy in regard to logical principles would seem to indicate that it is the data of experience which have jurisdiction over the factual content of a theory, whereas criteria of a very different kind are relevant for the adoption (or rejection) of the logical principles. In the customary view of the theories of the factual sciences, the principles of logic and pure mathematics are silent partners, presupposed but not explicitly listed among the postulates of the given theory (geometry, mechanics, electrodynamics, quantum mechanics, etc.). They are, to use a Kantian phrase with greater propriety than we find it used by Kant himself, the necessary conditions for the very possibility of any theory whatsoever. To ensure definiteness of meaning for our symbols, to ensure (the related) conclusiveness of deductive inference we have no choice but to conform to the principles of identity, of noncontradiction, and of the excluded middle. No matter whether we understand these principles as tautologies of the object language (as we do in propositional and functional logic) or whether we understand them as semantical precepts (formulated in the metalanguage), it is impossible to abandon, e.g., the law of the excluded middle, without at the same time abandoning the other two principles (as well as the principle of double negation, or the principles "$p \vee p \equiv p$," "$p \cdot p \equiv p$," etc.). Only if we allow ourselves to tamper with the implicitly understood meanings of "proposition," "negation," "equivalence," "disjunction," "conjunction," etc., can we responsibly deviate from one principle without affecting the others. And even if, upon modifying some of these meanings, we arrive at an "alternative logic," we shall yet have achieved no more than if, for example, we had perversely decided to replace the numeral "4" by th numeral "5" in arithmetic. That under such conditions "$2 + 2 = 5$" becomes a true statement is not in the least surprising. Actually, the parallel with arithmetic is (as everybody should have realized, at least since Frege's contributions) not merely a superficial analogy but genuinely a consequence of the fact that arithmetic (in ordinary interpretation) is a branch of logic (in ordinary, i.e., in Frege-Russell-Whitehead interpretation). Even if in some other world putting two and two objects together resulted invariably in a total of five objects, we should need ordinary (good old) arithmetic in order to formulate the rather peculiar natural laws of that world. Thought experiments of this kind reveal that the fundamental principles of logic are indeed independent of the data of experience. They show that these principles are indispensable not because of some pervasive features of the world that is to be symbolized, but because of the requirements of the process of symbolization itself. Every symbolic system has its tautological equivalences, based on conventional synonymities.

What is it then that accounts for the unique and ineluctable character of the principles of logic? If it is not the data of experience or the facts of the universe at large, what is it that makes compliance with them imperative and their violation a sin against the spirit of Reason? Neither the Ten Commandments nor the Law of the Land prescribes any rules of logic or language. What then is the "authority," what are the "sanctions" that dictate conformity with these principles? It will be suggested that at least part of what we mean by "mental sanity" consists precisely in compliance with those laws. Assuredly so, but this merely shows that "mental sanity" is (in part) defined by conformity with logic. The appeal to sanity therefore amounts to begging the question.

It is obvious that we have reached the limits of justification. Justification in the sense of validation involves reliance upon the principles of logic and can thus not provide their validation. Justification in the sense of a pragmatic vindication of the adoption of, and compliance with, the rules of logic would then seem to offer itself as a further opening, if we insist on pursuing our quest to the bitter (because trivial) end. If we wish to give such a justification, it too must be given by reasoning and will thus have to rely upon the very standards whose adoption is now the issue at stake. Will this involve us in a vicious circle? It will not, if we are perfectly clear that we are not seeking a *validation* of the principles of logic. If pragmatic *vindication* is sharply distinguished from validation, then all it can provide amounts to a recommendation of a certain type of behavior with respect to certain ends. We may say to ourselves: If we wish to avoid the perplexities and discomforts that arise out of ambiguity and inconsistency, *then* we have to comply with the rules of semantics and logic. If we wish to derive true propositions from true premises then we must conform to the rules of inference and the rules of substitution. The reasoning concerning these means-ends relations utilizes, as any such reasoning must, the forms of deductive and inductive inference. Perhaps in the extreme case—the degenerate case, as it were—only deductive inference is required.

There is only one more question that the dialectical process will finally bring forth: Why should we accept the ends which we took for granted in the vindication of compliance with logical rules? If the end is a means to further ends, then the question merely shifts to those further ends. And just as in the reconstruction of validation we disclose ultimate validating principles, so in the reconstruction of vindication we encounter ultimate ends or purposes. Whether definiteness and conclusiveness of reasoning are to be viewed as ultimate ends or as means to certain other values is a question of psychology. The well known transformation process of means into ends has brought it about that for many persons, especially of the scientific type of mind, the virtues of logicality have become ends in themselves. But for the vast majority of mankind logicality is primarily a means in the struggle for existence and in the pursuit of more satisfactory ways of living. These ends we pursue as a matter of stark fact; they are part of our human nature. The question whether this ought to be our nature, if not altogether preposterous, falls at any rate outside the domain of logical justification. If there is a meaningful question here at all, it is one for *ethical* considerations to decide.

Justification involving appeal to principles of methodology. It is generally granted that consistency and conclusiveness of reasoning are necessary conditions for arguments purporting to substantiate knowledge claims. It is almost equally well agreed that while consistency and conclusiveness may be sufficient in the purely formal disciplines, they are not sufficient in the realm of factual knowledge. The sort of justification that the claims of factual knowledge require leads us then to a consideration of principles outside the domain of formal logic. These principles belong to the field of inductive logic.

One qualification may be in order here. Inductive logic is not required for a justification of factual-knowledge claims that involve no transcendence beyond the completely and directly given. Perhaps a better way to state this contention is in the subjunctive mood: If there were knowledge claims susceptible to complete and direct verification (or refutation), their justification would involve appeal only to immediate data, to designation rules, to definitions, and to the principles of formal logic. We shall not attempt here to clean up this particular corner of the Augean stables of philosophy. In any case the doctrine of immediate knowledge seems to me highly dubious. The very terms in which we formulate observation statements are used according to rules which involve reference beyond the occasion of direct experience to which they are applied. If they involve no such reference, then they are not terms of a language as we usually conceive languages. Terms referring exclusively to the data of the present moment of a stream of experience could not fulfill the function of symbols in observation statements that are connected with symbols in other statements (of laws and/or other observation statements). If we are not to be reduced to mere signals indicating the individual occurrences of direct experience, we must formulate our statements regarding these individual occurrences in such a manner that they are capable of revision on the basis of other observation statements and of laws that are confirmable by observation.

Appeal to the justifying principles of inductive logic is inevitably made if the dialectic question "How do you know?" is pursued to the limit. An engineer may rest satisfied with reference to specific physical laws when he justifies his claims as to the efficiency (or inefficiency) of a particular machine. A physicist in turn may justify those specific laws by deduction from very general and basic laws, such as those of thermodynamics or electromagnetics. But when pressed for the reasons of his acceptance of those more (or most) general laws, he will invariably begin to speak of verification, of generalization, or of hypothetico-deductive confirmation. A researcher in medicine will proceed similarly. In order to justify a particular hypothesis, e.g., one according to which a certain disease is caused by a virus, he will quote evidence and/or will reason by analogy and induction. Justification of knowledge claims in the historical disciplines (natural as well as social) conforms to the same pattern.

A given item of observation is evidence not in and by itself, but only if viewed in the light of principles of inductive inference. On the level of common sense and on the more "empirical" levels of scientific inquiry those principles are simply the accepted laws of the relevant field. Utilizing some items of evidence and some pertinent laws we justify our assertions concerning past events in history, concerning the causes of diseases in pathology, concerning the existence of as yet unobserved heavenly bodies in astronomy, concerning motivations or learning-processes in psychology, and so on. The search for causes quite generally presupposes the assumption that events do have causes. The investigator of a crime would give us a queer look (if nothing worse) if we asked him how he could be so sure that the death under investigation must have had *some* cause or causes. He takes this for granted and it is not *his* business to justify the principle of causality. Philosophers however have felt that it is their business to justify the belief in causality.

We need not review in too much detail the variety of attempts that have been made in its behalf. The assimilation of causal to logical necessity was definitely refuted by Hume. Kant's transcendental deduction of a causal order depends on the premise that the human understanding impresses this order upon the data of the senses. Part of this premise is the tacit assumption that reason will remain constant throughout time and that it therefore can be relied upon invariably to bestow (the same) causal order upon the data. In this psychologistic version of Kant's epistemology we thus find that the lawfulness of the world is demonstrable only at the price of an assumption concerning the lawfulness of Reason. (We shall not press any further questions concerning the credibility of this ingenious but phantastic account of the nature of cognition.) Turning to the presuppositional version of the *Critique* we gladly acknowledge that Kant, more incisively than any of his predecessors, disclosed the frame of justifying principles within which the questions of natural science are raised as well as answered. But the elevation of strict determinism and of Newtonian mechanics to the rank of synthetic a priori principles proved to be a mistake. The development of recent science provides, if not a fully cogent refutation, at least a most serious counterargument against any such attempt at a rationalistic petrifaction of the laws of science of a given epoch. More crucial yet, Kant did not achieve what he proposed to do: overcome Hume's skepticism. The presuppositional analysis furnishes no more than this: "Knowledge" as we understand this term connotes explanation and prediction. Therefore, if knowledge of nature is to be possible, nature must be predictable. This is true enough. But do we establish in this fashion a synthetic a priori guarantee for the order of nature? Not in the least. All we have attained is an *analytic* proposition drawn from the definition of "knowledge."

Can *intuition* justify the belief in causality? Even if we granted that we have an intuitive acquaintance with causal necessity in some of its instantiations, how can we assure ourselves without *inductive* leap that the intuited samples are representative of the structure of the world at large?

It should scarcely be necessary to point out that the again fashionable attempts to rehabilitate the concept of Real Connections will not advance the problem of the justification of induction. We grant that problems such as those regarding the meaning of contrary-to-fact conditionals show that Hume's (and generally the radical empiricist) analysis of causal propositions is in need of emendation. Indeed, it seems inevitable to establish and clarify a meaning of "causal connection" that is stronger than Hume's constant conjunction and weaker than entailment or deducibility. Perhaps the distinction between laws (nomological statements) and initial conditions will help here. Our world, to the extent that it is lawful at all, is characterized by both: its laws and its initial condition. Counterfactual conditionals tamper with initial conditions. The frame of the laws is left intact in asking *this* kind of hypothetical question. The "real possibilities" which are correlative to the "real connections" are precisely the class of initial conditions compatible with the laws of our world (or of some other fancied world). These considerations show that the laws of a given world may be viewed as something stronger than can be formulated by means of general implication. They are the very principles of confirmation of any singular descriptive statement that is not susceptible to complete and direct verification. They are therefore constitutive principles of the conception of a given world, or rather of a class or family of worlds which are all characterized by the same laws.[2]

But the reconstruction of laws in terms of modal implications does not alter one whit their status in the methodology of science. Clearly, besides counterfactual hypotheticals we can equally easily formulate counternomological ones. Here we tamper with the laws. And the question of which *family* of worlds our world is a member can be answered only on grounds of empirical evidence and according to the usual rules of inductive procedure. Upon return from this excursion we are then confronted, just as before, with the problem of induction.

Obviously the next step in the dialectic must be the lowering of our level of aspiration. We are told that it is the quest for certainty that makes the justification of induction an insoluble problem. But we are

---

[2] Cp. W. Sellars, "Concepts as Involving Laws and Inconceivable without Them," *Phil. of Science*, XV (1948), 287.

promised a solution if only we content ourselves with probabilities. Let us see. "Probability" in the sense of a degree of expectation will not do. This is the psychological concept to which Hume resorted in his account of belief, or that Santayana has in mind when he speaks of "animal faith." What we want is a justifiable degree of expectation. And how do we justify the assignment of probability ratios to predictions and hypotheses? That depends on how we explicate the *objective* concept of probability. But here we encounter the strife of two schools of thought. According to the frequency interpretation there is no other meaning of "probability" than that of the limit of relative frequency. According to the logical interpretation "probability" (in the sense of strength of evidence, weight, degree of confirmation) consists in a logical relation between the evidence which bestows and the proposition upon which there is bestowed a certain degree of credibility. The adherents of this logical interpretation urge that the statistical concept of probability presupposes the logical one. For the ascription of a limit (within a certain interval) to a sequence of frequency ratios is itself an hypothesis and must therefore be judged according to the degree of confirmation that such hypotheses possess in the light of their evidence. Contrariwise, the frequency interpretation urges that locutions such as "degree of confirmation" or "weight," whether applied to predictions of single events or to hypotheses of all sorts, are merely *façons de parler*. Basically they all amount to stating frequency ratios which are generalized from statistical findings regarding the events concerned (the occurrence of successful predictions).

We shall not attempt to resolve the issue between these two schools of thought. Our concern is with the justification of induction. And here perhaps the divergence of interpretations makes no fundamental difference. Inductive probability in the sense of a degree of confirmation is a concept whose definition renders analytic every one of its specific applications. If we use this concept as our guide, that is if we believe that it will give us a maximum of successes in inductive guessing, then this could be explicated as an assertion about the (statistical) structure of the world. We are thus led to essentially the same rule of induction which the frequentists propose: Generalize on the basis of the broadest background of available evidence with a minimum of arbitrariness. This principle of straightforward extrapolation in sequences of frequency ratios applies to a world which need not display a deterministic order. Statistical regularity is sufficient. Does the application of the rule guarantee success? Of course not. Do the past successes of procedures according to this rule indicate, at least with probability, further successes? No again. Hume's arguments refuted this question-begging argument before Mill and others fell victims to the fallacy. Only if we utilize the *logical* concept of probability can we achieve a semblance of plausibility in the criticized argument. But for the reasons stated before, mere definitions cannot settle the issue as to whether our world will be good enough to continue to supply patterns of events in the future which will support this definition as a "useful" one.

The presuppositional analysis sketched thus far has merely disclosed one of the ultimate principles of all empirical inference. Any attempts to validate the principle itself involve question-begging arguments. Its ultimate and apparently ineluctable character can be forcefully brought out by considering how we would behave in a world that is so utterly chaotic and unpredictable that any anticipation of the future on the basis of past experience is doomed to failure. Even in such a world after countless efforts at inductive extrapolation had been frustrated we would (if by some miracle we managed to survive) abandon all further attempts to attain foresight. But would not even this yet be another inductive inference, viz., to the effect that the disorder will continue? The inductive principle thus is ultimately presupposed but in turn does not presuppose any further assumptions.

The various attempts (by Keynes, Broad, Nicod, Russell, and others) to deduce or render probable the principle of induction on the basis of some very general assumption concerning the structure of the world seem to me, if not metaphysical and hence irrelevant, merely to beg the question at issue. Assumptions of Permanent Kinds and of Limited Variety, provided they are genuine assertions regarding the constitution of the universe, themselves require inductive validation. To assign to such vast hypotheses a finite initial (or "antecedent") probability makes sense only if "probability" means subjective confidence. But nothing is gained in this manner. Any objective probability (logical or statistical) would presuppose a principle of induction by means of which we could ascertain the probability of such world hypotheses in comparison with the (infinite) range of their alternatives.

We have reached the limit of justification in the sense of validation. Can we then in any fashion provide a "reason" for this acknowledged principle of "reasonability"? Obviously not, if "reason" is meant in the sense of validating grounds. What we mean (at least in part, possibly as the most prominent part) by "reasonability" in practical life as well as in science consists precisely in the conformance of our beliefs with the probabilities assigned to them by a rule of induction or by a definition of degree of confirmation. We call expectations (hopes or fears) irrational if they markedly deviate from the best inductive estimates. The attempt to validate one of the major principles of all validation, it must be amply obvious by now, is bound to fail. We would be trying to lift ourselves by our own bootstraps.

The only further question that can be raised here concerns a justification of the *adoption* of the rule of induction (or rather of one of the various rules of induction, or one of the various definitions of inductive probability or of degree of confirmation). Such a justification must have the character of a vindication, a *justificatio actionis.* Our question then concerns the choice of means for the attainment of an end. Our end here is clearly successful prediction, more generally, true conclusions of nondemonstrative inference. No deductively necessary guarantee can be given for the success of such inferences even if we follow some rule of induction. The probability of success can be proved, but that is trivial because we here utilize the concept of probability which our rule of induction implicitly defines. This probability cannot be construed as an estimate of the limit of frequency. We do not know whether such a limit exists. Only if we grant hypothetically that there is such a limit can we assign weights to its various values (i.e., to intervals into which the limit may fall) on the basis of (always finite) statistical samples. What then justifies our optimistic belief in the convergence of statistical sequences toward a limit? Since any attempt at validation would inevitably be circular, we can only ask for a vindication of the rule according to which we posit the existence of limits. Reichenbach's well known but widely misunderstood justification of induction[3] consists, as I see it, in a vindication of the adoption of that rule. It amounts to the *deductive* proof that no method of attaining foresight could conceivably be successful if every sort of induction were bound to fail. Perhaps there are alternative techniques of foresight that might even be more efficient or reliable than the laborious method of scientific generalization. But such alternative

---

[3] H. Reichenbach, *Experience and Prediction* (1938). See also his article "On the Justification of Induction," *Jour. of Phil.,* XXXVII (1940), 101. Also reprinted in H. Feigl and W. Sellars (eds.), *Readings in Philosophical Analysis* (1949).

methods (let us none too seriously mention crystal gazing, clairvoyance, premonitions, etc.) would themselves have to be appraised by their success; i.e., they would have to be accepted or rejected on the basis of statistical studies of the frequency ratio of correct predictions achieved by them. And our confidence in such "alternative" techniques of foresight would therefore ultimately be justifiable only on the basis of normal induction. *If* there is an order of nature at all (i.e., at least a statistical regularity), not too complex or deeply hidden, then a consistent application of the rule of induction will reveal it. This statement is of course a tautology. It should not be confused with such bolder and undemonstrable factual assertions as that the inductive procedure is the only reliable one, or that it is our best bet. Reliability and optimal wagering presuppose inductive probabilities and thus cannot be invoked for their justification. We cannot even say that straightforward generalization is a necessary condition (never known to be sufficient) for the success of predictions. The air of plausibility that this statement shares with its close relative, the common-sense slogan "Nothing ventured, nothing gained" arises only if we disregard (logically conceivable) alternative routes to predictive success, such as sheer inspiration, capricious guessing, intuition, premonition, etc. The unique character that the inductive procedure possesses in contrast with those alternatives rests exclusively in this: The method of induction is *the only one for which it can be proved* (deductively!) that it leads to successful predictions *if* there is an order of nature, i.e., *if* at least some sequences of frequencies do converge in a manner not too difficult to ascertain for human beings with limited experience, patience, and ingenuity. This is the tautology over again, in expanded form, but just as obvious and trivial as before. In the more ordinary contexts of pragmatic justification the validity of induction is invariably presupposed. If we want to attain a certain end, we must make "sure" (i.e., probable) that the means to be chosen will achieve that end. But if we ask for a vindication of the adoption of the very *principium* of all induction, we deal, so to speak, with a degenerate case of justification. We have no assurance that inductive probabilities will prove a useful guide for our lives beyond the present moment. But equally we have no reason to believe that they will fail us. We know furthermore (as a matter of logical necessity or tautology) that *if* success can be had at all, in any manner whatsoever, it can certainly be attained by the inductive method. For this method is according to its very definition so designed as to disclose whatever order or regularity may be present to be disclosed. Furthermore, since the inductive method is self-corrective, it is the most flexible device conceivable for the adaptation and readaptation of our expectations.

The conclusion reached may seem only infinitesimally removed from Hume's skepticism. Philosophers do not seem grateful for small mercies. In their rationist quest for certainty many still hope for a justification of a principle of uniformity of nature. We could offer merely a deductive (and trivial) vindication of the use of the pragmatic rule of induction. But for anyone who has freed himself from the wishful dreams of rationalism the result may nevertheless be helpful and clarifying. It is the final point which a consistent empiricist must add to his outlook. We refuse to countenance such synthetic a priori postulates as Russell (perhaps not with the best intellectual conscience) lately found necessary to stipulate regarding the structure of the universe. We insist that no matter how general or pervasive the assumptions, as long as they are about the *universe,* they fall under the jurisdiction of the rule of induction. This rule itself is not then a factual assertion but the maxim of a procedure or what is tantamount, a definition of inductive probability. In regard to rules or definitions we cannot raise the sort of doubt that is sensibly applicable to factual assertions. In order to settle doubts of the usual sort we must rely on some principles without which neither doubt nor the settlement of doubt makes sense. The maxim of induction is just such a principle.

Justification involving appeal to epistemological principles: the criteria of factual meaningfulness. The slogan *"De principiis non est disputandum"* is perhaps most emphatically invoked in the justification of theological and metaphysical doctrines. But since the rise of pragmatism, operationism, and logical positivism, those issues have been undercut. Prior to the examination of the validity of theological or metaphysical assertions is the question of the type of meaning with which they can justifiably be credited. It is generally admitted that the hypotheses of inductive metaphysics, e.g., cosmological speculations, may be merely more problematic than the kind of hypotheses that we call "scientific." The distinction is one of degree and concerns only the probability or strength of evidential support of those conjectures rather than their factual meaningfulness. It may likewise be granted that such theological arguments as the teleological, or the inferences from the facts of religious experience, can be so formulated that they conform to the inductive or hypothetico-deductive patterns of scientific reasoning. Empiricists like Hume or Mill were critical of such arguments because they felt that the supporting evidence was extremely weak. But, notoriously, some theologians and metaphysicians have thought they could protect their knowledge claims against such criticisms by severing their assertions from observational evidence altogether. This much more orthodox reliance on pure faith or intuition involves, however, a radical shift. The assertions are now completely transcendent, i.e., transempirical. They have lost whatever intersubjective testability was possessed by the previous "empirical" approaches. According to the logical positivists' analysis the significance of linguistic expressions that lack confirmability in principle may consist in pictorial, emotional, and/or motivational appeals. But the presumption of factual reference is (according to this analysis) erroneous or illusory. This is perhaps most strikingly obvious in connection with the uses of the word "belief." We say that we believe that the earth is a sphere or that the law of the conservation of energy holds for atomic processes or that unemployment causes social unrest. But we also say that we believe in the dignity of man or in equal rights for everybody. Clearly, the latter usage of "belief" is utterly different from the former. It formulates a commitment to certain values, while "belief" in the former (empirical) sense applies to confirmable hypotheses.

There is no space for more than just a few hints regarding some of the issues of traditional metaphysics and epistemology. The problems of the existence of an external world, of the past, of other minds, of substance, of causal necessity, etc., appear *prima facie* as factually meaningful because they are often assimilated to the problems of the existence of *specfic* physical objects, past events, other persons' particular mental states, physicochemically characterized substances, concrete instances of causal influence, etc. Problems of this latter type are indeed meaningful precisely because we raise them within the frame of a language and of (inductive or hypothetico-deductive) procedures that makes responsible answers possible. But the aforementioned problems of metaphysics are in principle insoluble because they confuse questions of fact with questions regarding the semiotic frame which is *presupposed*. The justification of this presupposed frame must therefore be radically different. The only sort of justification we can give for this ("realistic") frame of our language consists in showing the indispensability and the adequacy of the language required for the purpose of such sciences as physics, psychology, or history.[4] Since we deny that the data of religious experience require a wider frame than the one sufficient for science, we do not admit that any alleged theological presuppositions have a status co-ordinate with, or analogous to, that of the presuppositions of science.

The criterion of factual meaningfulness has been the issue of intense disputes for more than twenty years. We need not review the well-known arguments. The issue as it concerns us here turns on the so-called "weaker verifiability criterion," i.e., the condition of (at least) incomplete and indirect verifiability or refutability. Logical empiricists recognize today that this criterion formulated as a principle is a proposal and not a proposition. It could be expressed as an analytic proposition only in a metalanguage that in addition to syntactical and semantical concepts contains also such pragmatic concepts as verification and confirmation. Given such a sufficiently rich metalanguage (viz., of *pure pragmatics*) the term "factually meaningful sentence" can be explicitly defined in terms of confirmability.

Two questions seem quite generally pertinent in regard to proposed definitions or stipulations of this sort: (1) Does the definition explicate adequately what is, no matter how vaguely, intended by the term (the *explicandum*) in the language of common sense and of science? (2) Does the definition of a term that has an emotive halo ("meaningful" is certainly such a term) succeed in stipulating a meaning that, when consistently employed, will be fruitful in its application?

There is a great deal of opportunity for dispute on the first point. I am inclined to contend, however, that once the distinction between emotive appeals and cognitive meanings is accepted, there is much that can be said in favor of the adequacy of the confirmability criterion. It explicates what is quite commonly regarded as the distinction between what "makes sense" and what doesn't. The second point is at any rate much more important. It raises the question of a vindication of the proposed meaning criterion. The criterion may then be viewed as a rule for the delimitation of factually meaningful from factually meaningless sentences. The purpose of the rule is obviously to distinguish discourse

---

[4] For a fuller analysis of these issues see: H. Feigl, "Existential Hypotheses," *Phil. of Science*, XVII (1950), 35-62; and W. Sellars, "Realism and the New Way of Words," *Philos. and Phenom. Res.*, VIII (1948), 601 (also reprinted in Feigl and Sellars, *op. cit.*).

that can justifiably claim to embody factually true or false statements from discourse that does not fulfill this function—even if it serves other, viz., noncognitive purposes. The vindication of the criterion must then consist in showing that its adoption will produce the sort of clarity that we seek when we realize that confusion of the various functions of language leads only to endless perplexity and vexation with pseudo problems. In other words, if we do not wish to open the floodgates to countless questions which by their very construction are in principle unanswerable, then the adoption of the confirmability criterion is indispensable.

Justification involving appeal to ethical principles. Moral approvals and disapprovals are formulated in normative judgments. These judgments need not be, and usually are not, expressed in sentences that are explicitly in the imperative form. "This is a case of fraudulence," "You are cruel to your brother," "It is right to be loyal to your country," "All men have equal and inalienable rights"—these and countless other sentences contain words that have a normative significance in addition to a component of factual meaning. There is even a kind of tautology (and correspondingly a kind of contradiction) that is exclusively based on the normative significance of the terms used. For example: "Wanton cruelty is condemnable" is a tautology, and its denial a contradiction.

The justification of specific normative judgments may be sought along the lines of their validation. Suppose we have made sure of all the relevant empirical facts and we can state that someone charges 25 per cent interest on debts owed to him. This is then condemned as "usury." The use of this term is a specific way of classifying the previously described fact and combining this classification with moral disapproval. How do we justify the moral disapproval? We may do this deductively (syllogistically in this simple case): "All usury is morally wrong: this is a case of usury; therefore . . ." We may next try to validate the major premise of the proceeding argument by deducing it from two universal premises such as: "All types of action in which one person benefits himself by harming another are morally wrong." "Usury is a type of action, etc. . . ." Perhaps we can succeed in deducing the major premise of this last argument from a still more general moral principle, such as the golden rule, or some principle of justice, or the like. This kind of regressive reasoning will of course terminate with some premise which cannot plausibly or fruitfully be deduced from any still more general or fundamental principle. It is generally conceded, however, that Kant's categorical imperative in its first or second formulation is vacuous and that therefore his deductions of specific moral precepts were fallacious. But let us suppose that we could formulate some principle such as Kant intended (i.e., a principle of justice, impartiality, or of "no special privileges") in a form that is not vacuous and hence would yield specific moral judgments when applied to empirically characterized actions or attitudes. What can we say in answer to skeptical questions regarding such a supreme principle? Derivation from theological or metaphysical principles will not do. Apart from the epistemological criticisms (discussed in the previous section), the question of the goodness or rightness of divine commandments or of metaphysically founded imperatives can only be silenced but not answered in any intelligible or enlightening fashion. Appeal to intuitive self-evidence is equally fruitless, if not suspicious, in this age of cultural anthropology and social psychology. Obviously we have reached the limits of validation. Just as in the other domains of justification, we may disclose the ultimate presuppositions; we may explicate the principles of validation of moral judgments. We may say that these principles define the moral terms ("right," "wrong," "ought") and delimit the moral universe of discourse, just as the principle of induction defines the methodological terms ("evidence," "probability") and delimits the universe of discourse of empirical knowledge.

We could rest more easily satisfied with this conclusion if the idea of alternative ethical systems were as plausibly refutable as that of alternative deductive or inductive logics. The vindication of the principles of meaning and knowledge is so trivial precisely because, given the purposes of language and knowledge, there are no genuine alternatives for fulfilling them. But we do know of alternative systems of moral norms. An aristocratic ethics such as Nietzsche's and a democratic one such as Jefferson's are clearly incompatible with each other. The ethics of capitalism and the ethics of socialism may serve as a (related) further example.[5] Even if there are areas in which such ethical systems may have elements of agreement, there are others in which they irreconcilably diverge.

---

[5] We assume here that capitalist and socialistic ethics differ in their respective conceptions of social justice. This is of course debatable. (The difference between the two ideologies may consist merely in a disagreement in belief concerning economic and sociological facts.)

It is of no avail to criticize one ethical system on the basis of another. The issue is *logically* symmetrical here. Such criticisms would merely utilize implicit persuasive definitions of such terms as "true morality," "the really right attitude," etc. They would beg the question at issue. From a more rigorous analytic viewpoint it may be remarked that ethical criticism in the usual sense applies only to actions and attitudes, not to propositions but to belief in them ("belief" in the sense of disposition toward action). Moral criticism makes sense only *within* the frame of a set of basic moral standards. Any incompatible alternative basic standards are as much beyond criticism as are the axioms of a non-Euclidian geometry within the frame of the axioms of Euclidian geometry. Quite generally we may conclude that, granting our rational reconstruction of the hierarchy of levels of justification in ethics, the acceptance or rejection of the supreme principles can be only a matter of pragmatic justification. But this, in a sense, has been obvious to all those who approach ethics from the point of view of the interest theory of value, or from that of anthropology, or from the "emotive-meaning" school of analysis. The meaning of moral judgments has been such a troublesome and enigmatic issue because these judgments in their protean ways simulate (1) the analytic truths of logic, in that they may be construed as necessary implications holding between the general value criteria and their specific applications; (2) factual propositions, in that they must always refer to empirically characterized classes of actions or attitudes; (3) purely emotional or motivational expressions and appeals, in that they evince attitudes and/or contain an imperative component. No wonder that moral norms have been viewed as synthetic a priori propositions, as altogether *sui generis,* endowed with "normative meaning." But normative meaning is just as analyzable here as it is in logic or epistemology. Criticism presupposes norms, and norms (like any *rules*) differ from (description) laws in being *prescriptive.* To the extent that a purely factual ("naturalistic") interpretation of norms falls (inevitably) short of an adequate analysis, it must be amended by proper attention to their directive or motivational components. If the word "ethics" is not to be used for a descriptive socio-psychological study of human conduct and its actually occurring evaluations, if it is to stand for something that is not a mere account of past and present moral codes, their origins and evolutions, then "ethics" is used in the sense of a system of norms which makes criticism and justification possible. At least the supreme justifying principles in every domain of validation must have the status of norms which implicitly define the *critical terms* of the domain in question: "correct," "conclusive," "warranted" in logic; "meaningful" in epistemology; "right" in ethics. All these terms have directive significance, just as all (nominal) definitions have a motivational appeal, in addition to whatever cognitive meaning may likewise be present. Now according to our reconstruction, moral judgments are valid if they are in accordance with the relevant ethical norms. The supreme norms define the standards of morality of a given system. The terms "right" and "wrong," if not rigorously scrutinized, are apt to be applied in a doubly persuasive manner: first, in *accordance with the norms* of the given system; and secondly, *to the norms* of the system. But we have already warned against this confusion. It is just as nonsensical to approve of a definition of "right" as right, as it is to approve of a definition of "probable" by saying that it is probable. The mistake in the first case is not as obvious as in the second because of the greater ambiguity of the term "right." The other meanings of "right" that are apt to interfere here are (a) the adequacy of the explication achieved by the reconstruction of the system of norms and (b) approval (endorsement) of the supreme norm in the sense of expressing personal agreement with it. It is this latter sense that would result from a vindication of the norms.

Now just what does a vindication here amount to? It consists in showing that adoption of the norms of a given moral system fulfills a purpose. Well, then, what is the purpose that is fulfilled by adoption of, e.g., the golden rule, or a principle of impartiality? The answer clearly depends on the individual's personality. Perhaps he obeys the golden rule because of sheer prudence and "enlightened egoism." Perhaps he has by training, education, experience, or reflection developed genuinely altruistic interests and thus holds the ideal of the greatest satisfaction for the greatest number. Generally, no vindication will prove convincing unless it appeals to the needs, interests, or aspirations of the individual concerned. If there are fundamentally incompatible purposes, unmitigated by any purpose to eliminate divergence of purposes, then only segregation or, in the extreme case, coercion will be able to settle such disagreement in attitudes. But given an interest in avoiding conflict there are the techniques of (unilateral) persuasion or of (bilateral) compromise.

No matter what factual ("naturalistic") content we associate with the (otherwise emotively significant) value terms "good," "right," "ought," etc., and their contraries, it is of the utmost importance to distinguish the *rules* that serve as *justificantia cognitionis* in the validation of moral judgments from the *goals* that serve as *justificantia actionis* in the vindication of the adoption of such rules. This distinction enables us to see more clearly what is involved in the quarrel between "deontological" and "teleological" moral philosophies. This quarrel can be adjudicated by alloting to validation and vindication their proper roles. The usual formulations of utilitarianism, for example, are logically questionable because they attempt to combine validation and vindication by telescoping together rules (such as "Only kindly acts are right") with goals (such as "the greatest happiness of the greatest number").

An obvious objection to this analysis urges that the adoption of moral rules requires a justification that goes beyond a mere sanction by purposes. In other words, it may be asked whether those purposes are morally good. But clearly this question presupposes moral standards and without them remains unanswerable. If the moral standards drawn upon are those that formulate the system whose vindication is under discussion, then (given complete logical consistency) we obtain a validation of the value judgment concerning the adoption of its standards that is bound to be analytically true. If the standards are taken from a system that is incompatible with the one under discussion, we obtain an invalidation resulting from logical contradiction.

Another related but more serious question concerns the ethical relativism which the preceding analysis seems to support. Now "ethical relativism" is a phrase which exerts a strong negative emotive appeal because it is taken to imply that there are no grounds for preferring one ethical system to another. This is often exaggerated in the charge that for a relativist moral standards can be no more than a matter of arbitrary decision, of whim and caprice. But these are gross caricatures of a position which merely combines a sociological conclusion with the results of a logical analysis of the structure of justification. A judgment of indifference is still a value judgment and thus justifiable only within its own frame of reference. More significantly yet, the purposes that we adduce in the vindication of ethical standards are not a matter of personal caprice but are (usually) the resultants of age-long experience in the harmonization of intra- and inter-individual needs and interests, of experience, personal and social, guided by the adaptive and integrative influence of intelligence. Far from being "arbitrary" or "capricious" in the usual sense of these words, our terminal purposes are usually held with the most serious and profound conviction. The only sense in which the misnomer "arbitrary" could be sensibly interpreted here is in the sense of "ultimate," i.e., nonvindicable and resting on the (logically) contingent traits of human nature. Such standards[6] as those of justice and kindliness, as well as of self-perfection, are the counterpart of goals such as those of a harmonious, peaceful, and progressive humanity. The goals or purposes are in turn resultants of the nature of man and his needs and interests in ever widening and ever more interdependent social contexts. The evolution of a global code of morality out of its tribalistic precursors offers in many ways a striking parallel to the development of the norms of scientific method out of its magical, animistic, and metaphysical origins. In a continuous process means and ends underwent selections, revisions, replacements, focussings, diversifications, and harmonizations. Experience of ever widening scope teaches the lessons of cautious conservation and daring innovation, of sweeping synthesis and attention to specific detail. Well established knowledge and clarity of meaning are indispensable. But only if they are in the service of purposes which emerge from the broadest experience will their utilization be regarded as justifiable. In this sense, and perhaps in this sense only, can the etymological association of wisdom with philosophy be supported.

SOME OBSERVATIONS BY WAY OF CONCLUSION

The conclusions we have reached are neither new nor should they be startling. Justification is a form of argument which requires some platform of basic agreement on one level, even if on a different level there is doubt or disagreement. (Argument need not involve two persons. One may try to justify some belief for one's own acceptance.) In order to resolve doubt or disagreement we must not, at least in the given context and until further notice, call into question the very means by which such doubt or disagreement is to be resolved. The status of the validating principles (in logical reconstruction) is that of stipulations, definitions, or conventions. They differ from other less fundamental and less consequential conventions, in that they determine whole domains of justification. That is the reason why so many ration-

---

[6] Perhaps we should remind the reader that standards are ideal norms. We are under no illusion to what little extent actual conduct conforms with them. But the degree of universality of the ideals embodied in the "moral sense" of people all over the earth is remarkable.

alistically inclined thinkers feel tempted to view them as synthetic a priori. But like all definitions or conventions the *justificantia* are a priori precisely and only because they are analytic. Since they are definitional in character, we can not ask whether they are in any sense true to fact. Their virtue lies in fulfilling a purpose. And purposes are resultants of the very needs of our lives. The key terms which are defined by the justifying principles (e.g., "correct," "valid," "true," "confirmed," "good," "right," "meaningful," etc.) carry emotional prestige and therefore lend themselves to persuasive redefinitions. This indicates that the content of these terms depends on the purposes we pursue. It is diagnostic of the purposes and ideals of our (western) civilization and of this age of science that the term *"reasonableness"* has come to embrace (at least) the following five connotations: (1) logical consistency; (2) inductive plausibility; (3) reflective clarity; (4) impartiality; (5) abstention from violence in the settlement of disagreements.[7]

There are two familiar phrases that serve as a last resort to philosophers when challenged as to the grounds for their reasons: "ultimate presupposition" (or "basic postulate") and "pragmatic justification." The use of these phrases is often regrettably glib. They are often employed as rhetorical devices designed to intimidate the inquirer and to put a stop to further argument and questions. They serve only too often as verbal sedatives for the philosopher himself. Our analysis has given us a clearer idea of what is involved in the responsible use of these two modes of justification hinted at by those expressions.

We must also guard ourselves against slipshod notions of *presuppositions*. The term "presupposition" is far from clear and univocal. Sometimes it refers to premises that imply. At other times it refers to consequences that are implied. The latter sense would be in keeping with the idea of necessary or indispensable conditions. Combining both we have a third meaning, namely, sufficient and necessary condition (and this would amount to logical equivalence or mutual deducibility of that which presupposes and the relevant presupposition). None of these explications in purely logical terms will quite meet the intended meaning of "presupposition." The class of premises that imply and the class of consequences that are implied by a given proposition are in-

---

[7] Cp. Dennes, W. R., "The Appeal to Reason," *University of California Publications in Philosophy*, 21 (1939) and his "Conflict," *Phil. Rev.*, LV (1946).

definitely wide in scope. We mean something much more restricted than all that.

Let us consider some examples. We say that the rules of the categorical syllogism (or what is tantamount in symbolic logic: the rules of the propositional and the lower functional calculi) presuppose the laws of identity, noncontradiction, and of the excluded middle. This might quite correctly mean that these laws are logical consequences of those rules. As is well known, the reverse does not hold here. We have here a case of necessary condition. But since an indefinite number of other consequences follow equally rigorously from the rules mentioned above, the prominence and distinction traditionally attributed to the three (so-called) laws of thought cannot thus be explained or defended.

Our difficulty might be resolved by distinguishing between necessary conditions (logical consequences) within a system of statements and necessary conditions in the sense of requirements imposed upon the system as a whole. These requirements would have to be stated in a metalanguage and when so stated could still be read as necessary conditions, but with this difference: The *conditio sine qua non* concerns the semantical (and/or syntactical) structure of the language (i.e., the object language) in which we customarily formulate the laws of logic. For example, we might say: Only if the language used in syllogistic reasoning is constructed in accordance with the *semantical* rule of identity (univocality of symbols, i.e., unambiguous designation rules) will we be able to validate the rules of the syllogism. Likewise we could say: Only if the definition of "degree of confirmation" is so chosen that it incorporates what we usually call the principle of induction (i.e., the regulative maxim of simplest extrapolation or straightforward posits) can we justify the customary rules for the assignments of inductive probabilities. The same sort of analysis may be applied to epistemological presuppositions. The stipulation of criteria of meaningfulness is an indispensable prerequisite for the justification of the intended distinction between genuine and pseudo problems, and this precisely for the reason that only an object language that complies with those criteria will not contain sentences that are in principle unconfirmable.

We found it tempting to think that these considerations may equally well apply to the presuppositions of moral evaluations. Unfortunately very little has as yet been achieved in the formalization of ethical systems, so that our conclusions must here remain tentative. It does seem plausible, however, that the ultimate validating principles of a given system of moral evaluations are incorporated by definition (stipulation) in the very meaning of the basic terms of that system. In any case it is clear that whenever we are engaged in ethical evaluations we are, so to speak, operating within a system. This is of course an idealization, because in practice we are rarely aware of the logical structure of the system, nor do we ever approach anything like the consistency of a postulate system. (The situation is still more amorphous and unstable in aesthetics.) The important point, however, is this: Any doubt raised with respect to the presuppositions of a given ethical system or any comparative evaluation of different ethical systems requires a further frame of reference (in the ideal case an alternative system) for the responsible settlement of such doubt, or for a justifiable preference. It is one thing to compare ethical systems in the value-neutral manner of a logician. It is another thing to criticize them ethically. The latter endeavor relies on fresh presuppositions. This is analogous to the fundamental shift that is required when we criticize certain, now obsolete, criteria of truth (e.g., revelation, authority, intuition, self-evidence) in the light of our modern criteria. The presuppositions of the older justifications of knowledge claims may indeed have been the necessary conditions of justification as it was then conceived. Historically and psychologically speaking, we might say (cp. Collingwood) that the ultimate or absolute presuppositions (criteria, standards) vary from epoch to epoch. They remain unscrutinized and uncriticized within the given epoch of thought. As long as no alternative frame of justification is envisaged, we are seldom fully aware of the one that functions jurisdictively at the moment. But while the historian may legitimately establish the cultural relativity of basic presuppositions, the philosophical analyst will be interested in (1) their explicit formulation and the recognition of their logical function and (2) the criteria that justify their criticism and revision. It is precisely the possibility of revision of erstwhile ultimate standards that urges us to amend the view according to which "*de principiis non est disputandum.*" This view is unassailable as long as it maintains that the criteria which are definitive of a certain mode of justification can not themselves be justified *within that mode.* Attempts in this direction are bound to be fallacies of the vicious circle, either ordinary *petitiones principii* or else violations of a semantical rule of types.

The ultimate principles of logic, semantics, methodology, and axiology are (as *justificantia*) not susceptible to cognitive justification. But if the question be raised *why we should adopt* those, rather than some alternative principles, then this obviously concerns not the validity of the principles but the justifiability of our attitude toward them. We do not wish to elicit the trivial answer that the reason for adoption of those principles is that, once adopted, they enable us to carry out such justifications that it is the very business of the principles to make possible. This answer would merely amount to a restatement of the *conditio-sine-qua-non* character of the principles that was just explicated. Nor are we here concerned with the justification of any particular explication or formulation of the justifying principles. What we are looking for is, instead, a pragmatic justification of our adoption (choice, preference) of the given principle.

This question is best understood as the formulation of a highly artificially generated doubt. The quest for the ultimate justifying principles already exemplified this Cartesian procedure. We are now even one step further removed from the type of doubt that would arise on the common-sense level. We are asking what reasons we have for embracing the very principles whose function it is to help in removing the more familiar types of doubt. The often implausible, unconvincing character of the results of philosophical analysis does not detract from its value. In the case of explication it is the unfamiliar character of the *explicatum*. In the case of justification it is the remote and unconvincing character of the "reasons." Convincingness is at its strongest where it dispels the kind of doubts we are apt to raise against the background of the currently accepted beliefs. But where doubt (artificially pretended) concerns those beliefs themselves, reasons given to re-establish those beliefs cannot possibly convince more strongly than do reasons embodying those accepted beliefs.

What we want to know then are the practical reasons that justify our choice of an entire mode of justification. Now, a pragmatic justification amounts to showing that something serves as a means towards an end. It thus requires a prior agreement (1) as to the desiredness of the end and (2) as to the method or type of reasoning by which the appropriateness of the means to the end is to be shown. As to the first point it may be said that the ends which we here acknowledge (without questioning) are simply taken as objects of certain interests. In regard to the field of cognition we bluntly acknowledge that the multifarious experiences (successes and failures) in the enterprise of knowledge have gradually given rise to a strong interest in the following desiderata: (1) *clarity*, i.e., freedom from confusion as to types of significance; (2) *definiteness*, i.e., univocality of meaning, possibly enhanced by quantitative precision; (3) *consistency and conclusiveness*, i.e., absence of self-contradiction (by means of rules of inference that ensure the truth of conclusions derived from true premises); (4) *warranted (reliable) assertibility*, i.e., availability of evidence that confers a high degree of confirmation on our knowledge claims; and (5) *maximum scope*, i.e., as complete and detailed a coverage of fact as is compatible with the foregoing conditions. Now, if it be granted (as to our previous point) that we are entitled to employ deductive logic in showing that the listed virtues of knowledge can be attained (or approximated) *only if* we adopt certain principles as the norms of cognitive procedures, then we may manage to offer a pragmatic justification of the principles of formal logic and semantics, of the meaning criteria, and of the principle of induction. The ideals of cognition are, for our purposes, to be conceived and formulated in terms of pure syntax, pure semantics, and pure pragmatics. If so formulated it can obviously be shown deductively (and asserted as an analytic statement) that conformity with the principles is a necessary condition for the attainment of those ideals. But, as already hinted, such a demonstration relies in turn on the principles of deductive logic. Does this involve a vicious circle? I think not. Our argument was not to establish the validity of logical principles. It was to show that their acceptance as regulative standards is an indispensable prerequisite for the fulfillment of certain ideal requirements. And since such "showing" is intended as an argument (or demonstration), it could not possibly abstain from the utilization of logical procedures.

Just how far removed from triviality must a deductive argument be in order to escape the criticism of circularity? We suggest that an inference is *strictly* circular only if its conclusion appears *literally* among the premises. Many arguments that are free from strict circularity are of course extremely trivial nevertheless. Since triviality is a psychological feature, there can be no universal rule as to just what complexity an argument must have in order to be enlightening or helpful to a person of given intelligence and curiosity. Our Cartesian quest for justification may have to be satisfied with demonstrations that have the tang of utter obviousness. The extent to which these demonstrations may nevertheless prove clarifying depends in part on the measure of psychological novelty that attaches to the explications of the key terms of the given context. For example, to say that only confirmable statements make sense (have factual meaning) is not just an arbitrary definition but really explicates what in some fashion we have known all along—implicitly. To bring it into full focus is the merit of the explication. The vindication of the meaning criterion is therefore neither strictly circular nor so trivial as to be unenlightening.

The preceding analyses, especially the remarks on pragmatic justification, would be grossly misunderstood if they were projected upon (i.e., translated into) the customary reasoning and language of common sense. Common sense operates *within* a frame of presuppositions and purposes; it never raises questions concerning this frame. If philosophical analysis had no other task than that of a hygiene and therapy of language, it might well restrict itself to the procedures utilized by G. E. Moore and L. Wittgenstein (and their disciples). The extravagances by which we are apt to deviate from common good sense into uncommonly strange and bad sense may indeed be successfully attacked by those methods. But full awareness of the basic principles of knowledge and evaluation can be attained only by a systematic analysis of the "rational reconstruction" type. The language of rational reconstruction is legitimate in a strict sense only if it is governed by a set of metalinguistic rules. But in order to introduce this apparatus of analysis and to give it its proper points of application a few didactic fictions and deviations from common-sense language are practically very helpful. Unlike the metaphysician who seriously proposes statements concerning what things really are, we use those didactic fictions (like the famous Wittgensteinian ladder) merely as a makeshift which can be discarded after it has fulfilled its purpose. When we spoke of choosing the principles of an entire mode of justification, we did not wish to assimilate such a choice to the choice situations of ordinary life, any more than, for example, when we speak in semiotic of "conventional" in contrast to "natural" signs. No one who uses this phrase intends to suggest seriously that some time in the remote past primitive men convened around stone tables and decided upon the meanings of the words they were going to use. Even if, as we claimed, there are no genuine rivals or alternatives to the principles of deductive logic (nor, in a weaker sense, with respect to inductive logic and epistemology), it is instructive and enlightening to ask what from the point of view of common sense must indeed appear like silly or foolish questions, concerning the reasons for

their adoption. Such inquiries are as clarifying in philosophy as are
thought experiments with "outlandish" possibilities in science. They
bring out with distinct prominence the role of the presuppositions
which would otherwise· never be fully explicit.

A SUMMARY ON CIRCULARITY AND PRIMACY

The following diagram traces the characteristic tangle of circularities
which inevitably results if the distinction between cognitive and pragmatic justification is not properly attended to.

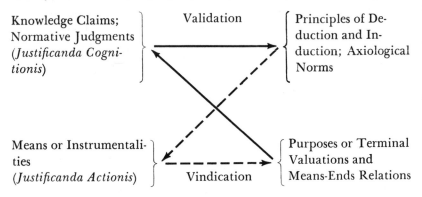

Knowledge claims are justified (validated) by (reference to data and)
appeal to the principles of deductive and/or inductive inference. Moral
(normative) judgments are validated by (reference to empirical facts
and) the axiological principles (norms) of the given moral code. The
adoption of these principles themselves may be justified pragmatically
(vindicated) by reference to purposes (terminal valuations) and the
(usually inductive or, in the degenerate case, deductive) relations between means and ends. These relations themselves may be asserted as
knowledge claims and thus require in turn cognitive justification. And
so we are apt to keep going merrily around, wherever we start with
our quest for justification. The first step toward disentanglement consists of course in the realization of the fundamental difference between
cognitive and pragmatic justifications. (The fully drawn arrows represent the former, the broken arrows the latter type of justification.)
Our purposes as formulated in terminal valuations as well as the
means-ends relations must be viewed as the unquestioned frame of
pragmatic justifications. However, since "terminal" is not intended in

the sense of "absolute," the terminal valuations may indeed, in a fresh context, be revised or replaced by alternative valuations. Obviously also our knowledge of means-ends relations (if inductive) is subject to revision. Correspondingly, the principles of deduction and induction form the unquestioned frame of cognitive justification. But this frame, too, as the history of logic, mathematics, and the empirical sciences amply demonstrates, is capable of revision and modification. Circularity and infinite regress can be avoided only if we reconstruct our justifications in such a manner that only one type is considered at a time and its corresponding frame taken for granted in that context and until further notice. The old puzzle of *primacy* thus resolves itself very simply in that we may realize that primacy is relative to the context of justification. Kant's insistence upon the primacy of practical reason is plausible enough within the context of pragmatic justification. But, clearly, in the context of cognitive justification "pure reason," i.e., the principles of deduction and induction, reigns supreme and functions as unquestioned presupposition. Hence, in arguments such as those of the present essay (and quite generally in philosophical analysis) the primacy of "pure reason" is a necessary and obvious consequence of the nature of the questions proposed for discussion. The structural analogies of the limits of justification in logic and in ethics must not obscure the equally important differences between the two fields. Violation of the logical principles vitiates the very purposes of reasoning and communication; a deliberate repudiation of the law of non-contradiction results in paralysis. But alternative moral codes are just as self-consistently conceivable as are alternative geometries. Clearly, there can be no alternative logics *in the sense* in which there are alternative systems of geometry or ethics.[8]

---

[8] For further analysis of related issues see W. Sellars, "Language, Rules and Behavior," in *John Dewey: Philosopher of Science and Freedom*, ed. by S. Hook (1950). Further applications may be found in my "Logical Reconstruction, Realism and Pure Semiotic," *Phil. of Science*, XVII (1950), 186-195.

Obligation and Ability

WILLIAM K. FRANKENA

It is well-known that we often withdraw such statements as "*A* ought to do *B*" or "*A* ought to have done *B* rather than *C*," when we become convinced that *A* cannot do or could not have done *B*. This undoubted fact has led many moral philosophers to say, in one way or another, that "ought" implies "can." Indeed, if there is anything on which philosophers are agreed with plain men and with each other, and goodness knows there is very little, it is Kant's dictum, "*Du kannst, denn du sollst!*" Sometimes it is asserted as a separate point of theory, more often simply as a step in some line of argument, but asserted it is. Almost always, however, it is affirmed with little further ado—with little examination, qualification, or explanation. It is asserted cryptically and unanalytically. This paper is an effort to do something to remedy this state of affairs.

Our dictum has many aspects, uses, and possible interpretations, and we cannot study them all. We shall not discuss nonethical senses of "ought," even though in some of them it seems to imply "can," as in "The train ought to be coming along any moment." We must also limit the scope of "can," partly to avoid the free-will controversy. (a) It has been understood to mean "I am free to choose or not to choose to do *A* (in the indeterminist sense of 'free')." (b) It may be taken to imply "My doing *A* is or will be a voluntary action on my part (in Moore's sense of 'voluntary,' according to which an action is voluntary if it is one which the agent would not have done or tried to do if he had chosen otherwise, no question being asked about the possibility of his choosing otherwise[1])." (c) It may be understood to entail "My doing *A* is or will be a voluntary action, not only in this sense of 'voluntary,' but also in the further sense that I can choose otherwise."[2] (d) Other things that may be meant by "can" are suggested by the fact that "I can't do that!" sometimes means "I have pressing engagements which prevent my doing it," "I should stand to lose too much if I were to do that," etc., and by Luther's *"Ich kann nicht anders."* We shall not be concerned, directly at least, with any of these meanings of "can." (e) In a very ordinary usage, "I can do *A*" means something that can be roughly expressed by "I know how to do *A* and am physically capable of doing it" or "I am able to do *A*, if I choose." Here, says Russell, "I can do *A*" means "*A* will occur if I will it."[3] According to Prichard it means "I can bring about a certain state of affairs indirectly," that is, "I can set myself to bring about a certain state of affairs, and my setting myself thus will bring about something which will have that state of affairs as its effect."[4] This is the meaning of "can" which is usually intended in our dictum, both by the philosopher and by the man on the street,[5] and the one with which we shall be concerned.

There is an ambiguity in the meaning of "can do" which must be noted before we continue. For we must distinguish between our latent and our active capacities, much as we do between our passive and our active vocabularies. My ability to skate is unfortunately, I am told, merely latent, not active, as is my ability to walk. I can skate in a sense, but not in the same sense in which I can walk; and I cannot, I suppose, run a mile in less than four minutes in either of these senses. Hence "I can do *A*" may mean either that I am actively capable of doing *A*, i.e., I can do *A* in the present stage in the development of my capacities, or that I am latently capable of doing *A*, i.e., I could do A, if the latent capacities which I actually have were further developed.

It is clear that "I can do *A*, if I choose" means "I am actively capable

---

[1] See G. E. Moore, *Ethics* (1912), pp. 13-16.

[2] See P. A. Schilpp (ed.), *The Philosophy of G. E. Moore* (1942), pp. 623-627.

[3] "The Elements of Ethics," *Philosophical Essays* (1910), p. 34.

[4] *Duty and Ignorance of Fact* (1932), pp. 4, 22. I am taking "can do" in what he calls the less strict sense.

[5] At least this is the meaning of "can" intended when our dictum is not associated with the free-will controversy.

of doing *A*"; and we shall, therefore, be dealing with the relation between having an obligation and being actively able to do. Our question, then, is: What are the ethically relevant senses of "ought" and how are they related to "can" in sense (e), that is, in the sense in which it is short for "can do, if I choose" or "am actively able to do"?[6]

We may begin with "ought" as it occurs in general statements or "moral rules." Such statements are of two sorts: rules enjoining certain feelings in certain situations, e.g., "A person ought to feel gratitude toward a benefactor," and rules requiring certain actions in certain circumstances, e.g., "We ought to keep our promises." Consider rules of the former kind. Cambridge philosophers have generally taken the position that "ought" is here used in a "wider" sense, which does not imply "can." Thus Sidgwick writes, "In a wider sense . . . I sometimes judge that I 'ought' to know what a wiser man would know, or feel as a better man would feel, in my place, though I may know that I could not directly produce in myself such knowledge or feeling by any effort of will. In this case the word merely implies an ideal or pattern which I 'ought'—in the stricter sense—to seek to imitate as far as possible."[7] The point which these writers have in mind is that feelings are not in control of the will in such a way that one can in a certain situation produce a certain feeling by willing to feel it; I cannot feel gratitude just because I choose to. Therefore in rules of feeling or "ideal rules," as Moore has called them,[8] "ought" does not imply "can" in our sense. If it did, they could not be true. If I have an obligation to feel gratitude toward my benefactors, this must then be an obligation which does not entail my being able to feel it toward them. On the other hand, while agreeing that our feelings are not directly controlled by our will, Sir David Ross maintains that, though the term "right" may properly be applied to feelings, the term "ought" may not—just because "ought" implies "can," and "right" does not. We actually use "ought" in connection with feelings as well as actions, he admits, but this is "an improper use . . . which we could not seriously defend." For we are only justified in saying "*A* ought to have felt sorrow then," if we are thinking that he might in the past so have disposed himself as to be able to feel sorrow at the time in question, and then the proper

---

[6] Hereafter "can" will be used in this way, unless otherwise specified.

[7] *The Methods of Ethics* (1907), p. 33. See also Broad, *Five Types of Ethical Theory* (1930), p. 161.

[8] *Philosophical Studies* (1922), p. 317.

thing to say is not "*A* ought to have felt sorrow then," but "*A* ought earlier so to have disposed himself as to be able to feel sorrow at the time in question."[9]

It is possible that "We ought to feel gratitude toward our benefactors" means "We ought so to cultivate our feelings that we will feel gratitude toward them," but it seems more plausible to hold that, if we ought so to cultivate our feelings, this is because we first ought to feel gratitude when benefited by others. To argue that, in saying this, we are using "ought" improperly will not do, for, as Ewing points out,[10] the criterion of proper use in such cases as this can only be usage, and we admittedly do apply "ought" to feelings. In fact, it may be a *petitio* to assert that we cannot seriously defend the use of "ought" in ideal rules unless we retranslate them in the manner indicated. For we *can* seriously defend it if we suppose that in this case "ought" does not imply "can," just as we can seriously defend the use of "dear" in "She is very dear to his heart," if we do not assume that "dear" always implies "expensive." In any event, our usage is so fluid that we not only use "right" where we should "more properly" use "ought" (as Ross himself points out[11]), but also use "ought" as a synonym of "right" in the sort of case in which he recognises that "right" does not imply "can." Hence in *actual* (if not in "proper") usage, there is a sense of "ought" in which ought-judgments do not presuppose possibility.

This, however, means only that to say we ought to feel in a certain way at a certain time is not to say we can so feel at that time if we choose. We should still all agree, I take it, that anyone who is constitutionally cut off from having the feelings in question at any time has not even this ideal duty to feel them at the time stipulated.[12] In the same way we should also admit that "We ought to love our parents" implies that we can cultivate feelings of love toward them and not only toward our fellow children. In other words, even in the present usage, "I ought" implies "I can" in the sense of being latently able.

While "We ought to feel gratitude toward our benefactors" does not entail "We can feel gratitude toward them, if we choose," it does entail "We ought to feel gratitude toward them, *if we can*." Here enters another sense of "ought," it should be noticed. For what we have is

---

9 Ross, *Foundations of Ethics* (1939), pp. 52-55.
10 *The Definition of Good* (1947), p. 131.
11 *Loc. cit.*
12 Cp. Ewing, *op. cit.*, pp. 165-166.

that "We ought (in a sense not implying 'can') to feel A" entails "We ought (in a sense implying 'can') to feel A, if we can." Moore goes farther. He distinguishes these two senses of "ought," and then says that "I ought to do A (in the first sense)" not only entails but means "I ought to do A (in the second sense), if I can."[13] In this he may be right, but, as we shall see when we discuss the general question of the relation of these two senses of "ought," another view is also tenable.

It is more plausible to hold that rules of action use "ought" in a sense implying "can, if I choose" than that rules of feeling do so, for actions seem to be in the control of the will in a way in which feelings are not. Hence Moore claims that in "rules of duty" we use "ought" in a can-implying sense, while in "ideal rules" we do not.[14] Yet Broad contends that, even in some rules prescribing actions, "ought" occurs in the "wider" usage in which it does not imply "can," e.g., in "Virtue ought to be rewarded."[15] To this contention Ross replies,[16] and Kant would certainly agree, that we can only say this seriously if we are thinking that some being can and ought so to act to reward virtue. Possibly the answer to Ross is that, of course, we should not *say seriously* that virtue ought to be rewarded unless we thought there was such a being, for our *saying* it would be pointless if there were not. However, it seems sufficient to remark that "Virtue ought to be rewarded" does not entail "There is a being who can reward it" but only "If anyone can reward virtue, he ought to do so," observing that in *this* sentence "ought" implies "can," while in the original it does not.

The Oxford neointuitionists or deontologists commonly conceive of the more basic rules of action, not as enjoining us actually to proceed to do certain things, but as asserting what they variously call claims, *prima facie* duties, responsibilities, and obligations.[17] For example, they hold that "We ought to keep our promises" says, not that keeping our promises is always our actual duty in the relevant circumstances, but that in those circumstances it is our actual duty to keep our promises *if other things are equal*.[18] Without committing ourselves to neoin-

---

13 *Philosophical Studies*, pp. 317-318.

14 *Ibid.*

15 *Loc. cit.*

16 *Op. cit.*, pp. 45-46.

17 For the conception here involved, see Ross, *The Right and the Good* (1930), ch. ii. For a brief history of the term used to designate it, see Carritt, *Ethical and Political Thinking* (1947), p. 3n. I shall use Ross's phrase "*prima facie* duty."

18 "If other things are equal" means, roughly, "if no other moral features of the situation prevent its being an actual duty."

tuitionism, we may make use of this conception. For the opposed principle of utility can be conceived as a *prima facie* duty in the fortunate
situation of having no rivals, so that other things being always equal,
the action which it requires will always be our actual duty. In fact, an
ideal utilitarian may even admit a number of *prima facie* duties, because for him there are many characteristics (besides pleasure) which
are ought-implying, where by an ought-implying characteristic is meant
one "such that, when a state of affairs possesses it, then the fact that an
action, which an agent could do, would produce that state of affairs is
favourably relevant (though only in a very weak degree) to the hypothesis that that agent ought to do that action."[19]

The point is that statements like "Promises ought to be kept" and
"Pleasure ought to be promoted" may alike be conceived as asserting
prima facie duties—as affirming that the characteristics in question are
ought-implying in Moore's sense. Taking them in this way, we may ask
whether or not "ought" as here used implies "can" in the sense of "can
do, if I try." Prichard would presumably answer (a) that if a moral
rule requires us even *prima facie* to *do* acts of kind *A* in the relevant
situations, then it presupposes that we can *do* them, if we set ourselves
to, and (b) that moral rules do not require us to do acts of kind *A*
in those situations but only to set ourselves to do them. Point (b) we
shall discuss later. Just now, assuming that moral rules enjoin us to
do and not merely to try, we may briefly consider (a). To justify it
Prichard simply says, "We never think that an action can be a man's
duty unless he is able to do it."[20] His wording suggests that he is here
thinking only of actual, and not of *prima facie,* duty; and in any case
his statement is not obviously true for the latter, though it may be for
the former. It may be that "We ought (*prima facie*) to keep our promises" does not entail "We *can* keep our promises, if we choose" but only
"We ought (actually) to keep our promises, *if we can,* and if other
things are equal." In fact, this seems to be not only a possible view but
a plausible one, especially if we conceive moral rules as stating that
certain characteristics are ought-implying in Moore's sense. And it
would appear to be almost certainly true, if moral rules require us
(*prima facie*), not merely to set ourselves to do, but to do; for then, if

19 Moore, in *The Philosophy of G. E. Moore,* pp. 603-604. I shall neglect Moore's
distinction between saying something is a *prima facie* duty in Ross's sense and saying a certain characteristic is ought-implying (cp. pp. 565, 596 f.) as being unimportant for our purposes.
20 *Op. cit.,* p. 6.

they imply that we can do, if we choose, they cannot be true without exception, as they are supposed to be.

There are here two alternatives. One may hold that "We ought (*prima facie*) to do an action of kind *A* in a situation of kind *B*" implies "We can do actions of kind *A*, if we choose," and that, therefore, when one cannot do an action of kind *A*, one has not even a *prima facie* duty to do it, despite the fact that one is in a situation of kind *B*. Or one may contend that one still has a *prima facie* duty to do the action of kind *A* then, though no actual duty, and that "ought (*prima facie*)" does not imply "can." The latter alternative is possible in any case, but it is pretty clearly true on the assumption that (b) is false, unless we admit that moral rules (even as statements of *prima facie* duties) have exceptions, which neointuitionists are reluctant to do. We may add that, on both views, *X*'s being an actual duty will presuppose that it can be done by the agent and that other things are equal. This is all that is essential. It is not essential that "ought" imply "can" in moral rules. We shall, therefore, adopt the latter position.

On this position "ought to do" in the general statements in question implies, not "can do, if I choose," but "ought to do, if I can." Thus, in discussing rules of action, we have come upon two senses of "ought," presumably the same two senses we came upon in dealing with rules of feeling, one implying "can," and one "ought (in the other sense), if I can (and if other things are equal)." Let us call the latter—which occurs in *prima facie* duties—sense (1), and the former sense (2).[21] Then it may be asked, again, whether "ought(1)" not only implies but means "ought(2), if I can (and if other things are equal)." Moore thinks so; Ewing, making use of the concept of "fittingness," thinks not. He admits that some justification for the view in question "is provided by Ross's suggestion that *prima facie* duties are to be viewed as *tendencies* to be absolute duties." "But," he argues, "to say that something is a *prima facie* duty is surely already to say not merely that there is a tendency for it to be fitting that we should adopt a certain attitude to it, but that it is absolutely fitting that we should do so, and also absolutely obligatory on us as far as it is in our power to take up the attitude at all."[22] If Ewing is correct, then "We ought(1) to do *A* (or it is fitting that we do *A*)" does not imply "We can do *A*, if we choose,"

---

[21] For reference purposes, the four main senses of "ought" dealt with in this paper are listed below. See final footnote.

[22] *Op. cit.*, p. 194.

and does not mean "We ought(2) to do *A*, if we can, and if other things are equal," though it entails this. It should be noted that fittingness may be an indefinable relation, as Ewing and others take it to be, but may also be definable. For all that is said here, "fitting" may mean "optimific," "commanded by God," or "approved by an impartial spectator." Ewing's position is an attractive one, and for a long time seemed to me to be obviously true. It is tempting to think that if something ought to be done if possible, this is because in some sense not involving "can" in its definition, even hypothetically, it already ought to be done. Unfortunately this is not necessarily true. What is obvious is that "I can do *X*" does not entail "I ought(2) to do it." Before I have an obligation to do *X* something more must be true of it than that I am able to do it. This something more may be that *X* is antecedently ("categorically, not merely hypothetically") fitting, but it need not be. It may only be the fact that *X* is pleasant, or keeps a promise, or has some other property which is ought-implying in Moore's sense.

On Ewing's view the situation is this: "being the keeping of a promise" entails "being fitting" and "being fitting" entails "being obligatory(2), if possible, and if other things are equal." On the other, and more economical, view: "being an act of promise-keeping" directly entails "being obligatory(2), if possible, and if other things are equal." Both positions seem to be consonant with common usage, and I now see little ground for choosing one rather than the other, apart from considerations, aesthetic and otherwise, which would take us too far afield for present purposes, since we are not dealing with the problem of trying to define "ought" in its various senses.

So much for "ought(1)," which occurs in our more general judgments of obligation. What of "ought" in particular judgments? Here it may also appear in sense (1). Consider the syllogism:

(a) I ought to make reparations for my wrongful acts.
(b) Doing *A* will make reparations for my wrongful act *B*.
(c) Therefore I ought to do *A*.

"Ought" occurs in sense (1) in the particular conclusion as well as in the general first premise, else the argument is invalid. In neither case, if we are right, does "ought" imply "can, and other things are equal." But one may judge that a certain action is my "actual duty," in the sense in which Ross used this phrase in *The Right and the Good*,[23] as I do when I review my situation and my various *prima facie* duties in an effort to find out what I really ought to do, and conclude that I ought to do action *C*. Here I use "ought" in sense (2), which presupposes at least that other things are equal and perhaps also that I can do *C*, and so cannot be identical with sense (1), even though it may be definable in terms of sense (1) or sense (1) in terms of it. The act which I ought(2) to do is the act which actually fulfills most fully my *prima facie* obligations in the situation in question. On the utilitarian theory, of course, this will always be the optimific or optimizing act, but on the neointuitionist view it may not be. This act has often been called the materially or objectively right act,[24] and has sometimes been referred to as the "fortunate" act, because it is only by luck that we ever do it.[25]

That we use "ought" in sense (2) is clear.[26] When we say that a man ought to do what he thinks he ought to do, we are using "ought" in two senses—in the second case in sense (2). When we say that a man thinks he ought to do *A*, but is mistaken, we are using "ought" in sense (2).[27] In fact, it seems to be admitted by those who deny the objective view of obligation that we actually do use "ought" in this sense, though we should not.[28] Moore even proceeds as if this were the only sense of "ought."[29] To hold this is to hold the objective view of obligation, and is clearly mistaken, as has been shown by Prichard and as we shall see below.[30] But Prichard's arguments show merely that (2) cannot be the only sense of "ought"; they refute the objective *view* of obligation but do not show that "ought" is not actually and defensibly used in an objective *sense*. They seem to show this only because Prichard implicitly assumes "ought" to have but one sense; as soon as it is seen that it has more (especially the three senses recognized by

---

[23] P. 28.

[24] Cp. Sidgwick, *op. cit.*, p. 207; Broad, "Some of the Main Problems of Ethics," *Philosophy*, XXI (1946), pp. 109 ff.

[25] Cp. Russell, *op. cit.*, p. 22; Ross, *The Right and the Good*, p. 31.

[26] See also Carritt, *op. cit.*, ch. ii; Ewing, *op. cit.*, pp. 118-120. On p. 119 Ewing seems to confuse senses (1) and (2).

[27] Or in sense (3), but this presupposes sense (2).

[28] Cp. Prichard, *op. cit.*, p. 24.

[29] So does Lucius Garvin in "Obligation and Moral Agency," *Ethics*, LVIII (1948), 188-194 and "Duty as External," *Jour. of Phil.*, XLV (1948), 549-555.

[30] In *The Right and the Good*, Ross defended the objective view of obligation; in *Foundations* he takes the subjective view.

Ewing[31]) it becomes plain that they show nothing of the sort.

Does "ought(2)" imply "can"? We have so far assumed so, as does the usual formula for what ought(2) to be done, viz., "The act which I ought(2) to do is that act, among all those which are possible to me, which will most fully fulfil my obligations(1)."[32] It is, however, possible to find a formula for what ought(2) to be done which does not introduce any reference to what the agent can do, if he chooses. Let "X is open to the agent" mean, not "X is possible for him to do, if he chooses," but "X can be chosen and entered upon by the agent." Then we can describe the act which an agent ought(2) to do as the act which, of all those open to him, will most fully fulfil his obligations, without implying that this act is one which he can carry out successfully. Thus there seem to be two possible descriptions of the objectively right act: (a) the usual one, (b) the one just suggested.[33] If we adopt the former, "ought(2)" implies both "can" and "other things are equal"; if we adopt the latter, "ought(2)" implies "other things are equal" but not "can."

It is not easy to see what should be said at this point. Perhaps we should recognize two subsenses of "ought," namely, (2a) and (2b). Discussing this question, Carritt writes, "I think it would be improper to speak of an obligation we *could* not fulfil *if we tried* [as we should if we used "ought" in sense (2b)], such as to move in two directions at once or to learn Chinese in a week. . . ."[34] In so far as Carritt is thinking that "ought(1)" implies "can" [for he fails to distinguish senses (1) and (2)] we may take him to be mistaken; there is no real difficulty about a *prima facie* duty which we cannot carry out. As far as "ought(2)" goes, he may be right. There is little point in recognizing sense (2b) if we have already admitted sense (1), and although it is a possible meaning of "ought," we may well not have adopted it in actual use, not being concerned to say of anything impossible that it is an actual duty in any sense.

Understanding "ought(2)" to imply "can," then, we must ask if "ought(2)" may not be defined in terms of "ought(1)," as well as the other way around. For it would seem that "A ought(2) to be done by

---

[31] *Op. cit.,* pp. 118-123.

[32] Cp. Ross, *The Right and the Good,* p. 41.

[33] Russell gives both kinds of descriptions of the objectively right act in *his* sense, *op. cit.,* pp. 25, 36.

[34] *Op. cit.,* p. 24.

me now" may mean "I ought(1) to do *A,* I can do *A,* and other things are equal," since it does at least imply this. One who holds Ewing's position might well claim that "ought(2)" is thus definable by reference to "ought(1)," rather than vice versa. So far as I can see, this suggestion may quite well be correct; here again there seems to be little reason for choosing between the rival views unless we bring in aesthetic considerations or others which are not within the scope of this paper. Apart from such considerations, it seems to be arbitrary which use of "ought" is taken as basic to the others. Of course, it may also be held that "ought(1)" and "ought(2)" cannot be defined by reference to one another, being either indefinable or definable only in terms of other concepts, ethical or nonethical. Then "ought(1)" will not mean "ought(2), if I can, and if other things are equal," though it will imply this; and "ought(2)" will not mean "ought(1), and can, and other things are equal," though it will imply this.

We may now proceed to study other senses of "ought" in relation to "can." The action which I ought(2) to do is the one which I do and should have before my mind, as the ideal, when I ask, "What should I do in the situation I am now in?" But, as everyone sees, we cannot know what act is right or obligatory in this sense, and we must be and are in a manner morally content with less. Hence moralists have often spoken of the act which will *probably* be most beneficial or which will *probably* most fully fulfil the relevant obligations. Russell, for instance, describes the wise or objectively right act as "that one which, of all that are possible, will probably have the best consequences."[35] They have also spoken of the act which it seems preferable to choose in the light, not of all the evidence available to a wise man with plenty of time, but of the evidence which the agent can reasonably be expected to have, or to get in the time at his disposal. This is the act which Russell calls the subjectively right act, and which Ewing describes as obligatory in his third sense.[36] No doubt there are other possibilities. We have here, in fact, a family of possible senses of "ought," which we might refer to as (3a), (3b), etc., and which all involve the notion of what probably ought to be done relatively to some body of evidence or other, which may not coincide with the body of evidence of which the agent actually makes use. Their differences lie in the way in which this body of evidence is defined. That we use "ought" in such senses is shown by the

---

[35] *Op. cit.,* pp. 25, 31-32.
[36] *Loc. cit.*

fact that we often say that a man ought not to have done a certain action, which, though successful, could not have been expected to be so.[37]

An action may, therefore, be one which I ought(3) to have done, even if it was wrong(2), though not, of course, if I knew it was wrong(2). Hence senses (2) and (3) are distinct and may be differently related to "can." Yet sense (3) presupposes sense (2), inasmuch as "I ought(3) to do A" presupposes that it is probable, relatively to a given body of evidence, that A ought(2) to be done by me. Perhaps "ought(3)" is definable in terms of "ought(2)," and "I ought(3) to do A" just means "It is probable that I ought(2) to do A." But all that concerns us is the connection between "ought(3)" and "can." "I ought(2) to do A" implies "I can do A." "I ought(3) to do A," however, does not imply "I ought(2) to do A" but only "It is probable on evidence E that I ought(2) to do A," and therefore may not imply "I can do A." In fact, to say that I ought(3) to do A is not to say that of the actions which I *actually* can do A is the one which will probably most fully fulfil my *prima facie* duties. I can no more know, except with probability, what I can do than what I ought(2) to do. Hence, in saying "I ought(3) to do A," I must be implying, not "I can do A," but "I probably can do A"; and it may, then, be that I ought(3) to do A even if I cannot do A, just as it may be that I ought(3) to do A even if it is wrong(2). Suppose it to be probable, relative to the body of evidence in question, that I ought(2) to do A. This will imply that it is probable I can do A. Then I ought(3) to do A. Suppose also that I set out to do it, and it turns out that I am unable to. Then, of course, I no longer have an obligation(3) to do A, and I never had an obligation(2) to do it. But it still remains the case that it was my obligation(3) to do A until the additional evidence came in (because of my setting out to do it) which established my inability to do it. What absolves me from being obliged(3) to do A is not the fact that I am unable to do it, but the fact that the body of evidence in question testifies that I am unable.

This brings us to another sense of "ought," often referred to as the peculiarly moral sense, even though it is not the only one which is relevant to ethics.[38] In all of the above senses of "ought," what I am re-

[37] Cp. Carritt, *op. cit.*, p. 15; Ewing, op. cit., pp. 121-122. Ewing answers Prichard's objection to admitting this sense. Cp. pp. 125-128. Ross in effect admits this sense, *Foundations*, pp. 156 f.

[38] See Ewing, *op. cit.*, pp. 128-132, on the relevancy of senses (2) and (3) (his first and third) to ethics.

quired to do is not simply what I as a matter of fact think I ought to
do, but what I objectively ought to do or what some body of evidence,
perhaps not possessed or used by me, makes it probable that I objectively ought to do. However, as Russell says, "There is certainly a
sense in which a man ought to perform any act which he ap-
proves. . . ."[39] A man, we say, ought always to obey his conscience.
We may label this use of "ought" sense (4). The act which ought to be
done in this sense (i.e., the act which the agent thinks he ought to do)
has usually been called the subjectively right act;[40] lately Carritt has
called it the putatively right act and Ewing the morally obligatory act.
Prichard is right as against Moore in insisting that this subjective sense
of "ought" must be recognized, but wrong in implying that there is no
more objective sense. For "ought(4)" clearly presupposes another sense
of "ought," as is shown by the fact that A is my duty(4) only if I already believe it to be my duty in some other sense, viz., (2) or (3).[41]

There is a complexity here which is not always realized. What one
thinks right depends partly on his beliefs about the nonethical features
of his situation and partly on his beliefs as to its ethical aspects. Hence
one may distinguish three cases: (a) the act which one ought to do if
the nonethical aspects of the situation are as he thinks they are, (b) the
act which the actual situation requires if one's *prima facie* duties
therein are what he thinks they are, and (c) the act which one thinks
to be required by the situation as he takes it to be. The last is the act
which we have said we ought(4) to do and is, perhaps, the only one
of the three with which we need be concerned here.

Obviously, an action may be right in sense (4) and wrong in all of
the above senses, or right in those senses and wrong in this. Should one,
then, if there is a discrepancy, do the action which is right in sense (4)
or the action which is right in some other sense? The answer, in part,
is that it depends on the sense in which "should" is being used in the
question. If it is used in sense (2), the reply can only be that we should
do the action which we ought(2) to do, etc. But the main part of the
answer is that one has no choice in the matter; one can (in a sense, not
ours) do only what he thinks he ought(2) to do. Further thought may
lead him to revise his opinion about this, but he will never *find* a dis-

---

[39] *Op. cit.*, p. 17; cp. Carritt, *op. cit.*, p. 15; Ewing, *op. cit.*, pp. 120 f.

[40] E.g., by Sidgwick, *op. cit.*, p. 207.

[41] Thinking it to be my duty in sense (2) and thinking it to be my duty in sense
(3) will in practice amount to the same thing.

crepancy between what he finally judges to be right(2) and what is really right(2).[42]

It is often held that if one does what one ought(4) to do one acquires merit and deserves praise and reward and that if one neglects to do it one gains a demerit and deserves blame and punishment. This is not so clearly true as it appears to be, but, in any case, we need not linger over this matter. Our question, as usual, concerns the relation of "ought(4)" and "can." Since it is sometimes regarded as the moral sense of "ought" *par excellence,* one might think that it is the most likely to entail "can." Actually the matter is somewhat complex. "I ought(4)" does not entail "I ought(2)." It entails "I think I ought(2)." Hence it presumably implies, not "I can," but "I think I can." If so, then, if I think I can and ought(2) to do *A,* even if I cannot. But this seems incredible! To resolve this difficulty we must distinguish between doing *A* and trying or setting ourselves to do *A.* It will, then, be observed that all we are really required to do when we are told that we ought(4) to do *A* is to try or set ourselves to do it. If I think I ought(2) to do *A* and try to do it but fail, I may say to you, "I failed my duty," and so I have in sense (2); but you will reply, if you are not unfriendly, "No, you tried, and that is all that can be asked of you," and so it is—in sense (4). It now becomes evident (a) that if I cannot do *A,* I have no obligation(4) to do it, but may have an obligation(4) to try, (b) that if I think I can and ought(2) to do *A,* I ought(4) to try to do it, even if I cannot in fact do it, and (c) that if I think or know that I cannot do *A,* I have no obligation(4) even to try to do it. One is also tempted to assert (d) that if I can do *A* and believe I can and ought(2) to do it, I ought(4) to do it and not merely to try. If so, we have here an exception to the rule that our obligation in sense (4) is only to try and not to do. But perhaps this case is not really an exception, for one may claim that even here I am obliged only to try, although if I try I shall succeed in doing, and that, while I am in this case to blame if I do not do, it is only because this means I did not try. Even if it were an exception, of course, it would be true that I have no obligation(4) to do *A* if I cannot do it. In short, "I ought(4) to do *A*" does not entail "I can do *A,*" because it does not really ask me to do *A* but only to try, and "I ought(4) to try to do *A*" does not imply "I can do *A,*" but only "I think I can do it, and I can try to do it." However, if it did ask me to do *A,* "I ought(4) to do *A*" would entail "I can

---

[42] Cp. Sidgwick, *loc. cit.*

do *A*." What it asks of me is possible to me; in this respect "ought(4)" implies "can." But it does not ask me to *do,* and therefore does not imply "can do."

Some writers have distinguished yet another sense of "ought," saying that I have not done what I ought if I do what is otherwise right from a wrong or bad or nonmoral motive. They have, therefore, introduced such notions as "the formally right act," "the virtuous act," etc.[43] So far as I can see, however, there is nothing new to be learned from a study of this sense or family of senses (5) of "ought" in its relation to "can." To say "I ought(5) to do from motive *M,* what I think I ought(2) to do," for example, seems to be explicable in terms of other senses of "ought" as follows: "I ought(4) to do what I think I ought(2) to do, *and* I ought(1) to feel motive *M* in situations of this sort." More interesting is "the perfectly right or completely right act," as it is sometimes called.[44] This may be variously defined by reference to other meanings of "ought" or "right." If "the perfectly right act for me to do here and now" is defined as "the act which I ought here and now to do, in senses (2)-(5)," then "*A* is the perfectly right act for me to do in this situation" implies "I can do *A,* if I choose." For "the perfectly right *A*" is just "the most completely right act of those possible to the agent." On the other hand, if being perfectly right involves, among other things, fulfilling all of the *prima facie* duties relevant to the situation, it may well be impossible for the agent to do the perfectly right act—and so not obligatory(2).

Now that we have studied the senses of "ought" and their relations to "can do, if I choose," it is time to examine Prichard's point (b)— "that an obligation must be an obligation not to do something but to set ourselves to do something."[45] We have admitted this in the case of "ought(4)." But we have also held that one has an obligation(1) to keep promises, for example, and not merely to try to keep them, even when he is unable to do so; and we have affirmed that "ought(2)" implies "can do, if I choose." Both of these conclusions will be false if Prichard is correct, the former because then even obligation(1) is only to try, the latter because then my having an obligation(2) to do *A* does not imply that I can do it, since it does not really enjoin doing,

---

[43] See Sidgwick, *op. cit.,* pp. 206-207; Broad, *loc. cit.;* Carritt, *A Theory of Morals* (1928), ch. xvi.

[44] See Sidgwick, *loc. cit.;* Broad, *loc. cit.;* Ross, *Foundations,* pp. 52-53.

[45] *Op. cit.,* p. 25.

but only that I can set myself.[46] Is Prichard right? The case is turned somewhat in our favor by the fact that we have seen reason for admitting three (plus) senses or families of senses of "ought" in addition to the subjective one (4) which Prichard recognizes. For while it is clear that an obligation in sense (4) is fulfilled by merely trying or setting ourselves, it is not clear that obligations in the other senses are. Moreover, his argument for his position, as well as the one added by Ross, loses its force if these other senses are kept in mind, although this cannot be shown here, for we must limit ourselves to the reasons for believing Prichard and Ross to be mistaken.

It can, I think, be granted that we may speak of an obligation to try or to set ourselves in senses other than (4).[47] But surely I have no obligation to try if I have no obligation to do. Trying is always trying to do; and, if I have an obligation to try, this is because I first have an obligation to do or think I have. I have an obligation in senses (1) or (2) to try, if and only if I have an obligation in senses (1) or (2) to do; and I have an obligation(4) to try, if and only if I think I ought in senses (1) or (2) to do. To this last point it may be replied that it is enough if I think I ought in senses (1) or (2) to *try*. But thinking this presupposes the thought that I ought in senses (1) or (2) to do. This is shown by the fact that if I know I cannot *do*, I have no obligation to *try* in any sense, and if I think I cannot *do*, I have no obligation(4) to try.

In general, it would seem that, if we were obliged only to *try*, then the fact that we cannot *do*, or know or think we cannot *do*, could not disoblige us, for we can (in our sense) always try. Suppose, however, that we have a straight-out obligation in senses (1) and (2) to try or to exert ourselves to do. What will this mean? It will mean that I ought(1) to perform that act of self-exertion or trying which will bring about, say, the keeping of my promise, and that I ought(2) to perform that act of self-exertion or trying which will come closest to bringing about what would be brought about by the various acts of self-exertion or trying which I ought(1) to perform.[48] For it will not suffice in senses (1) or (2) to perform the act of self-exertion or trying which I think will have the effects in question, since that is the one which I ought in

---

[46] I do not mean to imply that there are no problems about being able to set oneself. There are, but we are not concerned with them here.

[47] Carritt denies this for sense (2), *Ethical and Political Thinking*, p. 23.

[48] The term "self-exertion" is Ross's. See *Foundations*, p. 160.

sense (4) to perform. But to ask me to perform the self-exertion which *will* bring about a certain state of affairs is the same as to ask me to *do* a certain action.[49] Thus, asking me to make the self-exertion which will keep my promise is asking me to keep my promise; it is not asking me merely to try to keep it.

There is another line of thought which leads to the conclusion that we have obligations to do as well as to try. In an illustration used earlier, we found a man saying, quite naturally, "I failed to do my duty." Now, why did he fail to do his duty in the situation? Not because he did not try, for he did; but because, although he tried, he did not accomplish the required result. We must, therefore, have here a sense, namely (2), in which one ought, not simply to try, but also to accomplish.[50] And, if we have obligations(2) to do, then we have obligations(1) to do, for these two senses must be alike in this matter.

About "ought(3)" I am more doubtful, as it is intermediate between "ought(2)" and "ought(4)." But perhaps it need not be discussed. I have argued that one may have an obligation(3) to do *A*, even if one cannot in fact do *A,* although it ceases as soon as one's inability is revealed, and this still seems to me to be the case. In any event, however, Prichard's article (b) is not true for "ought(1)" or "ought(2)," and nothing more than a minor change of doctrine would be required, if it should be that obligation(3) like obligation(4) is merely to try and not to do.

To summarize: We have found the dictum that "ought" in its ethical uses implies "can" (in the sense of "can do, if I choose") not to be true *simpliciter*. "Ought" has several ethically relevant senses, of which four have been particularly discussed.[51] Only in the second of these does "I ought" imply "I can do, if I choose." In the first, it implies "I ought(2) to do, if I can" and "I am latently able to do," but not "I am actively able to do." In the third, "I ought" implies, not "I can," but "I probably can." In both cases, "I ought to do" entails a statement in-

---

[49] See the account given earlier of Prichard's analysis of being able to do.

[50] Cp. Carritt, *loc. cit.*

[51] The following sentences will serve to identify, distinguish, and relate these four senses:

    a. I ought(1) to do what I ought(2) to do, if I can, and if other things are equal.

    b. I ought(2) to do what will most fully fulfil my obligations(1) of the actions which I can do if I choose.

    c. I ought(3) to do what, relatively to evidence *E*, I probably ought(2) to do.

    d. I ought(4) to [try to] do what I think I ought(2) or ought(3) to do.

volving "can" in one way or another, but not "I can do, if I choose."
In the case of sense (4) the matter is still more complicated. "I ought(4)
to *do A*" does imply "I can *do A,* if I choose," for if the latter is false
the former is also. However, it is never true that I ought(4) to *do A,*
but only that I ought(4) to try (though we often say loosely "*B* ought(4)
to 'do' *A*"); and "I ought(4) to try to do *A*" does not imply "I can
do A" but only "I think I can do *A* (and I can try to do *A*)." Therefore,
understood in a way in which it may be true, "I ought(4) to 'do' *A*"
does not imply "I can *do A.*"

These are our main results. We have also tried to show two points in
Prichard's theory of obligation, accepted by Ross in his later work, to
be false. And we have suggested, somewhat tentatively, that, with the
help of "can" (in our sense), "ought(1)" and "ought(2)" are interdefinable. We have left for other occasions such further questions as:
(a) Are the various ethical senses of "ought" all interdefinable, with
or without the help of "can"? (b) Is "ought" in all of its ethical senses
definable in nonethical terms, with or without the help of "can"? (c)
What is meant by "implies" when it is said that "ought" implies "can"?

In arriving at these results we have sought to avoid making any
commitments to any particular theory of obligation, naturalistic or nonnaturalistic, neointuitionist or utilitarian. They may and should, therefore, if we are not mistaken, be accepted by and incorporated in any
ethical theory which is concerned to accord with common usage.

Substratum

MORRIS LAZEROWITZ

One of the most troublesome problems in the literature of philosophy concerns "the ancient and honorable notion of substance." As is well known, the metaphysical problem about the nature of material things, the question, that is to say, as to the *ultimate* constitution and structure of such objects as books and pennies and soap bubbles, has given rise to different theories none of which has, in essentials, turned out to be universally acceptable to professional philosophers. It has to be pointed out in this connection that each theory has its convinced adherents and that the arguments for each theory, though not convincing to some philosophers, are accepted as conclusive by others. This is a bewildering state of affairs and we may well wonder what has happened to create it: we may well be curious to discover what it is about some demonstrations that makes it possible for one group of able philosophers who have studied the problem to reject them and another group to accept them. In this paper the main object is to examine the theory which Aristotle expressed by saying that "matter is unknowable in itself." And I wish to examine it in connection with only one of the sources from which it derives. The theory has one source in the conception of a thing as being the invariant subject of change: "The thing, to be at all, must be the same after a change, and the change must, to some extent be predicated of the thing."[1] It has another source

---

[1] F. H. Bradley, *Appearance and Reality* (1925), p. 72.

in the distinction between a thing and its appearances, and still a further one, which is perhaps the basic source, in the distinction between a thing and its attributes. Only the last source will be of concern to us here.

According to the theory, a thing such as an apple or a pebble is composed of a substance in which a variety of attributes inhere, or which supports them or is their bearer or their owner. The substance itself is held to be something distinct from the sum of its properties. It is also held that our "experience" of a thing is confined to its qualities, so that it is possible for us to know what attributes the thing has; but what the possessor of the attributes, the substratum itself, is, remains hidden from us. Substratum lies beyond the bounds of possible experience: "We cannot say anything at all about its nature."[2] When a philosopher says "We do not know that things really are,"[3] one cannot help feeling that he utters these words with deep regret. It is not too much to imagine that some people feel themselves to be living in a world of impenetrable mystery and have the intolerable thought, though it may also give them a certain amount of pleasure, that their curiosity about the world can never be satisfied.

Not all philosophers have been able to accept this theory. Instead, some have been attracted to a different view about the composition of physical things, one from which it follows that there are no unknowable substances. This view is to the effect that a thing is composed of nothing more than the properties which, in ordinary language, "it" is said to have: "What would commonly be called a 'thing' is nothing but a bundle of co-existing qualities, such as hardness, redness, etc."[4] On this theory we can know what things really are, because there are no substances distinct from the experienceable qualities. There is nothing behind the barrier of knowable attributes, nothing to be an inner mystery which forever frustrates our curiosity.

Philosophers who adopt the view that a thing is just a bundle of properties sometimes reject the substratum theory in a way which throws it into an unexpected light. We quite naturally take the theory that a thing is made up of a substance together with a collection of attributes inhering in it to be a hypothesis with regard to the material facts about such things as tables and inkwells. And undoubtedly most

---

[2] G. Watts Cunningham, *Problems of Philosophy* (1924), p. 167.

[3] A. E. Taylor, *Elements of Metaphysics* (1912), p. 131.

[4] Bertrand Russell, *An Inquiry Into Meaning and Truth* (1940), p. 120.

philosophers, regardless of whether they hold the theory or reject it, conceive it to be about "the structure of reality." Some philosophers, however, appear to view it in a different light, which, if that is the right way to view it, makes it out to be utterly different from what we take it to be. Thus, one philosopher has written: "The introduction of an unknowable can generally, and perhaps always, be avoided by suitable technical devices, and clearly it should be avoided whenever possible."[5] The sort of device by the use of which unknowables are to be avoided or "got rid of" consists of making up a new form of speech, one not found in the language of ordinary conversation, and substituting it for the familiar, common form of speech which, it is claimed, introduces unknowables:

> Common sense regards a "thing" as having qualities, but not as being defined by them; it is defined by spatio-temporal position. I wish to suggest that, wherever there is, for common sense, a "thing" having the quality *C*, we should say, instead, that *C* itself exists in that place, and that the "thing" is to be replaced by the collection of qualities existing in the place in question. Thus "*C*" becomes a name, not a predicate.[6]

Our interest in the question as to what the metaphysical theory actually comes to, what its *nature* is, is justifiably aroused when we learn that some philosophers think it to be of a kind that can relevantly be dealt with by the use of a linguistic device, which consists in altering a current mode of speech. If the introduction of a new way of speaking will "get rid" of the unknowables claimed to exist by the theory, then the theory is only apparently about things, not actually about them at all. For no sort of change in language could, by itself alone, alter the inaccessibility to us of facts about material things, just as no tinkering with our language will make accessible to us information about the topography of the dark side of the moon. The idea that behind the experienceable attributes we meet with in our everyday perception of things there exist unknowable substrata could only be got rid of by linguistic means if the idea of such substrata were produced by the language we used, not by the things we perceived. An appropriate change in language may very well destroy an illusion produced by the use of words, but it will not remove an idea genuinely connected with the perception of things. Thus, the ordinary sentence "This is red," which seems to ascribe an attribute to something referred to by the

---

5 *Ibid.*, p. 122.
6 *Ibid.*, *pp.* 121-122.

subject word "this" creates, according to some philosophers, the misconception that the substantive stands for an unknowable something, a bare particular behind the attribute "red": "One is tempted to regard 'this is red' as a subject-predicate proposition; but if one does so, one finds that 'this' becomes a substance, an unknowable something in which properties inhere, but which, nevertheless, is not identical with the sum of its properties."[7] The way to destroy this unreal notion, which has no relation to the facts about the "structure of reality," is to replace expressions like "this is red" by expressions of the form "redness is here" and treat adjectives like "red" as names, not as predicates.

According to this conception of the source and nature of the theory, many thinkers have been deceived by language into holding a *Scheintheorie* while laboring under the notion that they were advocating a deep hypothesis about the constitution of things, were taking a verbal shadow for an actual theory about the ultimate nature of material objects. What has happened has been summed up in the following way: "It happens to be the case that we cannot, in our language, refer to the sensible properties of a thing without introducing a word or phrase which appears to stand for the thing itself as opposed to anything which may be said about it. And, as a result of this, those who are infected by the primitive superstition that to every name a single real entity must correspond assume that it is necessary to distinguish logically between the thing itself and any, or all, of its sensible properties."[8] Another philosopher has put it in this way: " 'Substance,' in a word, is a metaphysical mistake, due to the transference to the world-structure of the structure of sentences composed of a subject and a predicate."[9] Like a chronic psychological obsession which cannot be removed by confrontation with fact, the transference persists despite our familiarity with chairs and the like. And the explanation of the stubbornness with which the delusive idea persists is, apparently, that the source of the idea does not lie in the perception of things or in experiments conducted on them. The conception of substratum is a *metaphysical* mistake, not a scientific one, and not correctable by scientific means.[10] It would seem that the technique designed to destroy the transference and

---

[7] *Ibid.*, p. 120.

[8] A. J. Ayer, *Language, Truth and Logic* (1936), p. 32.

[9] Bertrand Russell, *A History of Western Philosophy* (1945), p. 202.

[10] "If science keeps to its own sphere, it cannot clash with any metaphysical theory," J. McT. E. McTaggart, *Some Dogmas of Religion* (1906), p. 91.

cure the linguistic delusion consists of reframing language in such a way that it will no longer offer the temptation to make the transference. One is reminded of Freud's comments about some neurotic people who become well only after changing their environment. The linguistic neurosis, so to speak, is also to be cured by changing the linguistic environment, by making part of the language aseptic, to use John Wisdom's expression.

By no means, of course, are all or even most philosophers in agreement with this version of what the substratum theory of the nature of material things comes to. Where it is maintained that the substance theory is an illusion caused by the subject-predicate structure of language, many other philosophers make the claim that the established language in everyday use is itself the natural result of an antecedent belief about the composition of material things. They, instead, explain the fact that language has a subject-predicate structure by reference to a prior hypothesis about reality. Thus: "When we ask how, if a 'thing' is merely the sum of its attributes, and possesses no underlying unity to which the attributes belong, the whole of our ordinary language about things comes to be constructed on the contrary assumption, how it is that we always talk and think as if every 'bundle' of attributes were owned by something of which we can say that it *has* the quality. . . ."[11]

Some philosophers maintain that the substratum theory is only the semblance of an empirical hypothesis into which we are tricked by language; others maintain that the theory is an actual hypothesis about the structure of things and that it determined the form of our language about things. How is one to decide between these two versions of what it comes to? What sort of observation or experiment or purely intellectual consideration will show that the words "Material things are constituted by substances in which attributes inhere" express a theory about material objects or are a verbal fraud which successfully masquerade as a theory? A little thought leads to the disconcerting conclusion that perhaps there is no way of definitely and conclusively deciding between the two versions. For those who insist that it is a theory about things are in no better position to make relevant observations than those who deny this: the disagreement does not arise because of any difference in observation or from different results of experimentation. And those who maintain it is a verbal counterfeit know no more

---

11 Taylor, *op. cit.*, p. 133.

facts about grammar and the accepted usages of words than those who hold the opposite view; there is no linguistic fact about ordinary discourse they can point to of which the others are not aware, and such that their acquaintance with it would compel them to give up their view. Neither knowledge of actual language nor sense-observation of things seems adequate to settling the matter, and it would consequently seem that there is no way of settling it. For what else is there to turn to?

Where different hypotheses have been proposed without agreed success, it is certainly permissible to try out still another hypothesis. The worst thing that can happen is that we shall again fail to arrive at an acceptable solution, which is something we are all hardened against in philosophy. I propose to take the view, in partial agreement with one of the two contending versions, that the substance "theory" is only the verbal imitation of a theory and entirely different from what we are inclined to think it is. But I shall argue that it is not ordinary, everyday language that causes us to think this. Instead, I shall try to show that the illusion of its being a theory about things is produced by a concealed *revision* of ordinary subject-predicate sentences, by a maneuver with language, and not by the subject-predicate form of discourse itself. It is what *metaphysicians* have done with words, their metaphysical artistry, that creates the appearance of a theory about the structure of things; but what they have done is hidden from our conscious awareness, as well as their own. The theory may be compared to a dream; indeed, in this case, the metaphysician may be said to dream with words. As in the case of an ordinary dream, the linguistic metaphysical dream is consciously enjoyed or disliked but only secretly understood. And in order to see how the illusory effect of a theory about the nature of things is produced, the language of the metaphysical fantasy has to be interpreted.

It is important, first of all, to see that the theory is not factual; i.e., it is important to see that it is not a theory about the constitution of material objects. Consider what Locke said:

> It is the ordinary qualities observable in iron or a diamond, put together, that make the true complex idea of those substances, which a smith or a jeweler commonly knows better than a philosopher; who, whatever substantial forms he may talk of, has no other idea of those substances than what is framed by a collection of those simple ideas which are to be found in them. Only we must take notice, that our complex

ideas of substances, beside all these simple ideas they are made up of, have always the confused idea of something to which they belong and in which they subsist. And therefore, when we speak of any sort of substance, we say it is a thing having such or such qualities. . . . These and the like fashions of speaking intimate that the substance is supposed always something besides the extension, figure, solidity, motion, thinking, or other observable ideas, though we know not what it is.[12]

Not imagining how these simple ideas can subsist by themselves, we accustom ourselves to suppose some *substratum* wherein they do subsist, and from which they do result, which therefore we call *substance*.[13]

So that if any one will examine himself concerning his notion of pure substance in general, he will find he has no other idea of it at all, but only a supposition of he knows not what support of such qualities which are capable of producing simple ideas in us; which qualities are commonly called accidents. If any one should be asked, what is the subject wherein colour or weight inheres, he would have nothing to say, but the solid extended parts: and if he were demanded, what is it that that solidity and extension inhere in, he would not be in a much better case than the Indian before mentioned. . . .[14]

Hume's challenge, which seems based, in a soundly empirical manner, on the sense-observation of things, is well known:

I would fain ask those philosophers, who found so much of their reasonings on the distinction of substance and accident, and imagine we have clear ideas of each, whether the idea of *substance* be derived from the impressions of sensation or reflection? If it be conveyed to us by our senses, I ask, which of them, and after what manner? If it be perceived by the eyes, it must be a colour; if by the ears, a sound; if by the palate, a taste; and so of the other senses. But I believe none will assert, that substance is either a colour, or sound, or a taste. The idea of substance must, therefore, be derived from an impression of reflection, if it really exists. But the impressions of reflection resolve themselves into our passions and emotions; none of which can possibly represent a substance.[15]

At first glance, Hume appears to have rejected the idea of substance as a "fiction" on the basis of observation. He seems to have come to his conclusion as the result of a closer, more careful, examination of things, a process comparable to inspecting a box to see whether it has a secret compartment. It looks as if he has made a thorough inventory of his

---

12 *An Essay Concerning Human Understanding*, bk. II, ch. xxiii, sec. 3.
13 *Ibid.*, sec. 1.
14 *Ibid.*, sec. 2.
15 *A Treatise of Human Nature*, bk. I, pt. I, sec. 6.

sense-experiences of such a thing, say, as a table, experiences we should express by saying "This table is brown," "This table feels smooth," and the like, and discovered that he actually experienced *only* brownness and rectangularity, smoothness and hardness, etc. He never, in connection with any of his senses, perceived the *thing* that is brown and smooth and rectangular, the substance in which the perceived attributes inhere. His description of what happened is the description of a person who in no instance of the sense-perception of objects comes upon anything over and above and in addition to attributes, a further something which owns them; and in consequence rejects the notion that any such entities as substances exist. The impression his words give is that they describe the rejection of an empirical claim on empirical grounds, a rejection based on reasons similar to those which finally makes us give up the belief in ghosts; we have never come upon one, not even its shadow. But this impression is erroneous.

It may first be noted that if the substratum hypothesis regarding the constitution of material objects is empirical and if what Hume did, to test it, was really to make a series of observations, then his rejection of the theory was quite unwarranted. For if this was his procedure, we have to suppose that he looked for what he should have realized, if the theory were correct, he would not be able to find and, after looking for substance and not finding it, concluded that it did not exist. Those who hold the theory claim that we "experience qualities but not the substance in which they inhere." How, then, could his failure to perceive substance have led Hume to make the claim of having demonstrated the notion of substance to be a fiction? How can you refute a hypothesis by not finding what the hypothesis states you cannot find? No scientist would think of rejecting the atomic theory because he failed to see an atom through the microscope, and it is hard to believe that it was something like this that Hume was actually doing. It is hard, in spite of the empirical descriptive language he used, to think that his claim is empirical and that he based it on processes of looking at things, feeling them, tasting them, and so on.

Locke would certainly not have found his consideration impressive. For he *agrees* with Hume about what we discover from an examination and inventory of our experiences of things. In his own words:

> Everyone upon enquiry into his own thoughts will find, that he has no other idea of any substance but what he has barely of those sensible qualities, which he supposes to inhere, with a supposition of such a sub-

stratum, as gives, as it were, a support to those qualities or simpler ideas, which he has observed to exist united together. Thus the idea of the sun, what is it but an aggregate of those several simple ideas, bright, hot, roundish, having a constant regular motion, at a certain distance from us, and perhaps some other?[16]

How, then, is the difference of opinion between the two philosophers to be explained? Is it to be explained as resulting from the fact that not all information relevant to the refutation or establishment of the substratum hypothesis is available, so that the lack of complete information leaves room for a divergence of beliefs? Is it to be hoped that examinations through future supermicroscopes, refined experiments, etc., will ever bring the metaphysical problem of substratum to an end? It is not difficult to see that laboratory science holds out no hope for its solution in the future. If physicists and chemists had satisfied themselves that at least they had reached the end of their quest and knew everything about matter, philosophers could show that the *metaphysical* problem of substance still remained unsolved. Nor would more ways of sensing things than the usual five be of the slightest help. A new and yet further way of perceiving a thing like an orange would only reveal new *qualities* of the thing; we still would not be able to perceive the substance itself, and the controversy over its existence would remain.

Consider again what Hume appears to have done, namely, to have looked for something by means of a series of careful observations. In the case of an actual search for anything we always have *some* idea of what it is we are looking for. We know, for example, what it would be like to look for and discover (or fail to discover) the unknown cause of a disease. But if we had no idea whatever, however rough, no inkling, of what it is we were trying to discover, we should not know where to begin nor where to turn, nor would we be able to recognize the thing as answering to what we want. The experiment Hume invites us to make is utterly different in this respect from an ordinary instance of looking for something. In this case, not finding what we are looking for implies that we had, to begin with, no idea whatever of what we were trying to discover. And it implies, moreover, that no process of looking had been resorted to. The search was only a sham. For when Hume points out that the supposed idea of substance derives neither from sensation nor reflection, which both he and Locke are agreed are the only sources of our ideas, he in effect tells us, not that it, like the

---

16 *Op. cit.*, bk. II, ch. xxiii, sec. 6.

idea of a centaur, is *fictitious,* but that there is *no such idea.* He tells us that the phrases "substance in which attributes inhere," "owner of attributes," "support of qualities" describe nothing actual or imaginable and are literally empty phrases to which no application has been given. Of course, then, there can be no looking for a bearer of properties, no examination of anything for the purpose of trying to discover a substratum, any more than there can be a search for binomial scarlet or for a slithy tove.

When it is claimed that none of our senses acquaint us with substance, that they all fail to reveal to us a support of such experienced qualities as shape, color, and taste, what this claim has, then, to be construed as coming to is that it is *logically impossible* to perceive in any way the subject of attributes. When it is said "We experience qualities but not the subject in which they are supposed to inhere," what these words must be taken to be stating is that under no conceivable circumstances could we ever experience substance, that this is a logical impossibility, however much they look to be asserting an empirical fact about what we fail to perceive. No one could seriously be supposed to be maintaining that we do not perceive substratum because as a matter of fact it does not exist or that we are prevented from experiencing it by a physical obstacle or some sort of physiological inadequacy. Nothing can be said to be a goal if we cannot describe what it would be like to attain it, and nothing can be said to be a barrier preventing us from attaining a goal unless we can describe overcoming it and reaching the goal. And what makes it certain that the inaccessibility of substance is not to be explained on physical or physiological grounds is that there are no descriptions in philosophy of what it would be like to perceive substance or of what it is that prevents our experiencing it.

A familiar argument, which is substantially Hume's, helps make clear what it is that stands in the way of our experiencing the substratum support of attributes. It goes as follows: If, in our imagination, we take away the various properties of a thing, for example, the shape, size, and other attributes of an orange, we find that there is nothing left; there is no residue, which is the owner of properties and distinct from them, for us to imagine. There is no difficulty about imagining Voltaire deprived of all his possessions, his garments, his money, books, and snuff box; bare Voltaire remains after this process. But when Voltaire's attributes are taken away from the substance in which they inhere, nothing whatever, no bare something, is left. This shows that the seemingly descriptive expression "substance in which properties inhere but which is distinct from them" is not used to describe anything thing. The impossibility of imagining substratum is a logical impossibility, which has its source in the linguistic fact that the word "substratum," in the sense of something "in which properties inhere but which is distinct from them," has been given no application. It might, of course, be urged that "substratum" does denote something, though what it denotes eludes us; but then we should have to accept the absurd consequence that the word has an application which it has never been given and is not known to have. It is clear, then, that we cannot perceive substratum for the same reason that we cannot see binomial scarlet: "perceives substratum," like "sees binomial scarlet," is a literally senseless expression. Hence, when a metaphysician says, "we do not know what things really are," his plaint would seem to be against language, namely, that to say such a thing as "A knows what it is, the substratum, that attributes ϕ_1, ϕ_2, ϕ_3 . . . . inhere in" is not to say anything. And when another metaphysician states that "we cannot say anything about its nature," he seems to be remarking that there do not exist words for describing substratum, which is to say that the word "substratum" is connected with no descriptive phrases.

It would appear now that the explanation of the substance hypothesis which construes it to be the distorted recognition of a linguistic fact, the recognition of such a fact displaced, so to speak, onto the world of things, is correct. The idea that the theory is a mistake due to the transfer to the world structure of the structure of subject-predicate sentences needs, apparently, to have a further point added: namely, it is this sentence structure taken in conjunction with the linguistic fact that it makes no sense to speak of knowing what it is that is the subject of attribution which is responsible for the mistake. Can this explanation be the right one, however? It is sufficiently plain that the theory is not an account of the nature of things and that its appearing so is an illusion due to the form of words used to express it. But is the source of the theory to be found, as is claimed, in the language we use in everyday conversation, the language of ordinary discourse?

The claim would be correct if in ordinary language it made sense to speak of perceiving colors, shapes, etc., but did not make sense to speak of perceiving things. But this is not the case at all; and it must be a mistake to think that the metaphysical idea of unknowable substance could be produced by the subject-predicate structure of *ordinary* sentences like "The dog is barking" or "This table is heavy." For it makes perfectly good sense to speak not only of hearing the barking of the dog and feeling the weight of the table but also of seeing the dog and of seeing the table, i.e., of perceiving the *thing* that is barking and the *thing* that is heavy. Moore has said: "Some people may no doubt think that it is very unphilosophical in me to say that we *ever* can perceive such things [as doors and fingers]. But it seems that we do, in ordinary life, constantly talk of *seeing* such things, and that when we do so, we are neither using language incorrectly, nor making any mistake about the facts—supposing something to occur which never does in fact occur."[17] Ordinary, *unphilosophical* people who speak in subject-predicate sentences do not have the idea that things, as opposed to attributes, are unknowable. How then could it possibly produce such an idea in the minds of metaphysicians? It seems plain that ordinary language could not have produced the idea; the source has to be discovered elsewhere. When a person who maintains that we do perceive things and that to say that we do is not a misuse of language is condemned as being unphilosophical, then we have to think that being *philosophical* consists in doing something unusual with words, not mistakenly, but with purpose, whether or not with awareness. It becomes highly plausible to think that metaphysicians have, if not consciously then with unconscious skill, *introduced* "linguistic unknowables." If substratum is unknowable, then the word "substratum" does not mean what is ordinarily meant by the phrase "subject of attribution." In some way that is obscure to us, language has been altered; and it is this altered language which is responsible for the theory that things are unknowable substrata in which attributes inhere.

What has happened? How has the metaphysical dream been produced? Fortunately, there are statements to be found in the literature which give us insight into what has taken place. Consider the following statement:

> Those who maintain that there is an ultimate plurality of substances, and yet hold that characters are, as such, universals, seem logically bound to deny that a substance is the complex unity of all its qualities and relations. Thus Mr. McTaggart, who occupies this position, asserts in his *Nature of Existence*, ch. V, that the complex unity is itself only a com-

---

17 G. E. Moore, *Philosophical Studies* (1922), p. 226. Moore said this in a different connection.

plex adjective, and therefore presupposes a subject ultimately distinct from itself.[18]

And also this statement:

> If we . . . suppose that his kind and all his particular attributes as well *belong* to the individual, the individual, to which they all belong, becomes a mere uncharacterized *something*. For in saying *what* it is, we should merely assign to it a fresh predicate; whereas we want to get not at its predicates but at that which "has" them. Thus we should reach a new way of considering the subject of predication. Originally it was the concrete individual, Socrates or Plato; but of what he is, one part was distinguished as what he is essentially, and the rest reduced to attributes or "accidents" of him, not necessary to his being, and not to be included in an account of his essence. Now what he is essentially is also reduced to the position of attribute and mere predicate, and the subject becomes a mere subject of which as such nothing more can be said that it exists and is unique in each individual.[19]

What these quotations, on careful reading, can be seen to tell us is that the substratum theory expresses the linguistic result of juggling with words. The illusion that things are unknowable in themselves has its source in a linguistic creation. In almost so many words, these quotations explain the mechanics of the illusion as consisting of the change brought about in language by *reducing* general names to the status of "mere adjectives," that is to say, the change brought about by reclassifying general substantives as "complex adjectives," while retaining the subject-predicate form of sentence.

It appears that some metaphysicians wish to recompose language, for some reason or other. Ordinary grammar does not satisfy them; and they wish to change it by depriving general substantives of their grammatical noun function and give them the status of adjectives without, however, giving up the subject-predicate form of sentence. In order to do this, it is quite plain that linguistic reparations will have to be made. If the substantive "penny" is counted as a "complex adjective" which "presupposes a subject ultimately distinct from itself," then, since in English there is no term distinct from it which it presupposes as a subject term, a new term will have to be invented to supply the need. If we wish to deprive "penny" of its noun place in the sentence "The penny is round" and at the same time wish to keep the gram-

---

18 G. F. Stout, *Studies in Philosophy and Psychology* (1930), p. 394.
19 H. W. B. Joseph, *An Introduction to Logic* (1931), p. 54.

matical structure of the sentence intact, without replacing the noun by a synonym, then our only resort is to find a structural replacement for the deleted term. For obviously there cannot be a sentence which has a subject-predicate structure but fails to have some sort of subject term, if only one which plays the role of subject in purely formal respects. A subject-predicate sentence *must* have a subject; this is the "necessity of thought" of which Locke speaks.

The introduction of a term which is only the formal, and not a material, substitute for a general noun is made possible by the fact that general names have two distinct functions. A word like "mouse" has, for one thing, a meaning; in this respect it has a semantic function which enables us to say *what* a thing is, e.g., that a thing is a mouse, or that a thing is a ball or a penny. In addition to this, it also has the formal syntactical function of serving as the subject of predication in sentences. If, now, general names are deprived of the syntactical use to which they are at present put, and given adjectival classification under parts of speech, the subject-predicate form of sentence in which they occur as subjects can nevertheless be preserved by introducing a term that will do part of the work of a general name, i.e., do its syntactical work without doing its semantic work. It will be sufficient if the new term is made to behave syntactically like an ordinary subject term and is otherwise a pseudo term, having no application to phenomena. Thus, to revert to the former example, the *structure* of the sentence "The penny is round" can be kept intact after its noun has been deleted, by letting the mark "x" occupy the place of "penny." We then have the new subject-predicate sentence "The x is round,"[20] where "x" differs from ordinary subject terms in respect of having been given no application. It is the failure to give "x" a meaning that makes it a "mere subject" or, to use Bertrand Russell's word, a *hook* on which to hang adjectives.

One philosopher seems to have divined what has happened when he observed that "Our idea of a substance, in fact, turns out to be no more than an unknown x, to which we refer the contents of experience."[21] The new subject term *is* an unknown x, which is to say it is a symbol that has no known meaning assigned to it; it has no semantic use, though it has the appearance of having such a use. It is a term by

---

20 "x" is not to be taken as representing a variable.
21 James Gibson, *Locke's Theory of Knowledge and Its Historical Relations* (1917), p. 95.

means of which we cannot say *what* a thing is, although, in the subject-predicate sentences of the substratum language invented by metaphysicians, it supplants words with which we can, and in ordinary language do, say what things are. It is this new form of subject-predicate language that causes the idea of unknowable substratum: the new term is a "linguistic unknowable." The complaint that we cannot say anything about the nature of substance, about what things really are, is not the factual complaint about things it may at first have seemed to be, nor is it about our everyday language, which, of course, contains general names. It is the expression of dissatisfaction with the substratum language of metaphysics and is of the same order as complaining that we cannot say what a "tove" is. The term "*x*" tells us nothing, conveys no information, about the thing described by the adjectives of a sentence in which it occurs as subject. Nor, of course, we can explain its meaning, in the way in which we can explain the meaning of a general name. If we are asked what a kangaroo is we can answer the question by describing the animal to which the word "kangaroo" applies, which is to say, by giving roughly the meaning of the word. This is impossible in the case of the metaphysical subject, which has no application; there is no explaining what an *x* is. The observation that on the substratum theory ". . . the individual becomes a mere uncharacterized *something*. For in saying *what* it is, we should merely assign to it a fresh predicate; whereas we want to get not at its predicates but at that which 'has' them"[22] comes to the same thing as the above complaint. It is easy to see why we cannot "get at" substance with a language in which general names have been reduced to adjectival status and have had their former position taken over by a term which does only their syntactical work. We can state what attributes a thing has but we cannot say what it is in which they inhere, except that it is an *x*, an "uncharacterized something." We can "get at" some animals with the word "kangaroo," but we get at nothing with the term "*x*."

The idea of substance as being that which remains after a thing has been stripped bare of its qualities—the idea, in other words, of "bare substance" or the "bare particular"—turns out to be a disguised expression of a linguistic fact. That which remains, after a general name has been deprived of its application to things by depriving it of the meaning it has in common with an indeterminate set of adjectives, is a term which has only a syntactical use, an equivalent of the formal sub-

---

22 Joseph, *loc. cit.*

ject term of substratum metaphysics. "Bare substance" is nothing more than a "bare" substantive word, the metaphysical ghost of a general name. This is the conception of substratum as something *distinct* from its properties and in which they inhere. It is a symbol that is *completely* distinct from its predicates by virtue of the fact that it has no meaning of its own, a fact which also makes it impossible to say, by means of it, what things are. It is possible in this language to say what properties a thing has, but not what it is. This fact, it may be noted, rids philosophers of the need of trying to distinguish the essence of a thing from its accidents. For without the ordinary distinction between general substantive words like "penny" and "horse" and adjectives like "round" and "roan"—a distinction which can be destroyed either by eliminating general nouns or by changing them into adjectives—there is no distinction between the essence and accidents of a thing. There is left only the distinction between a term which is a "pure" subject term (the pure abstract being of medieval metaphysics) and adjectives.

Consider, again, the familiar arguments used to demonstrate the unknowability of substance, the argument, namely, that we cannot envisage the entity that is left after a thing has been stripped of its attributes, or, what amounts to the same thing, Hume's argument that in addition to the perceived qualities of color, shape, odor, taste, and the like we never experience the thing which has them. This argument rests on and, indeed, is a distorted way of calling attention to actual points of difference and similarity between general names and adjectives. General names differ in their formal, syntactical use from adjectives, but also they are like them in important respects. For one thing, like adjectives, they have multiple applicability; or, to express this fact in metaphysical language, the universals for which they stand are capable of having a number of instances or of being possessed in common by a number of things. Thus, we can say that many things are grey and we can say that there are many mice. Also, and what is more specifically relevant in connection with the argument, the application of a general noun is determined by a variable set of adjectives, not sharply defined or specified. To put it roughly, as regards their meaning, general names are "complex adjectives." This is what Locke was pointing out when he remarked that "everyone upon enquiry into his own thoughts will find, that he has no other idea of any substance but what he has barely of those sensible qualities, which he supposes to inhere . . . Thus the idea of the sun, what is it but an aggregate of those several simple ideas, bright, hot, roundish . . . ?" Hence, to speak of an experiment, conducted in the imagination, of stripping a thing of its attributes is a disguised and more colorful way of expressing the linguistic fact that the meaning of a general noun like "mouse" is the same as that possessed by a complicated set of adjectives, so that by "stripping away" its adjectives, i.e., by depriving the noun of its adjectival meaning, we deprive it of its application to things. Noticing the impressive similarity between general nouns and adjectives makes some people wish to assimilate them to the class of adjectives. It is much as if, by their argument, they were to say: "See, the difference between general nouns and adjectives is mainly a difference in the way they function syntactically in sentences. By comparison with their semantic similarity, this difference is trivial, but it hides their similarity." And to correct this state of affairs and bring out what is hidden by the structure of subject-predicate language, general nouns are reduced to adjectival status. The syntactical function of nouns is turned over to a new symbol, and in this way the structure of subject-predicate sentences using general names as subjects is preserved and also the mystifying illusion of a deep theory about the structure of reality is created. Undoubtedly, the motivation for the change goes deeper than the linguistic considerations; we may well think that psychological needs play an important role in the production of the illusion.

Metaphysicians who find the substratum theory unacceptable also feel the importance of the semantic similarity that grammar tends to conceal, and are dissatisfied with the grammar that conceals it. What impresses these philosophers seems mainly to be the fact that both sorts of words, adjectives and nouns, have multiple applicability, that, e.g., "white" and "snow" are each applicable to a number of things. They see, however, the possibility of a different reconstruction, to which they are attracted. They see the possibility of assimilating adjectives to the class of substantive words. Instead of reducing general names to complex adjectives they change adjectives into abstract nouns, "red" into "redness," "round" into "roundness," and so on, and dispense altogether with the subject-predicate form of sentence. In this way they get rid, not of linguistic unknowables, in ordinary language (which has none), but of the pseudo unknowables, the introduced metaphysical subjects of the substratum language. Instead of having philosophical sentences like "The x is white," they have philosophical sentences like "Whiteness is here," or "Whiteness, here, now."

Entailment and
Necessary Propositions

C. LEWY

Consider the following two propositions: (A) "The proposition that there is nobody who is a brother and is not male is necessary," and (B) "There is nobody who is a brother and is not male." It is, I think, obvious that (A) entails (B): if the proposition that there is nobody who is a brother and is not male is necessary, it follows, of course, that there is nobody who is a brother and is not male. But does (B) entail (A)? This is the main question I wish to discuss, although I am afraid that my answer to it may well be wrong.

Now when I ask whether (B) entails (A), I am not using "entails" to mean "strictly implies": if I were so using it, then in order to shew that (B) entails (A), it would be enough to shew that (A) is itself a necessary proposition: for a necessary proposition is strictly implied by *any* proposition. But I am not using "entails" in this way. I am so using it that in order that P should entail Q, it is not enough, though it is necessary, that P should strictly imply Q. In order that P should entail Q, in this use of "entails," it is also necessary, though it is not enough, (1) that the propositional function "R counts in favour of P" should strictly imply the propositional function "R counts in favour of Q," and (2) that the propositional function "R counts against Q" should strictly imply the propositional function "R counts against P." In other words, in order that P should entail Q, in this use of "entails," it is not enough that P should strictly imply Q: it is also necessary, but not enough, that the proposition, with regard to any evidence R, that R counts in favour of P, should strictly imply the proposition that R counts in favour of Q, and that the proposition, with regard to any evidence R, that R counts against Q, should strictly imply the proposition that R counts against P. And this can also be expressed, more simply though less unambiguously, by saying that in order that P should entail Q, in this use of "entails," it is necessary, first, that any evidence which counts in favour of P should also count in favour of Q, and, secondly, that any evidence which counts against Q should also count against P.

Both (1) and (2) are necessary conditions for the truth of the assertion that P entails Q, althougm their conjunction is still not a sufficient condition; but neither (1) nor (2) is a necessary condition for the truth of the assertion that P strictly implies Q: for the truth of *this* assertion (1) by itself is sufficient, and (2) by itself is sufficient: hence, neither (1) nor (2) is necessary.

Perhaps the force of these two conditions will become clearer if we apply them to some examples. Consider the propositions: (A) "The proposition that there is nobody who is a brother and is not male is necessary," and (C) "There is nobody who is a sister and is not female." It is clear that (C) is necessary; hence, it is strictly implied by (A) and by any other proposition. But it is not *entailed* by (A), in my use of "entails": for it is not the case that the propositional function "R counts in favour of (A)" strictly implies the propositional function "R counts in favour of (C)." There are clearly evidential propositions which do count in favour of (A), but do not count at all in favour of (C): there is clearly no contradiction in saying, "The evidence at our disposal counts in favour of supposing that the proposition that there is nobody who is a brother and is not male is necessary; but it is quite irrelevant to the truth or falsehood of the proposition that there is nobody who is a sister and is not female." Of course, the propositional function "R counts against (C)" does strictly imply the propositional function "R counts against (A)": since (C) is necessary, the propositional function "R counts against (C)" is self-contradictory, and therefore strictly implies any propositional function whatever. In other words, the condition (2) is satisfied, and therefore (A) strictly implies (C); but the condition (1) is not satisfied, and therefore (A) does not *entail* (C).

Let us now take another example. Consider the following two

propositions: (D) "There is somebody who is a brother and is not male," and (E) "Cambridge is larger than London." It is clear that (D) is self-contradictory: hence, it strictly implies (E) and any other proposition. But it does not *entail* (E), in my use of "entails": for whilst the propositional function "R counts in favour of (D)" does strictly imply the propositional function "R counts in favour of (E)"—since the first function is self-contradictory—the propositional function "R counts against (E)" does not strictly imply the propositional function "R counts against (D)." There is no contradiction in saying, "The evidence at our disposal counts against supposing that Cambridge is larger than London, but it is quite irrelevant to the truth or falsehood of the proposition that there is somebody who is a brother and is not male." In other words, whilst the condition (1) is satisfied in the present case, the condition (2) is not satisfied.

This explanation of my use of "entails" is, of course, incomplete; but it does, I think, succeed in distinguishing entailment from strict implication; and it does this not merely by stating—as has often been done—that strict implication, whilst a necessary condition for entailment, is not a sufficient condition, but also by giving two further conditions which are necessary as well.

It is clear, then, that we cannot shew that (B) entails (A) merely by shewing that (A) is necessary. But the question whether (A) is necessary is important because unless (A) *is* necessary, (B) *cannot* entail it. For (B) is clearly necessary, and a necessary proposition cannot entail a proposition which is not necessary. This, I think, would be generally admitted; and one way of shewing it, though not the only one, is this. If a necessary proposition, P, entailed a contingent proposition, Q, of course, the negation of Q would have to entail the negation of P: but if Q is contingent, then the negation of Q is also contingent; and if P is necessary, then the negation of P is self-contradictory. Hence, if the negation of Q entailed the negation of P, it would follow that a contingent proposition entailed a self-contradictory proposition. But it is quite clear that if a proposition, say *not-Q*, which appeared to be contingent, entailed a self-contradictory proposition, this would provide a conclusive proof that it was itself self-contradictory, and thus that its negation, Q, was necessary.

It is clear, therefore, that (B) cannot entail (A), unless (A) is itself necessary. I think, however, that (A) *is* necessary, and I think I can shew that it is. But before doing this it may be worth while to mention one argument which seems to me to be fallacious. It has sometimes been said that if P entails Q and Q is necessary, it follows that P is also necessary: in other words, it has been said that a contingent proposition cannot entail a necessary proposition—that a necessary proposition can be entailed only by a necessary proposition. And if this were true, then it would follow, of course, that if (A) entails (B) and (B) is necessary, (A) is also necessary. But as I shall try to shew in the course of the present paper, this is *not* true: hence, to argue that (A) is necessary because there is a necessary proposition which is entailed by it would be fallacious. I think, however, that it is possible to shew that (A) is necessary in the following way. Consider the two propositions: (F) "The last proposition asserted by John before he left the room was not a necessary proposition," and (G) "The last proposition asserted by John before he left the room was not the proposition that there is nobody who is a brother and is not male." It seems to me that the first proposition entails the second: that we can truly say, using the expression "logically follows" quite correctly, "If (F) is the case, then it logically follows that (G) is the case." But if (A) were contingent this would be wrong, and we should have to say, "If (F) is the case, *and* it is also the case that the proposition that there is nobody who is a brother and is not male is necessary, then it logically follows that (G) is the case." Perhaps there is something wrong with this argument; but I can't see *what* is wrong with it, and in any case I have another argument which also seems to me to shew that (A) is necessary. It is briefly this. So far as I can see, in order to find out whether (A) is true, there is no need to make any empirical inquiry: we can find out the truth of (A) simply by *reflecting* on (A)—just as we can find out the truth of (B) by reflecting on (B), and the truth of *any* necessary proposition by reflecting on that proposition. And if this is so, then I think it *follows* that (A) is necessary: if it were not necessary, some empirical evidence would clearly be needed to establish its truth.

Finally, perhaps one could shew that (A) is necessary also in this way. If (A) is *not* necessary, it must, of course, be contingent. But to suppose that (A) is contingent is to suppose that it is logically possible that (A) should have been false: in other words, to suppose that (A) is contingent is to suppose that it is logically possible that the proposition "There is nobody who is a brother and is not male," although it is in fact necessary, should not have been necessary. But is this logically possible? I do not think so. It is obviously possible that the *sentence*

"There is nobody who is a brother and is not male" should have been used to express a contingent proposition and not a necessary one. But, if it had been so used, it would follow, I think, that it was not used to express the proposition that there is nobody who is a brother and is not male. It is quite true that the proposition "The proposition expressed by the sentence 'There is nobody who is a brother and is not male' is necessary" is not necessary; but this is not the same proposition as (A): it neither entails (A) nor is entailed by it.

Thus one argument against supposing that (B) entails (A), namely, the argument that whilst (B) is necessary (A) is contingent, is disposed of. And before considering another argument against this supposition, I should like to digress for a moment in order to explain why I think that a contingent proposition *can* entail a necessary proposition (in the sense in which "entails" does not mean "strictly implies"), although a necessary proposition cannot entail a contingent proposition. Consider the following two propositions: (H) "The proposition that there is nobody who is French and is not under fifty years of age is not necessary," and (J) "There is somebody who is French and is not under fifty years of age." It seems to me that if (A) is necessary, then (H) is also necessary: the reasons which I have given in favour of supposing (A) to be necessary apply also, *mutatis mutandis,* to (H). In other words, if to say of a proposition which is necessary *that* it is necessary is to make a necessary proposition, then to say of a proposition which is not necessary *that* it is not necessary is also to make a necessary proposition. It is clear, however, that (H) is entailed by (J); and since (J) is contingent, it follows that a contingent proposition can entail a necessary proposition. And I think, further, that this will also follow if we suppose (H) to be contingent: for if (H) is contingent, (A) must also, I think, be contingent; and yet (A) certainly entails (B), and (B) is certainly necessary. I think, therefore, that a necessary proposition *can* be entailed by a contingent proposition, although it is not the case that a necessary proposition is entailed by *any* contingent proposition, and still less by any proposition whatever: for instance, (H), although necessary, is certainly not entailed by the proposition "There is somebody who is English and is not under fifty years of age." And I think, similarly, that a self-contradictory proposition *can* entail one which is not self-contradictory, although it is not the case that a self-contradictory proposition entails any proposition whatever. For let us consider the proposition (K) "The proposition that there is nobody

who is French and is not under fifty years of age is necessary." If (H) is
necessary, then (K) is self-contradictory: more generally, if to say of a
proposition which is not necessary *that* it is not necessary is to make a
necessary proposition, then to say of a proposition which is not necessary that it *is* necessary is to make a self-contradictory proposition. Yet
(K), although self-contradictory, does, I think, entail the proposition
"There is nobody who is French and is not under fifty years of age," a
proposition which is false but *not* self-contradictory. At the same time,
(K) does not entail the proposition (L) "There is nobody who is English and is not under fifty years of age." For here, whilst our condition
(1) is satisfied, our condition (2) is not satisfied: the propositional function "*R* counts against (L)" does not strictly imply the propositional
function "*R* counts against (K)."

Let us now return to the question whether (B) entails (A). I have
criticized *one* argument purporting to shew that this entailment does
not hold; but there is another argument which leads to the same conclusion and which we must now discuss. This argument is as follows.
It may be said that (A) is a proposition *about* a proposition: it is a
proposition about the proposition (B), to the effect that (B) is necessary. But (B) itself is not *about* a proposition: (B) is simply the proposition that there is nobody who is a brother and is not male. We may
call (B) a "first-order" proposition, and (A) a "second-order" proposition. And it may be said that whilst a second-order proposition can
entail a first-order proposition, a first-order proposition cannot entail a
second-order proposition.

Now I see no objection to saying that whilst (A) is *about* a proposition (in some sense of "about"), (B) is not; and if this is all that is
meant by saying that (A) is a second-order proposition, whilst (B) is a
first-order proposition, I see no objection to using these expressions.
But if we do use them in this way, then it seems to me that the principle that a first-order proposition cannot entail a second-order proposition is simply false. For if (A) is a second-order proposition, so is the
proposition (M) "The proposition that London is larger than Cambridge is true." Yet it is certainly entailed by (N) "London is larger
than Cambridge," which is a first-order proposition. Of course, this
does not shew that (B) entails (A): but it shews that a first-order
proposition *can* entail a second-order proposition, and that therefore
the principle under discussion is false.

There is one other point in this connexion which I should like to discuss. It may be said that (B) cannot entail (A) because (A) contains the concept of necessity and (B) does not contain it. Now if "containing the same concepts" (however this may be defined) is a necessary condition for identity of propositions, and if (A) does contain a concept or concepts which (B) does not contain, then it will follow, of course, that (A) and (B) are not one and the same proposition. But even if (A) and (B) are not one and the same proposition, it does not follow that they are not logically equivalent: for it may just as well be said that whilst (M) contains the concept of truth, (N) does not contain it, and that therefore (M) and (N) are not one and the same proposition; yet it is quite certain that (M) and (N) *are* logically equivalent.

Perhaps, however, it may be claimed that, unlike (A), (M) is *not* a second-order proposition, and that therefore the fact that (M) is entailed by (N) does not shew that a second-order proposition can be entailed by a first-order proposition. For it has often been said that the word "true," at least in certain contexts, is "redundant" and can be "eliminated"; and perhaps it may be said that the word "necessary" is never redundant and can never be eliminated. But in the sentence expressing (M), the word "true" is certainly not redundant in the sense that we could cross it out without producing nonsense; and if by saying that it is redundant, one means merely that (M) and (N) are logically equivalent, then *if* (A) and (B) are logically equivalent, the word "necessary," in the sentence expressing (A), is redundant in precisely the same sense. Similarly, if by saying that the word "true," in the sentence expressing (M), is redundant, one means that (M) and (N) are one and the same proposition, then *if* (A) and (B) are one and the same proposition, the word "necessary," in the sentence expressing (A), is again redundant in precisely the same sense. We cannot therefore assume, without begging the question, that whilst the word "true" in the former sentence is redundant, the word "necessary" in the latter sentence is not redundant; and hence, we cannot maintain, without begging the question, that whilst (A) *is* a second-order proposition, (M) is *not* a second-order proposition.

There are, of course, important differences between our use of the word "true" and our use of the word "necessary." One such difference, especially important in the present connexion, is this. If in the sentence "The proposition that London is larger than Cambridge is true," we replace the sentence "London is larger than Cambridge" by any other sentence, then the proposition expressed by the *whole* new sentence will be logically equivalent to that expressed by the new component sentence. But if in the sentence "The proposition that there is nobody who is a brother and is not male is necessary," we replace the sentence "there is nobody who is a brother and is not male" by the sentence "there is nobody who is a brother and is not bald," the proposition expressed by the *whole* new sentence will certainly not be logically equivalent to that expressed by the new component sentence. Hence, it is certainly that case that whilst the word "true" may be said to be redundant, in a certain sense, in *all* instances of a certain type of context, the word "necessary" is not so redundant. But the fact that the proposition "There is nobody who is a brother and is not bald" does not entail the proposition "The proposition that there is nobody who is a brother and is not bald is necessary"—and that therefore the word "necessary" in the last sentence is in no sense redundant—this does not seem to me to shew that (B) does not entail (A), and that therefore the word "necessary," in the sentence expressing (A), is not redundant. For from the fact that a *contingent* proposition of the form "There is nothing which has ϕ and lacks ψ" does not entail the corresponding proposition of the form "The proposition that there is nothing which has ϕ and lacks ψ is necessary"—from this it in no way follows that a *necessary* proposition of the first form does not entail the corresponding proposition of the second form.

Yet I think there *is* a good reason for supposing that (B) does not entail (A), and it is this. I said at the beginning of this paper that I am so using "entails" that, in order that P should entail Q, it must be the case (1) that the function "R counts in favour of P" strictly implies the function "R counts in favour of Q" and (2) that the function "R counts against Q" strictly implies the function "R counts against P." And it seems to me that the first of these two conditions is not satisfied in our case. In other words, I think we can imagine evidence which would count in favour of (B), but would not count in favour of (A). For let us suppose that there is nobody who is a *sibling* and is not male: the proposition "There is nobody who is a sibling and is not male" is a contingent proposition which happens to be false; and I am simply imagining that it is true. For instance, we can imagine that, because of some odd law of nature, if a woman's first child is female, she can have no other children, whilst if her first child is male, all her subsequent children, if any, are also male. And we can also imagine that, in these circumstances, the word "sibling" still retains its present meaning and that people still envisage the possibility of *female* siblings. All this seems to me to be fully imaginable. But now the proposition "There is nobody who is a sibling and is not male" does seem to me to count in favour of (B), but not at all in favour of (A): it is, I think, quite irrelevant to the truth or falsehood of (A). And that the proposition "There is nobody who is a sibling and is not male" does count in favour of (B) can be seen by noticing that we can say, quite correctly, "If there is nobody who is a sibling and is not male, then there is nobody who is a brother and is not male." And we can say, also quite correctly, "If there is nobody who is a sibling and is not male, then it *must* be the case that there is nobody who is a brother and is not male." But it would be quite absurd to say, "If there is nobody who is a sibling and is not male, then the proposition that there is nobody who is a brother and is not male is necessary." And it would also be quite absurd to say, "If there is nobody who is a sibling and is not male, then it *must* be the case that the proposition that there is nobody who is a brother and is not male is necessary." And further, we can, I think, also say, quite correctly, "That there is nobody who is a sibling and is not male provides no reason at all for supposing that the proposition that there is nobody who is a brother and is not male is necessary."

But now if I am right in thinking that the proposition "There is nobody who is a sibling and is not male" counts in favour of (B) but does not count in favour of (A), then it follows that (B) does not entail (A). And if so, then an assertion which is frequently made, namely, the assertion that every necessary proposition is either itself an entailment proposition or is logically equivalent to an entailment proposition, is simply untrue. For (B) is certainly a necessary proposition; it is not itself an entailment proposition; and if it is not logically equivalent to (A), it cannot be logically equivalent to the proposition "The proposition that somebody is a brother entails the proposition that that person is male." Also if (B) does not entail (A), there follows another consequence which seems to me to be of some importance. It is sometimes maintained that to say of a necessary proposition that it is true entails that it is necessarily true; and that therefore the use of the word "true," when it is applied to necessary propositions, is different from the use of this word when it is applied to contingent propositions. But if I am right in thinking that (B) does not entail (A), then to say of a necessary proposition that it is true does *not* entail that it is necessarily true, and there is therefore no reason for supposing that the word "true" is ordinarily used in two different ways. For it is quite clear that (B) is logically equivalent to (B') "The proposition that there is nobody who is a brother and is not male is true." Hence, if (B) does not entail (A), it follows that (B') does not entail (A).

II

There is one other question which I should like to discuss, although I am not at all certain that I can do so satisfactorily. I have pointed out that, although our two conditions, (1) and (2), are *necessary* for the truth of the assertion that P entails Q, their conjunction is not a *sufficient* condition. And that this is so can be seen quite easily. The first condition enables us to exclude those strict implications the truth of which is due merely to the necessity of their consequents; in other words, if one proposition strictly implies another, merely because the latter is necessary, then the first condition assures us that the former proposition does not *entail* the latter. The second condition, on the other hand, enables us to exclude those strict implications the truth of which is due merely to the self-contradictoriness of their antecedents; in other words, if one proposition strictly implies another, merely because the former is self-contradictory, then the second condition assures us that the former proposition does not *entail* the latter. It follows that the conjunction of (1) and (2) will exclude those strict implications the truth of which is due merely to the necessity of their consequent or merely to the self-contradictoriness of their antecedents. But our conjunction will *not* exclude those strict implications the truth of which is due merely to the necessity of their consequents *and* the self-contradictoriness of their antecedents. Let us take some examples. I have pointed out that the proposition "There is somebody who is a brother and is not male" does not entail the proposition "Cambridge is larger than London," since here the second condition fails to be satisfied. And we can easily see, also, that the proposition "London is the capital of England" does not entail the proposition "There is nobody who is a brother and is not male," for here the first condition fails to be satisfied. But now consider the two propositions which I have labelled (D) and (C), namely, the propositions (D) "There is somebody who is a brother and is not male" and (C) "There is nobody who is a sister and is not female." Here *both* our conditions are satisfied: the function "R counts in favour of (D)" strictly implies the function "R counts in favour of (C)"; and the function "R counts against (C)" strictly implies the function "R counts against (D)." Yet I certainly do not wish to say that (D) entails (C) or that (C) follows from (D). I do not wish to discuss here whether or not there is *an* ordinary sense of "follows from" in which it is correct to say that a necessary proposition follows from any proposition whatever; but I am quite certain that there is no ordinary sense of this phrase in which, whilst it is *not* correct to say that a necessary proposition follows from any proposition whatever, yet it *is* correct to say that (C) follows from (D). I think, therefore, that if anyone maintained not only that (1) and (2) are *necessary* conditions for the truth of the assertion that P entails Q, but also that their conjunction is a *sufficient* condition, he would certainly not be using "entails" as the converse of "follows from."

Of course, some philosophers may say, and probably will say, that there is no ordinary sense of "follows from" in which it is *not* true that a necessary proposition follows from any proposition whatever: in any ordinary sense of this phrase, they will probably say, if P strictly implies Q, then Q can correctly be said to follow from P. But this, it seems to me, is simply wrong. For consider the following four propositions: "The proposition that there is nobody who is a brother and is not male is necessary"; "There is nobody who is a brother and is not male"; "The proposition that there is nobody who is a sister and is not female is necessary"; and "There is nobody who is a sister and is not female." Assuming that all these propositions are necessary, they are all strictly equivalent; but isn't it clear that there is *some* logical relation which holds between the first proposition and the second and also between the third and the fourth, but which does not hold between the first and the fourth or between the third and the second? It is obvious that the second proposition can correctly be said to follow from the first, and the fourth from the third; but even if it is also correct to say that the fourth proposition follows from the first and that the second follows from the third, is there no sense of "follows from" in which the second does follow from the first, but the fourth does not, and in which the fourth does follow from the third, but the second does not? It seems to me that the answer must be that there is such a sense: and it is *this* sense of "follows from," or "is entailed by," or "is deducible from," that I am trying to explain.

I think it may be worth while, at this point, to draw attention to a passage in Frege's *Grundgesetze der Arithmetik* which seems to me to be of interest in the present connexion. Frege says:

> Wie lautet nun eigentlich der Grundsatz der Identität? etwa so: "Den Menschen ist es im Jahre 1893 unmöglich, einen Gegenstand als von ihm selbst verschieden anzuerkennen" oder so: "Jeder Gegenstand ist mit sich selbst identisch"? Jenes Gesetz handelt von Menschen und enthält eine Zeitbestimmung, in diesem ist weder von Menschen noch von einer Zeit die Rede. Dieses ist ein Gesetz des Wahrseins, jenes eines des menschlichen Fürwahrhaltens. Ihr Inhalt ist ganz verschieden, und sie sind von einander unabhängig, so dass keins von beiden aus dem andern gefolgert werden kann.[1]

Now Frege is considering two propositions, (a) "In 1893 it is impossible for human beings to acknowledge that an object may be different from itself," and (β) "Every object is identical with itself." Assuming that the sentence "Every object is identical with itself" does express a proposition at all, we must, I think, agree that (β) is a "law of truth"; and I don't think that Frege would deny that any proposition which states a "law of truth" must be necessary: clearly, there can be no contingent "laws of truth." But if (β) is necessary, then it is strictly implied by any proposition; hence, assuming that the sentence "In 1893 it is impossible for human beings to acknowledge that an object may be different from itself" also expresses a proposition, we must conclude that (β) is strictly implied by (a). It follows that in supposing that (β) is not deducible from (a) Frege is either guilty of error or is so using "deducible" (or rather the synonymous word in German) that to say that one proposition is deducible from another does *not* mean that the latter strictly implies the former. And if he is so using it, and I think he is, I cannot persuade myself that he is using it incorrectly.

But to return to our question. We have seen that the conditions (1) and (2) are not sufficient for the truth of the assertion that P entails Q, in the use of "entails" we are concerned with. Is it possible to formulate any conditions which would be sufficient? I think it is. It seems to me that, in order that P should entail Q, it is necessary and sufficient (1) that the function "R counts in favour of P" should strictly imply the function "R counts in favour of Q," and (1′) that the function "X knows that the function 'R counts in favour of P' strictly implies the function 'R counts in favour of Q,'" should *not* strictly imply the function "X knows that the function 'R counts in favour of P' is self-

---

[1] I, xviii.

contradictory." To put the point more simply, though less unambiguously: In order that P should entail Q, in this use of "entails," it is sufficient as well as necessary that any evidence which counts in favour of P should also count in favour of Q, *and* that it should be possible for a man to know that this is so without knowing that no evidence *can* count in favour of P—without knowing that to suppose, with regard to any evidence whatever, that it does so count is self-contradictory.

The conjunction of (1) and (1') enables us to exclude not only those strict implications the truth of which is due merely to the necessity of their consequents or merely to the self-contradictoriness of their antecedents, but also those the truth of which is due merely to the necessity of their consequents *and* the self-contradictoriness of their antecedents. And this is so because, whilst (1) excludes strict implications of the first kind, (1') excludes those of the second and third kind.

Further, I think we can also formulate an equivalent set of conditions by reference to our earlier condition (2). We can say that, in order that P should entail Q, it is necessary and sufficient (2) that the function "R counts against Q" should strictly imply the function "R counts against P," and (2') that the function "X knows that the function 'R counts against Q' strictly implies the function 'R counts against P,' " should *not* strictly imply the function "X knows that the function 'R counts against Q' is self-contradictory." More simply, in order that P should entail Q, in this use of "entails," it is sufficient as well as necessary that any evidence which counts against Q should also count against P, *and* that it should be possible for a man to know that this is so without knowing that no evidence *can* count against Q—without knowing that to suppose, with regard to any evidence whatever, that it does so count is self-contradictory.

The conjunction of (2) and (2') also enables us to exclude those strict implications which we wish to exclude, without excluding any which must not be excluded. For whilst (2) excludes those the truth of which is due merely to the self-contradictoriness of their antecedents, (2') excludes those the truth of which is due merely to the necessity of their consequents, and also those the truth of which is due merely to the necessity of their consequents *and* the self-contradictoriness of their antecedents.

Let us now apply these two sets to one of our former examples. Consider again the propositions: (D) "There is somebody who is a brother and is not male," and (C) "There is nobody who is a sister and is not female." I have pointed out that here our earlier conditions, (1) and (2), are both satisfied; but our new conditions are not satisfied: (1') is not satisfied because "X knows that the function 'R counts in favour of (D)' strictly implies the function 'R counts in favour of (C)' "—this does strictly imply that X knows that the function "R counts in favour of (D)" is self-contradictory. In other words, it is impossible to know that the first condition is here fulfilled without also knowing that no evidence *can* count in favour of (D). And similarly, (2') is also not satisfied: it is impossible to know that the function "R counts against (C)" strictly implies the function "R counts against (D)," without knowing that the former function is self-contradictory.

There still remain two points which I must mention. I have been talking about the *conjunction* of (1) and (1'), and about the *conjunction* of (2) and (2'). But so far as I can see, (1) follows from (1'), and (2) follows from (2'). For any proposition of the form "X knows that P" entails the corresponding proposition of the form "It is true that P"; hence, if P is self-contradictory, "X knows that P" is also self-contradictory. And since any true proposition of the form "P strictly implies Q" is necessary, any false proposition of this form is self-contradictory: it follows that unless the function "R counts in favour of P" does strictly imply the function "R counts in favour of Q," the antecedent of (1') will be self-contradictory and will strictly imply the consequent. Hence if (1') is satisfied, (1) must also be satisfied. And a precisely similar argument shews that if (2') is satisfied, (2) must also be satisfied.

I do not know whether all this is correct; and perhaps, even if it is, it will not be found very enlightening. But I must point out that, in any case, one difficulty still remains. Consider the propositions: (S) "There is nothing which is scarlet and is not red," and (T) "There is nothing which is scarlet and is not coloured." Here the condition (1') is satisfied, and of course the condition (2') is also satisfied. And I think it would be perfectly correct to say that (S) entails (T), or that (T) logically follows from (S). But although this would be perfectly correct, it would *not* be correct to say that (S) *by itself* entails (T) or that (T) logically follows from (S) *alone*. It is quite clear, I think, that (S) *by itself* does not entail (T), although the conjunction of (S) and (U) "There is nothing which is red and is not coloured" does, by itself, entail (T). Of course, it may be said that if (S) does not, by itself, entail (T), then "My tie is red" does not, by itself, entail "My tie is coloured"; and it may therefore be said that if what we wish to explain is that sense of "entails" in which "My tie is red" *can* be said to entail "My tie is coloured," then it is no objection to our explanation that it compels us to say that (S) entails (T). But this, I think, would be wrong. For it seems to me that "My tie is red" can be said, quite correctly, not only to entail "My tie is coloured," but also to entail it by itself; yet although (S) can be said, quite correctly, to entail (T), it cannot be said to entail it by itself. I think, therefore, that there are at least two different ordinary uses of "(logically) entails" and of "(logically) follows from"; and what I have said gives an account only of the wider of these two uses. I am afraid I do not see quite clearly how to explain the narrower use.

Ethics and the Ceremonial Use of Language

MARGARET MACDONALD

When men take an oath, deliver a verdict, recite a creed, utter a curse, or cast a spell, they are using forms of speech much older than those of dispassionate narrative or scientific discourse. For oaths, curses, judgments, incantations, and similar utterances are not designed for the disinterested statement of fact. They exemplify a use of language not as a vehicle of information about nature, but as, itself, one of the powers of nature. The invention of writing and general literacy disguise from us that words are primarily breath, and breath, like steam, can be used as well as escape.

But what have speculations about the primitive uses of language to do with philosophy? It is, I conceive, at least one of the tasks of ethics, or metamorals, to determine the logical type of moral judgments. There is, in common use, a set of sentences containing the words "good," "bad," "right," "wrong," "ought," "duty" with a peculiar significance. What do such sentences say and how do they say it?

Given such a set of any common-sense utterances a philosopher may begin with internal comparison. He may distinguish particular from general assertions and the logical dependence of some upon others. He may try, by definition, to reduce the number of ultimate words. He may, e.g., define "right" and "ought" in terms of "good," or "good" in terms of "ought." He may thus simplify and systematize his data. But if he is philosophically puzzled, this purely formal procedure will not satisfy him. For however internally organised, the class will still present peculiarities. At best, there will remain an undefined term and the type of sentence in which it occurs. This must finally be interpreted by comparison with sentences outside the set. Hence the use of models. For most ethical theories are attempts to show that moral judgments function in a manner logically similar to some other type of sentence, by which they may be ultimately understood.

Every ethical theory or any model by which moral judgments are interpreted must account, I think, for at least the following characteristics of these judgments, as ordinarily used. For as so used they are certainly (1) normative, (2) authoritative, (3) public,[1] (4) indicative in grammatical form, (5) practical. This is, doubtless, not an exhaustive characterisation but I think it includes the most important features and those with which most ethical theories have tried to come to terms, though none has completely succeeded.

Nor have I a perfect alternative to offer. I do not lament this, however, since I believe that past theories have been based on a misconception of the nature of philosophical analysis. For, like most traditional philosophical theories, they seem to have exalted some one feature of a group of sentences, e.g., sentences expressing moral judgments and to have taken as model another type of sentence exemplifying this feature with which type the original group of sentences is then identified. The subsequent attempt to construe the remaining features in terms of the model has resulted either in sheer falsity or unintelligible metaphysics.

It is unlikely that any type of sentence can be a perfect model for any other type. If it could they would not be different types of sentence. Is the conclusion, then, that nothing can be said except that moral judgments are moral judgments, general propositions are general propositions, laws are laws, statements about material objects are just statements about material objects, everything is what it is and not another thing? That the business of the philosopher is to show that philosophical theories, including moral theories, are mere linguistic confusions? This is certainly a useful move in some contexts, but it does not, nevertheless, exhaust the philosopher's task. For the comparison of different types of utterance is illuminating, not because it

---

[1] I prefer this to the word "objective" for reasons which will appear later. It is intended to signify that moral judgments are used by us with something like common reference.

shows that one is exactly like another, but that it may be like a great many others in different respects. The philosopher's temptation is to simplify. But, as Wittgenstein once said, "It can never be our task to reduce anything to anything else." That may be the business of scientists; the philosopher's task is pure description.

There are, perhaps, family likenesses among *all* our utterances; some more, some less: even the notion of a "type" may be vague. Nevertheless, we do seem to start with relatively isolable groups which cause philosophical puzzlement. The treatment of this by philosophical analysis is not, however, the reduction of the complex to a set of simple elements, I suggest, but the disentangling of the complex by a variety of different comparisons, without identification. The result is more like (but, again, not *exactly like*) the same scene painted by Constable, Cézanne, and Picasso, or the character of Hamlet portrayed from Burbage to Olivier.

Whether this constitutes a satisfactory "explanation" of puzzling features depends, I suppose, upon interest and temperament and perhaps, also, on the use of the word "explanation" itself. For, in ordinary life, "explanation" is demanded of what is unclear or imperfectly understood. Moral judgments, however, are not a whit less clear or less well understood than those with which they are compared in a philosophical analysis. We have used them, perfectly correctly, from childhood. But, just as a word which we know how to spell and have written quite correctly suddenly "looks queer," so may any sentence or group of sentences, in ordinary language, to a philosophic frame of mind. "Why should it be so spelt?" and "What exactly are we saying by these sentences?" we exclaim, as if the cataract had been removed, or the veil of the familiar indecently withdrawn. It is then no answer to be told, "Well, it just *is* spelt like that" or "Don't be silly, you know quite well what moral judgments say." The philosopher is rightly unimpressed by the sensible cave men who have never seen the sun, the model of reality. Plato was quite right; the answer is found in more reality. The spelling of one word is not more strange than that of any of its fellows. A glance at its neighbours soon restores a momentary loss of faith. Similarly, a sentence, or type of sentence, which causes puzzlement may be compared with many others, in order to reveal, without simplifying, its complex nature. This procedure may likewise restore the security of the philosophically disturbed and so constitute for them an "explanation" of its apparently bewildering features. Only the philosophically disturbed, however, can judge whether this procedure will allay their disturbance and so constitute an "explanation" of the puzzling.

Moral Judgements and Truth

It is perhaps because philosophers are intellectually sophisticated persons that most ethical theories have tried to interpret moral judgments by analogy with factual statements. As already suggested, moral judgments are usually expressed by indicative sentences. They appear to state, e.g., "Courage is a virtue"; "Cruelty is evil"; "Lying is wrong"; "Men ought to be treated justly." Moral imperatives are justified only by corresponding indicative assertions. It is because false witness is wrong that men are commanded to abstain from it, because justice is right that the laws enforce fair dealing. In many other uses indicative sentences state what is true or false. They are the vehicles of factual communication, the means by which information is preserved and transmitted. I include among them, for this purpose, the formulas of mathematics and logic as well as natural laws and descriptions of empirical facts. An indicative statement of fact thus tends to be for most philosophers the paradigm of significant utterance. Moral judgments are certainly significant. To understand them, therefore, the philosopher asks, "About what subject matter do these judgments inform us?" "What facts do they state?" The answers may be roughly divided —since detailed treatment of each is impossible—into (a) naturalistic and (b) nonnaturalistic. The first identify moral judgments with a species of biological, sociological, psychological, or physical generalisations; the second, with statements about a special kind of subject matter called Value constituting a region of fact beyond the evidence of sense perception and known only by intellectual intuition.

For both types of theory, moral judgments are part of a public language having a common reference about which it is theoretically possible to reach agreement, either by sense perception or reason. They are true or false, independent of individual hopes, wishes, or feelings. They emphasise that personal desires can no more change an obligation than alter the movement of the tides. The model preserves the *hardness* and inescapability of moral judgments, their independence of personal preferences. For in these respects they do resemble factual statements.

But not in others. It is generally agreed that naturalistic theories of morals fail to account for either their normative or their authoritative character. Assertions about what exists are not simply identifiable with those about what is good. Nor does natural law *oblige* us to perform any action—not even a law connecting feelings of approval with such action. Nonnaturalistic theories try to remedy these defects, while keeping the statement model, by interpreting normative judgments as statements about norms or values as a peculiar kind of fact or constituent of facts. The normative character of moral judgments sets them apart from all empirical generalisations about verifiable fact. They have a special, almost mysterious, character. This is preserved if they are statements about what does not exist in space or time[2] from which also they derive authority. The result, however, is a queer distortion. I shall not enter into the mysteries of the realm of intelligible Values, for in the absence of any independent evidence of its existence, it seems more plausible to conclude that philosophers have misused a model than discovered a Newfoundland.

But if moral judgments are indicative sentences which state what is true or false, this conclusion will seem arbitrary and due merely to a dislike of metaphysics. There is, however, another alternative, viz., that not all indicative sentences are statements. Moral judgments do not assert what is true or false of natural fact. That they do so of nonnatural fact is obscure and unplausible. I suggest that there are no facts of which they are true or false, for they are not true or false at all. They, therefore, have no subject matter.

Philosophers assume that the plain man would be shocked to learn that no moral judgments are true. I have never seen this defended by any examination of ordinary moral discourse. It is at least disputable.

We often ask questions about morals. The philosopher knows that the proper answer to a question is a statement. The object of questioning is to learn the truth and to become better informed. If this is correct then "Is *p*?" and "Is *p* true?" are equivalent. And so they are in many uses. "Are prices rising?" and "Is it true that prices are rising?" differ in some important respects, no doubt, but are equivalent in meaning. At least, they are equally natural and intelligible forms of question. So are "Was Bernadotte murdered?" and "Is it true that Bernadotte was murdered?" It is also sensible to ask "Is murder wrong?" Now, however, the parallel seems to fail. For it does not seem equally sensible to ask "Is it true that murder is wrong?" or "Is it

2 Cp. Moore, *Principia Ethica* (1903), pp. 40, 41.

true that he ought not to have been murdered?" These forms are quite unnatural and, I suggest, would puzzle the plain man. For he does not use them. The example selected, however, may be thought tendentious. No one would question that murder is wrong. Therefore, it seems silly to ask whether this is true. Then consider more disputable examples. "Is it a duty to return good for evil?" "Is adultery wrong?" Would these be normally questioned in the form "Is it true that . . ."? I think no plain man would so question them. Nor would he naturally assert that "It is true that debts ought to be paid" or "It is true that nothing is worth the sacrifice of intellectual integrity" or so formulate any other moral judgment.

No one who is deliberating about a moral issue would describe himself as trying to discover the *truth* about what is right or wrong. He is trying to find out what *is* right or wrong; but if he were asked "And how much more have you discovered since last week about whether you ought to cheat the revenue?" he would rightly dismiss such a question as ignorant or frivolous. For he is not seeking information, but trying to make up his mind, to reach a decision about what is required of him. When he knows all the relevant natural facts, there are not some more nonnatural varieties which will solve the moral problem.

True replies to requests for information increase knowledge, and a person is well informed in proportion to the number of true propositions he knows about a subject matter. If then we are told that Professor Smith is a very learned man, it would be natural to ask "In what subject?" We should, however, be very surprised by the reply "Moral duties" or "What is good and evil" or "He is a great authority on right and wrong." I think the hearer would be inclined to retort "But aren't we all?" "In what does his superiority consist?" "Is he a very good man?" And if the reply were "No, he is very vicious, but morally very learned," we should surely be indignant or amused. This must be a bad joke. If, however, moral judgments are statements of any variety of fact, it should be possible to become well-informed, expert in this subject. Not even an intuitionist moral philosopher claims to be a greater moral expert than his fellows. For no sane person admits that he is incapable of knowing what he ought to do, though he may cheerfully confess to being quite incapable of understanding higher mathematics or the minutiae of classical scholarship.

No chairs are endowed or research grants solicited for investigations to extend moral knowledge. True, there are professors of moral phi-

losophy; but none, so far as I know, has yet announced the discovery
of a new moral law or unearthed another intrinsic value. Nor do they
consider this to be their task. But, why not, if the appropriate field of
fact exists?

Finally, that the statement model is inadequate is shown by our use
of the phrase "moral judgment." The findings of scientists, historians,
policemen, and other informed persons are reported in propositions or
statements. No one, however, normally speaks of "moral statements"
or "moral propositions" but of "moral judgments." Philosophers sometimes talk of the propositions of ethics or ethical statements, but these
terms refer to the language of ethical theory or metamorals. They are
technical, not ordinary, expressions. A parallel may be drawn with legal
usage. The deliberations of a court, like our own deliberations about
conduct, issue in judgments, not statements. Neither make disclosures.

But if moral judgments cannot be identified with any sort of factual
statement, is there another model which will completely illuminate
their usage? One has recently been suggested by the emotive theory of
ethics.[3]

Moral Judgments and Emotion

This view recognises that language has at least two functions: to
describe facts and to express feelings about them and what are, rather
vaguely, called "attitudes" towards them. Informative statement is descriptive. Moral judgments are descriptive so far as they inform. "You
ought not to have broken that promise" tells that a promise was made
and broken, but adds what does not inform, that the breach *ought not*
to have occurred. This *expresses*, but does not *state* the speaker's moral
disapproval of the action. It seeks also to change the delinquent's attitude so that he will not default again. The object of normative speech
is to express and influence nonintellectual attitudes, to improve morals,
not minds. Moral judgments may be better understood as poems than
as scientific discourses. Their model is the lyric, not the lecture. They
address the heart rather than the head.

Questions in morals are thus not requests for information but for
guidance about the cultivation of feelings, sentiments, dispositions by
the questioner. They are not asked from scientific curiosity, but from

---

3 Cp. A. J. Ayer, *Language, Truth and Logic* (1936), ch. vi; C. L. Stevenson, *Ethics
and Language* (1944).

anxiety about a personal state. Similarly, moral judgments are not colourless statements but utterances alive with personal acceptance or repudiation. Disputation in morals is not confined to the polite exchange of factual evidence but is dramatic dialogue used with all the devices of rhetoric to affirm, persuade, and convert. We are not satisfied merely to state that an action or policy is unjust. By calling it *wrong* we vigorously denounce it, thus expressing our own repugnance and seeking to persuade others to share our attitude.

This model certainly restores much of the flavour of moral judgments. To say that things are valued is not to state another fact about them, not even the fact that human beings feel concern for them, but rather to *show* that such concern *is* their value. It also rightly emphasises, I think, that moral judgments are more usually, and effectively, spoken than written. Is it not significant that it is always the voice and not the letters and treaties of conscience which admonishes? The ideal of scientific statement is the mathematical equation. I suggest as one reason for this that mathematical formulas are more naturally written or printed than uttered. They thus, quite rightly, exclude personal bias, but also personal concern. A mathematical equation does not lend itself to utterance in provocative, soothing, or indignant tones. So it may as well be written; no one cares. But many typographical devices of italics, exclamation marks, etc., must be employed if moral judgments in print are not to lose half their life.

The emotive theory does not, however, imply that moral judgments are purely irrational exclamations. They are articulate utterances, not mere cries and shouts. Though the head is subordinate, it is not entirely inactive. For expressions of attitudes may be "supported" by other assertions and devices which though they cannot "prove" may yet "persuade" to genuine conviction of superiority. Nevertheless, the perverse may remain unconvinced though neither crazy nor stupid. There are no rules of persuasion as of deductive and inductive argument. Its criterion of validity can be only success.

The theory, too, has the important consequence of connecting the normative character of moral judgments with their *power* to produce effects. It emphasises that moral assertions are never purely theoretical. But it overemphasises emotional effects. Moral judgments, on this view, are like symptoms of a fever with which the infected person may cause an epidemic. But proper isolation may prevent this consequence; the victim's fever will then take its lonely course. Romantic poets cherish their ardour and seek sympathy by lyrical expression. But the duty of fidelity is not a private passion or a fever which I seek to spread. It is an imposition which neither I nor you can morally escape. Moral judgments, like other eloquent expressions, do convey and rouse emotional attitudes but, unlike poems, moral judgments have *authority*. Personal feelings and attitudes have no authority for others. No one else is obliged to heed my approvals and disapprovals. Nor indeed am I obliged to heed them myself any more than I am obliged to feel terror in a burning building. I do, but that is irrelevant.

Moral judgments have a public and impersonal character and carry authority, all of which are absent from expressions of personal attitudes. Their identification with such expressions is, therefore, inadequate. We are concerned about moral issues but we seem forced, rather than choose, to be. The rightness of justice is not *my* attitude, nor its obligation dependent on my choice. Our feelings may be roused and strongly expressed on moral issues, but our feelings do not constitute their morality. Neither do we fuss overmuch about the approval of others, as Stevenson's analysis seems to suggest. "Do approve of this as I do" is the occasional cry of the morally insecure. And this is not because we assume that most people will approve, but because whether they do or not an action is right or wrong, a policy good or evil, an obligation exists or does not. We are all equally constrained. The emotive theory dissolves the hardness of moral judgments into the softness of a romantic preoccupation with a personal gospel and a private missionary society. It is a lucky accident that our gospels sometimes agree and that intercommunion occurs between the one-man sects. This seems an exaggerated moral protestantism.

Finally, moral judgments, unlike poems, do not merely inspire but, in some sense, imply action. Indeed, the relation is closer than that between premises and conclusion in inference. I have not forgotten that, on some versions of the emotive theory, moral judgments issue commands as well as express attitudes. Both are interpretations, however, for a judgment in indicative form is not ostensibly a command. True, there are moral imperatives. They are used when authorities command subjects, parents children, teachers pupils; but outside certain relationships rational adults do not command each other to be moral. To do so would be impertinent. And it is surely absurd, despite Kant, to speak of commanding oneself. The practical force of moral judgments does not then consist in this, that they are disguised commands.

Men made moral judgments long before they formulated scientific laws or expressed their souls in romantic verse. Children learn to respect and deliver such judgments at an earlier age than they become chemists, engineers, or artists. I shall now suggest that there are models other than either descriptive statements or emotive expressions with which they may be compared. I do not, however, wish to identify the use of language to express moral judgments with its use in these forms of utterance but only to suggest that comparison with them may illuminate features which have escaped both too intellectual and too sentimental analyses.

Moral Judgments and Action

There is a use of speech ancillary to the performance of common tasks. Among a group of dockers unloading a ship, miners working a seam, farm labourers haymaking, apart from chaff and chat (itself of unexplored logical interest), there will be speech essential to the task. This may be instruction, warning, announcement; but of whatever form it directs the task and may be as necessary to its efficient performance as the hands and tools of the workers. Their total activity is a complex of words and actions. Illustrations of this are difficult to give in print just because the words perform their function when spoken on the job and are out of work on the printed page. Everyone who has engaged in such tasks, however, knows how much success depends upon verbal interchange. To ask whether, "Look out! It's falling"; "No! The smaller one will do"; "Tip it this way!"; "There is your wagon"; "That's the load now; drive away!" have meaning apart from their roles in the task, the tones in which they are uttered, the effects they produce, is like asking for the function of a battle axe in a museum. Are they not then, it may be asked, mere substitutes for shouts and gestures which might have the same effects? Surely, if they are words and sentences they must be understood and not merely operate? They are very different from pitchforks or battle axes. If they are understood, they must be commands, statements, questions having general significance and not mere ingredients in performances? I suggest that speech so used is not a substitute for animal noises and gestures. Human beings perform their tasks with the help of words and sentences, not mere grunts and shrieks; but their purpose is not to inform or instruct, disinterestedly, but to complete the task. That these words can be used again as part of another task or even independently of any task does not show that they do not have a particular use as part of *this* task or that one important function of language is not to form part of practical tasks. They are then used to get work done in company with other workers. It is absurd to ask whether a common task has a common language or whether each worker uses his private jargon.

Another example of this use of words is in drill and training, the result of which is to knit words into a new pattern of behaviour. Words are linked with new processes, are reiterated, emphasised, injected into the training situation so completely that response to them becomes habitual or automatic. "Fire alarm!" is not a piece of news or merely a warning but a verbal signal which works to produce a series of actions from firemen who have been trained to their use. Indeed, an important part of training consists in acquiring the performatory uses of certain words.

Sentences which form part of practical performances have an entirely nontheoretical use. Their users do not speculate or inform for the sake of pure knowledge. Their form may be indicative but their use is quite different from similar sentences in narrative discourse. They tell what is to be done, by whom, how, and when. The question of their truth or falsity hardly arises and when it does is promptly settled. "This hose will do"; "No, it does not reach the roof"; "That case weighs a ton"; "No, look at the scales." It may be logically inappropriate to call such sentences expressions of propositions. They are certainly different from narrative statement.

Performatory sentences may be uttered with feeling. Their function, however, is not to express feeling but to assist a task, though the tone in which the words are uttered and the way in which the task is done may show the feelings of the workers.

Finally, while narrative may be spoken or written, performance is guided only by actual speech. The performers do not write to each other, not even if they are deaf mutes. Manuals of drill and instruction in various trades exist for the use of the literate but these are aids to training, not indispensable for its successful acquisition. It is unlikely, however, that knowledge of general laws and abstract relationships could occur without the invention of writing and special symbolisms. There seems no evidence of the existence of mathematics before the use of graphic symbols. But words are effective in executing a task or acquiring a skill because they are spoken and heard. Speech, not writing, is primarily performatory.

The Language of Rites and Ceremonies

Some performances have the special character of rites and ceremonies. A rite is a series of actions, prescribed by a rule, performed with great attention to form, whose purpose is not purely practical, theoretical, or recreational. Several workers building a boat or a team playing football are not performing a rite or ceremony although their actions are determined by a purpose or governed by rules.

The object of ritual and ceremonial is to give a special character to certain occasions and actions, to set them apart from ordinary life. It is, therefore, a special kind of performance. Language plays an important part in these performances but ritual language differs in function from that of normal intercourse. I shall illustrate this by brief accounts of three forms of ritual language, those of magic, law, and religion.

The ostensible object of a magical rite[4] is to control supernatural power for the benefit of the performers. An indispensable element in this control is the uttering of words. Malinowski records that magical language combines intelligibility with weirdness. Spells and charms are rarely pure gibberish. They usually contain, e.g., ordinary names of the objects to be affected. So far they can be understood. But they are also set apart from normal discourse. They do not occur in conversation. Their exalted character is preserved by various devices. The words are chanted or uttered in a special tone of voice; some may be meaningless; others, with the sentences in which they are used, may be obsolete or of antique grammatical construction. All these combine to give them special *power*. For they are conveyed by the breath into whatever they are required to affect which is thus charged with their life and gives the desired result.

The performers of a rite believe that it can produce this result. Nevertheless, the sentences they use do not function as detached statements of this or any belief. The words *make* the garden fertile or *kill* the enemy; they do not state that these effects usually follow the uttering of such words. They are not causal laws or even particular

---

[4] I am much indebted in the discussions of this section to Malinowski, *Coral Gardens and Their Magic* (1935) and his supplement on the primitive use of language in *The Meaning of Meaning* (1930).

causal propositions. Their meaning just consists in doing what cannot be done by ordinary methods and the common everyday use of language. Thus what is said is less important than that it be said correctly in the form prescribed by tradition. The value of the performance is its ceremonial, not its informative, character.

The results of magic are ardently desired by the performers, but the rite does not express these feelings of its individual participants. Rites are public enactments, not vents for personal emotions. They are common possessions, not private creations. The origins of magic are placed with legendary ancestors whose ceremonies have since been preserved intact. A magician is the vehicle of this tradition, not an individual artist. Rites are thus independent of all particular performers and even of all particular groups of performers. They are neither statements of natural fact nor expressions of personal attitudes.

Anthropologists often tell us how much magic survives in the languages of the most advanced societies. They intend by this to show how very primitive we remain despite our boasts of civilisation. No doubt we are often more foolish than primitive people. But sometimes this criticism is due to the common intellectualist preoccupation with scientific statement. It is, however, just another myth, that the pages of "Nature" or the *Proceedings of the Royal Society* contain the only valid forms of utterance. That our language has practical and ceremonial, as well as scientific, uses is not a mere relic of savagery. For we work, play, and celebrate as well as know. Ceremonial is very widespread and may be essential to social life. It cannot be conducted by scientific discourse. Special forms for its purposes must, therefore, be retained in any language.

Certainly no society can exist without law and justice. A trial conducted by correspondence in which no one was ever *seen* and nothing was *said,* even though all the correspondence were subsequently published, would be an interesting investigation, but a travesty of justice. It is true that in the course of a trial facts are investigated and interpreted according to laws. This might be done in chambers and the result communicated to the Home Secretary—or other appropriate official—as the results of a scientific experiment are communicated to the president of the Royal Society. Why then this parade of accusation, prosecution, defence, verdict, sentence in open court? I suggest that it is because a trial is not merely investigation, interpretation, condemnation or acquittal, but these only according to a proper procedure, a public ritual or ceremony. The accused must be seen and heard by his accusers and judges. He must hear and reply, in person, to their accusations. He must be brought forward to be tried, sentenced or acquitted in person. Even if the accused has fled and is tried in absence the same formalities are observed as if he were present. If the semblance of a *trial* be maintained, he must be represented and some defence made in his name.

A trial, then, is a public, spoken ceremonial whose object is a verdict on the accused. Significantly, it proceeds as a contest between the accused or his representatives and his accusers. Words are the weapons, and words in the final verdict determine victory or defeat. But the battle has its rules and the justice of the outcome is very closely connected with having been reached by the proper ceremony. The practical end of a trial is to determine a breach of law and punish the offender. But the ceremonial does more. It sets the performance apart from common life. By means of it personal conflicts are sublimated into impersonal issues settled by verbal victory. Peace replaces brawling. Ceremony is the majesty of the law and differentiates justice from any mere factual investigation. The verdict and sentence, though related to evidence, are not *conclusions* from it. They may be reversed by another trial. They are effective because pronounced in a setting which gives *authority*. There would be no point in challenging or defying them unless they were binding and must be observed. They are binding as words uttered in a special context which gives them power, akin to that of a magical formula and derived from a similar source, a ceremonial performance.

This, I expect, will be hotly contested as obscurantist distortion! The authority of a judgment derives from the justice of a law and not from the mere accidental ceremonies of its pronouncement. I reply that between law and judgment is procedure. A fair trial according to bad law is better than the summary enforcement of good. For the unregulated implementing of private decisions about just and unjust was the situation which legal ceremony was introduced to remedy.

If judicial procedure derives its authority from the laws it administers, from whence could come the authority of those laws? Again, I think, from another ceremony. Early law claimed the sanction of utterances—very different from common discourse—by divinely inspired or divine kings and heroes. Modern laws issue from legislative assemblies. But legislation is a tissue of verbal ceremonies. The authority of the English Parliament, e.g., derives from the manner of its election and the methods of conducting its business. These are largely traditional ceremonies. They are not determined by the fancies of individual members. Even in an authoritarian state, the Leader must distinguish, by some formalities, laws from other personal decisions. So the authority of law itself is inexplicable without the ceremonies conducted by their characteristic modes of utterance, which attend its introduction.

Ceremony is thus important to the creation and execution of law and, I suggest, constitutes the distinction between an expression of personal opinion or feeling and authoritative pronouncement. The decrees of legislative bodies and the verdicts of courts are not the private beliefs and explosions of M.P.'s, senators, judges, and juries. They transmit the authority of the public performances by which they were reached and on account of this are accepted as binding on those whom they concern. They have the general validity of impersonal, because official, utterances.

Newton was a great scientist; he was also a devout Christian. Did he believe the law of gravitation as he believed the Apostles' Creed? He discovered the first by personal toil; he would have been shocked to be told that anyone thus discovered the second. For the first he chose a formulation and communicated his results to the scientific world. The forms of the second he accepted and repeated as part of the services of the Christian church. When he did so he did not suppose he was learning or teaching others a law of nature. For religious language is not statement of natural fact. Whether or not there are supernatural facts, I suggest that the language of creeds, sacraments, articles of faith, etc., is not used in the manner either of everyday discourse or theoretical statement. Religious services differ from private conversations and scientific conferences. But neither can their utterances be simply labelled "emotive." There are poems of religious emotion and accounts of private mystical experiences. These, however, are not the staples of religious utterance, which are found rather in the common affirmations of the faithful in the public ceremonies of their churches. The poet and mystic, like the scientist, is free to choose the language which describes his experiences. He does not choose the words of the ceremonies by which he publicly affirms his faith. These are, normally, of set, traditional forms, recited, chanted solemnly and impressively, often to the accompaniment of music. They are part of the rite which, whatever else it may be, is certainly a public *act* of adherence to an institution. Ceremonial invests the performance with authority and binds the adherents to whatever further action may be required of them by this allegiance. Religious ceremonies may be performed with emotion, especially in time of persecution, but to relieve feelings is not their object. As in magic and law, ceremonial separates the public, official, authoritative affirmation from private opinion and feeling.

I suggest that to compare moral judgments with performatory and ritual speech may illuminate the impersonal, authoritative, and practical features unaccounted for or distorted in other analyses. I am, however, aware that my suggestions are sketchy and that the differences may be so great as to make the comparison more dangerous than useful. Moral judgments certainly commit their users to do or refrain from certain actions. They do not, however, invariably form part of the performance to which they oblige, for we do not always do as we ought. Nevertheless, as committing, they are more like acts than theoretical statements or lyric verse. Hume made this point long ago: "A promise is *a certain form of words* . . . by which we bind ourselves to the performance of any action" and "by making use of *this form of words* [a man] subjects himself to the penalty of never being trusted again in case of failure."[5] The use of this formula *is* the obligation to perform. Hume goes on to expatiate on this curious situation by comparing a promise with the use of words in the mass and holy orders where they are conceived to change entirely the nature of a substance and even of a human being. These, of course, are examples of ceremonial usage.

Moreover, if moral judgments are like ceremonial utterances, it is not possible to specify the precise ceremonies in which they occur as we can describe those of law courts, parliament, presidential elections, churches, or primitive rites.

It is sometimes useful when making philosophical comparisons to consider how we learned to use puzzling words. We learned to use such words as "red," "sour," "loud" by being presented with perceptible samples which served as ostensive definitions. We learned the use of "feel sick," "feel sleepy," "am depressed" by the occurrence of samples of our own to which we did not need to point. On the statement model of moral judgments, it would seem to follow that we learned moral words as we learned sensory words, though the samples were

---

[5] *A Treatise of Human Nature*, bk. III, pt. II, sec. 5.

nonsensory and presented to an internal, instead of an external, sense. On the emotive view, we learned them in connection with some peculiar inner perturbations. I think, however, that we learned them in neither of these ways. We learned them, mainly, by behaving to others in ways which gained praise or rebuke. Words and actions formed a pattern as in any other task or skill. Thus moral judgments never meant (and do not mean) for us things, qualities, or states, but performances. And the performances were in company. Our morality plays always had (and have) other actors. We performed in a public theatre, not a set of private theatricals. But the play was, and is, not of our choosing.

Moral behaviour is, however, a special sort of skill and its utterances have peculiar significance. To learn cooking, sewing, engineering, football is to learn a fairly definite range of actions which constitute those activities. But to learn to be unselfish, honest, courageous, loyal is to learn tasks of indefinite extent and to be moral in general is a task of absolutely unlimited range. In other words, morality covers the whole of life and may invade every other activity. How then can we liken it to a specific ceremonial performance?

Whenever a thing or action is called good or bad, right or wrong, it is morally evaluated, that is, separated, set apart from the rest. We have rejected as reasons for this that it has a peculiar quality or causes a peculiar state in us. But is it not as if these words cast a spell, invest their objects with something like ceremonial, have ritual significance? The effect of ceremony in the examples examined was just that of separating, setting apart from everyday affairs certain performances. Moral judgments too, then, involve a ceremonial use of language. Moral values are not a peculiar set of objects or emotions, but the ceremonial treatment of a wide variety of natural facts and situations.

To make a mistake in a game and to cheat at a game are not treated as failures on the same level, though the same action may occur in both situations. The first may be a nuisance, but the second will evoke from others something like the ceremony of anathema. To call an action *wrong*, in a characteristic tone of voice, accompanied by frowns, cold-shouldering, and more serious penalties, is not to give a further account of it but to treat it ceremonially and thus to invest the judgment in respect of it with an authority to affect action. This obtains a result not otherwise obtainable. And it could not be obtained by a statement of fact or an expression of personal disapproval. Moral judgments are thus, as it were, impersonal verdicts of a common moral ritual.

This comparison must not be confused with a return to the model of sociological generalization. I am not maintaining that moral judgments are statements of sociological facts, not even facts about moral codes and ceremonies. For they are not statements. Still less am I insisting that the moral codes we accept must be right because they exist. I have no moral axe to grind. This is an attempt at philosophical analysis in a series of metamoral statements, not an essay in sociology or practical morals. What seems plain and must be recognized in any analysis is that our moral judgments are common property. They make no statement of objective fact, but neither are they the expression of personal preferences and feelings. However adopted they claim the allegiance of all moral agents. To use moral words is not merely to entreat your agreement but to expect it if these words are correctly used. For they are the language of a rite in which we are all lifelong performers.

Introspection and Analysis

C. A. MACE

Do I not then believe, after all, in a method of systematically controlled introspection? Very emphatically I do; with all my heart, with all my mind, and with all my strength. My belief in introspection is old enough to have attained its majority; for it was in 1888, when for the first time I was reading James Mill's *Analysis,* that the conviction flashed upon me—"You can test all this for yourself!"—and I have never lost it since.[1]—Edward Bradford Titchener

The troublesome nature of "the problem of introspection" arises from the fact that it is not just one problem, but a tangle of many. Roughly, we have been taught that introspection is a peculiar and distinctive way of observing a peculiar and distinctive set of objects. In introspection we are said to turn round on ourselves and observe our own mental states. The "turning round" is contrasted with the ordinary procedure of making an observation through our senses, and our "mental states" are contrasted with the material objects in the "external world." All this clearly raises both methodological and metaphysical issues. It takes for granted a long and complicated story about the various sorts of things that may be observed, about the ways in which these things may be observed, and

---

[1] *Lectures on the Experimental Psychology of the Thought Processes* (1909), p. 96. Permission to use the quotations occurring in this paper has been given by The Macmillan Company and the estate of the late E. B. Titchener.

about the conditions to which a "scientific" statement must conform.

This long, and very complicated, story begins in the jungle. It began, according to the plausible suggestions of anthropologists, in primitive man's attempts to explain his dreams and other odd phenomena. These explanations in the western world grew into Greek philosophy, which in turn was displaced by the Christian revelation and the interpretations placed upon this revelation by the Fathers of the Church. Even with the emergence and progress of the natural sciences, dreams and the other odd phenomena did not become appreciably easier to explain, and professional philosophers were encouraged to reinterpret the facts in a variety of surprising ways. Common to many forms of philosophical synthesis was the attempt to co-ordinate all the odd phenomena, dreams, hallucinations, mirages, mirror images, and what not, as possessions of the observer, since most of them at least seemed to depend in part on him and his point of view. They seemed to connect themselves in some strange way with his activities and feelings, which "feelings" themselves shared the character of oddness and were difficult to place in the relatively simple and clear-cut picture of the world which progressively emerged from scientific research.

The reflective observer was accordingly encouraged to think of himself, of his palpable bodily self, as inhabited by a ghost—in fact to think of himself as *being* that ghost. He pictured himself the ghost of his own body having as its own immediate environment a ghost of the "external" world.

The story is of course fantastic, but it has left its mark upon nearly every attempt to give a systematic account of the introspective act. The theory of introspection in its most characteristic form is a theory about the way in which a ghost directly observes itself, as contrasted with the way in which it (less directly) observes the outside world through the mediation of the body it inhabits.

The nucleus of fact upon which this elaborate superstructure rests is the fairly obvious fact that there is something distinctive in the situation in which a scientific observer includes himself within his field of observation, when he not only observes the things around him but also observes himself observing them and observes his own reactions to them. He has sources of information about himself over and above his sources of information about other persons. He knows what it is like to feel hot or cold, whereas he can in general only observe other people when they sweat or shiver. It is accordingly very natural to expect that a scientist who is interested in the effects of changes in temperature upon the human organism might learn from his own experiences something that he could not learn so readily from the behaviour of other persons in situations similar to his own. The total field of such possible observations would appear to be extensive. This is the sole but sufficient factual basis for drawing a distinction between "introspection" and "external observation."

So stated, the distinction appears to be only a special case of the general principle that an empirical observation through one of the bodily senses may be supplemented by an empirical observation through another bodily sense. The state of a man's lungs may be observed by the use of a stethoscope. Such an observation may be supplemented by the use of X rays. But if the lungs observed are the lungs of the observer, this observer may further place on record what it feels like when he takes a deep breath. It may be said that this third empirical observation differs from the other two in that the observation cannot be checked by any second person; and this, of course, is so.[2]

Such observations, however, are plainly observations concerning the state of the observer's body. There are, in addition, observations which an observer can make about himself which do not seem to be observations about the *state* of his body, but rather observations about things he does and about things that happen to him. Many observations of this latter kind have been recorded by novelists and by all who have written autobiographies. We all, in fact, record them whenever we state that at a certain time we noticed something, remembered something, or tried to produce some effect or other. In nearly all these cases the observer who makes such reports about himself has sources of information more accessible to him than to anybody else, and there are many such observations such that if the facts are not observed by the person to whom they relate, no one else is likely to observe them. Titchener, for example, has described what he calls "his vivid and persistent auditory imagery" in the following way:

---

[2] This point need not here concern us. It has methodological significance only in conjunction with the thesis that an observation which cannot be checked is not a "*scientific*" observation. There may be a priori or conventional reasons for so defining the expression "scientific observation" that this thesis will be true, but there would appear to be no a priori or conventional reason why "empirical observation" should be so defined that an observation which cannot be checked cannot be described as "empirical."

If I may venture on a very sweeping statement, I should say that I never sit down to read a book, or to write a paragraph, or to think out a problem, without a musical accompaniment. Usually the accompaniment is orchestral, with a preponderance of the woodwind,—I have a sort of personal affection for the oboe; sometimes it is in the tone-colour of piano or violin; never, I think, is it vocal.[3]

Similarly, he writes:

Whenever I read or hear that somebody has done something modestly, or gravely, or proudly, or humbly, or courteously, I see a visual hint of the modesty or gravity or pride or humility or courtesy. The stately heroine gives me a flash of a tall figure, the only clear part of which is a hand holding up a steely grey skirt; the humble suitor gives me a flash of a bent figure, the only clear part of which is the bowed back, though at times there are hands held deprecatingly before the absent face. A great many of these sketches are irrelevant and accessory; but they often are, and they always may be, the vehicles of a logical meaning. The stately form that steps through the French window to the lawn may be clothed in all the colours of the rainbow; but its stateliness is the hand on the grey skirt. I shall not multiply instances. All this description must be either self-evident or as unreal as a fairy-tale.[4]

And certainly, however slight the degree to which we may share these experiences, they are "self-evident" enough. The facts may be odd, but they are not odd because they are unfamiliar or because there is any doubt about them. We understand what Titchener is saying and we have no doubt that he is telling the truth. They are odd chiefly in the sense that they are difficult to "relate" to the no less familiar facts concerning events in the observer's body and to events in the surrounding material world. They are also odd in the sense that it is not easy to state how the observation of these facts is connected with the observation of other things. A theory of introspection might fairly be expected to throw some light on these connections.

Titchener not only gave his introspections; he also attempted to tell us what introspection is. In fact, for an oecumenical exposition of the theory and practice of introspection as a scientific method, we cannot do better than consult his works, and in particular the *Lectures on the Elementary Psychology of Feeling and Attention* and the *Lectures on the Experimental Psychology of the Thought Processes*. In the former work we find this interesting passage:

---

[3] Titchener, *Experimental Psychology*, p. 9.
[4] Titchener, *Experimental Psychology*, p. 13.

We are agreed, I suppose, that scientific method may be summed up in the single word "observation"; the only way to work in science is to observe those phenomena which form the subject-matter of science. And observation means two things: attention to the phenomena, and record of the phenomena; clear experience, and communication of the experience in words or formulae. We shall agree, further, that, in order to secure clear experience and adequate report, science has recourse to experiment, —an experiment being, in the last resort, simply an observation that may be repeated, isolated, and varied. What, then, is the difference between natural science and psychology? between experimental inspection and experimental introspection?

We may set out from two very simple cases. (1) Suppose that you are shown two paper discs, the one of an uniform violet, the other composed half of red and half of blue. Your problem is, so to adjust the proportions of red and blue in the second disc that the violet which appears on rotation exactly matches the violet of the first disc. You may repeat this set of observations as often as you will; you may isolate the observations by working in a room that is free from other, possibly disturbing colours; you may vary the observations by working towards the equality of the violets first from a two-colour disc that is distinctly too blue, then from a disc that is distinctly too red; and so on. (2) Suppose, again, that the chord *c-e-g* is struck, and that you are required to say how many tones it contains. You may repeat this observation; you may isolate it, by working in a quiet room; you may vary it, by sounding the tones first in succession and then all together, or by striking the chord at different parts of the scale. It is clear that, in these cases, there is no difference between introspection and inspection. You are using the same method that you would use for counting the swings of a pendulum, or for taking the readings from a galvanometer scale, in the physical laboratory.

Now let us take some instances in which the material of introspection is more complex. (3) Suppose that a word is called out to you, and that you are asked to observe the effect which this stimulus produces upon consciousness: how the word affects you, what ideas it calls up, and so forth. The observation may be repeated; it may be isolated,—you may be seated in a dark and silent room, free from disturbances; and it may be varied,—different words may be called out, the word may be flashed upon a screen instead of spoken, etc. Here, however, there does seem to be a difference between introspection and inspection. The observer who is watching the course of a chemical reaction, or the movements of some microscopical creature, can jot down from moment to moment the successive phases of the observed phenomenon. But if you try to report the changes in consciousness, while these changes are in progress, you interfere with consciousness; your translation of the mental processes into words introduces new factors into the experience itself. (4) Suppose, lastly, that you are observing a feeling or an emotion: a feeling of disappointment or annoyance, an emotion of anger or chagrin. Experimental control is still possible; situations may be arranged, in the psychological laboratory, such that these feelings may be repeated, isolated and varied. But your observation of them interferes, even more seriously than before, with the course of consciousness. Cool consideration of an emotion is fatal to its very existence; your anger disappears, your disappointment evaporates, as you examine it.[5]

We may pare this argument, first of all, of the pardonable hocus-pocus concerning experimental procedures, the controlled conditions of quiet rooms, etc. Titchener was writing at a time when introspective psychologists felt it to be important to establish their scientific status. But whilst since that time experimental psychology has justified itself in quite a variety of ways, it has not established a single introspective observation in a laboratory which was not equally apparent to those who have carried out introspection in a psychoanalyst's consulting room or for that matter in the homely armchair.

Nor need we take very seriously the rather tedious argument concerning the way in which the act of introspection disturbs the process which is being observed. The argument in fact is silly in the sense of being self-refuting. The fact reported is itself discovered by introspection, and it is not easy to see how it could be established in any other way.

What then remains is the central thesis that *"observation means two things: attention to the phenomena and record of the phenomena; clear experience and the communication of the experience in words or formulae"* and the final conclusion drawn in a later paragraph: *"there is no difference between inspection and introspection. Attention in psychology and attention in natural science are of the same nature and obey the same laws."*

What, however, Titchener failed to make clear—what in fact he failed to see and what introspective psychologists generally have failed to make clear or even to see—is that the difficulties reside not so much in observing the facts as in knowing how to describe them.

It is indeed extremely difficult to obtain a satisfactory record of an introspective observation. It is, for example, extremely difficult to report upon the experience of recalling an event in early childhood or to explain what is "in one's mind" in using the word "but." The reaction of psychologists to this difficulty has been to concentrate attention, to elaborate techniques of observation, and to train observers to introspect.

---

[5] *Lectures on the Elementary Psychology of Feeling and Attention* (1908), pp. 175-178.

These endeavours have been in the main ineffective, because misdirected. The facts are there for everyone to "see," but we do not know how to *say* what we "see." That this is where the trouble lies can best be shown not by a general argument but by examining representative cases. Three such cases may be selected: the classical problem of "abstract ideas," the question of the nature and status of "mental images," and the problem of the "mental acts."

ABSTRACT AND GENERAL IDEAS

Again, let us quote the admirable Titchener:

> You will recall the main heads of the controversy. Locke had maintained that it is possible to form the general idea, say, of a triangle which is "neither oblique nor rectangle, neither equilateral, equicrural, nor scalene; but all and none of these at once." Berkeley replied that "if any man has the faculty of framing in his mind such an idea of a triangle, as is here described, it is in vain to pretend to dispute him out of it, nor would I go about it. . . . For myself, I find indeed I have a faculty of imagining, or representing to myself, the ideas of those particular things I have perceived, and of variously compounding and dividing them, . . . [but] I cannot by any effort of thought conceive the abstract idea described above. . . . The idea of man that I frame to myself must be either of a white, or a black, or a tawny, a straight, or a crooked, a tall, or a low, or a middle-sized man." The dispute has lasted down to our own day. Hamilton calls the Lockean doctrines a "revolting absurdity." Huxley finds it entirely acceptable.[6]

The point of interest in this is not so much who was right and who was wrong but the question: What sort of argument was this? and why should the dispute have lasted to this day?

It is clear, of course, that the issue does not turn on any differences in the constitutions of Berkeley and Locke or on any differences in what was open to their observation when they considered what happened to them when they thought of a man or a triangle. Berkeley obviously had his tongue in his cheek when he pretended that Locke might have some peculiar faculty which he himself lacked. He was in fact quite sure that Locke could not think of the nondescript triangle any more than he could; and what Locke thought he could think of he had every reason for supposing that Berkeley could too. In fact, it is one of the odd features in these disputes that the difficulties do not in general

---

[6] *Experimental Psychology*, p. 14.

arise with regard to the experiences in respect of which we have reason to suppose that individuals differ. They arise as acutely as anywhere in connexion with the experiences which we all have in common, experiences with which we are all familiar. What Locke and Berkeley were at cross-purposes about was not an issue of fact but a question as to how the facts should be reported. This is clear from the way in which Titchener himself proceeds to comment. He does not adduce fresh empirical evidence from the Lovelace papers or from Berkeley's Commonplace book. He does not cite his own introspections nor the evidence obtained in his own laboratory. He proceeds to *argue* the question, and to argue it like this:

> All through this discussion there runs, unfortunately, the confusion of logic and psychology that is characteristic of the English school. It is no more correct to speak, in psychology, of an abstract idea, or a general idea, than it would be to speak of an abstract sensation or a general sensation. What is abstract and general is not the idea, the process in consciousness, but the logical meaning of which that process is the vehicle. All that we can say of the idea is that it comprises such and such qualities; shows these and these temporal and spatial characters; has a certain degree of vividness as focal or marginal, clear or obscure; has the vague haziness of distant sounds and faint lights or the clean-cut definiteness of objects to which the sense-organ is accommodated; is arranged on a particular pattern.[7]

His own solution is that Locke was describing a "logical meaning" and that Berkeley was describing a "psychological idea." Again, it does not matter whether this solution is correct. The question is: What sort of solution was it and how was it obtained? The sort of solution it was is seen by examining how it was obtained. It was obtained not by any observational procedure but by considering how one should "speak correctly" of an abstract or general idea. And from this we begin to get some inkling of what happened on the occasion of Titchener's blinding revelation when he read James Mill. "I can test all this for myself!" he said. Of course he could. He, too, could guess what words in the English language mean. He, too, could play the analytic game.

There is, accordingly, a prima facie case for the hypothesis: *The problems of introspection are in part at least problems of analysis.* Given "clear experience" the problem is to communicate the experience in words.. To do this one must, of course, consider what words mean. Other cases may be examined with this hypothesis in mind.

---

[7] Titchener, *Experimental Psychology*, p. 15.

"Mental Images"

Tough Behaviourists cornered have sometimes denied that there are such things as "mental images," but the courage of would-be Behaviourists has sometimes failed them at this point. What, to begin with, are the facts—the facts, that is to say, stated as nearly as may be in a non-committal way?

Conversations such as the following are frequently overheard:

> *A.* "Do you remember your Aunt Elizabeth?"
> *B.* "Only vaguely. I was quite young when she died. I have only a vague recollection of a rather tall stately lady in some sort of shawl. She used to visit us every Christmas."
> *A.* "I remember her well. I can see her now sitting in that high-backed chair—wearing that Paisley shawl. It seems as though it were only yesterday."

And so on. We can all understand the sort of experience which *A* and *B* are talking about and we can understand how they differ. We have all at some time had some vivid recollection like *A*'s memory of Aunt Elizabeth and we know what it is to have only vague recollections like *B*'s.

In regard to such reports, arguments of the following kind arise. The fact that *A* "can see Aunt Elizabeth now" sitting in the high-backed chair wearing her Paisley shawl (despite the fact that Aunt Elizabeth has been dead for twenty years) entails that *A* is seeing a kind of "picture" of Aunt Elizabeth. And the fact that *A* is seeing a kind of picture of Aunt Elizabeth entails that this picture exists at the time that *A* is seeing it—and from this point we can go on to ask such questions as where the picture is, what it is made of, and a host of other questions similar to those which we might ask about the picture of Aunt Elizabeth hanging on the wall.

This line of thought may be countered along the following lines. The fact that *A* can recall Aunt Elizabeth in the vivid way described does not entail that any such "picture" exists either at the time of recall or at any other time. The metaphor fails to make sense. The existence of a "picture"—in any natural sense—is not attested by a single observation but depends upon a vast collection of supporting evidence. The existence of a picture on a wall is not established until we have established by suitable physical and chemical tests what it is made of—canvas, paint, paper, crayon, or what you will. Its existence requires to be attested by historical evidence—evidence to the effect that it was once in a different place and was put at a certain time where it now is. No such supporting evidence can be given for the alleged "mental" picture. No one can say what it is made of, nor where it came from. Its alleged existence depends upon an a priori argument— "You can't see a picture that isn't there." But clearly this begs the question. People often seem to see what isn't there. What requires to be established is precisely that in such cases what they see is a "picture." This is not made easier by the fact that it is in any case agreed that in the natural sense of the word they do not "see" anything at all. They could experience all that they claim to experience even if they had no eyes.

The argument could be indefinitely prolonged. What concerns us is again not who is right and who wrong in this argument—but: What sort of argument is it? On what does the issue turn?

And, again, it is clear that the issue does not turn simply upon making an observation. It is not by "looking" more closely at the experience of recalling Aunt Elizabeth that we can decide whether an image of Aunt Elizabeth exists. We have all the facts we need when we recall in the ordinary way what Aunt Elizabeth looked like. To settle the issue we have to "look" more closely not at our experience but at the meanings of the word "exist" and consider more carefully the criteria by reference to which the existence of a picture is established. The Behaviourist who denies that images exist may well be right, but he will establish his position not by getting *negative* results from an attempted observation but by getting *positive* results from an attempted "philosophical analysis."

MENTAL ACTS

One of the prettiest examples of the entanglement of introspection and analysis is provided by the controversy regarding "mental acts." Sensationists in psychology and phenomenalists in philosophy allowed themselves to be unnecessarily disturbed by Brentano's thesis that "every psychical phenomenon is characterised by what the scholastics of the Middle Ages have termed the intentional . . . in-existence of an object, and what we should term . . . reference to a content, direction upon an object, or immanent objectivity."[8]

---

[8] F. Brentano, *Psychologie vom Empirischen Standpunkte* (1874). Quoted by Titchener, *Experimental Psychology*, p. 43.

It was perhaps understandable that they should have been disturbed by the language employed, but here as elsewhere we have first to notice the obvious facts by which such language is provoked.

The argument proceeds through three fairly well defined stages. Proposition I lays the bait: "You agree that you can't just see. If you see you must see something—a light, a patch of colour, or what not. And so, too, you can't just hear. If you hear you must hear a sound." The bait is readily accepted.

Proposition II leads the victim on. "And if you introspect carefully, you will notice that this applies in other cases. You can't just wish; if you wish, you wish *for* something. And you can't just be pleased or sorry. When you are pleased or sorry, you are pleased or sorry that so-and-so is the case—just as when you believe, you must believe that so-and-so is the case or believe *in* something." This stage evokes some demur and a certain amount of argument about "objectless emotions" and about James's case of the man whose soul sweats with conviction but who does not know what he is convinced of; but subject to certain reservations, the point is sooner or later accepted.

Proposition III is the generalised formulation, more or less in Brentano's terms or in some other version, of the doctrine of "mental acts" and "mental contents." But the generalised formulation is apt to provoke open revolt.

Titchener's own reaction to the argument conforms to the type. At each stage he exhibited the appropriate and expected response. He accepts Proposition I. He demurs at Proposition II but gives in at the end. It is only at the third step that hesitancy becomes determined. All this, he says, "is a psychology not of observation but of reflection"— "a psychological fact, a datum of observation has been cast into logical form."[9] What can this mean?

One point at any rate is clear. No fresh information is required in passing from Proposition II to Proposition III. Viewed as a piece of philosophical technique, the three stages may be described in another way. The first step draws attention to a fact—a fact with which something can be done. The second step starts to do something with it— by pointing out that the fact is not unique, that there are others rather like it, though perhaps not obviously so. The third step combines a sort of generalisation with a sort of transformation. The fact is not merely generalised but is also stated in another way, as a rule in terms

---

[9] Titchener, *Experimental Psychology*, p. 50.

of philosophical technicalities. The generalisation and the transformation are connected since terms do not exist in common language appropriate to the generalised expression. Perceiving implies something perceived; feeling angry implies something to feel angry about; so, too, all mental acts and attitudes imply—what? How shall we put it? Shall we say that all acts and attitudes imply "the intentional existence of their objects" or "reference to a content"? The generalisation will always sound queer and always convey the suggestion that something has been slipped in. It is this perhaps that led Titchener to say that the datum of observation has been cast into logical form. But where in all this is the appeal to introspection? At most, surely, in the first and second stages of the argument; and even here the introspection is of an extremely simple kind and the appeal is not to introspection alone.

The "problem of introspection" is, it appears, in part a problem that arises from a mislocated difficulty. It is, of course, difficult to say what you see when you "look into your own mind." But this is not because it is difficult to see what is there. The difficulty is to say what you see —to say it in a clear, correct, and illuminating way. The difficulty is not overcome either by straining or by training. It does not help to look harder, and nothing much is gained by trying to train the "inner senses" as you train the palate.

Scientific observation, generally, is "attention to the phenomena and record of the phenomena." You look, you listen, you taste, you smell, you feel, and then you state what you have seen, heard, tasted, smelt, or felt. You may have no doubts about what you have experienced, but there will always be grounds for doubt about the ways in which you have described the experience.

There's the rub, indeed. What, apparently, Titchener failed to notice was that the *formulation* of experience was not peculiar to the statements of those with whom he disagreed. All psychology is a "psychology of reflection" in the sense that a psychologist observing a fact needs to reflect upon the way this observation may be suitably expressed. For that matter every science is a science of "reflection" in this sense. Every statement of fact, in any science, contains a datum of observation "cast into logical form."

By way of comment on any question of fact, it is always relevant to say "It depends on what you mean." "Is the sky blue?" "Is the lawn green?" It depends on what you mean by "blue." It depends on what you mean by "green." With the passage of the weeks in a scorching summer, there will be a decreasing percentage of observers who will describe the lawn as "green"; and we can roughly define the range of application of the term in good English usage.

The troublesome cases are those in which the permissible applications of a term do not correspond with any continuous variable, but rest upon a variety of "analogies" and subtle similarities. Problems of introspection are apt to assume the form: "Do you feel blue on Monday mornings? If so, is it always the same shade of blue?" If the question is difficult to answer, it is not because it is difficult to observe our feelings but because it is difficult to describe them. We could better frame the question in the following form: "Is 'blue' the most applicable adjective for your feelings on Monday morning, or can you think of a better way of describing them?" In the same way we could reformulate many of the classical questions of introspective psychology. How can we best describe the way in which we think about men when we are not concerned with any particular man? How can we best describe the various ways in which we think about a person who is not within the field of view? How can we best describe in a generalised way the sort of fact that we observe when we observe, for instance, that, whenever we are angry, we are angry *with*? By such restatement we effect a relocation of the problem. Problems of introspection are seen to be in part problems of analysis. This would seem to be the case whatever we may hold analysis to be.

The Verification Argument

NORMAN MALCOLM

A number of arguments have been used by various philosophers to prove that the truth of no empirical statement is absolutely certain. In this paper I wish to examine *one* of these arguments. The argument has, to the best of my knowledge, been stated more forcefully by C. I. Lewis than by any other writer. I will quote from him in order to obtain a strong presentation of the argument.

While engaged in discussing the statement "A piece of white paper is now before me," Lewis says the following:

This judgment will be false if the presentation is illusory: it will be false if what I see is not really paper; false if it is not really white but only looks white. This objective judgment also is one capable of corroboration. As in the other example [the other example, to which Lewis refers, is the statement "There is a flight of granite steps before me"], so here too, any test of the judgment would pretty surely involve some way of acting—*making* the test, as by continuing to look, or turning my eyes, or grasping to tear, etc.—and would be determined by finding or failing to find some expected result in experience. But in this example, if the result of any single test is as expected, it constitutes a partial verification of the judgment only; never one which is absolutely decisive and theoretically complete. This is so because, while the judgment, so far as it is significant, contains nothing which could not be tested, still it has a significance which outruns what any single test, or any limited set of tests, could exhaust. No matter how fully I may have investigated this objective fact, there will remain some theoretical possibility of mistake; there will be further consequences which must be thus and so if the judg-

229

ment is true, and not all of these will have been determined. The possibility that such further tests, if made, might have a negative result, cannot be altogether precluded; and this possibility marks the judgment as, at the time in question, not fully verified and less than absolutely certain. To quibble about such possible doubts will not, in most cases, be common-sense. But we are not trying to weigh the degree of theoretical dubiety which common-sense practicality should take account of, but to arrive at an accurate analysis of knowledge. This character of being further testable and less than theoretically certain characterizes every judgment of objective fact at all times; every judgment that such and such a real thing exists or has a certain objectively factual property, or that a certain objective event actually occurs, or that any objective state of affairs actually is the case.[1]

The same argument is stated more dramatically by Lewis in *Mind and the World Order*. He says:

> Obviously in the statement "this penny is round" I assert implicitly *everything the failure of which would falsify the statement*. The implicit prediction of *all* experience which is essential to its *truth* must be contained in the original judgment. Otherwise, such experience would be irrelevant. All that further experience, the failure of which would lead to the repudiation of the apprehension as illusory or mistaken, is predicted in the judgment made. Now suppose we ask: How long will it be possible to verify in some manner the fact that this penny is round? What totality of experience would verify it completely beyond the possibility of necessary reconsideration? . . . it seems to be the fact than *no* verification would be absolutely complete; that all verification is partial and a matter of degree. . . . Is it not the case that the simplest statement of objective particular fact implicitly asserts something about possible experience throughout all future time; that theoretically every objective fact is capable of some verification at any later date, and that no totality of such experience is absolutely and completely sufficient to put our knowledge of such particulars beyond all possibility of turning out to be in error?[2]

For the purpose of refuting it, Lewis considers the supposition that at a certain time, designated as t_1, the verification of such a statement as "this penny is round" could be complete. He continues the argument:

> Now suppose further that at some date, t_2, we put ourselves in position to meet the consequences of this fact, which was accepted as completely established at t_1. And suppose that these consequences fail to appear, or

---

[1] C. I. Lewis, *An Analysis of Knowledge and Valuation* (1946), p. 180.
[2] *Mind and the World Order* (1929), pp. 279-281.

are not what the nature of the accepted fact requires? In that case, will there still be no doubt about the accepted fact? Or will what was supposedly established at t_1 be subject to doubt at t_2? And in the latter case can we suppose it was absolutely verified at time t_1? Since no single experience can be absolutely guaranteed to be veridical, no limited collection or succession of experiences can absolutely guarantee an empirical fact as certain beyond the possibility of reconsideration.[3]

Many other philosophers have made use of this argument.

Carnap, for example, uses it in his paper, "Testability and Meaning."[4] He says:

> Take for instance the following sentence "There is a white sheet of paper on this table." In order to ascertain whether this thing is paper, we may make a set of simple observations and then, if there still remains some doubt, we may make some physical and chemical experiments. Here . . . we try to examine sentences which we infer from the sentence in question. These inferred sentences are predictions about future observations. The number of such predictions which we can derive from the sentence given is infinite; and therefore the sentence can never be completely verified. To be sure, in many cases we reach a practically sufficient certainty after a small number of positive instances, and then we stop experimenting. But there is always the theoretical possibility of continuing the series of test-observations. Therefore here . . . *no complete verification* is possible but only a process of gradually increasing *confirmation*.[5]

He continues: "For such a simple sentence as e.g. 'There is a white thing on this table' the degree of confirmation, after a a few observations have been made, will be so high that we practically cannot help accepting the sentence. But even in this case there remains still the theoretical possibility of denying the sentence."[6]

Before proceeding to an analysis of this argument, which I will call "the Verification Argument," I wish to say something about the nature of the conclusion which it is thought to prove. Previously I said that it is thought to prove that no empirical statements are absolutely certain. But this remark is not sufficiently clear because of a haziness in the

3 *Ibid.*, pp. 281-282.

4 Rudolf Carnap, "Testability and Meaning," *Phil. of Science*, III, IV (1936, 1937). This argument is also used by Carnap in *Philosophy and Logical Syntax* (1935), pp. 11-13 and in *Logische Syntax Der Sprache* (1934), p. 246; by A. J. Ayer, in *Foundations of Empirical Knowledge* (1940), pp. 42-45; by K. Popper, in *Logik der Forschung* (1935), pp. 60-62.

5 Carnap, "Testability and Meaning," *Phil. of Science*, III (1936), 425.

6 *Ibid.*, p. 426.

meaning of the expression "empirical statements." Certainly no philosopher who has used the Verification Argument has intended that the argument should apply to necessary or a priori truths. But there is a class of statements with regard to which philosophers have had difficulty in deciding whether to classify statements of that class as empirical statements; and among those philosophers who have used the Verification Argument there would be disagreement and hesitation about saying whether the argument applies to statements of that class. Statements of the class in question have been called "incorrigible propositions" or "basic propositions" or "expressive statements" or "sense statements." The sentence "It *seems* to me that I hear a scratching sound at the window," when used in such a way as not to imply that there is a scratching sound at the window, would express a statement of this class. The sentence "It *looks* to me as if there are two candles on the table," when used in such a way as not to imply that there are two candles on the table, would express another statement of this class. I will call statements of this class "incorrigible statements," and henceforth I will use the expression "empirical statement" in such a way that the class of empirical statements will be understood to exclude incorrigible statements as well as necessary truths and necessary falsehoods. It is in this sense of "empirical statement" that the conclusion of the Verification Argument will be understood to be the proposition that every empirical statement is "less than absolutely certain."

The class of empirical statements is, of course, enormous. The following are examples of such statements: "There is an ink bottle on that table," "I see a goat in the garden," "We were in Lugano last winter," "I closed the door a moment ago," "There is no milk in the ice box," "Gottlob Frege was not a Spaniard," "Michelangelo designed the dome of St. Peter's," "Water does not flow uphill," "Chickens are hatched from eggs," "This man's neck is broken," "My wife is angry." The Verification Argument is thought to prove that whenever any person has ever asserted that the truth of any one of these statements is absolutely certain his assertion was false or mistaken, and also to prove that if anyone should, in the future, make such an assertion his assertion will be false or mistaken.

It is to be noted that the phrase "it is absolutely certain" is only one of several phrases which are used synonymously in certain contexts. Some of the other synonymous phrases are "it has been completely verified," "it has been established beyond a doubt," "I have made absolutely certain," "I have conclusively established," "I know for certain," "it has been proved beyond any possibility of doubt," "it is perfectly certain." The Verification Argument is thought to prove something with regard to each and every one of these phrases. It is thought to prove that whenever anyone applies one of these phrases to any empirical statement the assertion which he thereby makes is false or mistaken or incorrect or unjustified. It is thought to prove, for example, that if any art historian has ever made the assertion that it is conclusively established that the dome of St. Peter's was designed by Michelangelo, his assertion was false or mistaken or incorrect or unjustified; and if any art historian should, at any time in the future, make this assertion, his assertion will be false or mistaken or incorrect or unjustified. It is thought to prove that if a physician who has just examined a man struck down by a bus should ever assert "I have made absolutely certain that his neck is broken," what he asserts is wrong or improper or unjustified, *no matter how careful his examination has been.*

It is common knowledge that assertions of this sort are *often* mistaken and that it frequently happens that someone asserts that he has made absolutely certain that so-and-so is true, when either so-and-so is not true or else, even if so-and-so is true, he has not made so thorough an investigation as to justify his assertion that he has made absolutely certain that so-and-so is true. The Verification Argument is thought to prove, not simply that many assertions of this sort are mistaken or unjustified, but that *all* such assertions are, *in all cases,* mistaken or unjustified. In short, it is thought to prove that it is not even *possible* that anyone should, in *any* circumstances, make such an assertion without the assertion being false or unjustified or improper or mistaken or incorrect.

In order to state the Verification Argument as clearly as possible I will make use of an example. Let us suppose that a dispute has arisen between a friend and myself as to whether William James used the phrase "the stream of thought" as the title of a chapter in his book *The Principles of Psychology,*[7] my friend contending that James did not use that phrase, but did use the phrase "the stream of consciousness" as the title of a chapter. Whereupon I take from a bookshelf

---

[7] Two volumes, 1890.

Volume I of James's book, turn the pages until I come to page 224, where I see the title "The Stream of Thought" occurring just under the heading "Chapter IX." Then I say, "You are wrong. Here is a chapter entitled 'The Stream of Thought.'" He says, "Have you made absolutely certain?" I reply, "Yes, I have. Here, look for yourself."

I believe that this example provides a natural usage of the expression "I have made absolutely certain." It is, furthermore, a good example for my purposes because I do wish to maintain that on June 17, 1948, I did make absolutely certain that the phrase "the stream of thought" was, on that day, on page 224 of my copy of Volume I of James's *The Principles of Psychology*. The statement "The phrase 'the stream of thought' was, on June 17, 1948, on page 224 of my copy of Volume I of James's *The Principles of Psychology*" I will call "*S*." The Verification Argument is thought to prove that I did *not* make absolutely certain that *S* is true. Let us see whether it does prove this.

The first step in the argument consists in saying that *S* has "consequences" or "expected results in experience," or that from *S* one can infer statements which are "predictions about future observations." It seems to me that it is not difficult to see an important thing that is mean by these expressions. If, for example, someone said "Just now a cat went into the closet," and I believed the statement, I should *expect* that if I were to search about in the closet I should see or hear or touch a cat. If I did not believe his statement he might naturally say "I assure you that if you look in the closet you will see a cat." And if I did look and did see a cat it would be natural to regard this as *confirming* his first statement "Just now a cat went into the closet." Another way of expressing this matter would be to say that if it is true that a cat went into the closet just now, then it *follows* or is a *consequence* that if I were to search about in the closet I should see or hear or touch a cat. This is a natural use of "follow" and of "consequence." And it is easy to understand what is meant by saying that the conditional statement "If I were to search about in the closet I should see or hear or touch a cat" states a "prediction about future observations." Henceforth I will use the word "consequence" to express these relationships. I will say that it is a "consequence" of the statement "Just now a cat went into the closet" that if I were to search in the closet I should see or hear or touch a cat; and I will say that the conditional statement "If I were to search in the closet I should see or hear or touch a cat" expresses a "consequence" of the former statement. In this use of "consequence" it is a consequence of the statement, S, that if now, on June 18, 1948, I were to look at page 224 of my copy of Volume I of James's *Principles* I should see the phrase "the stream of thought." I should certainly expect to see that phrase if I were to look at that page now, and I should be greatly astonished if I did not see it.

It may be said that what I have called a "consequence" of S is not a consequence of S alone, but of S conjoined with some other statements. If I thought that since yesterday someone had erased from page 224 of James's book the phrase "the stream of thought," then I should not expect that if I were to look on that page I should see that phrase. Also I should not expect to see it if I knew that my vision was abnormal or that the room was so dark that I could not make out printed words. The statement "If I were to look on that page now I should see that phrase" expresses a consequence, not of S alone, but of the conjunctive statement "The phrase was on that page yesterday, and there is no reason to think that the printing on that page has been altered or has changed since then, and my vision is normal, and the light is good." I cannot see any objection to saying this. I believe that it is a natural way of speaking to say that if S is true then it is a consequence that if I were to look at page 224 now I should see that phrase; and I will continue to speak in that way. But it will be understood that this consequence of S is not a consequence of S alone, but of S conjoined with the other statements mentioned.

A difficult question now arises, namely, what *kind* of statements are the conditional statements that express consequences of S? Consider the statement "If I were to look now at page 224 of my copy of James's book I should see the phrase 'the stream of thought.'" I will call this statement "c." c is of the form "If A then E." Now a view has been put forward by Lewis that implies that this consequence of S should really be expressed in these words: "If it were the case that it should *seem* to me that I was looking at page 224 of James's book then it would be the case that I should *seem* to see the phrase 'the stream of thought.'" I will call this statement "k." Lewis holds that in a conditional statement which expresses a consequence of an empirical statement, both A and E (that is, both antecedent and consequent) must be regarded as what I call "incorrigible statements" and what he calls "expressive statements."[8] Lewis calls the statements which express consequences of an

---

[8] "The hypothesis 'A' must here express something which, if made true by adopted action, will be *indubitably* true. . . . And the consequent 'E' represents an even-

empirical statement "predictions"; and so does Carnap. Lewis talks about his believing such a statement as "there is a piece of paper before me." He says that this belief involves numerous predictions, e.g., that if he were to fold it, it would not crack; that if he were to try to tear it, it would tear easily.[9] A moment later, however, he says that he has not expressed himself accurately. He says

> But it was my intention to mention predictions which, though only partial verification of the objective fact I believe in, could themselves be decisively tested. And there I have failed. That the paper, upon trial, would really be torn, will no more be evidenced with perfect certainty than is the presence of real paper before me now. It—provided it takes place—will be a real objective event about which, theoretically, my momentary experience could deceive me. What I meant to speak of was certain expected experiences—of the *appearance and feeling* of paper being folded; of its *seeming* to be torn.[10]

He is saying that the statement "If I were to try to tear this, it would tear easily" is not a "prediction" and does not express a "consequence," in his use of "prediction" and "consequence," of his belief that there is paper before him. This passage and the one which I quoted from page 184 show that he would regard the statement "If it *seemed* to me that I was trying to tear this, then it would *seem* to me that it was tearing easily" as the sort of statement that is a "prediction" and expresses a "consequence" of his belief and if it were true would partially confirm or verify his belief. Thus it is clear that Lewis's use of "consequence," as this word occurs in his presentation of the Verification Argument, is such that he would say that k is a "consequence" of S, and c is not. There is, of course, an enormous difference between k and c. The difference could be expressed in this way: If I were to look now at page 224 of James's book and were to see there the phrase "the stream of thought," that would *entail* that page 224 of James's book does exist and that the phrase "the stream of thought" is on that page. But if now it were to *seem* to me that I was looking at page 224 of James's book and if it were to *seem* to me that I was seeing there the phrase

---

tuality of *experience*, directly and certainly recognizable in case it accrues, not a resultant objective event, whose factuality could have, and would call for, further verification. Thus both antecedent and consequent of this judgment "If A then E," require to be formulated in expressive language . . ." (*An Analysis of Knowledge and Valuation*, p. 184).

9 *Ibid.*, p. 175.
10 *Ibid.*

"the stream of thought," that would *not* entail that page 224 of James's book exists or that that phrase is on any page of any book.

No other philosopher who has used the Verification Argument has, to the best of my knowledge, expressed himself on this point. Carnap, for example, says that when we are trying to verify an empirical statement what we do is to infer from it statements that are "predictions about future observations."[11] But he does not say whether these "predictions" are statements like *c* or statements like *k*. Since he does not even allude to the distinction it would be natural to assume that by "predictions" he means statements like *c*. Whether this is so or not I will henceforth mean by "statements which express consequences of *S*" statements like *c* and not like *k*. I have two reasons for this decision. One is that statements like *k* are awkward and unnatural. The other and more important reason is that I am not sure that there is any natural usage of "confirm" or "verify" according to which the discovery that *k* is true would confirm or verify that *S* is true. Suppose that I were in doubt as to whether *S* is true. If I were to look now at page 224 of James's book and see there the phrase "the stream of thought," that would indeed confirm that the phrase was on that page yesterday. But if it were merely the case that it *seemed* to me now that I was looking at page 224 of James's book and that it *seemed* to me that I was seeing there that phrase, in a sense of the preceding words that is compatible with its being the case that I am dreaming now or having an hallucination and am not seeing any page or any printing at all, then how would this confirm that the printed words "the stream of thought" were on page 224 of James's book yesterday? It is not clear to me that it would in the least confirm *S*, in any natural sense of "confirm." This is, however, a difficult point and I do not wish to argue it here. I believe that no important part of my treatment of the Verification Argument is affected by the decision to interpret the statements that express consequences of *S* as statements like *c* and not like *k*, and it is open to anyone reading this paper to interpret them in the other way.

There is, however, a fact about the relationship between *S* and the statements that express consequences of *S* which should be clearly understood. This is the fact that *S* does not *entail* any statement that expresses a consequence of *S*, in whichever of these two ways one interprets these statements. For example, *S* does not entail *c*, i.e., the state-

---

11 "Testability and Meaning," *Phil. of Science,* III (1936), 425.

ment "S but not c" is not self-contradictory. It is not self-contradictory
to say "The phrase 'the stream of thought' was on page 224 of James's
book yesterday but it is not the case that if I were to look on that
page now I should see it there." Nor is c entailed by the conjunctive
statement "The phrase 'the stream of thought' was on page 224 of
James's book yesterday, and there is no reason to think that the printing
on that page has changed or been altered since then, and my vision
is normal, and the light is good." Even though there is no reason to
think that the phrase "the stream of thought" has disappeared from
that page since yesterday it *may* have disappeared, and if it has, then
if I look at that page now I shall not see it there. It should be even
clearer that S does not entail k. The whole statement "The phrase 'the
stream of thought' was on page 224 of James's book yesterday but it is
not true that if it were the case that it should *seem* to me that I was
looking at that page it would be the case hat I should *seem* to see that
phrase" is not self-contradictory. Nor is k entailed by the previously
mentioned conjunctive statement of which S is one conjunct. When
Carnap says that in order to verify an empirical statement we "infer"
or "derive" from it statements that are "predictions about future observations,"[12] the words "infer" and "derive" must be understood in a
sense in which to say that one infers or derives q from p is *not* to say
that p entails q. When Lewis speaks of the "implied consequences"[13]
of a belief, it is to be understood that to say that a belief "implies"
certain consequences is not to say that it entails the statements that express those consequences. Whenever the word "consequence" occurs in
my discussion of the Verification Argument it is to be understood that
an empirical statement does not entail any statement that expresses a
consequence of it. This being understood, I see no reason for not accepting the first step in the Verification Argument. When it is said that
S, or any similar statement, has "consequences" or "expected results in
experience," or that from S one can infer "predictions about future observations," it seems to me that this has a fairly clear meaning and is
also true.

The second step in the argument consists in saying that the number
of "consequences" or "expected results in experience" or "predictions
about future observations" that can be inferred from S is "infinite" or
"unlimited." This step in the argument offers some difficulty, but the

---

12 *Ibid.*

13 *An Analysis of Knowledge and Valuation*, p. 176.

following considerations may help to explain it. I said before that it is a consequence of S that if I were to look now at page 224 of this book I should see the phrase "the stream of thought." But it is also a consequence that if I were to look a second from now I should see that phrase, and if I were to look two seconds from now I should see it, and three seconds from now, and so on for an *indefinite* number of seconds. What it means to say that this number of seconds is "indefinite" is that *no* number of seconds from now can be specified such that, after that number of seconds had elapsed, I should no longer expect that if I were to look at that page I should see that phrase. At some future time that page may be destroyed. But for as long a period of time as it continues to exist and is not injured or tampered with, and provided that during that period my vision remains good, I should expect that if at *any* moment during that period I were to take a good look at that page in a good light I should see that phrase, *however long* that period of time shall be. There is a second consideration: I do not expect merely that if *I* were to look at that page now *I* should see that phrase, but also I expect that if my wife were to look at that page now she would see that phrase, and that if the man who lives on the floor below were to look at that page he would see that phrase, and that, in short, if anyone of an *indefinitely* large number of persons of good vision were to take a good look now at that page he would see that phrase. What is meant by saying that the number of persons in question is "indefinitely" large is that *no* number of persons, however large, can be specified such that I should not expect that if any person of this number were to look at that page he would see that phrase. There is a third consideration that is a combination of the preceding two and may be stated as follows: I should expect that if anyone of an indefinitely large number of persons of good vision were to take a good look at that page either now or at any second of an indefinite number of seconds from now, he would see that phrase, provided that the page had not been injured or tampered with and that he looked at it in good light. I think that the statement that the number of "consequences" or "predictions" or "expected results in experience" that can be inferred from S is "infinite" or "unlimited" or "indefinitely large" means what I have expressed in these three considerations; and if that is so I am prepared to accept the second step in the Verification Argument.

The third step in the argument consists in saying that any of these "consequences" or "expected results in experience" may not turn out as expected and that any of these "predictions about future observations" may prove to be false. What this implies with regard to *S*, for example, is that if I were to look now at page 224 of James's book I might not see the phrase "the stream of thought," or that if I were to look a second from now I might not see it, or if my wife were to look now she might not see it, and so on. This proposition in the Verification Argument seems to me to require very careful examination, and I shall return to it later.

The fourth step in the Verification Argument consists in saying that if some of these "consequences" or "expected results in experience" or "predictions about future observations" that can be inferred from *S* should not turn out as expected or should prove to be false, then doubt would be thrown on the truth of *S*. Lewis expresses this when he says: "And suppose that these consequences fail to appear, or are not what the nature of the accepted fact requires? In that case, will there still be no doubt about the accepted fact?"[14] This fourth proposition in the argument seems to me to express an important truth but one that is difficult to state. If I were to take a good look now at page 224 of James's book and were *not* to see the phrase "the stream of thought," I should not simply conclude that I was mistaken when I asserted previously that it is there, and so dismiss the matter. The truth is that I should at first be too dumbfounded to draw any conclusion! When I had recovered from my astonishment what I should conclude or whether I should conclude anything would depend entirely on the circumstances. Suppose that if I were to look now on that page I should see, or seem to see, the phrase "the stream of *consciousness*" occurring as the title, under the heading "Chapter IX," instead of the phrase "the stream of thought." As I said, I should at the first moment be enormously astonished and not know what to say. But suppose that I looked again and again and that I still saw, or seemed to see, the phrase "the stream of consciousness"; that everything else in the room and the things seen through the windows appeared to look the same and to be placed as I remembered them to be the moment before I looked at the page; that I did not feel ill, dizzy, or queer but perfectly normal; that I had assured myself that the book *was* my copy of Volume I of James's *Principles* and that the page *was* page 224; and that there was no reason to believe that the printing on that page had

---

14 *Mind and the World Order*, p. 282.

been altered since the last time I had looked at it. If all of these things were to occur, then I must confess that I should begin to feel a doubt as to whether the phrase "the stream of thought" ever was on page 224 of James's book. What is more important is that this would be a *reasonable* doubt. When Lewis asks the rhetorical question, "Will there still be no doubt about the accepted fact?"[15] he means to imply, of course, that there would be a doubt. But, furthermore, he must mean to imply that the doubt that would exist in those circumstances would be a *reasonable* doubt, i.e., that there would be *good* grounds for doubting. For if the doubt were not a reasonable one then the fact that it existed would be no evidence that that which had been accepted as a fact was not a fact. Now when I say that if certain things were to happen I should doubt whether the phrase in question ever did appear on the page in question and that this would be a reasonable doubt, I am accepting the fourth step of the Verification Argument. I am accepting the statement that if certain consequences of S should "fail to appear" then I should have good grounds for believing that I was mistaken when I asserted previously that I had made absolutely certain that S is true. I should have good grounds for believing that the phrase "the stream of thought" was not there on page 224 of James's book, but also for believing that that phrase *never* had been on that page. I do not see any mistake in this fourth step in the Verification Argument.

There is a fifth step in the argument that is also difficult to state. It is implied, I believe, in these remarks by Lewis:

> Now suppose . . . that at some date, t_2, we put ourselves in position to meet the consequences of this fact, which was accepted as completely established at t_1. And suppose that these consequences fail to appear, or are not what the nature of the accepted fact requires? In that case, will there still be no doubt about the accepted fact? Or will what was supposedly established at t_1 be subject to doubt at t_2? And in the latter case can we suppose it was absolutely verified at time t_1?[16]

The last two sentences in this quotation express the proposition which I have called "the fifth step" in the argument. This proposition may be stated as follows: If at any time there are good grounds for believing that a given statement, p, is false then at no previous time was it

---

15 *Ibid.*
16 *Ibid.*

known with certainty that p is true. This proposition is implied by the rhetorical question, "And in the latter case can we suppose it was absolutely verified at time t_1?" The "latter case" referred to is the time t_2 at which there is supposed to exist a reasonable doubt as to whether something that was accepted at t_1 as a fact is really a fact. What the rhetorical question implies is that if there is a reasonable doubt at t_2 as to whether something is a fact then it cannot have been the case that at t_1 it was absolutely verified that that something is a fact. This proposition will, perhaps, be clearer if expressed in the following way: The proposition "There are now good grounds for doubting that p is true" *entails* the proposition "At no previous time was it known with absolute certainty that p is true."

Should we accept this proposition which is the fifth step in the Verification Argument? Let us substitute for "p" the statement "Hume was the author of *An Abstract of A Treatise of Human Nature.*" Is there any contradiction in supposing that some person, say a publisher, had made absolutely certain in 1740 that Hume was the author of *An Abstract of A Treatise of Human Nature,* but that in 1840 some other person, say a historian, had good grounds for believing that Adam Smith, and not Hume, was the author of it? Is there any contradiction in supposing that some person at one time should possess a body of evidence that conclusively established that so-and-so was the case, but that at a later time another person should possess none of that evidence but should possess *other* evidence on the basis of which it was reasonable to doubt that so-and-so was the case? I cannot see any contradiction in this supposition. Consider this actual example: Some competent Greek scholars are unable to decide whether Plato was the author of the *Lesser Hippias.* They can cite grounds for saying that he was and grounds for saying that he was not. The view that he was the author is subject to a reasonable doubt. But Plato may have been the author. If he was the author then Plato himself, or a contemporary, may have known with certainty that he was the author.[17] Now are the two statements, (a) "Someone at some time in the past knew with absolute certainty that Plato was the author of the *Lesser Hippias,*" and (b)

---

[17] This statement might be thought to beg the question. It *does* conflict with the conclusion of the Verification Argument. It does *not* beg the question with regard to any premise in the argument. It could do so only if some premise in the argument contained the assertion that no one can know with certainty that any empirical statement is true. But if this were contained in a premise then the Verification Argument itself would beg the question.

"Someone now has good grounds for doubting that Plato was the author of the *Lesser Hippias*," incompatible with one another? They are not at all. The proposition that is the conjunction of (*a*) and (*b*) is not self-contradictory. Nothing is easier to imagine than that it should be the case *both* that Aristotle knew with absolute certainty that Plato was the author of that dialogue *and* that 2400 years later a professor of Greek, not having the evidence which Aristotle had and noticing in the dialogue certain features of style uncharacteristic of Plato, should have a reasonable doubt that Plato was the author. There is no contradiction whatever in this supposition, although it may be false. If this supposition is not self-contradictory, then (*b*) does not entail that (*a*) is false. Therefore, the fifth step in the Verification Argument is an error.

Why should anyone fall into the error of thinking that the proposition "There are now good grounds for believing that *p* is false" entails the proposition "At no previous time was it known with absolute certainty that *p* is true"? I believe that there is something which may explain why this error should be made. What I have in mind is the following: If some person were to make the assertion "Aristotle knew with absolute certainty that Plato was the author of the *Lesser Hippias* but I doubt, and with good reason, that Plato was the author," then his assertion would contain an odd absurdity. The most ordinary use of the phrase "knew with absolute certainty" is such that "*x* knew with absolute certainty that *p* is true" entails "*p* is true." Therefore, the above assertion *entails* the assertion "Plato was the author of the *Lesser Hippias* but I doubt that he was." But if anyone were to assert "Plato was the author of the *Lesser Hippias*" he would *imply*, by his assertion, that he *believed* that Plato was the author of the *Lesser Hippias*. By his assertion "Plato was the author of the *Lesser Hippias* but I doubt that he was" he would *assert* that he doubted something, but also *imply* that he did *not* doubt that something but believed it.[18] The same absurdity would be contained in the assertion "It is raining but I doubt it." If a philosopher had sensed the peculiar absurdity of this sort of assertion he might be led to conclude that since it would be absurd for anyone to *assert* "At a previous time someone know with absolute certainty that *p* is true but I doubt, and with a good reason,

---

[18] Moore has called attention to the peculiarity of this sort of statement. Cp. G. E. Moore, "Russell's 'Theory of Descriptions,'" *The Philosophy of Bertrand Russell* (1944), p. 204.

that p is true," that therefore the proposition "At a previous time someone knew with absolute certainty that p is true and now someone
doubts, and with good reason, that p is true" is self-contradictory.

It would be a mistake, however, to draw this conclusion. Although
it would be absurd for anyone to assert "It is raining but I doubt, and
with good reason, that it is raining," it does not follow that this proposition is self-contradictory. That it is not self-contradictory is shown
from the fact that the proposition "It is raining but *he* doubts, and
with good reason, that it is raining" is clearly not self-contradictory.
Since the latter proposition is not self-contradictory, how can the
former one be so? Indeed, I can easily imagine that it should happen
both that it was raining *and* that, at the same time, I had a reasonable
doubt as to whether it was raining. This supposition is certainly not
self-contradictory. Thus the proposition "It is raining but I doubt, and
with good reason, that it is raining" is not self-contradictory, although
it would be an absurdity if I were to *assert* it. If this proposition *were*
self-contradictory then "I doubt, and with good reason, that it is raining" *would* entail "It is not raining." But once we see clearly that this
proposition is not self-contradictory then, I think, all temptation to
believe that this entailment does hold is removed.

It would also be absurd for anyone to assert "Aristotle knew with
absolute certainty that Plato was the author of the *Lesser Hippias* but
I doubt, and on good grounds, that he was." But it does not follow that
the proposition "Aristotle knew with absolute certainty that Plato
was the author of the *Lesser Hippias,* but someone now doubts, and
on good grounds, that Plato was the author" is self-contradictory. It
would be a great mistake to think that the statement "Someone now
doubts, and on good grounds, that Plato was the author of the *Lesser
Hippias*" entails the statement "It is false that Aristotle knew with absolute certainty that Plato was the author of the *Lesser Hippias.*" Lewis
makes this mistake, I believe, when he assumes that if something was
accepted as a fact at time t_1 but that at time t_2 there arose a reasonable
doubt as to whether this something was a fact, then it follows that it
was not absolutely verified at t_1 that this something was a fact. With
regard to S, which is the statement, "The phrase 'the stream of thought'
was on June 17, 1948, on page 224 of my copy of Volume I of James's
The Principles of Psychology," this fifth step in the Verification Argument claims the following: *If* today, June 18, 1948, those things which
I have imagined as happening *should* happen, so that I should have

good reason to believe that S is false, then it would follow logically that I did not make absolutely certain yesterday that S is true.

I have tried to show that that claim is false. It is true that it would be an absurdity for me, or anyone, to assert "I made absolutely certain on June 17 that S is true but today, June 18, I doubt, and with good reason, that S is true." This assertion would have the same peculiar absurdity as the assertion "S is true but I doubt that S is true." But it does not follow in the least that the proposition "On June 17 I made absolutely certain that S is true and on June 18 I doubted, and with good reason, that S is true" is self-contradictory. It does not follow at all that the proposition "On June 18 I doubted, and with good reason, that S is true" entails the proposition "It is false that on June 17 I made absolutely certain that S is true." It might be objected that if I had made absolutely certain on June 17 that S is true, then on June 18 I should remember this fact and, therefore, should not be able to doubt that S is true. But it is logically possible that I should not remember on June 18 that on June 17 I had made certain that S is true. There is no logical contradiction whatever in the supposition that on June 18 I should have a reasonable doubt that S is true, although on June 17 I had made absolutely certain that S is true. Thus it seems to me that there is no reason to accept the fifth step in the Verification Argument and that, in fact, it is a definite error.

Can the Verification Argument be restated in such a way as to avoid this error? It seems to me that this can be done by the following two measures. The first measure consists in *strengthening* the fourth step in the argument. The fourth step is the proposition that if certain things were to happen then I should have good grounds for doubting that S is true. This step could be strengthened by substituting the proposition that if a sufficient number of things were to happen I should have *absolutely conclusive* grounds for thinking that S is false. It seems to me that if the fourth step were strengthened in this way it would still be a true proposition. When discussing the fourth step I imagined certain things as happening such that if they *were* to happen I should have grounds for doubting that S is true. But let us imagine that certain additional things should occur. Let us imagine that, being astonished and perplexed at seeing the phrase "the stream of consciousness' on page 224 of James's book, I should ask my wife to look at that page and that she too should see the phrase "the stream of consciousness." Let us suppose that I should examine the manuscript of this paper in order to verify that there was in it the statement that I had made absolutely certain that the phrase "the stream of thought" was on page 224, but that I should find instead that in the manuscript was the statement that I had made absolutely certain that the phrase "the stream of consciousness" was on page 224. Let us imagine that I should then examine other copies of Volume I of *The Principles of Psychology* and see that in each of them the title of Chapter IX was "*The Stream of Consciousness*"; that I should find a number of articles written by psychologists and philosophers which quoted from page 224 of James's book and that each of them quoted the phrase "the stream of consciousness" and that not one quoted the phrase "the stream of thought"; that my wife should declare sincerely that she had read page 224 of my copy of James's book on June 17, 1948, and that she recalled that the phrase "the stream of consciousness" was on that page and not the other phrase; that every one of several persons who had recently read Chapter IX in other copies should declare sincerely that to his best recollection James had used the phrase "the stream of consciousness" in that chapter and had not used the other phrase. *If* all of these things were to happen then there would be *more* than good grounds for doubting that S is true; there would be, I should say, absolutely conclusive grounds for saying that S is false. In other words, it would be absolutely certain that the phrase "the stream of thought" was not on page 224 of my copy of James's book on June 17, 1948; and it would be absolutely certain that my seemingly vivid recollection of seeing it there was a queer delusion. The fourth step of the Verification Argument could, therefore, be reformulated as saying that *if* a sufficient number of things were to occur then there would be absolutely conclusive grounds for saying that S is false.

The second measure involved in revising the Verification Argument would be to change the fifth step by substituting for the false proposition "If at any time there should be a reasonable doubt that S is true then at no previous time did anyone make absolutely certain that S is true," the true proposition "If at any time there should be absolutely conclusive grounds that S is false then at no previous time did anyone make absolutely certain that S is true." The latter proposition is clearly true. It is a plain tautology. In ordinary discourse the expressions "I made absolutely certain that p is true" and "there are absolutely conclusive grounds that p is false" are used in logical opposition to one another. It would be a contradiction to say "There are absolutely conclusive grounds that p is false but I made absolutely certain that p is true." The statement "I made absolutely certain that p is true" entails "p is true"; and the statement "There are absolutely conclusive grounds that p is false" entails "p is false." Thus the statement "There are absolutely conclusive grounds that p is false but I made absolutely certain that p is true" entails the contradiction "p is false and p is true." Therefore the proposition "If at any time there should be absolutely conclusive grounds that S is false then at no previous time did anyone make absolutely certain that S is true" is a tautology.

If the Verification Argument were revised by strengthening the fourth step and changing the fifth step, in the way that I have suggested, then the argument *would* prove (provided that there were no other error in the argument, which, I think, there is) that on June 17, 1948, I did not make absolutely certain that S is true. But if the argument were revised in this way then it could not be used to prove the *general* proposition that *no* empirical statement can be conclusively established as true, for an obvious reason. In its revised form the argument would contain as a premise the proposition "If at any time there are absolutely conclusive grounds that S is false then at no previous time did anyone make absolutely certain that S is true." Even if the argument could be used as a valid proof that I was mistaken when I asserted that I had made absolutely certain that S is true it could not be used as a valid proof that no empirical statement can be conclusively established as true, *because* one premise of the argument relies on the supposition that a particular statement, the statement "S is false," can be conclusively established as true. The situation with regard to the Verification Argument is, therefore, as follows: When stated in its original form, as presented by Lewis, the fifth step in the argument is a logical error. When the argument is revised so as to avoid this error, then it cannot be used to validly prove the proposition that no empirical statement can be conclusively established as true, which is the conclusion that it was intended to prove.

II

I wish to point out another error in the Verification Argument, an error that I believe to be of very considerable philosophical importance. The whole argument may be stated as follows:

I. *S* has consequences.

II. The number of consequences of *S* is infinite.

III. The consequences of *S* *may* fail to occur.

IV. *If* some of the consequences of *S* *were* to fail to occur, then there would be a reasonable doubt that *S* is true.

V. If at any time there should be a reasonable doubt that *S* is true then at no previous time did anyone make absolutely certain that *S* is true.

Conclusion: No one did make absolutely certain that *S* is true.

I will call this the "original" Verification Argument. Before I try to show the second error in the argument I wish to make some remarks. In the first place, I have stated the argument as if it applied only to the statement *S*. But it is intended, of course, to be a perfectly general argument. There could be substituted for *S* any other empirical statement. If the argument as stated is sound, then by substituting any other empirical statement for *S* we could obtain a parallel, sound argument. In this sense the Verification Argument, if it were sound, would prove, with respect to any empirical statement whatever, that no one did make absolutely certain that that statement is true. Indeed, it would prove that no one *can* make absolutely certain that that statement is true, because the argument applies at any *time* whatever. In the second place, I have tried to show that premise V is false. I suggested that this false step could be eliminated by the adoption of these two measures: First, to substitute for IV the proposition, which I will call "IV*a*," "If a sufficient number of the consequences of *S* were to fail to occur, then it would be absolutely conclusive that *S* is false"; second, to substitute for V the proposition, which I will call "V*a*," "If at any time it should be absolutely conclusive that *S* is false then at no previous time did anyone make absolutely certain that *S* is true." It seems to me that both IV*a* and V*a* are true. If these substitutions are made then the whole argument may be restated as follows:

I. *S* has consequences.

II. The consequences of *S* are infinite in number.

III. The consequences of *S* may fail to occur.

IV*a*. If a sufficient number of the consequences of *S* were to fail to occur then it would be absolutely conclusive that *S* is false.

V*a*. If at any time it should be absolutely conclusive that *S* is false then at no previous time did anyone make absolutely certain that *S* is true.

Conclusion: No one did make absolutely certain that *S* is true.

This second statement of the argument I will call the "revised" Verification Argument. The revised argument is different from the original argument in two respects. First, premise V of the original argument is false but the corresponding premise of the revised argument is true. Second, premise IV*a* of the revised argument contains the assumption that an empirical statement, "*S* is false," can be conclusively established as true. If we substituted for *S* in the revised argument any other empirical statement, *p*, then IV*a* would contain the assumption that it can be conclusively established that the contradictory of *p* is true. No premise of the original argument, however, contains the assumption that any empirical statement can be conclusively established as true. This difference between the two arguments might be expressed in this way: If all of its premises were true the original argument would prove, with regard to any empirical statement that was substituted for *S*, that that statement cannot be conclusively established; and no premise of the argument assumes that any empirical statement can be conclusively established; therefore it could properly be said that if all of its premises were true the original argument would prove the general proposition that *no* empirical statement can be conclusively established. If all of its premises were true the revised argument would also prove, with regard to any empirical statement that was substituted for *S*, that that statement cannot be conclusively established; but since one premise assumes that an empirical statement can be conclusively established, it would be wrong to say that the revised argument, if its premises were all true, would prove the general proposition that *no* empirical statement can be conclusively established. No matter what statement was substituted for *S*, premise IV*a* would assume that the contradictory of that statement can be conclusively established. The revised argument has this peculiar logical character, that if all of its premises were true it would prove, with regard to *any* empirical statement, that that statement cannot be completely verified, but it would not prove that *no* empirical statement can be completely verified.

The revised argument, however, does *seem* to prove, with regard to my statement *S*, that no one can make absolutely certain that *S* is true. If it does prove this then it follows that I was mistaken when I asserted that on June 17, 1948, I made absolutely certain that *S* is true. I have previously accepted premises I, II, IV*a*, and V*a*. This leaves premise III. I believe that III contains a serious mistake. I expected III in this way: "The consequences of *S may* fail to occur." Lewis makes use of III in the following passage:

> No matter how fully I may have investigated this objective fact, there will remain some theoretical possibility of mistake; there will be further consequences which must be thus and so if the judgment is true, and not all of these will have been determined. The possibility that such further tests, if made, might have a negative result, cannot be altogether precluded; and this possibility marks the judgment as, at the time in question, not fully verified and less than absolutely certain.[19]

When Lewis says, "The possibility that such further tests, if made, might have a negative result, cannot be altogether precluded" he is asserting the proposition which I have called "III." Carnap, in discussing the statement "There is a white thing on this table," says that "the degree of confirmation, after a few observations have been made, will be so high that we practically cannot help accepting the sentence." When he adds, "But even in this case there remains still the theoretical possibility of denying the sentence"[20] he is, I believe, making use of III. It is unlikely that he is merely saying that it is possible that someone should deny the statement to be true, because the fact that someone had denied the statement to be true would in no way tend to show that the statement cannot be completely verified. It is likely that what he is asserting is that there "remains still the theoretical possibility" that some of the statements, which are "predictions about future observations" and which can be inferred from the statement in question, should turn out to be false. If this is a correct interpretation of his remarks then he is asserting III.

In order that we shall be clear about the meaning of III let us remind ourselves of what are some of the "consequences" or "expected results in experience" or "predictions about future observations" that can be inferred from *S*. If *S* is true then one consequence is that if I were to look now at page 224 of James's book I should see the phrase "the stream of thought." Another consequence is that if I were to look

---

19 *An Analysis of Knowledge and Valuation*, p. 180.
20 "Testability and Meaning," *Phil. of Science*, III (1936), p. 426.

again two seconds later I should again see it; another is that if my wife were to look a second later at that page she would see that phrase; and so on. What proposition III says is that it is *possible* that some or all of these things should fail to occur, that it is *possible,* for example, that if I were to look at page 224 now I should *not* see that phrase. Although it may appear obvious to some philosophers what is meant by saying that such a thing is "possible," it does not appear at all obvious to me, and I wish to scrutinize proposition III.

In order for the Verification Argument to be a valid deductive argument (i.e., an argument in which the premises entail the conclusion) III must be understood in such a way that it implies the following proposition, which I will call "IIIa": "It is not certain that the consequences of S will occur." Why must III be understood in this way? For this reason, that someone might agree that it is *possible* that some or all the consequences of S should fail to occur but at the same time maintain that it is *certain* that they will occur. I might agree, for example, that it is *possible,* in some sense of "possible" that if I were to look at page 224 of James's book now I should not see the phrase "the stream of thought," but maintain, nevertheless, that it is certain that if I were to look at that page now I should see that phrase. The assertion of proposition IIIa is, therefore, a required step in the argument. If III is understood in such a way that it implies IIIa then the revised argument is a valid deductive argument. This will be seen if we substitute IIIa for III and write down the whole argument, which I will call the "finished" Verification Argument:

I. S has consequences.

II. The consequences of S are infinite in number.

IIIa. It is not certain that the consequences of S will occur.

IVa. If a sufficient number of the consequences of S should fail to occur then it would be absolutely conclusive that S is false.

Va. If at any time it should be absolutely conclusive that S is false then at no previous time did anyone make absolutely certain that S is true.

Conclusion: No one did make absolutely certain that S is true.

It seems to me that the conclusion does follow logically from the premises. To put the argument more briefly: If it is the case that were certain things to happen then it would be conclusively established that *S* is false, and if it is not certain that those things will not happen, then it follows that no one has made certain that *S* is true. I have accepted premises I, II, IV*a*, and V*a*. I have admitted that the conjunction composed of these premises and of III*a* entails the conclusion. Therefore, if I were to accept III*a* I should be agreeing that the finished argument is sound and that its conclusion is proved. I should have to admit that I was mistaken when I asserted that I had made absolutely certain that *S* is true. I do not see, however, any good reason for accepting III*a*. I believe that it has seemed obvious to the proponents of the Verification Argument both that III is true and that III implies III*a*. I wish to show that this is a mistake. I wish to show that III may be understood in several senses, that in some of these senses III is true and that in some it is false, and that only in the senses in which III is false does III imply III*a*.

I expressed proposition III in the words "The consequences of *S* *may* fail to occur." I could have expressed III in several other ways. I could have expressed it by saying "It is *possible* that the consequences of *S* will not occur," or by saying "The consequences of *S* *might* not occur" or by saying "*Perhaps* the consequences of *S* will not occur," or by saying "It *may be* that the consequences of *S* will not occur," or by saying "The consequences of *S* *could* fail to occur." The words "may," "possible," "might," "perhaps," "may be," "could," "can" are related to one another in such a way that for any statement that uses one of these words there may be substituted an equivalent statement that uses another of them. But whichever one of this class of statements we employ to express III, its meaning will be open to several different interpretations.

Let us consider some of the different things which might be meant by the proposition "It is possible that the consequences of *S* will not occur." One thing which might be meant is that the statement "The consequences of *S* will not occur" is not self-contradictory. Frequently in philosophical discourse and sometimes in ordinary discourse when it is said "It is possible that so-and-so will happen" or "So-and-so may happen," what is meant is that the statement "So-and-so will happen" is not self-contradictory. If, for example, I were to say that it is possible that beginning tomorrow the temperatures of physical objects will vary with their colors, or that it is possible that in one minute the desk on which I am writing will vanish from sight, one thing which I should mean is that the statements "Beginning tomorrow the temperatures of physical objects will vary with their colors" and "In one minute this desk will vanish from sight" are not self-contradictory. When III is interpreted in this way what it says is that it is not the case that the contradictory of any statement which expresses a consequence of S is self-contradictory. It says, for example, that the statement "If I were to look now at page 224 of James's book I should *not* see the phrase 'the stream of thought' " is not self-contradictory. This interpretation of III I will call "III_1."

Another thing which might be meant by III is that no statement that states the *grounds* for holding that any consequence of S will occur *entails* that it will occur. Let me make this clearer by an example. If someone were to ask me why I am sure that if I were to look now at page 224 of James's book I should see the phrase "the stream of thought," I might reply "I saw it there yesterday and there is no reason to believe that the page has changed or been altered since then and my vision is normal and the light is good." But what I offer as reasons or grounds for saying that if I were to look at that page now I should see that phrase, does not *entail* that if I were to look at that page now I should see that phrase. In the sense of "possible" which is used in III_1, it is possible that the following statement is true: "I saw the phrase on that page yesterday and there is no reason to believe that the printing on that page has changed or been altered since then and my vision is normal and the light is good, *but* if I were to look on that page now I should *not* see that phrase." This statement is not self-contradictory. I have called the following statement, "c": "If I were to look now at page 224 of James's book I should see the phrase 'the stream of thought.' " c expresses one of the consequences of S. Let us call the statement that I have just used to state the reasons for holding c to be true, "R." The proposition "R but not c" is not self-contradictory. In other words, R does not entail c. It is possible, in the sense of "possible" that is used in III_1, that c is false even though R is true. It is possible, in this sense, that the phrase "the stream of thought" has vanished from page 224 even though there is no reason to think that it has; and if it had vanished I should not see it there. It is not self-contradictory to suppose that it has vanished although there is no reason to think that it has. It seems to me, that with regard to any statement p that expresses a consequence of S, it is the case that it is not entailed by any statement q that states the grounds for saying that p is true. This is one natural interpretation of the meaning of III. I will call it "III$_2$." It must not be supposed that III$_1$ and III$_2$ are equivalent. With regard to c, for example, III$_1$ says that the statement "not c" or "c is false" is not self-contradictory. What III$_2$ says, with regard to c, is that the statement "R but not c" is not self-contradictory. III$_1$ says that the negative of c is not, by itself, self-contradictory. III$_2$ says that the conjunction of R and the negative of c is not self-contradictory, or, in other words, that R does not entail c. III$_1$ and III$_2$ are entirely different propositions and both of them seem to me to be clearly true. The conjunction of III$_1$ and III$_2$ is, I believe, what would ordinarily be meant by the statement "It is *logically* possible that the consequences of S will not occur."

I wish now to point out other uses of "possible" and the correlative words that are of quite a different *kind* than the two so far mentioned. When it is said in ordinary life that "It is possible that so and so will happen," what is very frequently meant is that *there is some reason to believe* that so-and-so will happen. Suppose that my wife were to say, "It's possible that Mr. Jones will come to see us this evening." If I were to ask "Why do you think so?" she might naturally reply "He said to me this morning that he would come if he did not have to work." In this example the reply consists in stating a piece of *evidence* in favor of saying that he will come. Suppose that a friend, who looks to be in perfect health, should say "I may be extremely ill tomorrow." To my question "Why do you say that?" he might reply "Because I ate scallops for lunch and they have always made me very ill." Here again the reply offers a *reason,* some *grounds* for saying that he will be ill. This usage of "possible," "may," "might" and their correlatives is enormously frequent in ordinary discourse, and it is strikingly different from the usages noted in III$_1$ and III$_2$. When my friend replied to my question "Why do you say that you may be ill tomorrow?" his reply did not consist in pointing out the logical truth that the statement "I shall be ill tomorrow" is not self-contradictory; nor did it consist in pointing out the logical truth that no statement which expressed grounds for saying that he will not be ill tomorrow would entail that he will not be ill tomorrow. It did consist in giving some reason, or evidence, or grounds, for believing that he will be ill tomorrow. My question "Why do you think so?" or "Why do you say that?" would be naturally understood as a request for the reason for believing that he will be ill tomorrow. It would be quite absurd for him to reply to my question by saying, "Because the statement 'I shall be ill tomorrow' is not self-contradictory" or by saying, "Because it does not follow logically from the fact that my health is excellent and that I feel perfectly well that I shall *not* be ill tomorrow." If he were to reply in this way it would be regarded as a joke. If a Greek scholar were to remark "It's possible that Plato was not the author of *The Republic*" we should ask "Why do you say so?" and it would be only a joke if he were to reply "The statement 'Plato was not the author of *The Republic*' is not self-contradictory," or to reply "The evidence we have for saying that Plato was the author does not *entail* that he was the author." We should naturally interpret his first remark to mean "There is evidence that Plato was not the author of *The Republic*"; and our question "Why do you say so?" would be naturally understood as a request for him to say what the evidence was. His reply gave no evidence. He failed to show that it is *possible* that Plato was not the author of *The Republic*, in the sense of "possible" which was appropriate to the context.

A radical difference between the use of "possible" that I am now describing and its uses in III$_1$ and III$_2$ consists in the fact that the kind of "possibility" now being described admits of *degree,* whereas those other kinds do not. The ordinary expressions "There is some possibility," "It is barely possible," "There is a slight possibility," "There is a considerable possibility," "There is a greater possibility that so-and-so than that such and such," "It is very possible," "There is a strong possibility," all belong to the use of "possible" now being described and not to its uses in III$_1$ and III$_2$. If the man who says "It is possible that I shall be ill tomorrow" supports his statement by saying that he had just eaten scallops and scallops had always made him ill, then he could have correctly expressed his statement by the words "It is *very* possible that I shall be ill tomorrow" or "There is a *strong* possibility that I shall be ill tomorrow." But if he supports his statement by saying that "I shall be ill tomorrow" is not self-contradictory, or by saying that the fact that he is in excellent health does not entail that he will not be ill tomorrow, then he could *not* have correctly expressed his statement by the words "It is *very* possible that I shall be ill tomorrow" or "There is a *considerable* possibility that I shall be ill tomorrow." The expressions "There is some possibility," "There is a considerable possibility," "There is a greater possibility that so-and-so than that such and such" mean roughly the same as the expressions "There is some evidence," "There is a fair amount of evidence," "There is more evidence that so-and-so than that such and such." The expressions of both types are expressions of *degree*. If the man who says "It is possible that Plato was not the author of *The Republic*" means that the statement "Plato was not the author of *The Republic*" is not self-contradictory, then he is not using "possible" in a sense that admits of degree. There can be more or less evidence for a statement, the reasons for believing it can be more or less strong, but a statement cannot be more or less self-contradictory. The statement "There is a slight possibility that the Smiths are in Paris this week but a greater possibility that they are in Rome" illustrates a use of "possibility" which is totally different from *logical* possibility. The statement obviously does not mean that "The Smiths are in Rome" is *less* self-contradictory than "The Smiths are in Paris." It does not make sense to say that one statement is "less" self-contradictory than another. And it obviously does not mean that the evidence as to the whereabouts of the Smiths entails "The Smiths are in Rome" *more* than it entails "The Smiths are in Paris." It does not make sense to say "*p* entails *q* more than it entails *r*." The statement obviously means that there is some reason to think that the Smiths are in Paris but greater reason to think that they are in Rome.

I hope that I have made it sufficiently clear that there is a common use of the word "possible" and of the correlative words, according to which the statement "It is possible that so-and-so" means "There is some reason to believe that so-and-so." When proposition III is interpreted in this sense it is equivalent to the proposition "There is some reason to believe that the consequences of S will not occur." I will call this interpretation of III, "III_3."

There are other common uses of "possible" closely analogous to its use in III_3. Suppose that the members of a committee are to meet together. All of the committee, save one, turn up at the appointed time and place. Someone asks "Does K. (the missing member) know that there is a meeting?" Inquiry reveals that no one recalls having notified K. of the meeting. It is also pointed out that, although an announcement of the meeting appeared in the local newspaper, K. frequently does not read the newspaper. A member of the committee sums up the situation by saying "Then it is possible K. does not know about the meeting." This latter statement means that *there is no reason* to think that K. does know about the meeting; and this seems to me to be a very common usage of the word "possible" and its correlatives. The proposition "It is possible that the consequences of S will not occur," which is proposition III, if interpreted in the sense just described, would mean "There is no reason to think that the consequences of S will occur." This interpretation of III, I will call "III$_4$."

Suppose that the question arises as to whether M. was in a certain theater at the time when a murder was committed there. It is known that he left a bar only fifteen minutes before and that it would be extremely difficult for any man to go from the bar to the theater in fifteen minutes. The situation might be summed up by saying "It is unlikely that M. was at the theater at the time of the murder but it is *possible* that he was." This statement means that there is good reason to believe that M. was not at the theater but that the reason is not absolutely conclusive. It is a very common use of "possible" to say that although there are strong grounds for believing that so-and-so is the case, it is still *possible* that so-and-so is not the case, where this is equivalent to saying that although the grounds for saying that so-and-so is true are strong, they are not absolutely conclusive. If III were interpreted in this way it would mean "The grounds for saying that the consequences of S will occur are not absolutely conclusive." This interpretation of III, I will call "III$_5$."

I have wished to show that sentences of the sort "It is possible that so-and-so," "It may be that so-and-so," "Perhaps so-and-so," have several different uses. The very same sentence has, in different contexts, quite different meanings. I do not know that there are not still other uses of those sentences; but if there are I cannot think of them. The third premise of the Verification Argument is expressed by a sentence of this sort. When it is said "It is possible that the consequences of S will not occur," the question arises, therefore, in which of these different ways is this sentence being used? When Lewis says "The possibility that such further tests, if made, might have a negative result, cannot be altogether precluded" his statement is equivalent to "It is possible that further 'tests,' if made, will have negative results." How are we to understand the use of "possible" in this important premise of the argument? In what sense of "It is possible that so-and-so" is it possible that if I were to look now at page 224 of James's book I should not see the phrase "the stream of thought"? A proponent of the Verification Argument cannot reply that it is possible in the *ordinary* meaning of "It is possible." There is not such a thing as *the* ordinary meaning of that phrase. A sentence of the sort "It is possible that so-and-so" does not have just *one* meaning that is the same in all contexts. The only course open to us is to examine each of the several different interpretations of the third premise in order to see whether there is any interpretation of it which will make the "revised" Verification Argument a sound argument.

III is the proposition "It is possible that the consequences of the statement S will not occur." IIIa is the proposition "It is not known that the consequences of S will occur." I pointed out previously that in order for the revised argument to be a valid deductive argument III must be understood in such a way that it implies IIIa. In order for the revised argument to be a *sound* argument it must also be the case that III is true. (I am using the phrase "a sound argument" in such a way that a deductive argument is a sound argument if and only if it is both the case that it is a valid deductive argument and that all of its premises are true.) Is there an interpretation of III in accordance with which III implies IIIa *and* III is true? The following are the different interpretations of III which arose from the description of the several meanings of sentences of the sort "It is possible that so-and-so":

III$_1$. The statement "The consequences of S will not occur" is not self-contradictory.

III$_2$. No statement, p, which expresses a consequence of S is entailed by any statement, q, which states the grounds for holding that p is true.

III$_3$. There is some reason to believe that the consequences of S will not occur.

III$_4$. There is no reason to think that the consequences of S will occur.

III$_5$. The grounds for holding that the consequences of S will occur are not absolutely conclusive.

With regard to these propositions I think that the following is the case: III$_1$ and III$_2$ are true. But neither of them implies IIIa. III$_3$, III$_4$, and III$_5$ each implies IIIa. But each of them is false. I wish to defend these statements, and I will do so by discussing each of these interpretations of III.

(III$_1$) It is clearly not self-contradictory to say either that all or that some of the consequences of S will not occur. It is possible, in one sense of "It is possible," that they will not occur. But it does not follow in the least that it is not absolutely certain that they will occur. Here is a source of philosophical confusion. With regard to any contingent statement, it is the case that "p is false" is not self-contradictory. A natural way to express this logical truth about p is to say "It is possible that p is false." This provides the temptation to say "Since it is possible that p is false, therefore it is not certain that p is true." But this is a confusion. From the sense of "It is possible that p is false" in which this means that "p is false" is not self-contradictory, it does not follow either that there is some reason to believe that p is false, or that there is no reason to believe that p is true, or that the reason for holding that p is true is not conclusive. The fact that it is possible that p is false, in this sense, *has nothing to do with the question of whether p is false.* In this sense of "It is possible that p is false" it is not self-contradictory to say "It is certain that p is true although it is possible that p is false." In the senses of "It is possible that p is false" that are expressed by III$_4$ and III$_5$ it *is* self-contradictory to say "It is certain that p is true although it is possible that p is false." In the sense of "It is possible that p is false" that is expressed by III$_3$ it is not self-contradictory to say "It is certain that p is true although it is possible that p is false," for the reason that I gave in discussing proposition V. But in the sense of III$_3$ to say "It is possible that p is false" *is* to say something that counts *against* saying "It is certain that p is true."

It is easy to be misled by these different uses of "It is possible" and to conclude that from the fact that it is possible that p is false, when this means that "p is false" is not self-contradictory, that therefore it is not certain that p is true. But in the use of "It is possible" that is expressed by III$_1$, "It is possible that p is false" only tells us what *kind* of statement p is. It only tells us that p is a contingent statement and not a necessary truth or a necessary falsehood. It tells us *nothing* about the state of the evidence with respect to p. In the uses of "It is possible" that are expressed by III$_3$, III$_4$, and III$_5$, the statement "It is possible that p is false" does tell us something about the state of the evidence. It tells us that there is some evidence for believing that p is false, or that there is no evidence for believing that p is true, or that the evidence for p, although strong, is not conclusive. In these latter uses the statement "It is possible that p is false" says something *against* its being certain that p is true. The statement " 'p is false' is not self-contradictory" says nothing whatever against its being certain that p is true. That statement is *neutral* with regard to the question of whether p is true or of whether it is certain that p is true. To say that " 'p is false' is not self-contradictory" entails "It is not certain that p is true," amounts to saying that "p is a contingent statement" entails "It is not certain that p is true." But to say the latter would be to say something false. It is not self-contradictory to say "There are many contingent statements which I know with certainty to be true." c is the statement "If I were to look now at page 224 of James's book I should see the phrase 'the stream of thought.' " c is a contingent statement; which entails that "c is false" is not self-contradictory. It is correct to express this logical fact about c by saying "It is *possible* that if I were to look now at page 224 I should *not* see the phrase 'the stream of thought.' " But although this statement expresses a truth it is not a truth which is even *relevant* to the question of whether it is certain that if I were to look now at that page I should see that phrase.

(III$_2$) Previously I said that the grounds for saying that c is true are expressed by the statement "I saw the phrase when I looked there yesterday, there is no reason to believe that the printing on that page has changed or been altered since then, my vision is normal, and the light is good." I said that this statement, R, does not entail c. A natural way of expressing this fact about the logical relationship of R to c is to say "Even though R is true it is *possible* that c is false." This expresses the fact that the inference from R to c is not a deductive or demonstrative inference. But it provides another great source of philosophical confusion. There is a temptation to conclude from the fact that it is possible, in this sense, that c is false even though R is true that, therefore, it is not *certain* that c is true. It does not, however, follow from the fact that R does not entail c either that it is not certain that c is true or that R does not state the grounds on the basis of which it is certain that c is true. The temptation arises from the fact that there are several uses of "It is possible that p is false" and that frequently these words mean that there is some reason to believe that p is false, or that there is no reason to believe that p is true, or that it is not absolutely conclusive that p is true. When one says "Although R is true c may be false" and expresses by this the fact that "R and not c" is not self-contradictory, it is easy to be misled by the variety of uses of "possible" and "may be" into supposing that one has said something that counts against its being certain that c is true. But the statement that R does not entail c, i.e., that "R and not c" is not self-contradictory, says nothing that counts either for or against its being certain that c is true. Whether it is certain that c is true depends upon the state of the evidence with regard to c. The statement "R does not entail c" says no more about the state of the evidence with regard to c than does the statement " 'c is false' is not self-contradictory." Both statements are irrelevant to that matter. The statement "The fact that R is true makes it absolutely certain that c is true" is in no way contradicted by the statement "R does not entail c." The two statements are perfectly compatible with one another. One statement describes the evidence concerning c. The other describes a logical relationship between R and c of which one could be aware even though one knew nothing whatever about the state of the evidence concerning c. The fact that R does not entail c provides no ground for doubting that c is true. It is a mistake to suppose that because it is possible that c is false even though R is true, in the sense of III_2, that therefore "It is possible that c is false," where these latter words imply that it is not quite certain that c is true. What I have said about c applies equally to every other statement which expresses a consequence of S.

(III_3) III_1 and III_2 provide no basis whatever for accepting $IIIa$. The same thing cannot be said of III_3. If there is some reason for believing that any consequence of S will not occur, this counts in favor of holding that it is not certain that it will occur. But is III_3 true? Is there some reason or ground or evidence for thinking that any consequence of S will not occur; for thinking, for example, that if I were to look now at page 224 of James's book I should *not* see there the phrase "the stream of thought"? There is none whatever. Let us consider what *would* be a reason for thinking that any consequence of S will not occur. If some person of normal vision had carefully looked for that phrase on that page a few minutes ago and had not found it there, then that would be a reason, and a powerful one, for thinking that if I were to look now I should not see it there. Or if my copy of James's book possessed the peculiar characteristic that sometimes the printing on the pages underwent spontaneous changes, that printed words were suddenly replaced by different printed words without external cause, then that would be a reason for doubting that if I were to look now at that page I should see that phrase. But there is no reason to think that any person has looked for that phrase and has not found it there, or to think that my copy of James's book does possess that peculiar characteristic.

It might be objected that although there is no reason to think that these things are true nevertheless they *may* be true. In which of the several senses of "may be" is it that these things *may* be true? If it is in the senses of III_1 and III_2 then it does not follow that it is not certain that they are false. It cannot be said that they may be true in the sense that there is some reason to think that they are true, for we are supposing it to be admitted that there is no reason. May they be true in the sense that there is no reason to think that they are false, or in the sense that the grounds for saying they are false are not conclusive? But there *is* reason to think that they are false. There is reason to think that no one has tried and failed to find that phrase on that page. The reason is that I did make certain that the phrase was there yesterday, and if those printed words were there yesterday then it is perfectly certain that they have been there as long as the book has existed. This is not only a reason but is what would ordinarily be regarded as a conclusive reason for saying that no one of normal vision who has carefully looked for that phrase on that page in good light has failed to see it there. The reason is obvious for saying that my copy of James's book does not have the characteristic that its print undergoes spontaneous changes. I have read millions of printed words on many thousands of printed pages. I have not encountered a single instance of a printed word vanishing from a page or being replaced by another printed word, suddenly and without external cause. Nor have I heard of any other person who had such an encounter. There is overwhelming evidence that printed words do not behave in that way. It is just as conclusive as the evidence that houses do not turn into flowers—that is to say, absolutely conclusive evidence.

It cannot be maintained that there is any particular evidence for thinking that the consequences of S will not occur. It might be held, however, that there is a *general* reason for doubting whether they will occur. The reason is that the consequences of *some* statements *do* fail to occur. It might be argued that, since sometimes people are disappointed in expecting the consequences of a certain statement to occur, therefore I may be disappointed in expecting the consequences of S to occur. This would be similar to arguing that since people are sometimes mistaken when they declare a statement to be true therefore I may be mistaken when I declare S to be true, or that since people sometimes suffer from hallucinations therefore I may have been suffering from an hallucination when I thought that I was making certain that *S* is true.

There is undoubtedly a temptation to argue this way. The following remarks by Russell are but one example of it. "Lunatics hear voices which other people do not hear; instead of crediting them with abnormally acute hearing, we lock them up. But if we sometimes hear sentences which have not proceeded from a body, why should this not always be the case? Perhaps our imagination has conjured up all the things that we think others have said to us."[21] Here Russell is arguing that since sometimes people imagine voices, therefore in every case when one "hears a voice" one may have imagined the voice. I cannot undertake to examine in this paper all of the sources of the temptation to argue in this way. They lie in some serious difficulties surrounding the philosophical question, "How do I know that I am not dreaming or having an hallucination?" To investigate them would lead us away from the Verification Argument.

I do want to point out that this sort of arguing is, on the face of it, entirely invalid. To argue that since people sometimes make mistakes therefore I may be mistaken when I say that *S* is true is like arguing that Francis Bacon may not have been an Englishman because some men are not Englishmen, or that Bismarck may not have been a statesman because some men are not statesmen, or that I may be blind because some men are blind. This is a travesty of correct reasoning. There are *some* circumstances in which reasoning of that sort is acceptable. If the door to the adjoining office is closed and we are wondering what the man in there is doing and someone says that surely he is sitting at his desk, one of us might reply "He may not be sitting at his desk because sometimes he sits on the floor." In these circumstances the fact that sometimes he sits on the floor *does* count against saying that it is surely the case that he is sitting at his desk. But if we were to open the door and see him sitting at his desk then it would be absurd for anyone to say "He may not be sitting at his desk because sometimes he sits on the floor." This sort of reasoning is acceptable in those circumstances where one has not yet investigated the question at issue, where one is not in a position to know the answer, where one can only make conjectures. If there is an unexamined chair in the closet and

---

21 Bertrand Russell, *An Outline of Philosophy* (1927), p. 9.

someone assumes that it is wooden, we might reply "It may be metal because some chairs are metal." But once we have looked at it, felt it, and scratched some splinters from it then it would be only amusing to say "It may be metal because some chairs are metal." Here is a type of reasoning that is appropriate in some circumstances but not in all circumstances. There might be circumstances in which it would be reasonable to say "I may be having an hallucination because people do have hallucinations" or to say "I have imagined that I heard a voice because sometimes I do imagine that I hear voices"; but it is an error to suppose that this is a reasonable thing to say in *all* circumstances.

These remarks apply to what we were considering as a general reason for doubting that the consequences of *S* will occur. The suggestion was that the consequences of *S* may fail to occur because the consequences of some statements do fail to occur, that since sometimes people make false statements and are disappointed when they expect their consequences to occur, that therefore when I asserted *S*, I may have made a false statement and may be disappointed in expecting its consequences to occur. There are circumstances in which it is highly reasonable to temper the confidence with which I assert something, by reminding myself that sometimes other people and myself make erroneous assertions. But it is a mistake to suppose this to be reasonable in *all* circumstances, to suppose, for example, that it is reasonable to conclude that, since sometimes I am mistaken therefore when I say that I am more than ten years old I may be mistaken and that it is not quite certain that I am more than ten. Thus the suggestion that there is a general reason for believing that the statements that express consequences of *S* are false, and that the reason is that *some* statements that people expect to be true turn out to be false, is completely in error and presents nothing more than a caricature of good reasoning. It would be a caricature of good reasoning if a member of a society of Greek scholars were to declare to the society that there is reason to believe that Plato was not the author of *The Republic* and when asked for the reason were to reply that people often believe propositions which are false.

I conclude that III$_3$ is false. It asserts that the consequences of *S* may fail to occur in the sense that there is some reason for thinking that they will not occur. But there is no reason at all, neither any particular reason nor any general reason, for thinking that any of the consequences of *S* will not occur.

(III$_4$) Proposition III$_4$, which expresses another common usage of "It is possible," says that there is *no* reason to believe that the consequences of S *will* occur. III$_4$ is false because there is a very good reason for saying that the consequences of S will occur. The reason is that S is true. What better reason could there be? Two objections might be made to this. First, it might be said that no empirical statement, *p*, is evidence for another empirical statement, *q*, unless *p* entails *q*; S does not entail any statement that expresses a consequence of S (e.g., S does not entail *c*); therefore the fact that S is true is no evidence that any statement is true that expresses a consequence of S. This objection, however, cannot be made use of by a proponent of the Verification Argument. The fourth premise in that argument says that if some of the consequences of S were not to occur then there would be some reason to think that S is false. But the contradictory of a statement which expresses a consequence of S does not entail that S is false (e.g., "*c* is false" does not entail "S is false"). Therefore, one step in the Verification Argument assumes what is clearly correct, that a statement, *p*, can be evidence for a statement, *q*, even though *p* does not entail *q*. The second objection that might be made is that if S is true then there is good reason to think that the consequences of S will occur, but that it is not absolutely certain that S is true. If a person made this objection it would be necessary to ask him what his reason is for saying that it is not absolutely certain that S is true. Is his reason that he has looked at that page of James's book and failed to find that phrase there? In other words is he saying that there are particular grounds for thinking that it is not certain that S is true? But there are no such grounds. Is his reason the general philosophical proposition that no empirical statement is absolutely certain? But that is the very proposition that the Verification Argument is meant to prove and so that proposition cannot be used as a step in the argument. There is no way in which it can be consistently upheld, within the context of the Verification Argument, that there is no reason to believe that the consequences of S will occur. III$_4$ cannot be accepted as an interpretation of proposition III in the argument, because not only is III$_4$ false but also its use as a premise would lead either to an inconsistency or to a circular argument.

(III$_5$) It is unlikely that any philosopher who has used the Verification Argument would wish to maintain either that there is some reason to believe that the consequences of S will not occur or that there is no reason to believe that they will occur. But undoubtedly he would wish to maintain that the grounds for saying that they will occur are not absolutely conclusive. The statements that express consequences of S are empirical statements and the Verification Argument is intended to prove that the grounds for no empirical statement are absolutely conclusive. If the conclusion of the argument is true then III_5 is true, and it would be inconsistent to accept the conclusion and not to accept III_5. But we are now regarding III_5 as a *premise* in the argument intended to prove that conclusion. Within the context of the Verification Argument the proposition that is the conclusion of it cannot be offered in support of premise III_5, because the argument would then be circular. What is to be offered in support of III_5?

The Verification Argument is subject to a serious logical difficulty. It cannot be a valid deductive argument unless it contains the premise that it is not certain that the consequences of S will occur. The fact that this premise is required is obscured by the ambiguity of proposition III, which is the proposition "It is possible that the consequences of S will not occur." The meaning of III is open to several interpretations. Only if III is interpreted in such a way that it implies III_a is the argument valid. III_5 is one natural interpretation of III, and III_5 implies III_a. In fact, III_5 and III_a are logically equivalent propositions. III_5 entails $IIIa$ and $IIIa$ entails III_5. But $IIIa$ (or III_5) is a proposition which requires *proof*. Proposition $IIIa$ is extremely similar to the proposition which is the general conclusion of the Verification Argument. The conclusion says something about every member of the entire class of empirical statements—it says that the truth of not one of those statements is completely certain. Proposition III_a says the same thing about every member of a certain subclass of empirical statements, namely, the class of conditional statements which express consequences of S. S was but one example of an empirical statement, picked at random, and could be replaced by any other empirical statement. Whatever statement may be substituted for S, proposition $IIIa$ would say that it is not certain that the conditional statements that express consequences of *that* statement are true. In effect, therefore, proposition $IIIa$ says that the truth of not one of an enormous class of statements—namely, all conditional statements which express consequences of any empirical statement—is completely certain. This sweeping and paradoxical claim requires to be justified as much as does the general conclusion of the Verification Argument. Every one of us in ordinary life frequently makes assertions of the following sort: "It is absolutely certain that if you look through these binoculars you will see a canoe on the lake," "We know for certain that if you pour that acid into this solution you will see a red precipitate form," "It is perfectly certain that if you were to touch that wire you would receive a shock." That is to say, every one of us frequently asserts of some conditional, empirical statement that its truth is entirely certain and beyond question. Shall it be said that the conditional, empirical statements which express consequences of *S*, or of any statement substituted for *S*, are not certainly true because *no* conditional, empirical statement is certainly true? What is the justification for the latter proposition? What is the justification for saying that every time anyone has made an assertion of the preceding sort his assertion has been false or mistaken or unjustified?

Here is a gap in the Verification Argument and the Verification Argument itself cannot be used to fill that gap. What is to fill it? Some other philosophical argument? Hume produced an argument that, if it were sound, would prove that it is not certain that any of the conditional statements that express consequences of *S* are true. But Hume's argument could not be used by a proponent of the Verification Argument to prove premise IIIa. Hume's argument was intended to prove that no inferences about matters of fact are "founded on reasoning."[22] He meant that there can be no reason to accept any inference about matters of fact—that there can be no reasonable inferences about matters of fact. But premise IV of the original Verification Argument asserts that if some of the consequences of *S* were not to occur then there would be reason to think that *S* is false. That premise implies that there can be reasonable inferences about matters of fact. Thus Hume's argument is incompatible with the Verification Argument. Perhaps there is some other philosophical argument that could be offered in support of IIIa; but until it has been presented we cannot determine whether it is sound or whether it is compatible with the Verification Argument.

The Verification Argument does not stand on its own feet. Proposition IIIa, a required premise, makes a claim which is of the *same nature* as the general conclusion of the argument and only slightly less grandiose. The philosophers who have used the argument have tended to tacitly assume IIIa. They have not clearly seen that IIIa needs to be

---

[22] *An Enquiry Concerning Human Understanding*, pt. II, sec. 4.

set down as a premise and to be *supported*. The explanation for this, I believe, is that these philosophers have been confused by the variety of uses of the phrases "It is possible," "It may be," and their equivalents. When they have said that "It is possible that further tests will have a negative result" or that "The predictions about future observations may prove to be false," they have thought that they were saying something that is so obviously true that it does not require support *and* that shows that it is not certain that those further "tests" will have a "positive result" or that those "predictions" will prove to be true. The fact is, however, that although there are natural interpretations of III according to which III is obviously true, none of those interpretations show that III*a* is true; and although there are natural interpretations of III which, if true, would show that III*a* is true, there is no reason to think that III is true in any of those interpretations. The result of this confusion is that III*a* although a required premise, is an unsupported premise.

There is one passage in his exposition of the Verification Argument in which it is clear that Lewis is asserting a proposition corresponding to III$_5$ and, therefore, to III*a*. He is discussing his "belief" that there is a piece of paper before him. He says:

> And my belief must imply as probable, anything the failure of which I should accept as tending to discredit this belief. Also it is the case that such future contingencies implied by the belief, are not such that failure of them can be absolutely precluded in the light of prior empirical corroborations of what is believed. However improbable, it remains thinkable that such later tests could have a negative result. Though truth of the belief itself implies a positive result of such later tests, the evidence to date does not imply this as more than probable, even though the difference of this probability from theoretical certainty should be so slight that practically it would be foolish to hesitate over it. Indeed we could be too deprecatory about this difference: if we interrogate experience we shall find plenty of occasions when we have felt quite sure of an objective fact perceived but later circumstance has shocked us out of our assurance and obliged us to retract or modify our belief.[23]

When he says "the evidence to date does not imply this as more than probable" ("this" refers to "a positive result of such later tests") it is clear that Lewis is asserting that the evidence for any statement that expresses a consequence of his belief is not absolutely conclusive. (If the evidence for a statement is not absolutely conclusive then it follows

[23] *An Analysis of Knowledge and Valuation*, p. 176.

that it is not certain that the statement is true, i.e., III$_5$ entails IIIa.)
What is his reason for saying that there is no absolutely conclusive
evidence that later "tests" will not have a "negative result"? I think
that part of his reason lies in the statement "However improbable, it
remains *thinkable* that such later tests could have a negative result."
It is clear that he is using "thinkable" as equivalent to "conceivable."
The phrase "It is conceivable" is used in ordinary language in exactly
the same way as are the phrases "It is possible" and "It may be." The
expression "It is conceivable that so-and-so" is open to the same variety
of interpretations as is the expression "It is possible that so-and-so."
How shall we understand the statement "However improbable, it remains conceivable that later tests will have a negative result"? If it
means that it is not self-contradictory to suppose that later "tests" will
have a "negative result," or that the evidence for saying that later
"tests" will have a "positive result" does not *entail* that they will, then
this statement is true; but it provides no ground for denying that the
evidence is absolutely conclusive that later "tests" will have a "positive result." If the statement means that there is *some evidence* that
later "tests" will have a "negative result," then the statement is false.
With regard to c, it is not true that there is some evidence that if I were
to look at page 224 of James's book I should *not* see the phrase "the
stream of thought." The statement does not mean that there is *no*
evidence that later "tests" will have a "positive result"; for Lewis
clearly holds that it may be probable or even highly probable that
later "tests" will have a "positive result." The only thing left for the
statement to mean, so far as I can see, is that the evidence, although
strong, is not absolutely conclusive that later "tests" will have a
"positive result." But if the statement "However improbable, it remains conceivable that later tests will have a negative result" has this
meaning, then it provides no justification at all for the statement that
"the evidence to date does not imply as more than probable that later
tests will have a positive result." The two statements are then *identical*
in meaning and the former statement can provide no justification for
the assertion of the latter statement. Both statements are equally in
need of support.

I believe that there is something else in the paragraph just quoted
from Lewis that he may have regarded as supporting his claim that
"the evidence to date does not imply this as more than probable, even
though the difference of this probability from theoretical certainty

should be so slight that practically it would be foolish to hesitate about it." He continues: "Indeed we could be too deprecatory about this difference: if we interrogate experience we shall find plenty of occasions when we have felt quite sure of an objective fact perceived but later circumstance has shocked us out of our assurance and obliged us to retract or modify our belief." In terms of my statement, S, I understand Lewis to be saying the following: It is no more than probable that the consequences of S will occur; but it may be so highly probable that there is no "practical difference" between this high probability and "theoretical certainty." It may be so highly probable that it would be foolish to hesitate over this difference and to feel any doubt that the consequences of S will occur. But then, he warns, perhaps we are deprecating this difference too much. ("Indeed we could be too deprecatory about this difference:") I understand him to be saying that we should remember that it is not certain that the consequences of S will occur and that perhaps we should hesitate a little, i.e., feel a slight doubt that they will occur. Why? *Because* there have been numerous occasions when we felt sure of something and then discovered later that we were mistaken. If I understand Lewis correctly, (he is using the latter fact both to reinforce his claim that it is not conclusive that the consequences of S will occur) and as a ground for suggesting that perhaps it would be reasonable to feel a slight doubt that they will occur. But if he is doing this then he is making a mistake that I mentioned in my discussion of proposition III_3. That mistake consists in thinking that there is a *general* reason for doubting any particular statement that we believe to be true, the reason being that it has frequently happened that what we believed to be true turned out to be false. I am not entirely confident that Lewis is arguing in that way; but if he is, then enough was said in our discussion of III_3 to show that this alleged general reason for doubt is no good reason at all for doubting that the consequences of S will occur and that to argue in this way is to commit a travesty of correct thinking.

The passage that I have just quoted contains the clearest assertion of proposition III_5 that I can find in Lewis' writing or in the writing of any other proponent of the Verification Argument. In this passage no good grounds are offered in defense of III_5 and the assertion of it seems to obtain its plausibility from the ambiguity of the expression "It is conceivable" ("thinkable"), which has the same ambiguity as the expression "It is possible." Almost anyone who reflects on these matters will, indeed, feel an inclination to say that III_5 is true. What is the source of this strong inclination? I believe that it lies exactly in that ambiguity. Consider c, which is the statement "If I were to look now at page 224 of James's book I should see there the phrase 'the stream of thought,'" and which expresses a consequence of S. One feels compelled to say that it is possible that c is false. And this is correct. It *is* possible that c is false *in the sense* that "c is false" is not self-contradictory, and *in the sense* that the grounds for affirming c do not entail c. Now feeling assured that the statement "It is possible that c is false" is undeniably true, one wants to conclude "Therefore it is not *certain* that c is true." And from the latter statement one correctly concludes "Therefore the grounds for affirming c are not conclusive." Reasoning in this way leads one to accept III_5. But this reasoning is fallacious. The error lies in the step from "It is possible that c is false" to "Therefore it is not certain that c is true." In the senses of "It is possible" in which it is undeniably true that it is possible that c is false, the fact that it is possible is irrelevant to the question of whether or not it is certain that c is true. The fact that, in those senses, it is possible that c is false is entirely compatible with the fact that the grounds for affirming c are perfectly conclusive and that it is perfectly certain that c is true. The grounds I should give for affirming c are that I saw the phrase "the stream of thought" when I looked at page 224 of James's book yesterday and that there is no reason to believe that the printing on the page has changed or been altered since then, and that my vision is normal, and that the light is good. These grounds would be accepted as absolutely conclusive by everyone in ordinary life. In what way do they fail to be conclusive?

It will be said "It is possible that you had an hallucination yesterday and did not see the page of a book at all." As I said before, there are connected with this statement problems of great importance which cannot be studied in this paper. I will limit myself to these remarks: The meaning of the statement is not that there is *some reason* to think that *I* had an hallucination yesterday. The philosopher who makes this statement does not intend to claim that by virtue of a particular knowledge of me and of my circumstances yesterday he has evidence that I suffered from an hallucination. This statement is intended to make the general claim that *everytime anyone* has believed that he did perceive a certain thing it is possible that he did not perceive that thing at all and that he had an hallucination instead.

Furthermore this statement does not claim merely that whenever anyone has believed that he perceived a certain thing it is possible that he
was having an *hallucination*. It is intended to claim that it is *also*
possible that he was *dreaming* or that he had an *optical illusion*, or,
in short, that he suffered from *an error of some sort*. The philosophical
statement "Whenever anyone has made a perceptual judgment it is
possible that he was suffering from hallucination" is a disguised way
of claiming "Whenever anyone has made a perceptual judgment it is
possible that his judgment was in error," or of claiming "It is possible
that every perceptual statement is false."

Now is it possible that every perceptual statement is false in any sense
of "It is possible" from which it follows that it is not *certain* that any
perceptual statement is true? Let us review the uses of "It is possible"
that we have described. Any perceptual statement may be false in the
sense that the contradictory of any perceptual statement is not self-
contradictory; but it does not follow that it is not certain that any
perceptual statement is true (III_1). It is true, I believe, that the evidence
that one could offer in behalf of any perceptual statement does not
entail that the statement is true; but, again, it does not follow that it
is not certain that any perceptual statement is true (III_2). It cannot be
maintained that with respect to each perceptual statement there is some
particular evidence that that statement is false; e.g., there is no evidence
at all that my statement that I saw a page of a book yesterday is false
(III_3). To argue that since some perceptual statements are false therefore it is not certain that any particular perceptual statement is true is
unsound reasoning (III_3). It would be absurd to contend that there is
no reason to accept any perceptual statement (III_4).

Nothing remains to be meant by the statement "It is possible that
every perceptual statement is false" except the claim that the grounds
for accepting any perceptual statement are never conclusive (III_5). As
I said, I believe that the grounds which one could offer in behalf of
any perceptual statement do not *entail* that the statement is true. It
does not follow in the least, however, that the grounds are not perfectly
conclusive. I can produce enormously good grounds for accepting my
perceptual statement that I saw the phrase "the stream of thought" on
page 224 of James's book yesterday. The best way to show that those
grounds are not conclusive would be to offer *some evidence* for saying
that I did not see that phrase yesterday. But no philosopher is prepared
to do this. Therefore, the philosophical claim that those grounds are

not conclusive does not rest on *evidence*. On what does it rest? On a confusion, I believe. One is inclined to argue "It is not conclusive that that perceptual statement is true because it is possible that it is false." But examination of this statement shows that the words "It is possible that it is false" do not mean that there is *evidence* that it is false. They mean that it is *logically* possible that it is false. But the fact that it is logically possible that it is false does not tend to show in any way that it is not conclusive that it is true.

The inclination to contend that it is possible that every perception is hallucinatory rests, in part at least, upon the same confusion which lies at the root of the Verification Argument, a confusion over the usage of the expression "It is possible." One can construct an argument intended to prove that it is not certain that I did not have an hallucination yesterday, which closely resembles, in an important respect, the Verification Argument. This argument may be stated as follows:

If certain things were to happen there would be good reason to believe that I had an hallucination yesterday.

It is possible that those things will happen.

Therefore, it is not certain that I did not have an hallucination yesterday.

The second premise of this argument corresponds to premise III of the Verification Argument. In order that the conclusion should follow, this second premise must be understood in such a way that it implies the proposition "It is not certain that those things will not happen." I contend that there is no natural interpretation of this premise in which it is both the case that the premise is true and that it implies that proposition.

I have tried to show that there is no sense of the expression "It is possible," and the correlative expressions, in which the statement "It is possible that the consequences of S will not occur" *both* is true *and* implies the statement "It is not certain that the consequences of S will occur." To show this is to expose the most important error in the Verification Argument. The Verification Argument is a very tempting argument. From the propositions that S has an infinite number of consequences and that it is *possible* that these consequences will not occur and that if a sufficient number of them did not occur it would be conclusive that S is false and that if it were conclusive that S is false then no one previously made certain that S is true, it *seems* to follow that I did not make certain yesterday that S is true. The proposition

that it is *possible* that these consequences will not occur is the premise
of central importance. When one first meets the argument one feels
that this premise cannot be questioned. It seems so obviously true that
there is scarcely need to state it. This apparently invulnerable premise
conceals a serious fallacy. This premise must be understood in such a
way that it implies that it is not certain that the consequences of S
will occur. Anyone who undertakes to examine carefully the several
ordinary usages of "It is possible" should see that in the usages expressed by III_1 and III_2 this premise does not imply in the least that it
is not certain that the consequences of S will occur. He should see that
in the usages expressed by III_3 and III_4 this premise is clearly false. He
should see that in the usage expressed by III_5 this premise stands in
need of support and that the proponents of the Verification Argument
have offered nothing valid in support of it and that if it were to be supported by philosophical argument it could not, without circularity, be
supported by the Verification Argument itself. The persuasiveness of the
Verification Argument arises from the failure to distinguish several usages of "It is possible" that occur in different contexts in ordinary discourse. The result of this failure is that in the philosophical context of
the argument one tries to make that phrase straddle several different
ordinary usages all at once. In the usages expressed by III_1 and III_2
the proposition "It is possible that the consequences of S will not
occur" is an obvious logical truth. In the usages expressed by III_3, III_4,
and III_5 this proposition expresses a *doubt,* implies an *uncertainty.*
Through neglecting to distinguish these two sets of usages one is led to
think *both* that the proposition "It is possible that the consequences of
S will not occur" is an obvious truth *and* that it implies that it is not
certain that the consequences of S will occur.

   The proponents of the Verification Argument have emphasized their
proposition that the consequences of an empirical statement are *infinite* in number. They have exerted themselves mainly in arguing for
that premise of their argument, while they have said hardly anything
at all about proposition $IIIa$. If, however, $IIIa$ is true then it does not
matter, in a sense, whether II is true or not. If S has only *one* consequence and if that consequence is such that if it failed to occur S
would be refuted and if it is not certain that that consequence will
occur, then it follows both that it is not certain that S is true and that
I did not make certain yesterday that S is true. It will be replied, of
course, that if S had only one consequence then we could put that one

consequence to the test. If *c*, for example, expressed the only consequence of *S* then we could find out whether *c* is true by my performing the action of looking now at page 224 of James's book. If we knew that *c* is true and if *c* expressed the only consequence of *S*, then we should know with certainty that *S* is true. But *S* has not just one or several consequences, but an infinite number. We cannot put an infinite number of consequences to the test. Therefore we cannot know with certainty that *S* is true.

This argument makes an important assumption. The assumption is that I cannot know that any consequence *will* occur. I can know that it *is* occurring and, perhaps, that it *has* occurred, but not that it *will* occur. It assumes that I cannot know that *c* is true *until* I perform the action of looking at page 224 of James's book. *This assumption is identical with proposition IIIa.* Why should we accept this assumption? The philosophers who use the Verification Argument have given us no reason at all. This assumption goes against our ordinary ways of thinking and speaking. I should say, for example, that it is certain that if I were to look now at page 224 of my copy of James's book I should see there the phrase "the stream of thought." My grounds for saying this are that I saw the phrase there yesterday, that there is no reason to think that the printing on that page has changed or been altered since then, that my vision is normal, and that the light is good. These are not merely "very good" grounds; they would ordinarily be regarded as absolutely conclusive. What grounds do those philosophers have for saying that it is not certain that if I were to look now at that page I should see that phrase? None at all! There is nothing whatever which prevents me from knowing now that *c* is true. *I do not have to perform the act of looking now in order to know that if I did perform it now I should see that phrase.* I should also say that it is certain that if my wife were to look at that page now she would see that phrase and that it is certain that if my neighbor were to look now he would see it and so on for an indefinite number of persons. If I can know now that *c* is true I can also know now that any number of other statements, which express consequences of *S*, are true. That this number of statements is infinite or unlimited or indefinitely large does not prevent me from knowing that they are all true. I cannot perform an infinite number of actions of looking; but it does not follow in the least that I cannot know what the results would be *if* any of an infinite number of possible actions of looking were performed. With regard to any one of an infinite number of statements which express consequences of S, I can give grounds for saying that it is certain that that statement is true and the grounds are what would ordinarily be regarded as perfectly conclusive. The philosophers who use the Verification Argument have put their emphasis in the wrong place. The critical step in the argument is not the proposition that an empirical statement has an infinite number of consequences; it is the unjustified assumption that it cannot be certain that those consequences will occur.

III

Our attention has been concentrated on the fallacies contained in propositions III and V of the original argument. There are, however, other errors involved in the thinking that surrounds the argument. One of these errors consists in a misunderstanding of the ordinary usage of expressions such as "verify," "establish," "make certain," "find out." The proponents of the argument say that if I want to find out whether a certain proposition is true I make a few "tests" or "observations." These few tests may be enough "for practical purposes" but, they say, I can go on making tests forever. "But there is always the theoretical possibility of continuing the series of test-observations. Therefore here also *no complete verification is possible* but only a process of gradually increasing *confirmation*."[24]

Let us take an example. Suppose that I think that *Paradise Lost* begins with the words "Of Man's first disobedience," but that I am not sure and wish to verify it. I take from the shelf a book entitled *Milton's Poetical Works.* I turn to the first page of verse and under the heading *Paradise Lost, Book I,* I see that the first four words of the first line of verse are "Of Man's first disobedience." It would ordinarily be said that I had verified it. The proponents of the Verification Argument would say that I had not "completely" verified it. They would say that I had not even "completely" verified the fact that the first four words of verse on *the page before me* are the words "Of Man's first disobedience." What shall I do to *further* verify this latter fact? Shall I look again? Suppose that I do and that I see the same thing. Shall I ask someone else to look? Suppose that he looks and that he sees the same thing. According to this philosophical theory it is still not "completely" verified. How shall I further verify it? Would it be "further verifica-

---

24 Carnap, "Testability and Meaning," *Phil. of Science*, III (1936), 425.

tion" if I were to look *again* and *again* at this page and have more and more other people look again and again? Not at all! We should not describe it so! Having looked once carefully, if I then continued to look at the page we should not say that I was "further verifying" or "trying to further verify" that the first four words of verse on that page are "Of Man's first disobedience." Carnap declares that although it might be foolish or impractical to continue "the series of test-observations" still one could do so "theoretically." He implies that *no matter what the circumstances* we should describe certain actions as "further verifying" or "further confirming" this fact. That is a mistake. Suppose that I continued to look steadily at the page and someone wondered why I was behaving in that way. If someone else were to say "He is trying to further verify that those are the first four words," this would be an absurd and humorous remark. And this description would be equally absurd if my actions consisted in showing the book to one person after another. In those circumstances there is nothing which we should *call* "further verification." To suppose that the "process of verification" can continue "without end" is simply to ignore the ordinary usage of the word "verify." It is false that "there is always the theoretical possibility of continuing the series of test-observations." It *is* possible that I should continue *to look at the page*. It is *not* possible that I should continue the verification of that fact because, in those circumstances, we should not describe *anything* as "further verification" of it. The verification *comes to an end*.

Carnap would say that the statement "The first four words of verse on this page are 'Of Man's first disobedience'" is not "completely" verified because "there remains still the theoretical possibility of denying the sentence."[25] What does he mean by "there remains still the theoretical possibility of denying the sentence"? Does he mean that it is logically possible that someone should *deny* that statement? This is true, but irrelevant to the question of whether it has been established that the statement is true. Does he mean that the contradictory of the above statement is not self-contradictory? This is also true and also irrelevant. Does he mean that there is *some reason* for thinking that the statement is false, or that there is *no reason* for thinking it true? But there is the best of reasons for saying it is true, namely, that I looked carefully at the page a moment ago and saw that those were the first four words; and there is no reason whatever for saying that it

25 *Ibid.*, p. 426.

is false. Does he mean that the fact that I looked at the page and saw
that those were the first four words of verse does not "completely" establish that the statement is true? In what way does it fail to establish
it "completely"? Shall we repeat that it does not "completely" establish
it because "there remains still the theoretical possibility of denying the
statement"? But this is circular reasoning. Carnap's statement "there
remains still the theoretical possibility of denying the sentence" embodies the same confusion that surrounds premise III of the Verification Argument, the confusion produced by the failure to distinguish
the several different usages of the expression "It is possible."

Some philosophers have thought that, when it is said in ordinary
discourse that it is absolutely certain that so-and-so, what this means
is that it is *practically* certain that so-and-so. This is clearly a mistake.
The ordinary usage of "practically certain" is quite different from the
ordinary usage of "absolutely certain." It is "practically certain"
normally means "It is almost certain." To say that it is practically
certain that so-and-so implies that it is *not* absolutely certain. "It is
practically certain that p is true" implies that it is reasonable to have a
slight doubt that p is true and implies that the evidence that p is true
is not absolutely conclusive. "It is absolutely certain that p is true"
implies, on the contrary, that the evidence that p is true is absolutely
conclusive and implies that in the light of the evidence it would be unreasonable to have the slightest doubt that p is true.

Lewis and Carnap do not, of course, make the mistake of identifying
absolute certainty with practical certainty. They make a different mistake. They identify absolute certainty with "theoretical certainty."
Lewis, for example, uses the expressions "absolutely certain" and
"theoretically certain" interchangeably.[26] Both he and Carnap say that
the truth of an empirical statement can be practically certain but not
"theoretically certain." How are they using the expression "theoretical
certainty"? What state of affairs, if it could be realized, would they
call "theoretical certainty"? In what circumstances, supposing that
such circumstances could exist, would it be "theoretically certain" that
a given statement is true? The answer is clear from the context of their
arguments. It would be "theoretically certain" that a given statement
is true only if an *infinite* number of "tests" or "acts of verification"
had been performed. It is, of course, a *contradiction* to say that an infinite number of "tests" or acts of any sort have been performed by

---

[26] Cp. *An Analysis of Knowledge and Valuation*, p. 180.

anyone. It is not that it is merely impossible in practice for anyone to perform an infinite number of acts. It is impossible *in theory*. Therefore these philosophers *misuse* the expression "theoretically certain." What they call "theoretical certainty" cannot be attained even in *theory*. But this misusage of an expression is in itself of slight importance. What is very important is that they identify what they mean by "theoretically certain" with what is ordinarily meant by "absolutely certain." If this identification were correct then the ordinary meaning of "absolutely certain" would be contradictory. The proposition that it is absolutely certain that a given statement is true would *entail* the proposition that someone had performed an infinite number of acts. Therefore, it would be a *contradiction* to say, for example, "It is absolutely certain that Socrates had a wife." Statements of this sort are often false, or they are often unjustified on the strength of the evidence at hand. But to say that such statements are one and all *self-contradictory* is perfectly absurd. A philosophical theory that has such a consequence is plainly false.

Phenomenalism

PAUL MARHENKE

In a recent re-examination of the tenets of phenomenalism, A. J. Ayer defines phenomenalism as the philosophical theory which holds that physical objects are logical constructions out of sense-data. Since this definition has been frequently misconstrued, Ayer adds the following explanation: "To say that physical objects are logical constructions out of sense-data . . . does not mean that physical objects are literally composed of sense-data. . . . It means simply that statements about physical objects are somehow reducible to statements about sense-data."[1] If this explanation is now substituted for the statement explained, we have a second definition of phenomenalism.

These two definitions illustrate what Carnap has called the material mode and the formal mode of speech. The first definition employs the material mode of speech: the statement that physical objects are logical constructions out of sense-data appears to convey information about the nature of physical objects. The second definition employs the formal mode of speech: the statement that statements about physical objects are reducible to statements about sense-data does not convey and does not appear to convey information about the nature of physical objects. The difference between the material and the formal mode is much more striking if the two definitions are formulated as follows: (*a*) A physical object is a com-

---

[1] A. J. Ayer, "Phenomenalism," *Arist. Soc. Proc.*, XLVII (1946-47), 169.

plex of sense-data. (*b*) Any statement containing the name of a physical object is synonymous with a statement that contains the names of sense-data but not the names of physical objects. Formulation (*a*) appears to make an assertion regarding the composition or constitution of physical objects. In reality it makes an assertion regarding the synonymity of two statements, since formulations (*a*) and (*b*) are identical in meaning. The two sentences "A physical object is a complex of sense-data" and "An organism is a complex of cells" appear to be strictly comparable. The first appears to convey information about the composition of physical objects, the second about the composition of organisms. But while the second really conveys the information it appears to convey, the first does not. Sentences of the second sort are genuine object sentences. Sentences of the first sort are object sentences in disguise; they are about words rather than objects and are accordingly called pseudo object sentences by Carnap.

It is Carnap's advice that the use of the material mode of speech be avoided, because of the ever-present temptation to interpret pseudo object sentences as statements regarding the composition of physical objects, rather than as syntactical statements regarding the analyzability of sentences containing the names of physical objects into sentences of another kind. Earlier phenomenalists showed a preference for the material mode of speech, and their formulation of phenomenalism as the thesis that physical objects are composed of sense-data or that they are collections of ideas has always impressed the non-phenomenalist as extremely paradoxical. Contemporary phenomenalists remove the air of paradox from the thesis of phenomenalism by adopting the formal mode of speech. When a contemporary phenomenalist tells us that a physical object is a family of actual and possible sense-data, he does not intend to give us information concerning the composition of physical objects. The determination of the composition of material objects he regards as the prerogative of the scientist and not as his concern. If he employs the material mode at all he does so because it is briefer and more concise than the formal mode. But if anyone is inclined to yield to the temptation to interpret his statement as a genuine object sentence, he had better translate it into the formal mode.

The preceding remarks regarding the definition of phenomenalism may now be summarized. Phenomenalism is currently defined by adopting either the material or the formal mode of speech. When the material mode is employed it is defined, e.g., as the philosophical theory which holds that physical objects are logical constructions out of sense-data. Some of the variants of this definition are obtained by substituting for the phrase "physical objects are logical constructions out of sense-data" one of the following phrases: (1) physical objects are permanent possibilities of sensations, (2) physical objects are complexes of actual and possible sensations, (3) physical objects are classes or families of sense-data. When the formal mode is employed it is defined, e.g., as the philosophical theory which holds that statements about physical objects are reducible to statements about sense-data. Some of the variants of this definition are obtained by substituting for the phrase "statements about physical objects are reducible . . ." one of the following phrases: (1) statements about physical objects are analyzable into statements about sense-data, (2) statements about physical objects are translatable into statements about sense-data, (3) statements about physical objects are synonymous with statements about sense-data. The defining sentences that are expressed by employing the material mode are identical in meaning with the defining sentences that are expressed by employing the formal mode. Nevertheless, the employment of the formal mode is preferable to the employment of the material mode in the definition of phenomenalism, because the employment of the material mode may prevent the recognition of the defining sentences as pseudo object sentences.

The foregoing definition of phenomenalism can be expressed in an especially succinct form by using the abbreviations "*M*-sentence" and "*S*-sentence," the former to denote any statement containing the name of a physical object and the latter to denote any statement containing the names of sense-data but not the names of physical objects.[2] With these abbreviations the thesis of phenomenalism receives the following formulation: Every *M*-sentence is analyzable into (synonymous with) an *S*-sentence.

In order to get an insight into the logical form of the *S*-sentence, it would be necessary to examine some specimen analyses of *M*-sentences. But such analyses are not likely to be available for inspection because of the excessive length of the *S*-sentence. At any rate specimen translations of *M*-sentences cannot be found in the writings of phenomenalists. The best they offer is always a very partial and fragmentary translation. Let us see how a phenomenalist begins the

---

2 Cp. Konrad Marc-Wogau, *Die Theorie der Sinnesdaten* (1945), p. 391.

translation of an *M*-sentence such as "There is now a wall behind my back." An expositor of the phenomenalistic thesis recently claimed that this sentence is synonymous with a class of sentences of which the following is typical: "If I shall turn my head (have certain kinesthetic experiences), then I shall also have the visual experience called 'seeing a wall.' "[3] But this *S*-sentence or rather the whole conjunction of *S*-sentences of this type (which is also an *S*-sentence), is quite obviously not synonymous with the given *M*-sentence. For the *M*-sentence says that there is a wall behind my back *now*, whereas the corresponding *S*-sentence speaks of the sense-data I *shall* sense, if I *shall* sense certain other sense-data (kinesthetic sensations). But the wall may very well have ceased to exist by the time I shall experience the kinesthetic sensation of turning my head. The *S*-sentence will then most likely turn out to be false, i.e., I shall not have the visual experience called "seeing a wall." In answer to this criticism a phenomenalist will perhaps reply that the general pattern of the proposed analysis is quite correct and that the only mistake is the choice of the wrong mood of the verb "to be." The *S*-sentence with which the given *M*-sentence is synonymous is a conjunction of *S*-sentences of the form "if . . . then . . . ," but the indicative mood of the verb "to be" should of course be replaced by the subjunctive. If a typical member of the conjunction is altered to read "If I were to turn my head . . . , then I would also have . . . ," everything is in order. The "were . . . would" idiom is required in the formulation of the *S*-sentences when the reference of the *M*-sentence is to the present. Similarly, the "had been . . . would" and the "should . . . would" idioms are required in the translation of *M*-sentences when the temporal reference is to the past and future. If, as phenomenalists seem to think, the *S*-sentence into which a given *M*-sentence is analyzable is a conjunction of conditionals, not all of these conditionals can be in the indicative mood. Some must be contrary-to-fact conditionals. The admission of contrary-to-fact conditionals into the *S*-sentence poses a new analytical puzzle, to be sure, but the phenomenalist, even if he does not solve this puzzle, has in any case proved his thesis, if he can now show that every *M*-sentence is synonymous with a conjunction of conditional sentences of the described sort.

The phenomenalist can prove his thesis most easily by producing a sample analysis of an *M*-sentence. This no phenomenalist has yet done. He has instead given us directions for constructing the *S*-sentence,

---

[3] Gustav Bergmann, "Remarks on Realism," *Phil. of Science*, XIII (1946), 261.

e.g., "form the conjunction of all the sentences of which the following is typical," but he has not constructed this sentence. The critics of phenomenalism have thought that the reason for this failure lies in the fact that it can not be done. Phenomenalists, needless to say, have not allowed these objections to go unchallenged. Let us examine some of the arguments of the critics of phenomenalism as well as the replies of its defenders.

The arguments against phenomenalism are of two types: (1) the direct arguments against the phenomenalistic thesis that *M*-sentences are analyzable into *S*-sentences; (2) the indirect argument to the effect that phenomenalism is committed to an erroneous theory of sense-perception. We begin with the indirect argument.

The indirect argument may be put roughly as follows: Phenomenalists think that *M*-sentences are analyzable into *S*-sentences, because they believe that what is directly perceived in a perceptual situation is always a sense-datum and never a physical object. If they had not been committed to this erroneous view they would have seen no plausibility in their thesis that *M*-sentences are analyzable into *S*-sentences. To be sure, it is possible to hold this erroneous view without holding this thesis about *M*-sentences. However, although phenomenalists are not unique in advocating this erroneous view, it is a view that follows from the phenomenalistic thesis. Hence if the view that what is directly perceived in a perceptual situation is always a sense-datum and never a physical object can be proved erroneous, it follows that the phenomenalistic thesis about the analyzability of *M*-sentences is false. For if there are cases of the direct apprehension of physical objects, then there is at least one *M*-sentence, namely the sentence describing this perceptual situation, that is not analyzable into an *S*-sentence.

The view that the perception of a physical object involves the apprehension of a sense-datum has been challenged repeatedly in recent discussions. The analysis of veridical perception, it is maintained, does not lead us to sense-data. When the perceptual situation is veridical we may claim that we are in direct perceptual contact with a physical object, and in analyzing this sort of experience we need never have recourse to sense-data. The sole argument in favor of the existence of sense-data, it is maintained, is the so-called argument from illusion. Whenever the perceptual situation is nonveridical, the object directly perceived is not a physical object. A hallucinatory perceptual situation, for example, contains a constituent that simulates a physical object of such and such a kind. This constituent, on which the deception is based, is a sense-datum (not a physical object). The opponents of sense-data do not regard the argument from illusion as conclusive. Many of them seem to be of the opinion that no perceptual situation, veridical or nonveridical, contains a sense-datum. Others concede that the analysis of hallucinatory perception leads us to sense-data, but they nevertheless maintain that this is not true of the analysis of veridical perception, that we have no reason to assume that the analysis of veridical perception must follow the pattern set for the analysis of hallucinatory perception.

The opponents of sense-data apparently also hold the opinion that sense-data would never have emerged in the analysis of perceptual situations if there had been no illusions (hallucinations, delusions, dreams). As against this opinion it is here maintained that the correct analysis of the perception of physical objects leads us to sense-data even if every perceptual situation were veridical. In order to show this we shall take as a typical example of a perceptual situation the visual perception of a physical object. We shall assume that the perceptual situation is veridical, that the object is opaque, and that no part of the object is hidden by other physical objects. Whenever I see a physical object under the specified conditions, it is obviously also the case that I see a part of its surface, for this follows simply from the supposition that the object is opaque. When I see a cube, for example, I see, let us say, three of its six faces. If the cube is opaque, the other three faces are certainly not seen in the same sense of the word "seen" in which the first three are seen. And both of these senses must of course be distinguished from the sense of "seen" in which the cube is seen. If all of this is correct, the relation of seeing between a person and a physical object is an analyzable relation. Let S_1 be the relation between A and X when A sees X, where A is a person and X a physical object, and let S_2 be the relation between A and Y, where A is a person and Y a physical surface. Finally, let P be the relation between Y and X when Y is a part of the surface of X. In this notation the analysis of AS_1X may now be rendered as follows: $(\exists Y) : AS_2Y . YPX$.

This analysis of the relation S_1 into the relative product of the relations S_2 and P should be common ground, it would seem, to all theories of perception. But however that may be, philosophical opinions begin to diverge when one raises the question whether the relation S_2 is analyzable or not. Those who hold that it can not be further analyzed

regard the Y that appears in the above analysis, i.e., the physical surface, as a sense-datum. In other words, those who maintain the ultimacy
of the above analysis believe that the sense-datum that is directly apprehended in visual perception is always a part of the surface of a
physical object. Those who hold that the relation S_2 can be further
analyzed challenge the view that visual sense-data can be identified
with physical surfaces. If we accept their arguments, we have to distinguish between the sense-datum Z and the surface Y with which Z
is correlated or which Z represents. In addition to the senses of the
word "seen" already discussed, we now have to distinguish two further
senses. The sense of "seen" in which a sense-datum is seen must be
distinguished from the sense of this word in which a physical surface
is seen. Let S_3 be the relation between A and Z when A sees Z, where A
is a person and Z a sense-datum, and let Q be the relation between Z
and Y when Z represents Y. The analysis of the component AS_2Y that
appears in the above analysis of AS_1X may then be rendered as follows:
$\exists Z) : AS_3Z . ZQY$.

The view that S_2 is an analyzable relation leads to the various forms
of the sensum theory. A visual sensum or sense-datum, according to
this theory, is something that is (1) immediately or directly apprehended and (2) distinct from the part of the surface of a physical object it represents. Whether both of these conditions should be required
in specifying the meaning of the term "sense-datum" is questionable.
If the sensum theory were false, the term "sensum" as employed in this
theory would be applicable only in the analysis of nonveridical perception. However, the analysis of veridical perception leads us to something immediately or directly apprehended whatever theory of perception we adopt. This something would not be a sense-datum if the
sensum theory were false, i.e., if it were a part of a physical surface.
Since veridical and nonveridical perceptual situations both contain
a component which is apprehended immediately and directly, it is
best to employ the term "sense-datum" for designating something that
satisfies condition (1) only. If we wish, the term "sensum" may then
be reserved for designating an entity that satisfies both conditions. If
the sensum theory is true, the sense-datum is always a sensum. But if
this theory is false, the sense-datum is a sensum only in nonveridical
perception; in veridical perception it is a part of the surface of a physical object.

Our formulation of condition (1) requires some further comments.

We say that something is directly seen when this relation is not analyzable as a relative product. Further, we say that something is directly seen when it is the subject of statements whose verification of falsification can be effected by a visual inspection of its properties and its properties alone. If in addition to the item in question other particulars have to be examined before the statement can be verified or falsified, then it is not directly seen. As an example of the difference let us consider the perception of a cube. We shall assume that we are sufficiently far away so that when we see (S_1) the cube, we also see (S_2) the three faces F_1, F_2, and F_3. Since the object seen is a cube, it has of course three other faces F_4, F_5, and F_6, which are not seen (S_2). The faces we do not see may in fact be colored red, but we can obviously not establish this without turning the cube over and around, i.e., without altering the perceptual situation. These faces could have been colored blue or they might not have existed at all (if the cube had been an hallucination or if the seeing of it had been induced by hypnosis) without any alteration in the sort of visual experience we have when we see a cube with the faces F_1, F_2, and F_3. In short, in order to determine the properties of the faces F_4, F_5, and F_6, e.g., their color, it is useless to investigate the properties of the sense-datum that is directly seen when the cube confronts us with the faces F_1, F_2, and F_3. No such disability exists in the instance of these three faces. If they are in fact blue, I can establish this by visual inspection (assuming that the perception is veridical and that the sense-datum is not a sensum). The faces F_1, F_2, and F_3 are thus directly apprehended, in the sense specified, while the cube as a whole is certainly not directly apprehended in this sense.

We are thus led to sense-data in the sense previously specified, even when we assume that visual perception is always veridical. When I look at a cube I do not see all of its six faces, and in this sense of "see" I see a part of its surface only. The six faces of the cube are joined to one another to form a three-dimensional whole. The three faces I see are ordered three-dimensionally but, unlike the six faces, they do not form a three-dimensional whole.

Obvious and trivial though this characterization of a visual sense-datum may seem, it has not gone unchallenged. It has been challenged on the ground that it is based on an inaccurate description of visual perception. In a recent work of Marc-Wogau it is alleged that the view we have advocated fails to distinguish between the following two kinds of perceptual situation: (1) We see a part of the surface of the object, and (2) We see the object as a three-dimensional (closed) whole.[4] We have an example of the first when we look at the wall of a house, when this is all we can see because we are too close to the house to see it as a whole. We have an example of the second when we see the house as a whole from a greater distance. Marc-Wogau points out that in the first example we may have the perception of a colored surface. In the second example, he maintains, we never have the experience of a colored surface or of a plurality of colored surfaces juxtaposed in a three-dimensional array. In the second example we do not have the perceptual experience of seeing only a part of the surface of the object as we do in the first. In certain cases, it is true, the perceptual experience of seeing a house may be indistinguishable from the sort of experience we have when we look at a stage set, and what is then directly apprehended will appear as a three-dimensional array of a roof and of walls. But this sort of experience is also not describable as the experience of something that is not three-dimensionally closed. For a stage set is also apprehended as three-dimensionally closed: the walls of the stage set are seen, not as a part of the surface of a house, but as physical objects having a farther side.

Marc-Wogau's objections to the view he rejects are not entirely clear. His allegation that there is a distinction between the perceptual situations (1) and (2) is correct, but not his allegation that this distinction is ignored by the philosophers who accept the analysis of perception we have sketched. The distinction exemplified by Marc-Wogau may also be made as follows. There is a usage of the locution "part of" according to which it is correct to say that I see only a part of the surface of a physical object when it is physically possible to see a part of its surface that contains the surface seen as a proper part. According to this usage, it is not correct to say that I see only a part of the surface of a physical object when it is physically impossible to see a part of its surface which contains the surface seen as a proper part. Hence, when I see three of the faces of a cube and then describe this situation by saying that I see only a part of its surface, I am using language incorrectly if I follow the above convention. For it is impossible to see a part of the surface of the cube of which the three faces seen are a proper part. That there is a correct and an incorrect usage of the locution "part of" is denied by no one, least of all by the

---

[4] *Op. cit.,* p. 44.

philosophers whose analysis of sense perception Marc-Wogau rejects. These philosophers will retort that they are not using the locution "part of" in accordance with the above convention but rather in accordance with a different convention of their own in their analysis of sense perception.

However, Marc-Wogau's complaint is evidently not merely that a convention is being flouted. His real objection he himself formulates as follows: "It is of course correct that we can not see the farther side of the house before us; we also do not see the interior of an opaque body. This means that we can not determine the color of its farther side or of its interior by analyzing what is directly seen. But it does not mean that the house is not directly seen as an object with a farther side and with interior sides."[5] C. D. Broad, in commenting on this statement in his examination of Marc-Wogau's theory of perception, suggests that Marc-Wogau's remarks are capable of the following interpretations. (*a*) What is directly apprehended in the perception of an opaque object is the whole of a closed outer surface. (*b*) What is directly apprehended is solid, i.e., filled with matter. (*c*) What is directly apprehended is always apprehended "as *part* of the *outer surface* of a three-dimensional object of *some form or other;* which may be either closed or open on the side invisible to the observer; which, if closed, may be either hollow or filled with matter; and which, even if it be open, or closed and hollow, has a certain finite thickness, and therefore a hind surface or an inner surface of some kind or other as well as a front surface or outer surface."[6]

Broad says he is not sure whether Marc-Wogau wants to maintain either (*a*) or (*b*). It seems incredible that in rejecting the thesis that what is directly seen has no seen farther side and no seen inner side or inside, Marc-Wogau should have meant only what Broad has included under (*c*). When one says that the sense-datum is apprehended "as part of the outer surface of a physical object," one presumably means only that it is believed to be continuous with the unseen parts of the outer surface of the physical object. And when Marc-Wogau maintains that the house "*is seen immediately as*" (this is his phrase) an object with a farther side or with an innerside, he may mean only that the object seen immediately (the sense-datum) is believed to have

---

5 *Loc. cit.*

6 C. D. Broad, "Professor Marc-Wogau's 'Theorie der Sinnesdaten' (II)," *Mind*, LVI (1947), 109.

a farther side and an inner side or that this is taken for granted. If this is all Marc-Wogau intends to maintain it would be difficult to find a philosopher or psychologist who disagrees with his description. But he seems to maintain much more than this. He seems to maintain that the farther side and the inside of an opaque physical object are directly apprehended in the same sense in which its hither side is directly apprehended. It is of course possible to specify the sense of the phrase "directly apprehended" in such a way as to make this statement true. But this is in any case not the sense involved when it is denied that the farther side and the inside of an opague physical object are directly apprehended,—and this is admitted by Marc-Wogau. We have to distinguish between (1) "The house is seen immediately as an object with a farther side and with an inner side" and (2) "The farther and the inner side of the house are seen immediately." When the house is viewed from the outside, (2) is obviously false, for otherwise I would be able to tell you what a house looks like on the farther side without going there or what it looks like on the inside without going in.

The descriptions philosophers have given of perceptual situations have often been ludicrously inadequate or downright erroneous. Marc-Wogau records some of their more glaring errors. He points out that the perception of a tomato is analyzed erroneously when it is said to involve the perception of a red patch. Anyone who is familiar with the perception of red patches knows that this sort of experience is certainly not part of the experience of perceiving a tomato. It is more nearly correct to say that what I directly apprehend is something tomatolike; this much at least seems to be guaranteed by an examination of the ingredients of the perceptual situation. Marc-Wogau also accuses philosophers of ignoring the fact of phenomenal constancy. They have inferred the geometrical properties of sense-data from the laws of optics and have maintained, against the empirical evidence, that a coin looks elliptical, i.e., that the sense-datum is elliptical, whenever the line of sight is not normal to the surface of the coin. The rectification of these and similar errors is undoubtedly a matter of great importance. But an increase in the accuracy and adequacy of the phychological description can not alter the epistemological distinction between the direct and the indirect, the immediate and the mediate.

That there is really no disagreement as to where the line between the direct and the indirect must be drawn may be illustrated with one further example. Suppose we consider the perceptual experience we have when we look at a match box across the face of which a pencil has been placed. Our description of what we see is perhaps formulated in the following terms: We see the face of the match box divided into two parts by the pencil. A Gestalt psychologist might now challenge the adequacy of this description. If he does, he will tell us that we do not see the face of the match box divided into two parts by the pencil. On the contrary, we see it as a single and unitary whole stretching under the pencil. Now if the first description is taken to imply that I am conscious of two surfaces, that I do not take it for granted that the two halves are connected, the description of the Gestalt psychologist is undoubtedly an acceptable correction. The fact is that the surface on the left of the pencil is seen as continuous with the one on the right, i.e., one takes it for granted that only one surface is seen. The perceptual experience of seeing the face of a match box behind a pencil is quite different from the perceptual experience of seeing the two fragments when the match box is cut in two. If the first description in interpreted as denying this fundamental difference it is of course erroneous. However, it need not be interpreted in this way. The two descriptions (1) "I see two surfaces separated by the pencil" and (2) "I see one surface, a part of it under the pencil" are not contradictory. The appearance of contradiction vanishes as soon as it is realized that two meanings of "see" are involved. The first description is in order when we wish to convey the information that the portion of the face under the pencil is not seen in the sense that I can not determine by visual inspection what is color is unless the pencil is removed. The second description is in order when we wish to convey the information that I am not conscious of a multiplicity of surfaces, that I see, in this sense of the word, the portion of the face covered by the pencil as well as the left and the right halves.

The elimination of errors from the description of perceptual situations is not going to be of help in proving that physical objects rather than sense-data are directly apprehended. No more is given to the Gestalt psychologist who describes the perceptual situation correctly than to the philosopher who describes it incorrectly. Physical objects are directly perceived if an *M*-sentence is directly verifiable (or falsifiable). And to deny that physical objects are directly perceived, when this is the meaning of the phrase "directly perceived," is not to deny that there are other uses of this phrase that permit one to say that physical objects are directly perceived. However, these other uses are not going to change the fact that an *M*-sentence is not directly verifiable. It follows that the phenomenalist cannot be refuted by pointing out inaccuracies and inadequacies in his description of perceptual situations. Unless we can show that physical objects are directly perceived, the claims of phenomenalism cannot be refuted by discovering errors in the analysis of perception to which it is committed. An attack on phenomenalism such as Stout's misses this point completely. Stout alleges that phenomenalism is inconsistent with the evidence of sense perception, because sense perception contains a factor—Stout calls it "perceptual seeming"—that is completely ignored by phenomenalism. In particular, he charges that phenomenalism is inconsistent with the following sorts of facts. (1) The top of the table seems to stretch under the book that lies on the table, although there is here no sensible appearance (sense-datum) of the part of the top that is covered by the book. (2) In distance perception there may be no sensible appearance of distance, although one object will seem to be behind another. It is even possible to "perceive one thing as behind another, although it is so hidden that there is no sensible appearance of it." (3) It is possible to "perceive things as having insides when they are not transparent." When the object is opaque there is a sensible appearance of its surface or of a part of its surface, but none of its inside. If I try to picture its inside mentally I get only images of surfaces. In the instance of the inside of an object "there is not a permanent possibility but a permanent impossibility of sensation."[7]

We have already dealt with the first charge in connection with Marc-Wogau. The answer to this type of objection is: "Let it be so; the portion of the table top covered by the book is still not directly apprehended in the same sense in which the visible portions are apprehended." A similar answer is appropriate in the instance of the second objection. If anyone finds it instructive to use the word "perceive" with a meaning that permits him to say that he perceives the objects in a closed room when he is on the outside, he can obviously not be prevented from doing so. But this verbal usage will not enable him to apprehend sense-data that other people do not apprehend. The last objection is of a different nature. The inside of an object cannot be directly apprehended on the ground that only surfaces can be directly apprehended. Nevertheless, the objects we apprehend appear to have insides. But, for the reason given, there can be no sense-datum of the

---

[7] G. F. Stout, "Phenomenalism," *Arist. Soc. Proc.,* XXXIX (1938-9), 11 f.

inside of an object. And this consequence, Stout thinks, refutes phenomenalism. Instead of finding this last objection difficult to deal with, the phenomenalist has always insisted that a physical object has an inside and that a statement to the effect that a physical object has an inside is analyzable into a statement about sense-data in which this property is not mentioned. Physical objects and sense-data are objects of different types and the property of having an inside can be predicated significantly only of a physical object.

We are not going to succeed with the refutation of phenomenalism by challenging its analysis of perception unless we are prepared to maintain that physical objects are directly apprehended in the epistemological sense. Phenomenalism is false if physical objects are directly apprehended, for there is then at least one M-sentence, namely the sentence that asserts the direct apprehension of this object, which is not analyzable into an S-sentence. If we are only prepared to maintain that physical objects are directly apprehended in some other than the epistemological sense, then what we maintain is not incompatible with the analysis of perception phenomenalism accepts. As long as we agree that physical objects are not directly apprehended, we have agreed in principle to the analysis phenomenalism accepts, however defective this analysis may be.

In an earlier portion of this paper we formulated two analyses of perceptual statements such as "AS_1X," namely, (1) $(\exists Y) : AS_2Y \, . \, YPX$ and (2) $(\exists Y) \, (\exists Z) : AS_3Z \, . \, ZQY \, . \, YPX$. Analysis (1) is accepted by those who hold that a sense-datum may be identical with a part of the surface of a physical object and analysis (2) by those who reject this view. But whether we accept analysis (1) or analysis (2) as correct, in either case the analysis makes reference to a sense-datum. It is therefore the first step in the phenomenalistic program of analyzing every M-sentence into an S-sentence. But its is obviously not the last step, as both analyses contain the name of a physical object and they as well as the sentence analyzed are therefore M-sentences. The acceptance of analysis (1) or of analysis (2) hence does not as yet commit one to phenomenalism. Phenomenalism holds further that these M-sentences are reducible to S-sentences. Hence, if phenomenalism is to be refuted, we must refute this thesis. This brings us back to the arguments of the first type, the direct arguments against phenomenalism.

The least cogent of these arguments is the objection that the phenomenalistic analysis of M-sentences is circular. The objection is not that it is logically impossible to analyze an *M*-sentence into an *S*-sentence, but rather that every attempted analysis has failed, inasmuch as it concluded with an *M*-sentence. Thus, one of the components of the sentence with which the *M*-sentence "There is a chair in the next room" is alleged to be synonymous may be given in this form: "If a person should look into the next room he would apprehend a sense-datum that he would take to be part of the surface of a chair." Here the conditional sentence refers to a person and to a room, both physical objects, and is therefore not an *S*-sentence. The objection that the phenomenalistic analysis of *M*-sentences is circular will prove to be baseless, if the reference to physical objects can be eliminated from the conditional sentences into which the *M*-sentence is analyzed. Phenomenalists are confident that a non-circular analysis of *M*-sentences is possible. They usually blame their failure to supply us with a sample of such an analysis on the poverty of language. If languages contained more terms designating sense-data, the appearance of circularity could easily be avoided. Many of the critics of phenomenalism are inclined to accept this reply as correct.

Another argument many philosophers have found convincing is based on a false interpretation of the phenomenalistic thesis that a physical object is a permanent possibility of sensations. The argument is that this thesis leads to absurd consequences regarding causation. Physical objects, so the objection runs, manifest their causal properties whether they are observed or not. A magnet, for example, affects a compass needle whether anyone observes the magnet or not. If phenomenalism were true we would therefore be committed to the absurdity that the movement of the compass needle is caused by a mere possibility (the unobserved magnet). Phenomenalism must therefore be rejected, because its fundamental thesis is incompatible with the proposition that actual sense-data can not have possible sense-data as causes.

The answer to this objection is quite easy when we remember that the thesis of phenomenalism when expressed in the form of an object sentence is a *façon de parler*. When the phenomenalist chooses the material mode of speech, he does not intend to make an assertion regarding the constitution of material things. He can therefore not be accused of holding the absurd view that actual sense-data have possible sense-data as causes, since he does not hold the view that physical objects are composed of possible sense-data. This becomes clear as soon as he shifts from the material to the formal mode of speech. In the formal mode of speech his claim is that the *M*-sentence "The deflection of the compass needle is caused by the magnet" is analyzable into an *S*-sentence. One of the stages by which this *S*-sentence is reached might be the *M*-sentence "If a person had seen that the compass needle was deflected, he would also have been aware of the sense-datum of a magnet, if certain conditions had been satisfied." When the material mode of speech is employed it is very easy to come to the conclusion that the phenomenalist is committed to a division of causes and effects into two *kinds,* actual and possible. If we permit ourselves this kind of nonsense, we are of course also obliged to give serious consideration to the question whether actual effects can have possible causes. The adoption of the formal mode prevents the formation of this kind of discourse. The causal relation between the magnet and the deflection of the needle is discovered by observing regularities among sense-data, but when I observe the deflection and infer the presence of the magnet I am not asserting that a sense-datum of the needle was *preceded* by a sense-datum of the magnet, of an actual sense-datum if the magnet was noticed and of a possible one if it was not.

Another objection, which Carnap has made[8] is based on a false view of the nature of the conditional sentences that make up the *S*-sentence into which the *M*-sentence is analyzed. We have argued that these conditionals must include so-called contrary-to-fact conditionals, i.e., conditionals expressed by means of the "were . . . would," "had been . . . would," "should . . . would" idioms. Carnap's objection to the phenomenalistic thesis is based on the assumption that these conditionals are material implications. Now a material implication is true when its antecedent is false. It will be remembered that the antecedents of the contrary-to-fact conditionals express the conditions under which sense-data that are referred to such and such a physical object are observed. If these conditions are never satisfied, the conditionals are all true and the *M*-sentence is conclusively verified. For example, the statement that there is a chair in the next room is conclusively verified if no one ever looks into the next room.

Carnap's objection need not shake a phenomenalist's conviction in the validity of his thesis. Contrary-to-fact conditionals are not material implications. Carnap's absurd conclusion would have to be derived from some other assumption.

---

[8] Rudolf Carnap, "Testability and Meaning," *Phil. of Science,* III (1936), pp. 420 f.

An argument offered by R. B. Braithwaite[9] is not so easily disposed of. Braithwaite maintains that phenomenalism lays itself open to the criticism that its proposed analysis of M-sentences is circular. Phenomenalism holds that M-sentences are synonymous with S-sentences, and the verification of an M-sentence is therefore the same as the verification of the corresponding S-sentence. Now an observer is verifying an M-sentence, e.g., the sentence "There is a chair in the next room," if both of the following conditions are satisfied: (a) he observes sense-data of the right sort when he is in the room; and (b) these sense-data are observed under *normal* conditions, i.e., he is not dreaming or he does not have an hallucination. The first condition without the second is obviously insufficient, for its satisfaction is compatible with the falsity of the M-sentence; even if the room were empty he might dream that he was in it and that he saw a chair, or he might look into the room and have the hallucination of a chair. If we now try to express the statement that the observer's perception is normally conditioned in terms of an S-sentence, we find that the verification of this S-sentence is again subject to two conditions: (a') Whoever verifies the S-sentence in question must observe sense-data of the right sort, e.g., that the observer's eyes are open, that he responds to changes in the environment in appropriate ways, that he makes appropriate verbal responses when questioned, that the sense-data he experiences are peripherally and not centrally conditioned, etc., etc., and (b') Whoever verifies the S-sentence has normal perceptions. If we now try to express condition (b') as an S-sentence, we are in turn led to a pair of conditions (a'') and (b''), and so on ad infinitum. This infinite regress becomes especially simple if we assume that an observer cannot establish his own normality. The normality of the first observer is then established by the properties of the sense-data of a second observer, provided the second observer's sense-data are normally conditioned. And the normality of the second observer is in turn established by the properties of the sense-data experienced by a third observer, provided his sense-data are normally conditioned. It does not seem possible to stop this regress at any point, and it therefore does not seem possible to eliminate all reference to physical objects from the analysis of M-sentences. The infinite regress can be avoided only by admitting an M-sentence to the

---

9 R. B. Braithwaite, "Propositions about Material Objects," *Arist. Soc. Proc.*, XXXVIII (1937-8), p. 275.

effect that an observer's perception is normal into the analysis of the given *M*-sentence.

The phenomenalist can meet this objection either by finding a satisfactory answer to it or by modifying the thesis of phenomenalism to the extent of including the *M*-sentence to the effect that an observer's perceptions are reliable in the analysis of the given *M*-sentence. But whichever answer he makes to the objection, he confronts a much more serious argument in the objection that the proposed analysis of the given *M*-sentence is impossible. An *S*-sentence can not be synonymous with an *M*-sentence, since every *M*-sentence entails an infinite number of logically independent *S*-sentences. The proposed analysis of an *M*-sentence into an *S*-sentence can therefore not be carried out. Every *S*-sentence we propose as the analysis of the given *M*-sentence will necessarily be of finite length and will therefore exclude an infinite number of conditionals that are also entailed by the given *M*-sentence. Since, by hypothesis, the M-sentence entails these conditionals, while the *S*-sentence does not, the one cannot be synonymous with the other. As an illustration of this situation let us attempt an analysis of the *M*-sentence "This is a cube." The corresponding *S*-sentence, let us say, begins with a conjunction of conditionals, all of them of the form "If a person were looking at the cube from the position *P* he would observe a sense-datum of such and such a kind." But since the cube is observable from an infinite number of positions, the *S*-sentence would have to contain an infinite number of conjuncts of this form. And this is impossible. The conditionals that follow from a given *M*-sentence are thus literally inexhaustible, and *M*-sentences are therefore not analyzable into *S*-sentences. For the same reason *M*-sentences are not conclusively verifiable. *M*-sentences are verified by verifying *S*-sentences. Hence, if an *M*-sentence entails an infinite number of logically independent conditionals, the conclusive verification of an *M*-sentence is impossible.

The objection that an *M*-sentence cannot be synonymous with an *S*-sentence has never been satisfactorily answered. However, philosophers have undertaken the more modest task of attempting a refutation of the consequence that an *M*-sentence is not conclusively verifiable. The most recent attempt to refute this consequence was made by A. J. Ayer. Ayer states the argument thus:

> No single sense-experience, taken by itself, ever proves that a physical object exists. From the bare fact that I am seeing these visual sense-data

it does not follow that this is a match-box. Nevertheless the occurrence
of these visual sense-data, taken in conjunction with what I remember,
fully justifies the statement that this is a match-box. . . . By itself the
occurrence of just these sense-data would not be sufficient, but in conjunction with previous experience it is. This previous experience may
consist of previous perceptions of the physical object in question, that is,
previous sensings of the appropriate sense-data, but it need not. In certain circumstances I might be fully justified in believing in the existence
of a physical object that I had never before perceived: and in such cases
the strength of the evidence would lie in the general character of my
previous experience.[10]

In so far as the statements Ayer makes in this passage are true, they
have no relevance to a refutation of the contention that M-sentences
are not conclusively verifiable. It is true that on the basis of certain
sense experiences we regard the assertion of a certain M-sentence as
fully justified. Thus, when I hear barking at night, I am fully justified
in asserting the presence of a dog, especially when the barking is loud
and clear. We do not need to investigate here what is meant by the
phrase "fully justified" as employed in this context, except to point out
that the statement "p fully justifies q" is not synonymous with the
statement "q is deducible from p." However, whatever it means, the
employment of this phrase under the circumstances indicated is sanctioned by English usage. I am similarly making correct use of the
English language when I say that the occurence of the bark is *sufficient to establish* or that it *proves* the presence of a dog. But the
existence of these conventions governing the usage of words such as
"proves," "justifies," etc., has nothing to do with the objection that
M-sentences are not conclusively verifiable. And in so far as Ayer thinks
he has disposed of this objection, his argument is an *ignoratio elenchi.*
The objection that an M-sentence is not conclusively verifiable is an immediate consequence of the fact that an M-sentence does not follow
from a finite conjunction of S-sentences. For an M-sentence entails an
infinite number of logically independent S-sentences, and any finite
collection of these therefore entails none of the S-sentences that are
not members of the collection. Let S_1 and S_2 be two logically independent S-sentences, and let M_1 be an M-sentence. By hypothesis we
have (1) M_1 entails S_1 and M_1 entails S_2, (2) S_1 does not entail S_2 and
S_2 does not entail S_1.

Logic allows us to assert (3) If S_1 entails M_1 and M_1 entails S_2 then

---

[10] *Op. cit.*, p. 173.

S_1 entails S_2 and, by applying the principle of transposition to (3), (4) If S_1 does not entail S_2 then either S_1 does not entail M_1 or M_1 does not entail S_2. By (2) and (4) we now have (5) Either S_1 does not entail M_1 or M_1 does not entail S_2. And finally by (1) and (5) we have (6) S_1 does not entail M_1. This demonstration that M_1 does not follow from S_1 is not intended to give the impression that there is not also a sense of "follow" in which the M-sentence does follow from a finite conjunction of S-sentences. But this sense, whatever it may be, is certainly not identical with the logical sense of "follow" that is involved in the assertion that an M-sentence does not follow from a finite conjunction of S-sentences. This assertion cannot be refuted by pointing out that some people use the word "follow" and its synonyms in accordance with a convention they do not share with the logicians.

It should be noted that Ayer does not claim to have shown that an M-sentence is synonymous with an S-sentence. He claims merely to have shown that M-sentences are entailed by certain S-sentences. If this were correct, the same M-sentence would of course follow from an indefinite (infinite) number of other S-sentences as well. This is due to the fact that the sense-data, whose occurrence justifies, in Ayer's opinion, the assertion of the M-sentence, are not unique. Thus it turns out again that the phenomenalistic thesis can not be upheld: even if the M-sentence followed from an S-sentence (of finite length), the M-sentence would be synonymous only with an infinite disjunction of such S-sentences.

Ayer was apparently prompted to attempt a refutation of the principle that no M-sentence is conclusively verifiable by a misinterpretation of the argument in favor of this principle. Ayer's own version of this argument is as follows: "No statement about a physical object can be conclusively verified; on the ground that, however much favorable evidence there may be for it, it is always conceivable that further evidence will show it to have been false all along."[11] Ayer confesses that he used to accept this argument, but that he is now inclined to reject it, because he is now doubtful about the validity of the assumption on which, in his opinion, the argument is based. "The assumption," he says, "is that if, for example, I am looking at my telephone and suddenly see it change into what appears to be a flower-pot, or vanish altogether, or what you will, that proves that it never was a tele-

---

11 *Ibid.*, p. 171.

phone."[12] Ayer thus seems to be of the opinion that the argument for the principle assumes that when we perceive that a physical object ceases to exist or that it changes into another physical object, we are bound to believe that the object never existed. Until the object ceased to exist or until it changed into another object, we had evidence favorable to the supposition that the object existed, while its cessation or change provides us with further evidence unfavorable to this supposition. Since this assumption is obviously absurd, it follows that the argument that entails it must be mistaken. On a certain interpretation of the argument as Ayer formulates it, this absurd assumption would indeed have to be made. The required interpretation becomes plain when we follow Ayer's reasoning to the end. Ayer tells us that he did not make the assumption when he lost his fountain pen. One moment he saw the pen; the next moment it was gone. If he had made the assumption he would presumably have reasoned as follows: "The hypothesis that I had a fountain pen was supported by the apprehension of sense-data of the right sort until a moment ago; but this hypothesis is obviously mistaken, since the further evidence I apprehend now consists of sense-data of an entirely different sort." Ayer found that he did not reason in this way when he met with a test case, and he concludes that the argument against the conclusive verifiability of *M*-sentences must therefore be defective.

Ayer's absurd assumption is entailed by the argument in favor of the principle that *M*-sentences are not conclusively verifiable only when the reference to *further evidence,* in Ayer's formulation of the argument, is interpreted as a reference to *future* sense-experience. Ayer seems to hold that, if the argument in favor of the principle were valid, I would be making a prediction regarding the sense-data that I shall apprehend in the future when I believe that this is a fountain pen; and hence I would have to regard a failure of this prediction as a proof that the fountain pen was hallucinatory. Ayer accordingly argues from the absurdity of this conclusion to the invalidity of the argument. He would have done better if he had argued from the absurdity of this conclusion to the incorrectness of his interpretation of the reference to further evidence. Unless the *M*-sentence makes an explicit or implicit reference to the future, the *S*-sentences it entails make no reference to the future. The sense-data I experience in the future are irrelevant, as evidence, to the

---

12 *Ibid.*

M-sentence that this is a fountain pen, and this becomes obvious as soon as we notice that this *M*-sentence does not entail the *S*-sentence to the effect that I shall apprehend sense-data of such and such a kind under such and such conditions. The truth of this *M*-sentence does not require the truth of the prediction that the fountain pen will last forever.

But even if Ayer's contention that *M*-sentences are conclusively verifiable be accepted, the thesis of phenomenalism must in any case be rejected as untenable. We cannot speak of the analysis of an *M*-sentence into an *S*-sentence, if the *S*-sentence cannot be produced. According to one view the *S*-sentence in a conjunction of conditionals, or an infinite disjunction of such conjunctions, and each conjunction consists of an infinite number of conjuncts. According to the other view, Ayer's view, the *S*-sentence is an infinite disjunction of conjunctions, though each of these conjunctions consists of a finite number of conjuncts. According to either view, then, it is logically impossible to construct the *S*-sentence that corresponds to a given *M*-sentence. An *M*-sentence therefore necessarily differs in meaning from every *S*-sentence. But although it is logically impossible to construct an *S*-sentence that is synonymous with an *M*-sentence, we are not entitled to conclude that the analysis of an *M*-sentence yields a residue of meaning that is not expressible as an *S*-sentence. In addition to the *S*-sentences an *M*-sentence entails, it does not also entail sentences of another type that are not verified by the observation of sense-data. The evidence by which *M*-sentences are verified is all of one kind. It is possible to define phenomenalism simply as the rejection of the view that "to speak about material things is to speak about something altogether different from sense-data, or . . . it is to speak about sense-data but about something else besides."[13] But if this is the definition, the thesis of phenomenalism becomes indistinguishable from the fundamental principle of empiricism that everything we can know and mean must be verified and exemplified in the directly observable.

---

[13] A. J. Ayer, *The Foundations of Empirical Knowledge* (1940), p. 241.

"If," "So," and "Because"

GILBERT RYLE

Logicians say oddly little about inferences. They prefer to
change the subject and talk instead about hypothetical statements. For instance, they shy off discussing what we do with
such dicta as "Today is Monday, so tomorrow is Tuesday"
and discuss instead such dicta as "If today is Monday, tomorrow is Tuesday." In consequence they are apt to misdescribe or
ignore the actual employments that we give to "if-then" statements. A good deal of light would be thrown upon the theoretical uses of "if-then" statements by an enquiry into some of
the nontheoretical uses to which we put other sorts of "if-then"
sentences, such as conditional promises, threats, injunctions,
wagers, requests, and counsels. In particular, the regulation of
our practical conduct by accepted rules, like the rules of games,
etiquette, morals, style, grammar, and technology, has much
in common with the regulation of our theorising conduct by
our acceptance of variable hypothetical statements (or "laws").
In this paper, however, I try to bring out at least part of the
force of some "if-then" sentences in another way, and shall
accordingly be limiting the discussion to hypothetical statements proper, namely, those which can or must appear in the
exposition of true or false theories. I try to exhibit the major
differences between our theoretical uses of "if-then" sentences
and our theoretical uses of "so" or "therefore" sentences, as
well as the connections between them. (But the distinction
between theory and practice is not hard-edged. Are we being

theoretically active or practically active when we converse? Or when we give verbal swimming-instructions? Or when we make requests and bets?)

There is a third class of theory-constituting sentences which also needs to be considered, namely, those of the pattern ". . . , because . . . ." For these are different as well from inferences as from hypothetical statements and yet are closely related to both. I shall call statements of this class "explanations."

In using "if-then" sentences and in using "because" sentences we are stating or asserting. "If today is Monday, tomorrow is Tuesday" is a true statement; "Tomorrow is Tuesday, because today is Monday" is another statement which may be true. But "Today is Monday, so tomorrow is Tuesday" is not a statement. It is an argument, of which we can ask whether it is valid or fallacious; it is not an assertion or doctrine or announcement of which we can ask whether it is true or false.

We can, indeed, ask whether its premiss is true, and whether its conclusion is true; but there is not the third question "Is it true that today is Monday so tomorrow is Tuesday?" An argument is not the expression of a proposition, though it embodies the expressions of two propositions.

By what criteria do we decide whether an expression is a statement or not? We cannot rest with the grammatical criterion that the verb is, or the verbs are, in the indicative mood and that the sentence ends with a full stop and not a question mark. For in some hypothetical statements, both verbs may be in the subjunctive mood; and conversely in arguments, both verbs are in the indicative mood. Neither of them is a question, but only one of them is a statement.

Another criterion would be this. Usually we should call a sentence a "statement" if by shifting its verb and replacing its full stop by a question mark a recognisable question resulted. "All men are mortal" is a statement, for "Are all men mortal?" is a question; "It is Tuesday tomorrow because it is Monday today" is a statement, for "Is the reason why it is Tuesday tomorrow that it is Monday today?" is a proper if not very natural question. Using this criterion we are helped to see that arguments are not statements, since there is no way of producing a question out of "Today is Monday, so tomorrow is Tuesday" by shifting verbs and replacing the full stop by a question mark. But then we should notice that there is no very natural way of converting an "if-then" statement into a question either. Indeed, where it is easy to formulate natural questions to which "because" statements are answers, e.g., by asking "Why is it Tuesday tomorrow?" or "Why do you say that it is Tuesday tomorrow?" it is not easy, though it is not impossible, to formulate any natural questions to which "If it is Monday today, it is Tuesday tomorrow" would be an answer. In this respect hypothetical statements seem to behave more like arguments than like explanations.

Next, when a person makes a statement to the effect that something is the case, it is always or usually appropriate to ask whether he knows, believes, or supposes that it is the case; we can ask whether he is lying or mistaken and so question the truth of what he has told us; we can contradict him; we can consider the evidence for and against what he has said; and we can thank him for the information that he has given us. But when he produces an argument, none of these responses is appropriate. We may consider whether he is right to draw that conclusion "q" from that premiss "p," but we cannot ask whether he knows, believes, or merely supposes that p, so q. Indeed " p, so q" cannot be the filling of any "that" clause. We may rebut his argument, but we cannot contradict it; we can contradict his premiss and his conclusion, but we cannot rebut them. We may describe his premiss and his conclusion as pieces of information; but his argument from the one to the other is not an extra piece of information. We can examine his evidence for his conclusion, but we cannot ask for evidence for or against his move from his evidence to his conclusion.

Finally, it is an important, if not the important, feature of our use of words like "statement," "proposition," and "judgment," that any statement, proposition, or judgment can function as a premiss or a conclusion in arguments. Suitability for what may be summarily called the "premissory job" is one of the main things that make us reserve the title of "statement" for some sentences in distinction from all the rest. Commands, reproaches, questions, laments, exhortations, and plaudits are not constructed for incorporation as they stand into arguments, either as premises or conclusions. By "a statement" we mean, at least *inter alia,* a sentence that is constructed for such incorporation. And then it is patent that arguments themselves are not statements. The conclusion of one argument may be the premiss of another argument, but an argument itself cannot be the premiss or conclusion of an argument. Nothing follows from "p, so q," nor does "p, so q" follow from anything. "p, so q" cannot perform the premissory job. Hypothetical statements and "because" statements, on the other hand, can be premisses and conclusions in arguments (though only in relatively high-level arguments).

We might say, provisionally, that an argument is no more a statement than a piece of multiplication is a number. An argument is an operation with statements, somewhat as a pass is an operation with a football. Since an argument is not a statement, it is neither a categorical nor an hypothetical statement; nor is it any third sort of statement, like a "because" statement, which though not classifiable as categorical or hypothetical must certainly rank as a statement.

But there is an important connection between the argument "Today is Monday, so tomorrow is Tuesday" and what is told in the hypothetical statement "If today is Monday, tomorrow is Tuesday." For in considering the argument, we can enquire not only whether the premiss is true and the conclusion is true, but also whether the conclusion is legitimately drawn from the premiss. And to ask whether the conclusion is legitimately drawn from the premiss is to raise the question whether it is true that if today is Monday, tomorrow is Tuesday. In some way the validity of the argument requires the truth of the hypothetical statement and to concede the truth of the hypothetical statement is to concede the argument. This already shows part of the point of making hypothetical statements. But just how does the validity of the argument require the truth of the hypothetical statement?

(a) It might erroneously be suggested that an argument requires the truth of the corresponding hypothetical statement in the way in which "That creature is a fox" requires the truth of "That creature is a mammal," namely, that the hypothetical statement follows from or is entailed by the argument. But this will not do. For an argument, not being a statement, is not the sort of thing that can be described as entailing or not entailing statements. Certainly "If today is Monday, tomorrow is Tuesday" follows from the statement "The argument 'Today is Monday, so tomorrow is Tuesday' is a valid one"; but it neither follows nor does not follow from the argument "Today is Monday, so tomorrow is Tuesday." An argument is not a statement about its own merits, and it cannot do what a statement about its merits can do.

(b) It might erroneously be suggested that an argument "p, so q" is nothing more or less than a stylistically veiled conjunctive statement, the candid expression of which would be "p, and (if p, then q) and q." So the argument requires the truth of the hypothetical statement in the way in which "Jack and Jill fell down the hill" requires the truth of "Jill fell down the hill." But this will not do. For conjunctive statements are true or false statements, not valid or invalid arguments. They can, *en bloc*, be premisses or conclusions of arguments; they can be asserted, questioned, and contradicted, known, believed, or guessed. A man with a good memory might remember that "*p, and (if p, then q) and q*" without having drawn a conclusion or followed the drawing of a conclusion by anyone else. If the hypothetical statement were false, its conjunction with "*p*" and "*q*" would render the conjunctive statement false, but it would not render it a fallacy; and a person who asserted such a statement would show that he was in error but not that he was illogical.

(*c*) It might, conversely, but equally erroneously, be suggested that "*p, so q*" requires the truth of "*if p, then q*" because the hypothetical sentence is just the argument "*p, so q,*" misleadingly worded; so that "*p, so q*" requires "*if p, then q,*" since that is simply to say that "*p, so q*" is equivalent to "*p, so q.*" But this will not do. In "*if p, then q*" no premiss is asserted and no conclusion is drawn. A person might say "*if p, then q*" and then accept "*but not-p*" and "*not-q*" without withdrawing what he had said. Moreover a hypothetical statement can function in the premissory way and in the conclusion way, which an argument cannot do. It can also with a change of style be contradicted or questioned. "It could be Monday today, without its being Tuesday tomorrow" (e.g., on the occasion of a calendar reform) contradicts "If it is Monday today, it is Tuesday tomorrow"; and "Can it be Monday today and not Tuesday tomorrow?" is the corresponding query.

(*d*) More plausibly but still erroneously, it might be suggested that an argument requires the truth of the corresponding hypothetical statement in this way. An argument "*p, so q*" is always invalid unless the premiss from which "*q*" is drawn incorporates not only "*p*" but also "*if p, then q.*" "*q*" follows neither from "*if p, then q*" by itself, nor from "*p*" by itself, but only from the conjunction "*p and (if p, then q).*" But this notoriously will not do. For, suppose it did. Then a critic might ask to be satisfied that "*q*" was legitimately drawn from "*p and (if p, then q)*"; and, to be satisfied, he would have to be assured that "*if (p and [if p, then q]), then q.*" So this new hypothetical would have to be incorporated as a third component of the conjunctive premiss, and so on forever—as the Tortoise proved to Achilles. The principle of an inference cannot be one of its premisses or part of its premiss. Conclusions are drawn from premisses in accordance with principles, not from premisses that embody those principles. The rules of evidence do not have to be testified to by the witnesses.

It is not merely that the officially recognized Rules of Inference cannot be given the rôle of premiss components in all the specific inferences that are made in accordance with them. The same thing is true of the most 'meaty' and determinate hypothetical statements, like "If today is Monday, tomorrow is Tuesday." This equally is not a premiss from which, together with "today is Monday" the conclusion "so tomorrow is Tuesday" is drawn. The argument "Today is Monday, so tomorrow is Tuesday" is an application of "if today is Monday, tomorrow is Tuesday"; and it is in this notion of application that lies the answer to our question "How does a valid argument require the truth of the corresponding hypothetical statement?"

Part of this last positive point may be brought out in this way. If we ask, "What is the point of learning cooking recipes, bridge conventions, or rules of the road?" the obvious beginning of the answer is "In order to be able to cook dishes properly, play bridge properly, and drive vehicles properly." Correspondingly, if we ask for evidence that someone knows these things, an obvious beginning of the answer is that he does cook properly, play bridge properly, and drive vehicles properly. But we may, though we need not, expect more than this. We may expect the learner not only to be able and ready to operate properly in the kitchen, at the bridge table, and on the road, but also to be able and ready to *tell* the recipes, the conventions, and the rules of the road; to tell them, for example, when someone else needs tuition, or to tell them when he has to justify his own operations, or to tell them when a debate is in progress about possible improvements in the methods of cooking, playing bridge, or using roads.

In the same sort of way, if we ask what is the point of learning "*if p, then q,*" or what is the evidence that someone has learned it, part of the answer would be a reference to the learner's ability and readiness to infer from "*p*" to "*q*" and from "*not-q*" to "*not-p,*" to acquiesce in the corresponding arguments of others, to reject affiliated invalid arguments, and so on. But we should also expect him on certain, perhaps rare, occasions to *tell* his hearers or readers "*if p, then q.*" He would be expected to be able and ready to make the hypothetical statement when someone else required to be taught, when he himself was under challenge to justify his inference operations, and so on.

The question "What is the point of learning '*if p, then q*'?" is quite different from the question "What is the point of making the statement '*if p, then q.*'" When we learn something, we cannot be learning *only* how to teach it—else there would be no "it." When we teach a lesson, we cannot be teaching *only* how to teach that same lesson, else there would be no lesson. Thus, making a hypothetical statement is sometimes giving an inference precept; and the first object of giving this precept is that the recipient shall make appropriate inferences. A posterior object of giving him this precept is, perhaps, that he shall in his turn give this inference precept to others, again with the same primary object, that they shall learn to perform the appropriate inferential operations.

Knowing "*if p, then q*" is, then, rather like being in possession of a railway ticket. It is having a license or warrant to make a journey from London to Oxford. (Knowing a variable hypothetical or "law" is like having a season ticket.) As a person can have a ticket without actually travelling with it and without ever being in London or getting to Oxford, so a person can have an inference warrant without actually making any inferences and even without ever acquiring the premises from which to make them. The question "What is the point of getting or keeping a railway ticket?" is quite different from the question "What is the point of showing or handing over a ticket?" We get and keep tickets in order to be equipped to travel from London to Oxford (on occasions when we are in London and wish to travel to Oxford). But we show tickets in order to satisfy officials that we have the right to travel, and we hand tickets over to other people in order to give them both the right to travel and the opportunity to satisfy officials that they have that right.

Neither buying a ticket, nor owning a ticket, nor showing or transferring a ticket is travelling. Nor are we making or following the inference "*p, so q*" when we get or retain the knowledge that "*if p, then q,*" or when we utter or write the statement "*if p, then q.*" But what we have learned, when we have learned it, and what we have taught, when we have taught it, is, in the first instance to argue "*p, so q,*" or else "*not-q so not-p,*" etc., and to accept such arguments from others. And as travel warrants can be invalid in various ways, so "if-then" statements can be false. Uncovenanted journeys can be made from London to Oxford, and from "Today is the 28th of February" to "Tomorrow is the 1st of March."

It must be realised that asserting *"if p, then q"* is not making a report of any inference or a comment on any inference. Nor is it recommending, exhorting, confessing, requesting, or commanding anything.
It is not talking about inferring any more than showing up a ticket or
transferring a ticket is talking about a railway journey.

We should now turn to consider briefly the force of dicta like "It
is Tuesday tomorrow, because it is Monday today," i.e., answers to
questions of the type "Why so-and-so?" Explanations are not arguments
but statements. They are true or false; they are answers to questions;
they can express what someone knows, believes, guesses, or queries;
and they can be premisses or conclusions of arguments. (But it should
be noticed that there is a didactic use of "because" sentences, in which
they function much more like arguments than like statements, namely
when a teacher wishes to lead his pupils by the hand from the premiss
to the conclusion of an argument familiar to him but new to them.
He may say "Because this and that, therefore so-and-so." He is then
synchronously leading them along the path and showing them the
signposts.)

Now the statement *"q, because p"* cannot be true unless *"q"* and
"p" are true. It also cannot be true unless *"if p, then q"* is true. In
these respects, that it requires the truth of *"p," "q,"* and *"if p, then q,"*
it has obvious analogies to the argument *"p, so q."* But the sense of
"requires" is different, since explanations are true or false, but not
valid or invalid, while arguments are valid or invalid but not true
or false. If a person accepts *"p, so q"* as not only valid but also correct,
in the sense both that its premiss and conclusion are true and that the
argument from the one to the other is legitimate, then he is committed
to accepting *"q, because p"* as true, and vice versa; yet *"q, because p"*
is not a paraphrase of *"p, so q,"* any more than surrendering one's
ticket to the ticket collector at one's destination is making a legitimate
train journey. To say *"q, because p"* is not to say, in other words, *"p,
so q."* But nor is it to say *"p, and q, and (p, so q)."* For, *"p, so q,"* not
being a statement, cannot be a component of a conjunctive statement.
Nor is *"q, because p"* equivalent to *"p, and (if p, then q) and q";* for
a person who said this would not have given the explanation of *"q,"*
though he would have provided material out of which such an explanation could be constructed. He would have mentioned what was in
fact the (or a) reason for *"q,"* but he would not yet have given it as the
reason for *"q."* (Nor, in real life, do we form conjunctive statements

out of component statements of such different constitutions as "*p*" and "*if p, then q.*") No, in saying "*q, because p,*" we are not just asserting but *using* what is expressed by "*if p, then q*"; we are putting it to work or applying it; we are attaching "*q*" to "*p*" in accordance with the license conveyed by "*if p, then q.*" For the question "Why '*q*'?" is the question "From what premiss is '*q*' legitimately drawn?"; and the answer to this question has to give not just the true premiss "*p,*" but, therewith, the title to infer from "*p*" to "*q.*"

In other words, just as the inference "*p, so q*" does not embody "*if p, then q*" as a component of its premiss, but rather applies it in being an operation with "*p*" and "*q*" executed in conformity with it, so "*q, because p*" does not embody "*if p, then q*" as a component of its "because" clause but applies it in another way.

Should we class explanations as categorical or as hypothetical statements? The answer must be "They are neither—nor are they conflations of categorical with hypothetical statements." The dichotomy "either categorical or hypothetical," though initially clarifying, is finally muddling. Is the umpire a player or a spectator? He is neither a player nor a spectator nor both a player and a spectator.

The still somewhat nebulous notion of application may now be clarified by a new consideration. There is an important respect in which at any rate some hypothetical statements differ both from inferences and from explanations; namely there can be what are called "variable hypotheticals," but there could not be variable inferences or variable explanations. We can say "If anyone is a man, he is mortal," but we cannot say either "Anyone is a man, so he is mortal" or "Because anyone is a man, he is mortal" or "Anyone is mortal, because he is a man." The premiss and conclusion of an inference are propositions, not propositional functions, statements and not statement skeletons; and the same thing is true of the clauses of a "because" statement. True, the premiss and the conclusion of an inference may be entire variable hypothetical statements. From "Whoever reads Plato in the original reads Greek" it follows that "Whoever reads Plato in the original reads a language other than Latin." But in the way in which the clauses of a variable hypothetical statement are themselves not statements but statement indents, inferences and explanations cannot have statement indents for their terminals.

Much as some railway tickets are season tickets, licensing their holders to make a given journey on any day during a stated period, so some hypothetical statements are, so to speak, seasonal inference warrants. And just as no journey can be a seasonal journey, so no inference or explanation can be a variable inference or a variable explanation. Permits can be open, but permitted actions cannot be open.

Now it is just this fact that such hypothetical statements are open that makes other statements, like premises and conclusions, eligible as fillings for them. That something is an eligible filling for (or satisfies) an open specification is part of what is meant by saying that the statement, rule, or warrant (etc.) incorporating the specification "applies" to that something. A certain local parking regulation applies to me and my car in this way. For though it does not mention us, it tells what any private car owner may or may not do about parking his car (no matter what its age, make, colour, or price). But I and my car do not then, in our turn, "apply" to anything further. What I do on a particular occasion with my car may comply with or be a breach of this regulation; but it makes no sense to suggest that there is something else that, in a similar way, complies with or is a breach of what I do with my car on this occasion. Or there may be exceptions to a rule, law, or maxim, but such an exception cannot, in its turn, be something to which there could be, in the same way, exceptions. "Save for . . ." can be tacked on to a variable hypothetical statement, but not on to an inference or an explanation. I shall try shortly to show that some kind of openness, variableness, or satisfiability characterises all hypothetical statements alike, whether they are recognised "variable hypotheticals" like "For all x, if x is a man, x is mortal" or are highly determinate hypotheticals like "If today is Monday, tomorrow is Tuesday."

Let me, however, first take stock. Part of what I have been trying to do is to show that the activities of asserting and following both hypothetical statements and explanations are more sophisticated than the activities of wielding and following arguments. A person must learn to use arguments before he can learn to use hypothetical statements and explanations. In arguing (and following arguments) a person is operating with a technique or method, i.e., he is exercising a skill; but in making or considering hypothetical statements and explanations he is, for example, giving or taking instruction in that technique or operation. Roughly and provisionally, he is not cooking, but writing or reading a cookery book, not practising an art but teaching it or receiving tuition in it.

Another, though connected, object has been this. Fascinated by the model of simple, singular, affirmative, attributive, or relational statements, theorists are apt to ask "What exactly do hypothetical statements assert to characterise what?" or "What exactly do 'because' statements assert to be in what relation to what?" or, more generally, "What do such statements describe?" or "What matters of fact do they report?" And they are apt to toy with verbally accommodating replies about Necessary Connections between Facts, or Internal Relations between Universals, and the like. But if such statements are, as I have argued, sophistications upon inferences, the corresponding rewording of their question shows clearly what has gone wrong. For if I ask "What exactly do arguments assert to characterise what?" or "What exactly do inferences state to be in what relation to what?" the reply is easy. Arguments are not assertions or statements at all and so are not attributive or relational statements. Hume might be doctored into saying: "Causality is not a relation; for '*p, so q*' is an inference and not a statement, and so is not the statement of a relation. 'So' is not a relation word, or a relational predicate, or a predicate of any sort. For '*p, so q*' is not a subject-predicate statement since it is not a statement at all. Predicting an event from another event is not describing a bond, for it is not describing." But this point has been generally overlooked, partly owing to the habit of ignoring inferences (which are not statements) and concentrating instead on hypothetical statements and explanations (which are), and partly owing to the tacit and false assumption that such statements belong to pre-inferential levels of discourse, instead of to post-inferential levels.

It is time now to harden the edges of the notion of application from another side. When I learn "*if p, then q,*" I am learning that I am authorised to argue "*p, so q,*" *provided that I get my premiss* "*p.*" But the hypothetical statement does not tell me "*p,*" any more than getting a ticket puts me on to the train. The statement "*if p, then q*" does not incorporate the statements "*p*" and "*q,*" as these statements certainly are incorporated in such dicta as "*p and q,*" "*q, because p,*" "*p, so q,*" and "*p, although q.*" In saying "if *p,* then *q,*" I am not stating "*p*" or "*q*" or in any way committing myself to the truth of "*p*" or "*q*"; I am stating or asserting something, but I am not stating or asserting them. Neither the statement "*p*" nor the statement "*q*" enters into the statement "if *p,* then *q.*" Yet, especially when so encoded, the hypothetical statement does very much look like a statement incorporating the two component statements "*p*" and "*q.*" If it does not incorporate them, then the coding must be highly misleading. I am going to argue for just this conclusion.

In ordinary English we very often so word our hypothetical statements, that the protasis expression after the word "if," and the apodosis expression after the word "then" (if this occurs) have both the vocabulary and the syntax of statements. The protasis and apodosis expressions in "If it is Monday today, (then) it is Tuesday tomorrow" look and sound exactly like the statements "today is Monday" and "tomorrow is Tuesday" as these might appear either by themselves or as components of a conjunctive statement, or as premiss and conclusion of an inference, or as explicandum and explicans in an explanation. But sometimes in ordinary English, often in old-fashioned English and commonly in languages like Latin, the protasis clause and the apodosis clause are worded subjunctively. And to say that they are worded subjunctively is to say that they are not worded as statements are worded. In "If it be Monday today, it is Tuesday tomorrow," one of the clauses does not look or sound like a statement. In "If it were Monday today, it would be Tuesday tomorrow," neither clause looks or sounds like a statement.

We have another familiar way of wording hypothetical statements. Although the standard textbooks discuss "modal propositions" in a different chapter from that in which they discuss hypotheticals, the differences between modal and hypothetical statements are in fact purely stylistic. There is only one colloquial way of correctly negating the superstitious hypothetical statement "If a person walks under a ladder, he comes to grief before the day is out," namely, by saying "No, a person may (might or could) walk under a ladder and not come to grief." And the only colloquial way of putting a question to which an "if-then" statement is the required affirmative answer is to ask, for example, "Can an Oxford Vice-Chancellor not be (or Need he be) a Head of a College?"

But if we reword, as we always can reword, an "if-then" statement as a statement of the pattern "It cannot be Monday today and not be Tuesday tomorrow," we see at once that what follows "cannot" and "and" has none of the appearances of a statement. The statementlike appearance of the clauses of those "if-then" statements which are not subjunctively worded is a deceptive appearance and one which always can be and often is obviated in stylistically different paraphrases. But if so, the logicians' code style (which I have myself been using) *"if p,*

then q" is deceptive. For the letters *"p"* and *"q"* as they occur here look
and sound just like the *"p"* and *"q"* that occur in conjunctive statements, inferences, and explanations. But if the clauses of a hypothetical
statement are not statements, then logicians ought not to flag them
so. The practice tempts their users and their pupils to assume the truth
of such falsities as these: hypothetical statements assert connections between statements or between judgments or between propositions or between facts or between aspects or features of the Real; they are truth
functions of atomic statements; and so on.

Cook Wilson was much more nearly right when he said that hypothetical statements assert relations between questions. This still will
not do, for just as nothing is stated or asserted, so nothing is asked in
the protasis or in the apodosis; and if no one is being asked anything,
no question is occurring. But he was right in seeing that no statement
is made by either clause and so that the hypothetical statement as a
whole is not telling us anything about any such incorporated statements. Nor is it a resultant, product, or truth function of any incorporated statements. But he was on the right track, too, in a further
and more positive respect. What the hypothetical statement does embody is not statements but statement specifications or statement indents—bills for statements that statements could fill. Similarly what
the parking regulations embody are not cars or drivers but specifications that cars and their drivers can satisfy. It is because hypothetical
statements embody statement specifications, that an inference from one
statement to another can be described as being "in accordance with"
or being "an application of" the hypothetical. The premiss fills the
protasis bill; the conclusion fills the apodosis bill. They "fulfil the
conditions." Now this notion of statement indents, or statement specifications is indeed very close to the notion of a question. For a question does contain a specification of what is required, and what is required is a statement, for an answer to a question is a statement. Of
course, asking a question does not consist merely in voicing a statement specification. Asking a question is doing a specific conversa-
tional job with such a specification. Uttering a hypothetical statement
is doing another specific job with a couple of statement specifications,
with either of which by itself, or with both of which conjointly, a
person with a different interest could have made a request for a specified piece of information. There are, I suppose, plenty of other con-

versational, administrative, and theoretical things which are done with statement specifications.

Now just as "Who . . . ?" can be answered by "Socrates . . . ," and the variable "*x*" in "*x* . . ." can have "Socrates" for one of its values, so "Is today Monday?" can be answered by "Today is Monday," and ". . . today be Monday" can have "Today is Monday" for one of its values. This is the sense in which I said earlier that all hypotheticals are variable hypotheticals. "Variable" and "hypothetical" are related as genus to species. (But this is not the sense in which logicians have separated some hypotheticals as "variable hypotheticals" from the rest.)

If a consignment of bicycles fills the bill in an export license, the bill that it fills is not itself that consignment of bicycles or a consignment of anything else; it is only the verbal specification of such a consignment. Similarly if a statement fills a bill, the bill that it fills is not that statement nor any other statement. Putting an export-license into an envelope does not involve putting a consignment of bicycles into that envelope; it involves putting into the envelope that part of the flimsy which carries the specification of the consignment. Putting the words "today is Monday" and "tomorrow is Tuesday" into a hypothetical statement does not involve putting a premiss or a conclusion into that statement; it is only putting in the specifications of such a premiss and conclusion. And as export licenses can be drafted, though no bicycles are manufactured, so hypothetical statements can be made though no premiss statement or conclusion statement is ever made.

Sometimes it is suggested that the difference between the occurrence of "it is Monday today" and "it is Tuesday tomorrow" in a hypothetical statement and their occurrence as answers to questions or as premiss and conclusion in an inference is merely this: In the hypothetical statement, "today is Monday" and "tomorrow is Tuesday" occur in an "unasserted" way, whereas in the other contexts they occur in an "asserted" way. The suggestion is that to be asserted is a luxury extra, like italicisation. But this will not do. If nothing is asserted, or no statement is made, then no question is answered, nothing is contradicted, no premiss is used, no conclusion is drawn, no information or misinformation is given. A statement bereft of its employments is not a statement and an expression debarred from doing any of the jobs of a statement has either no job or else a different job.

What tempts people to say this sort of thing, as well as to say such things as that hypothetical statements assert relations between statements, propositions, or facts, is the patent similarity between protasis expressions and apodosis expressions (as commonly worded) on the one hand and statements on the other. There need not be, though there can be, a vocabulary flag or syntax flag to show that they are not statements. The standard code symbolisation *"if p, then q"* reinforces this temptation. For surely logicians, of all people, would not symbolise completely disparate things by identical symbols. Or have they too assumed that indistinguishable styles prove identity of function?

In many ordinary cases there is no similarity whatsoever between bills and what fills them. The specification of a consignment of bicycles in an export license is not in the slightest degree like a consignment of bicycles. The specification is a bit of paper covered with typewritten letters; the bicycles are bits of iron, steel, rubber, and aluminium. A railway ticket from London to Oxford has nothing on it resembling London or Oxford.

But some specifications are very similar to the things that satisfy them. A cooking instructor may teach cookery not in words or diagrams, but in dumb show. He goes through the motions that his pupil is to go through. He is not telling her what to do, but showing her what to do. If she is inattentive or clumsy, he may complain that her actions do not comply with the requirements he had made of her. Yet he imparted these requirements to her only by making motions. It must be noticed that he is not cooking. He does with an empty spoon what she is to do with a full spoon; he does with a cold oven what she is to do with a hot oven. The difference between their operations is not to be described by saying that she is concocting edible ("asserted") puddings, where he had been concocting not-to-be-eaten ("unasserted") puddings. For he had not been concocting a pudding at all, but only showing her how to do it *when she had got the ingredients and the hot oven.*

Much as no concocting is done in the movements staged by the demonstrator, so no premises are used or conclusions drawn by a person making a hypothetical statement. But also, much as the operations to be done with ingredients are specified by the very similar but empty-handed operations of the demonstrator, so the inferential operations to be done with statements are specified by the very similar but empty-handed verbal operations of the author of a hypothetical statement. We might say that delivering a hypothetical statement is teaching in dumb show what to do with statements—save that in this case the demonstration cannot be in dumb show since the operation that is being taught is itself a talking (or writing) operation. In somewhat the same way, an actor manager may instruct his actors how to deliver their words, not by telling them, but by showing them what to do. He too cannot do this in dumb show.

The cooking demonstrator is neither handling ingredients and utensils nor talking about them. His activity is not one either of using or of mentioning flour, sugar, spoons, or ovens. The actor manager is similarly not mentioning or (strictly) using the utterances that he is showing his actors how to deliver. For he is not acting to an audience, but teaching his actors to do so. But even the actors in speaking their parts before the audience are not, strictly, using their words. They are not being defiant, remorseful, loving, or desperate, but only pretending to be so. Their utterances cannot be classified as either "use" or "mention." *A fortiori,* the actor manager's actions of teaching (by showing) how convincingly to seem defiant, remorseful, etc., are not classifiable as either "using" or "mentioning." In the same way, the author of a hypothetical statement is neither using nor mentioning any premiss statements or conclusion statements. He is showing, empty-handed, how to use them. We might say that he is making a dummy inference, with a didactic purpose. It may be noticed that showing what to do is a more sophisticated performance than doing it ingenuously, though a less sophisticated one than telling what to do.

Before concluding, I must mention some points which need to be borne in mind.

(1) "If" sometimes means "even if," or "although"; such an "if" clause functions not as a premiss indent, but as an indent for a "but" statement.

(2) The author of an unfulfilled conditional like "If Hannibal had marched on Rome, he would have taken it," does not work empty-handed. He commits himself to the falsity of "he marched on Rome" and "he took it." His assertion is, in consequence, not far removed from being an explanation why Hannibal did not take Rome. However I do not think that "If he had marched on Rome, he would have taken it" is a paraphrase of "The reason why he did not take it is that he did not march on it." It would not naturally be proffered as the answer to a "why" question or a "why not" question, though I think

that its truth would entail and be entailed by the truth of the "because" answer to such a "why not" question.

(3) I have said nothing about different varieties of inferences, hypothetical statements, and explanations. (*a*) For all three, we can find sets of specimens which are logically truistic, arguments "valid in virtue of their form alone" and hypothetical statements and explanations which are "true in virtue of their form alone." E.g., "Jack and Jill fell down the hill, so Jill fell down the hill," "If Jack and Jill fell down the hill, Jill fell down the hill," and "Jill fell down the hill, for both Jack and Jill fell down the hill." (*b*) For all three, again, we can find specimens which are valid or else true in virtue of some tight convention or arrangement, like those which yield inferences, inference warrants, and explanations about matters of calendar fact or matters of chess fact. (*c*) For all three, again, we can find sets of specimens the validity or truth of which require to be vouched for by observation and experiment.

(4) I have said nothing about statements of the kinds " '*p*' entails '*q*' " or " '*q*' does (or does not) follow from '*p*.' " Such locutions are used (roughly) not by the players in the field but by the spectators, critics, and selectors in the grandstand. They belong to the talk of logicians, cross-examiners, and reviewers. It should be noticed here too that the codification " '*p*' entails '*q*' " is uncandid where " '*p*' would entail '*q*' " would be candid. For " '*p*' entails '*q*' " could be, and in real life ordinarily would be construed to mean that the true conclusion "*q*" is legitimately drawn from the true premiss "*p*"; and to say this is quite different from saying that "If there were a true statement satisfying the protasis, there would be legitimately deducible from it a true statement satisfying the apodosis."

Interpretation and Evaluation in Aesthetics

CHARLES L. STEVENSON

Let us suppose that a critic is in doubt about the meaning of a certain poem. He is inclined to take it as an allegory, for if he were content with its literal meaning, he suspects, he would be understanding it too passively—he would be bringing too little to it. Yet the poem sometimes resists the allegory; so he fears that in his efforts to avoid bringing too little to it he has gone to the other extreme: he has read meanings into it. Whether or not the poem is allegorical, then, presents him with a problem, one that is familiar throughout literary criticism.

His decision will be closely related to his evaluation of the poem; but it will not in itself be a decision about the poem's value. If he subsequently concludes that the poem is allegorical, for instance, he may or may not conclude that the allegory enhances its beauty. His problem is one of *interpretation,* and we can conveniently use that term to distinguish it from any problem of aesthetic *evaluation* that normally attends it.

We shall encounter the same distinction, though in a somewhat altered form, in this further example: Suppose that a critic is studying a nonobjective painting. In certain of his moods, on attentively regarding it, he has experienced a subtle emotion and has felt that its lines form a unified design. These moods have been rare, however, and for the most part it has seemed emotionally weak, with lines moving awkwardly and pointlessly. So which reaction is he to trust—which reveals the emotion that the painting actually expresses or the design that it actually embodies? Are his rarer moods those of special discernment, enabling him to bring to the painting a proper sensibility; or are they forced, over-wrought moods, causing him to project into the painting various elements that are foreign to it?

In this case the *relation* of the problem to an evaluative one is even more obvious. If the critic decides that the painting expresses a subtle emotion or that it has a unified design, we shall expect him to evaluate it favorably. But the relation is presumably a contingent one. If he should go on to make an unfavorable evaluation, we should be surprised at his unusual taste; but we should not, I think, be inclined to say that he had contradicted himself. Or even if we should be so inclined—for the vagueness of our language does not permit a categorical decision about such a matter—we should not want to say that "subtle emotion" and "unified design" are *limited* to an evaluative function. We should want to separate, by abstraction, two aspects of their meaning. First they designate certain nonevaluative qualities of emotion or design; and then, as an independent step, they say that these qualities *possess* value or are *attended by* value. Hence the emotion and design are not *identical* with value, and questions about them can be considered as presenting distinct, nonevaluative problems.

Shall we say that the nonevaluative problems are concerned with an "interpretation" of the painting? If we do we shall perhaps be using the word in an extended sense. In our first example the use of "interpretation" was strictly conventional; but in the second, where emphasis on the cognitive meaning of a work of art gives place to emphasis on its expressiveness and design, the term has a way of seeming half-metaphorical. But however that may be, I propose to say that an "interpretative" problem is presented by the second example no less than by the first. For the examples have much in common: both require a decision about the way in which we are to experience a work of art— a decision about nonevaluative but aesthetically relevant elements that the work "has," as distinct, for instance, from those that are "read into it" or are "forcibly projected into it." The word "interpretive," no other familiar word being available, is convenient for emphasizing this important point of analogy.

We must be careful to distinguish this use of the term from another that is somewhat more familiar. An "interpretation" is often given by a *secondary artist,* such as a virtuoso or an actor, who re-creates the work of a primary artist by performing it. But as the term will here be used, an "interpretation" is given by a *critic*, whose aim is not to re-create the work but to decide how to react to it in an appropriate way and to guide others in doing so. In the first sense, which introduces topics that the present paper cannot discuss, one may interpret Beethoven or Shakespeare but not El Greco or Donatello; but in the second sense one may interpret the work of any artist whomsoever.

These remarks permit me to indicate, though still somewhat roughly, the scope of the present paper. It will be concerned with both interpretive and evaluative questions—though it will emphasize the former, the latter having had more than their share of attention in aesthetics. It will not attempt to *answer* these questions, however, since that is the task not of analytical philosophy but of art criticism. Its aim, which can be realized only in a partial way, will be to *clarify* the questions —to define the terms in which they are formulated. And it will draw certain conclusions, for which the study of terms will prepare the way, about the extent to which interpretation and evaluation involve matters of taste that are "not to be disputed."

II

If we generalize from the examples that have been given, we shall find that any problem of art criticism, whether interpretive or evaluative, can scarcely be formulated without reference to a fivefold distinction.

There is always (*a*) *a work of art,* which for the sense of words here in question will be a physical object or event. Let us assume that it undergoes no change during the time that it is being observed and criticized. In literature, music, and the ballet, the work of art can be identified with the physical events involved in various readings or performances. Let us assume that these undergo no change in the sense that any two readings or performances will be exactly alike. For although false, the assumption will conveniently exclude any question about the "interpretation" of a secondary artist, which the limited scope of this paper (it will be remembered) does not permit us to consider. Now the work of art will be contemplated by (*b*) *an observer,* and it will be obvious that (*c*) *the conditions of observation* under which he contemplates it will not be constant. For if there is no change in the more obvious physical conditions, there will at least be changes in the observer's state of mind—in his sensitiveness, his manner of paying attention, and so on. (It is convenient to include the latter under [c] even though they might, alternatively, have been included under a separate heading.) With these changes, even though the work of art undergoes no changes at all, there will be correlated certain changes in (d) *the appearances* that the work presents to the observer, where this term is to be understood quite broadly, designating not only visual and auditory experiences, but many others, including those that attend cognitive and emotional reactions. We may tacitly ignore, however, the appearances that obviously have no bearing on aesthetic appreciation. It is these changes in the appearances, and various other changes in them that may reasonably be expected to occur later on, that introduce the problem of art criticism. For the observer is trying to make a decision about (e) *the aesthetic properties that are possessed by the work of art itself,* such as its grace, spatial rhythm, beauty, and so on; and he does not wish to say that it has all the properties that are suggested, at one time and another, by its appearances. In some sense or another he must distinguish appearances that are "deceptive" from those those that are not. It is on that account, as the introductory examples have emphasized, that he finds the problem of interpreting or evaluating the work of art (of deciding what aesthetic properties it "really has") a difficult one.

The exact basis of this fivefold distinction, familiar though it is, could become the topic of a difficult and sophisticated analysis. It raises questions that fall within the problem of perception—of "appearance and reality"—which is only a little less perplexing to modern philosophers than it was to Socrates and Theaetetus. For our limited purposes, however, we may leave the earlier parts of the distinction unexamined, dealing only with the last one.

The reason is simply this: In aesthetics there is first of all the need for a middle degree of clarity—one that goes beyond common sense without yet aspiring to epistemology. For if epistemology must say the last word, it is not likely to say it tomorrow; and in the meanwhile, by accepting distinctions that in some sense must be recognized and by following out their implications, we can hope for a clarity which, if partial, is at least within our grasp.

Nor will the first four elements that we have recognized be suspected, on any familiar view of perception, of involving a distinction without a difference. If the physical work of art is repudiated as a Lockean substance, it is likely to be reinstated as a Berkeleyan sensible object. And if it is then identical with all its appearances, it is not identical with that particular set of its appearances in which we shall be principally interested. Thus our distinction continues to hold, as it does, *mutatis mutandis,* for other theories of perception. The controversy has not been about *whether* the distinction can be made, but about *precisely how* it can be made; and the latter question, important though it is, leads far beyond the middle degree of clarity that we must seek.

With regard to the last factor in our fivefold distinction, however—the aesthetic properties possessed by the work of art itself—we must proceed with greater care. For any misunderstanding there will be a misunderstanding of what is peculiar and central to interpretation and evaluation.

What can a critic reasonably be understood to mean, then, when he predicates this or that aesthetic term *of a work of art*—when he says (to take new examples) that it is "satirical" or that it "expresses nostalgia" or that "its perpendicular planes set up an internal tension" or that "in spite of its artistic imperfections, it achieves sublimity"? (Note that the first three terms emphasize interpretation and the last, evaluation.) We shall not be able to give separate attention to each of the many terms that are used in this way, but perhaps we can find the aspects of meaning that they have in common and that distinguish them from other terms.

III

Although factor (*e*) of our distinction is obviously different from the other factors taken separately, it may nevertheless be defined with reference to some combination of them: it may be defined, for instance, with reference to (*b*), (*c*), and (*d*). As we shall progressively see, that is a tenable assumption on which to proceed. A part of what we shall be assuming, then, is this: Whenever a term is predicated of a work of art, and assigns to it a property that is interpretive or evaluative, it will prove on analysis to refer to the *appearances* that the work of art presents to an *observer*. But it will not refer to all of these appearances; for, as has been indicated, the varying appearances simply *raise* questions of interpretation and evaluation, whereas a term predicated of a work of art is expected to *answer* them. So a further part of what we shall be assuming is this: The term will refer only to those appearances that arise under certain *conditions of observation,* and will itself implicitly specify what these conditions are. Thus a work of art must be capable of seeming as it is, but need not actually do so when the conditions of observation are *other* than those specified.

Should this assumption be made for all terms whatsoever and not just for those typical of aesthetics, it would imply that to be is to be perceiv*able* and would introduce epistemological issues that we must be content to avoid. When restricted to aesthetics, however, it cannot easily be questioned. A work of art that is beautiful but under no conditions can seem beautiful or that is unified, poignant, and true to life, but under no conditions can be seen, felt, or understood to have these characteristics, may be a fitting object of contemplation, if you will, for speculative minds; but for artists and critics it is devoid of interest.

How will our assumption work out on a concrete case? Since any interpretive or evaluative term will provide an example, let us arbitrarily select "cheerful," as it might be used in describing a musical theme. Now it will be obvious that our assumption is itself sufficient to suggest the *form* that the definition of this term must assume, namely, (*A*) "The theme is cheerful" has the same meaning as "The theme appears cheerful to those who listen to it under conditions *X*." And this in turn suggests where the next steps of analysis must lead.

Although "cheerful" is the term to be defined, it reappears in the definiens with a change of context. So we have the question: (1) What does "cheerful" mean as it occurs in the definiens? And there will obviously be this further question: (2) What terms, specifying the conditions of observation, must be put in place of the variable, "*X*"? Let us discuss these questions in turn.

The first question sounds paradoxical, giving the impression that any definition of the form (*A*) is destined to circularity. But the paradox is easily resolved. Like so many terms in our language, including all those that here concern us, "cheerful" changes its sense with certain changes in its context—an ambiguity that is not unfortunate, by the way, since its contribution to linguistic economy outweighs any perplexities that it may temporarily occasion. To see the nature of the ambiguity we need only examine (*A*) a little more closely.

In the definiendum the reference to an observer, the conditions of observation, and the appearances is only implicit; and the burden of the reference rests on "cheerful" itself. But in the definiens the reference is explicit; there "cheerful" does no more than assign a quality to certain appearances, the reference to the observer and to the conditions of observation being made by *other* words. So the definition implies (and in a way that many epistemological theories will sanction[1]) that there are at least two senses of "cheerful": there is a complicated sense which assigns a property to a theme (or painting, etc.), and there is a relatively simple sense which assigns a quality to *certain appearances* of the theme. The net effect of (A), then, is to show how the simple sense can be used in defining the complicated sense.

Let us use the term with the subscripts "c" and "s," depending on whether its complicated or its simple sense is in question. We can then rewrite (A) in the following way: (B) "The theme is cheerful$_c$" has the same meaning as "The theme appears cheerful$_s$ to those who listen to it under conditions X." Hence question (1) does not indicate that the definition of "cheerful$_c$" is circular, but simply goes on to ask about the meaning of "cheerful$_s$."

A study of (1) and parallel questions would be of great interest, for it would locate and perhaps minimize a troublesome vagueness in the language of criticism. But, having now seen its relation to the rest of our problem, we must be content to leave it without further discussion. We must pretend, in fact, that not only "cheerful$_s$" but also a great many other s-terms, including the controversial term, "beautiful$_s$," can safely be used without being clarified. This will be pardonable, so long as we *know* that we are pretending. And it will be practicable; for terms are characteristically interpretive or evaluative only when used in their complicated senses, and all that is common to their meanings can be seen by examining how they are related to their simple senses, no matter what the latter may subsequently prove to be.

Our attention must focus, then, on question (2). With regard to schema (A) or its reformulation (B), we must ask what terms, specifying the conditions of observation, can replace the variable, "X." Or rather, since the cheerfulness of a theme interests us only as an example, we must ask about "X" in the general schema: (C) "The work of art is Q_c" has the same meaning as "The work of art appears Q_s when

---

[1] See C. I. Lewis's distinction between properties and qualia, *Mind and the World Order* (1929), pp. 121 ff. Note that in *some* sense the distinction will reappear in epistemological theories that differ sharply from Lewis's. A materialist, for instance, can distinguish between properties of objects and qualities of their appearances, even though he takes the appearances as physiological reactions caused by the object in an observer's body. Once again, the question is not *whether* the distinction can be made, but *just how* it can be made, the latter lying beyond our present interests.

observed under conditions X," where "Q_c" is to be replaced, initially, by *any* of our interpretive or evaluative terms, and "Q_s" by the same term, used in its simple sense. It is this question that will be discussed in the following section and, more indirectly, in those that follow it. So for preliminary purposes I need only say this: The value assigned to "X" must contribute to a satisfactory analysis of the definiendum. And a satisfactory analysis (if I may speak with undue simplicity about a complicated topic) is one that is faithful to common usage without being bound by its confusions and without being insensitive to its flexibilities. In the present case we shall want to make the definiendum clearer than it normally is, but we shall not want to divert it from the purposes for which critics are accustomed to use it.

IV

Let us begin a definition which makes only a slight, almost imperceptible advance, but which is nevertheless of interest: (D) "The work of art is Q_c" has the same meaning as "The work of art appears Q_s when observed in the proper way." It is obvious that in some sense, and so far as it goes, this can be accepted. It is equally obvious that "proper" is not much better than the "X" that it replaces. It will be useful only if it can be defined, or at least partially clarified, in its turn.

And yet "proper" must not be dismissed as unworthy of our attention. Like its near synonyms, "appropriate," "fitting," and "correct," it has a normative sound, and hence seems to belong to the same family as "good." Now the meaning of "good" has long been a subject of controversy; so we must not assume that a clearer version of (D) will be easily obtained.

Even "good," however, has *certain* senses that are not at all perplexing. Good soil is fertile soil, good money is money backed by a solvent government, and so on. It is just possible, then, that we can define "proper" in an equally straightforward way, if not for all contexts then for the special context that (D) provides. Let us try this, experimentally.

If we bear in mind the phrase, "Time will tell," remembering that time tells nothing without the help of critics, we may be inclined to propose the following definition: (1) The "proper" way of observing a work of art is the way in which it will be observed, in the long run, by the majority of critics who have studied it. But to this there are many objections, of which I can here take time to mention only the one that is most important to the later parts of this paper.

If in ordinary conversation a man should say, "In the long run the majority of critics who have studied a work of art will always observe it properly," he would be taken as an aesthetic optimist, maintaining that criticism is *progressing.* An aesthetic pessimist would immediately disagree. And the disagreement, in any usual sense of words, would be one that involved many complexities. It could not be settled in the way that (1) would appear to settle it—merely by making the optimist's statement, in its essential respects, true by definition and the pessimist's self-contradictory. So if definition (1) is to be considered at all, it must be with the understanding that it is irrelevant to such an issue: it leaves out from the meaning of "proper" and suggestion of optimism, or any suggestion that what is proper is in some degree good or desirable or worth cultivating. Having accepted the definition, a man is free to say, if he wishes, that the proper way of observing a work of art is one that no sensitive person, no matter how justified he may be in cherishing the arts, ever ought to respect. And with that restriction the definition becomes pointless for the purpose of this paper.

We are interested in "proper" only for contexts provided by (*D*) at the beginning of this section, one of the logical consequences of (*D*), for example, being, "A work of art is beautiful$_c$ if and only if it appears beautiful$_s$ when observed in the proper way." But if the "proper" way may be one that no sensitive person ought to respect, etc., then neither this instance of (*D*) nor any other will be acceptable. Meanwhile there is obviously some other sense of "proper" that *will* make (*D*) acceptable; and that we have still to find.

Note that the element that (1) disregards is normative.[2] To return to our earlier parallel, (1) is comparable less to a definition equating good soil with fertile soil, where any normative force of "good" is gratuitous, than to a definition equating good laws with those that the

---

[2] This "normative" element has so far been indicated by the words "optimist," "progress," "worth cultivating," "ought," etc. Do they actually disclose an element which definition (1) of "proper" has omitted? My argument can appeal only to introspection on this point; and I think that no other argument, on such an issue, can avoid such an appeal. Indeed, it is less an "argument" than a way of directing attention: it supplies contexts which help the reader to become aware of his linguistic habits and to notice how the proposed definition would require him to change them.

legislators, judges, and juries will eventually establish. The latter is either a way of using words to forward (perhaps inadvertently, due to a confusion) a legal optimism[3] or else, when it deprives "good" of its normative force, a thoroughly misleading way of changing the meaning of a useful term.

Let us now turn to a further example. It is sometimes said, and often implied, that the intentions of the artist must be the critic's constant guide.[4] If we let our definition reflect this view we shall have: (2) The "proper" way of observing a work of art is the way that the artist intended. This is initially somewhat plausible, but is nevertheless open to serious objections. One of the objections, in fact, is similar to that just given for (1).

As ordinarily used, the statement, "The proper way of observing it is the way the artist intended," has the effect of suggesting that the artist's decision is authoritative—of a sort that *ought* to be taken, for aesthetic purposes, as beyond appeal. And that is a controversial suggestion. Certain critics might repudiate it, pointing out that not all artists are great artists and that some are impossibly vain and pretentious, intending us to observe their work in ways that are absurd. Now no matter what stand we ourselves may care to take on this issue, we must realize that the authoritative position of the artist, so long as it is to bring with it an obligation of other people to respect it, is nothing that can be established as a definition. So we may conclude, as before, that (2) is neutral on such an issue, allowing anyone to say, if he wishes, that the proper way of observing a work of art is one that no sensitive person ought to respect. And seeing this, we are no longer inclined to accept the definition as suitable to the context provided by (*D*).

Let me add that (2) is open to a further objection. Suppose that a painter, looking at a work that he has just completed, finds it strong and dignified; and suppose that later on he can discern neither of

---

[3] For a discussion of the semantic principles involved in such cases see my *Ethics and Language* (1944), ch. ix, or my paper "Persuasive Definitions," *Mind*, XLVII (1938), 331-350.

[4] A penetrating criticism of this view has been given by W. K. Wimsatt and M. C. Beardsley, "The Intentional Fallacy," *Sewanee Review*, LIV (1946), 468-488. They are discussing a different form of the view, however, from the one I am discussing. They ask: Must a critic compare what an artist actually expressed with what he intended to express, and judge his work accordingly? Whereas I am concerned only with what the artist's work actually expressed, and am asking, in effect, whether certain intentions of the artist are relevant even in determining that.

these qualities. He does not wholly trust his later reaction; but he also wonders whether he should trust his earlier one—his creative enthusiasm may have caused him to think he had succeeded in expressing what he had actually failed to express. He must now make a critical judgment of his own work, and there can be no doubt that the problem will often be as difficult for him as for others. What will happen, then, if he makes use of (D) supplemented by (2) and draws the conclusion: "My painting is strong$_c$ and dignified$_c$ if and only if it appears strong$_s$ and dignified$_s$ when observed in the way I intend"? He will only be perplexed, and simply because he *has* no fixed intentions. He may, to be sure, acquire them later on; but it is also true that he may not. Each year he may see his painting with new eyes, never quite certain that his present way of observing it is to be his ultimate one.

This second objection is, however, less important than the first. For we are not so much interested in examining this or that particular definition as in examining definitions of a certain *kind:* and the first objection to (2), which parallels, as we have seen, the objection to (1), holds equally well for many other definitions—for all those, in fact, that make "proper" a scientific or naturalistic term. So let me return to this objection, showing why it becomes relevant.

When used in contexts like (D), "proper" has a normative function which any naturalistic definition fails to make evident. In considering the definition, however, our familiarity with the term leads us to supply this element: we understand the definiendum in some other sense than the definiens provides. And then, in order to make the best of the definition, we take it less as a definition than as a judgment—one that weds the normative force of "proper" to the conditions mentioned in the definiens and thus favorably evaluates them. That is why (1) appeals only to optimists about the future of criticism, and (2) only to those who trust in the self-criticism of artists. But note that the definition, if we continue to call it that, now requires us to consider whether or not the naturalistic conditions, specified by the definiens, *deserve* the favorable evaluation that "proper" gives them. And like any normative question about the arts, this belongs not to analysis but to criticism. A well-founded answer to it cannot be obtained merely from a study of language. Since we want the definition to clarify criticism, not to legislate to its conclusions, we immediately proceed, as soon as we see this, to understand the definition in a strict way, taking it as ascribing to "proper" neither more nor less meaning than the word is to have. That is to say, we inhibit our tendency to supply the word, independently of the definition, with its usual normative force. And we then see that the analysis proposed by any such definition is not acceptable. What we must do, then, is to emphasize the normative force of the term. We must not tacitly use its normative force without analyzing it, nor must we leave it out. Rather, we must make clear what it is. And from the above discussion we may conclude—though not without the caution that this tangled issue demands—that we shall not be successful so long as we insist that "proper" be equated with purely scientific terms.

V

Although the above remarks have been negative, they have important implications. If they are correct—if "proper" is an other-than-scientific term and if (D), which defines the Q_c terms with reference to "proper," is in accordance with established usage—then this much is evident: All those questions of art criticism that are concerned with interpretation and evaluation, their nature being established by their key terms, will be (in part, at least) other-than-scientific questions. The critics who attempt to answer them will not be pure scientists; and the answers that they give, in the very nature of the case, will be of a sort that the methods of science cannot wholly establish.

This will be evident if we contrast the Q_c terms, which introduced "proper," with such a term as "red$_c$." Although the latter has an incidental use in criticism, I should classify it as neither interpretive nor evaluative, since it leads to a different sort of issue than any that "unified$_c$," "poignant$_c$," "beautiful$_c$," and so on, are likely to occasion. We may presumably accept, for "red$_c$," a schema like (C), page 325: "This is red$_c$" has the same meaning as "This appears red$_s$ when observed under conditions X." But here there is little doubt that "X" can be replaced by *scientific* terms—those referring to lighting conditions similar to daylight, to average eyesight, and so on. The vagueness of the term will allow us a certain freedom in replacing "X," to be sure; but the vagueness is like that of many other common terms and in this case causes no serious perplexity. So "This is red$_c$" is directly open to empirical tests, both with regard to (a) whether the specified conditions of observing obtain, and (b) whether, under these conditions, the object appears red$_8$. For any interpretive or evaluative judgment, however, we have a different situation. The conditions of observation are there specified by "proper," which resists a purely scientific definition; the test corresponding to (a) above will accordingly not be empirical in any ordinary way; and the judgment, to that extent, will be other than scientific.

This conclusion should not be surprising. A critic is not altogether unlike a creative artist; for if he does not re-create a work of art in a literal sense, as does an actor or a virtuoso, he does so in a figurative sense: he re-creates it in his own experience, constantly selecting, from the various ways in which it can be seen, heard, felt, or understood, those that are to be actualized and perpetuated. Now scientific knowledge is not "the" concern (even though it is often "a" concern) of a creative artist; so may we not fairly suspect that it is not "the" concern of a critic? Although not decisive, this analogy suggests that our conclusion is free from paradox.

We must make sure, however, that we do not leave a scientific conception of criticism too hastily. And we must make doubly sure that the other-than-scientific aspects of criticism, if we are indeed to recognize them, are free from chaotic implications. Should they make reflective criticism impossible—should they require us to say, for instance, that interpretation and evaluation depend on caprice or depend on some "insight" that defies intersubjective testing and hence is the practical equivalent of caprice—then for that very reason we should have to consider the possibility of rejecting them. We should have to question the previous steps in our analysis, seeking with greater care for definitions that were free of these implications. For an analysis that, to such an extent, undermined our everyday convictions would in all probability do so at its own peril and not at the peril of reflective criticism.

So our conclusion—that the key terms of art criticism introduce a problem which is partly other-than-scientific—can so far be accepted only in a provisional, tentative way.

VI

Since our discussion is becoming an extended one, it may be well to pause for a moment, summarizing what has preceded, and anticipating what is to follow. Our main problem, as stated in section 1, is to examine certain terms whose function is interpretive ("allegorical," "unified," etc.) or evaluative ("beautiful") and to clarify certain aspects of their meaning. We saw, in section 2, that we can hope only for a "middle degree" of clarity, which stops short of epistemology. But our epistemological neutrality still permits us, as we saw in section 3, to hold that any interpretive or evaluative term, although predicated of a physical work of art, refers indirectly to the *appearances* of the work. We thus have the following definitional schema: (C) "The work of art is Q_c" has the same meaning as "The work of art appears Q_s when observed under conditions X." Here the interpretive or evaluative term to be defined must be put in the place of "Q_c." The Q_s term will depend on the Q_c term and will normally be the same adjective used in a simpler sense. To complete the definition of any given Q_c term, accordingly, two steps are required: it is necessary (1) to clarify the corresponding Q_s term and (2) to replace the variable, "X," in a suitable manner, by a constant term. We decided (page 325) that step (1) lies beyond the limited scope of this paper. Hence our problem centers on step (2).

Now it is evident, as we saw in section 4, that "conditions X" can give place to "conditions that are proper." But that only raises a question about the meaning of "proper." We considered the possibility of defining "proper" with reference to the conditions that will be maintained, in the long run, by the majority of critics; and we also considered the possibility of defining it with reference to the artist's intentions. In both cases we found the definitions inadequate; and by generalizing from the objections to which they are open, we saw that "proper" cannot be equated, for our special context, with *any* set of purely scientific terms.

This led us to infer, in section 5, that the problems of interpretation and evaluation are, at least in part, other-than-scientific problems—a conclusion which, if true, is of much importance in forming our conception of a critic's methods. But *is* it true? Although our analysis seems to have established it, and in a way that initially seems free from paradox, we have just seen that we must not accept it without caution. For if it should prove to undermine the possibility of reflective criticism, then, rather than rest content with this implication, we should do better to reconsider the analysis that led to it. Up to the present point, accordingly, our discussion has prepared the way for a conclusion which cannot yet be drawn with full confidence.

What must be our subsequent steps? Clearly, we have no alternative but to broaden our inquiry: we must temporarily leave the definition of terms and examine the living contexts in which the terms are employed. We must, in other words, look directly to the nature of interpretive and evaluative *problems*. For only if these problems prove to include, without elements of chaos, the other-than-scientific aspect that we have envisaged, shall we be free to return to our definitions and to develop them in a positive way.

So section 7 will consider some of the critic's central questions; and it will emphasize the questions that obviously *are* scientific. This will prevent us from leaving a scientific conception of criticism too hastily. Sections 8 and 9 will then point out and describe the other-than-scientific aspect of criticism and estimate its importance.

Since these sections will be sufficient, in my opinion, to show that the other-than-scientific aspect of criticism does not prevent criticism from being reflective or "guided by knowledge," we shall then, in sections 10 and 11, return to the term "proper," establishing its meaning for the context that interests us and showing how our analysis of it bears out our study of the critic's problem. This will have immediate implications, of course, on the meaning of our interpretive and evaluative terms, whose analysis will be developed and tested in section 12.

The paper will conclude, in sections 13 and 14, with several observations (some of them foreshadowed in earlier sections) about the way in which matters of taste are open to reasoning and argument.

VII

What are the essential parts of a critic's problem, then, when he is interpreting or evaluating some given work of art? In the initial stages of his inquiry and perhaps, though in lesser degree, throughout all its stages, a critic is attempting to become familiar with the *possibilities* that lie before him. He is sampling, as it were, the apparent qualities of a work of art, seeking to determine the various ways in which it *can* be experienced. For if he ignores some of the possible Q_s's he will later ignore the corresponding Q_c's; hence certain interpretations or evaluations, of a sort that he might wish to accept, will not even occur to him. So he observes the work under varying conditions, attending to this rather than that, weakening these associations and strengthening those, and so on. In doing this he is not, *ipso facto*, deciding which of the conditions of observations are "proper." He is doing something preliminary to that and separable from it, if in no other way, at least by abstraction.

To this extent the critic's problem is obviously a scientific one: it is a problem of psychophysics. As dealt with by a professional psychologist, to be sure, it would lead to matters of great complexity. The last word of scientific explanation, if it were obtainable, would involve a tabulation of *all* the apparent qualities that a work of art can present, each of them specifically correlated with the conditions of observation under which it occurs. And it would involve knowledge not only of the remote conditions that determine aesthetic experience, but also of the immediate ones, including the physical and chemical states of the observer's nervous system. These are matters that lie well beyond the critic's interests or needs. But it does not follow that the critic is engaged in something foreign to psychology. He is engaged in the relatively simple, though still difficult, parts of it. In the same way a fisherman, learning about the weather from his own varied experience, is not doing something foreign to meteorology.

Having roughly familiarized himself with the ways in which a work of art *can* be experienced, a critic must proceed to make a selection from among them—a *decision* about how he is to observe the work in the course of his subsequent appreciation. There is no doubt that interpretation and evaluation require such a decision, in some sense of the word, and that it is a process of the utmost complexity. It involves a channeling, so to speak, of the critic's aesthetic sensibilities. The states of mind that he "brings to" the work he is appreciating—these in turn being among the factors that determine how he reacts to it—progressively become less subject to variation, certain of them becoming his own and others alien to him.

Although I use the word "decision" to refer to this process, let me say that I do so for want of a better one. For "decision" is likely to emphasize only those factors which immediately respond to volition and are relatively open to introspection, as when a man "decides" to walk to his office rather than to drive there. Now these factors by no means predominate when a critic "decides" to observe a work of art in this way rather than that. In certain cases, to be sure, they are not absent. Thus a critic of music can usually attend "at will" to the inner voices in a contrapuntal composition; and in listening to program music, he can deliberately control, within certain limits, the extent to which he permits himself to become preoccupied with the program rather than with the sounds. But in many cases—particularly in those where the channeling of the critic's sensibilities involves his receptiveness to certain emotions—the changes cannot be made "at will." They are subject to control only by indirect steps, in which voluntary effort is directed not to them but to certain factors which, cumulatively, may bring them about in the course of time. When I speak of the critic's characteristic *decision,* then, with reference to cases of the latter sort no less than the former, I must ask the reader to remember that I am using the term in a half-technical, forcibly extended sense.

The critic's decision is related to his problem in a very important way, as will be evident from this observation: Suppose that of the several possible conditions, C_1, C_2, C_3, under which a work of art can be observed, a critic decides to accept C_1; and suppose that under conditions C_1 the work of art appears Q_{s1}. In that case the critic will be inclined, so long as his decision does not alter, to say that the work of art has (or "really has") the property Q_{c1}. This last remark *presents* in verbal form his interpretation or evaluation. So between the critic's decision and his interpretation or evaluation there is a direct, intimate relation. (I shall return to this point in subsequent sections.)

So far we have seen that the critic must (*a*) learn about the *possible* C's and the Q_s's correlated with them; and we have seen that he must (*b*) make a *decision* between the C's. Now (*b*) immediately suggests a further part of the critic's problem. He will not wish (normally, that is) to make his central decision in ignorance. Hence he must (*c*) bring to mind or acquire knowledge that will serve to *guide* his decision. Let me explain by example.

In one of his elegies, John Donne writes,

> . . . my love is slaine, I saw him goe
> O'r the white Alpes alone . . .[5]

Do these lines represent the lover's death as serene and noble or as horrible? We may be temporarily uncertain, since the reference to the "white Alps" suggests the former interpretation, whereas the accompanying context (which I do not quote) suggests the latter. So we must make a decision; and we can here make use of knowledge, as mentioned above in (*c*), in order to *guide* our decision. An instance of rele-

---

5 "Elegie XVI," Nonesuch Press ed. of Donne's works, edited by John Hayward (1929), p. 90.

vant knowledge is easily given: The Alps, which to us are a relatively accessible region and a symbol of natural beauty, were in the seventeenth century virtually unexplored and a symbol of a forbidding barrier between one people and another. This knowledge, when called to mind, is likely to lead us to avoid an anachronistic reading of the poem and hence guide our decision in a way that favors the second of the two interpretations mentioned.

In just what sense can knowledge "guide" a decision? We must not suppose that a logical relation is involved. For a decision is a *process*, in which certain ways of responding to a work of art are accepted and others rejected. It is not, then, the assertion of a proposition (this being true for *any* usual sense of "proposition"). And only if it involved a proposition could it meaningfully be said to stand in a logical relation to knowledge.

Rather, the guiding relation is a *causal* one. The situation, when viewed with deference to the principle of parsimony, is simply this: Like any psychological process, the critic's decision has a great many causes; and among these causes we must include the critic's beliefs, which will not, of course, remain compartmentalized in a purely cognitive "portion" of his mind, but will influence him both conatively and affectively. Similarly, we must include among these causes the critic's knowledge; for his beliefs, when strongly confirmed, are the same as his knowledge. Now when his knowledge acts as a psychological *cause* of his decision—when it is *one* of the factors, that is to say, that determines him to make this decision rather than that—then it may also be said to "guide" his decision.

In many problems of interpretation or evaluation, it will be evident that the critic's characteristic decision can be guided by knowledge, and by knowledge of various sorts. In the above case, and in others roughly parallel to it, his decision can be guided by a knowledge of cultural history or of philology. In other cases it can be guided by a knowledge of psychology. Thus a critic may find that certain associations, though they intensify the mood of a work of art, do so in a way that is ephemeral; so he may decide to counteract these associations, preferring a mood that is less intense but more enduring. Note that the ephemeral or enduring character of a mood is one which psychology, often in its nontechnical aspects, can establish. Let me add that the critic may be guided, in part, by an inquiry into the artist's intentions (no matter whether these are fixed or variable) or by an inquiry into what the majority of critics are likely to say in the long run; for, although we have rejected these factors as unsuitable for a definition of "proper," we have not banished them from criticism altogether. Knowledge about them can serve, that is to say, as a part cause of the critic's decision. But since my general point will be clear, I need not multiply examples.

Now here the critic's problem has again its scientific aspects. The beliefs that guide his decision will be open to empirical tests and hence to scientific methods. Nor is it possible to overemphasize the extent to which science, in this special way, becomes relevant. In the part of the critic's problem that was first mentioned, where he is surveying the various alternatives (the various C's with their correlated Q_s's) between which he must decide, we have seen that his problem is essentially one of psychophysics. But in the part of his problem that was last mentioned, where he is seeking knowledge that will guide him in deciding upon this alternative rather than that, he can confine himself to no one science. Potentially, all sciences have a bearing on his problem.

VIII

Among these many scientific aspects of criticism, then, where are we to find something that is more than scientific? There are two sharply different ways in which we might hope to answer this question. We might hold either that criticism involves some more-than-scientific *knowledge* or that it involves some more-than-scientific *aim*. And the second of these possibilities, in my opinion, is far more promising than the first.

For if we should develop the first, we should find, sooner or later, that our recognition of more-than-scientific knowledge requires us to postulate some special entity—some unique object or quality, or some unique, synthetic, *a priori* relation—which this knowledge is about. And such a view, even if it could be stated in an intelligible way, would run the risk of multiplying entities beyond necessity. It would be tenable only as a last resort.

If we develop the second possibility, however, we shall be able to avoid this objection. For the critic's more-than-scientific aim need not be one that a scientist cannot describe. It may simply be one that a scientist, in his professional capacity, does not *share*. It may be a non-cognitive aim, not in the sense that it is unknowable, and not in the sense that it is unguided by knowledge, but only in the sense that it is not directed *to* the acquirement of knowledge. Thus it need not involve any unique subject matter. The principle of parsimony can be retained without compromise.

So let us consider only this second possibility, working it out in detail. And our first and central observation in doing so is an obvious one; in fact it is so very obvious that we have made it, almost inadvertently, in the preceding section. We were there trying to emphasize the aspects of the critic's problem that are scientific; but these lay so near to the nonscientific aspect that we could not help but notice the latter as well.

More specifically, we noted the presence of what I called the critic's "decision"—the channeling of his sensibilities in which he comes to accept certain ways of observing a work of art, when appreciating it, and to reject others. And this very decision introduces an aim that is not a pure scientist's aim. For the critic's task is not limited, in scientific fashion, to one of accepting or rejecting, as true or false, certain *descriptions of* the conditions under which works of art are observed; it is concerned with accepting or rejecting these very conditions. His decision culminates not in a new scientific *belief about* aesthetic sensibility, but in a new aesthetic sensibility. It culminates not in an "I shall" but in an "I will," not in a prediction but in a resolution. A scientist may wish to *study* the critic's decision and all the factors that make it possible or determine its outcome; but he is not called upon, in his professional capacity, to *make* it. His study is one thing and the decision that he studies is another, to say otherwise being a particularly transparent instance of the "psychologist's fallacy."[6]

We have, then, in the critic's efforts to make his characteristic decision, an aim which is "noncognitive" in the sense previously indicated: it is neither unknowable nor unguided by knowledge, but it is directed *to* something other than knowledge. And in contrasting it with a scientist's aim, let me add, we need not fear that we are misdescribing the work of a scientist, implying that he is a purely cogni-

---

[6] See William James, *Principles of Psychology* (1890), vol. I, ch. vii, last section. One is said to commit the "psychologist's fallacy" when, in describing a given state of mind, he erroneously ascribes to *it* the characteristics that attend his own state of mind as he studies it—when he confusedly assumes, as it were, that the proper study of mankind is man studying man.

tive being. The scientist too must make certain "decisions" in the very course of his studies; he must decide, for instance, what topics are *worth studying*.[7] But note that *his* decision bears directly on his knowledge: it requires him to accept or reject certain topics of cognitive inquiry and not, like the characteristic decision of a critic, to accept or reject certain ways of responding to a work of art.

So there is little that is controversial, so long as we hold that a special kind of decision is *one* factor that distinguishes criticism from science. The essential question, then, is whether or not this point of difference is the one that we have been seeking. Does it really color the critic's problem in an important way; and will it help us, once it is noticed, to find acceptable definitions of "proper" and of our interpretive and evaluative terms?

These questions will be answered presently and in the affirmative. We must begin by examining the critic's decision more closely, with attention to the scientific issues that surround it.

IX

Although we have just seen that the critic's decision is noncognitive, we have previously seen that it can be guided by knowledge. And it will be evident that for reflective critics, in whose work we are likely to be most interested, the decision will be guided in an elaborate way. It may be asked, then, why it is necessary to emphasize the decision at all. Could we not take it for granted and attend only to the knowledge that guides it?

Let me put the question more concretely. Suppose that a man, having for some years been a critic, now wishes to change his vocation and to devote his attention to purely scientific questions about the arts. He will no longer deliberately attempt, then, to make any aesthetic

---

[7] A judgment about what is *worth* studying, though one that a scientist makes, is not, as I see it, a scientific judgment. I should classify it as an evaluative judgment about science. Or should anyone wish to classify it as "scientific" in some broader sense of that term, then at least I should want to point out that it is not directly testable by inductive methods, but requires indirect and less definitive methods of the sort I have discussed in my *Ethics and Language*. So the similarity between a scientist's decision and a critic's (which is generic only) does not, in my opinion, show that a direct use of induction pervades science and criticism alike. It shows, rather, that an *in*direct use of induction, of a sort that will presently be recognized here for criticism, also attends certain problems of evaluation that are particularly interesting to scientists.

decision; but he will still be acquiring scientific knowledge that can guide a decision. Will there be any real change? Will not his decision, even though he is not concerned about it, attend his scientific inquiries as a kind of epiphenomenon?

A part of the answer is simply this: Since neither a critic nor a pure scientist can hope for complete knowledge, even about some individual work of art, each must emphasize certain beliefs and neglect others. Now a critic emphasizes those that bear upon his special aim—that of deciding how to observe a work of art aesthetically. Beliefs that he thinks will influence his decision are accepted as relevant and tested, the others being ignored as irrelevant. Although his decision is not immediately directed *to* knowledge, it has this *effect* on the sort of knowledge he seeks. A pure scientist, however, emphasizes beliefs for a less specific purpose: he is neither exclusively nor primarily concerned with selecting and testing just those beliefs that will alter his own aesthetic sensibilities or the sensibilities of others. So although the critic and the pure scientist may be alike in having beliefs that are empirically testable, they will differ in their manner of organizing them. And only when they are organized in the critic's fashion will they be likely to have a marked effect on aesthetic sensibilities. Even if an answer to all scientific questions were found and made available in a vast encyclopedia, a critic would still have the task of gathering together the limited part of this knowledge that is relevant to his interpretive and evaluative decisions and of bearing it in mind while deciding.

Thus the critic's decision is not epiphenomenal to his inquiries into pure science. It has its own effects, determining the extent and direction of his studies. We may conclude, then, that between the critic's aim and the scientist's there is not only a difference, but an important difference.

It remains the case, of course, that whenever criticism is reflective it is still closely related to science. Indeed, one might speak of it as an applied science. For in any applied science—in surgery, in bridgebuilding, or even in billiards—the same need arises for a special organization of knowledge, used for the purpose of influencing a *decision*. And if the term "decision," in such cases, has not the technical sense that has here been assigned to it, it nevertheless retains a sense that suggests interesting parallels.

But if we refer to criticism as an applied science—and I am not recommending that way of speaking, but only indicating that I have no strong objection to it—we must be careful to prevent the term "applied" from being deceptive. Now it will be deceptive, and strongly so, if it leads us to forget that we can say of most applied science precisely what is here being said of criticism: it is *more* than science. And it is more than science for the same reason. It requires a decision about what is to be done—and about what is to be done not merely for the purpose of acquiring further scientific knowledge, but for purposes that extend beyond the pursuit of knowledge. It requires a decision to make this surgical operation rather than that, or to build this kind of bridge rather than that, and so on. So, as before, the decision is guided by knowledge without being directed to knowledge; it is more than cognitive and hence more than scientific. But let us continue.

We must emphasize the critic's decision partly for the reason just given: it directs his inquiries, giving his knowledge a special scope and organization. And we must emphasize it for this further reason: it helps us to see that his knowledge, however carefully selected and organized it may be, does not guide him with the impersonal demands of logic. Between his beliefs and his decisions (as we have previously seen) there is not a logical but only a causal, psychological relation. Hence his beliefs guide him in a way that permits his decision to be colored by his own individuality.

Given certain beliefs about a painting, for instance, a critic may in fact decide to accentuate its colors and lines, letting its subject matter, with its various associations, occupy only the periphery of his attention. But if he had been of another temperament he might, with the same beliefs, have made the opposite decision. And the latter would have been neither more nor less "logical," neither more nor less "scientific," than the former. He is taking a step *from* knowledge *to* a way of observing—a step to which these terms, in any literal sense, simply do not apply.

We shall see this more clearly if we view the issue not as a personal but as an interpersonal one, as an issue that arises when two or more critics, interpreting or evaluating the same work of art, are attempting to come to a *mutual* decision about how to observe it. In the course of their discussion the critics will tend to extend and correct their beliefs, and in the light of their new beliefs some or all of them may be guided to new decisions. It is for that reason, in good measure, that they find discussion so profitable. But let us ask this question: Suppose that they should come to agreement about *all* beliefs that can in any way affect their decision, omitting no evidence and making no mistakes in logic. Will they, *ipso facto*, make the same decision? Clearly, their beliefs will not be the only factors that guide them, for their training and native sensibility will also be relevant. So they will make the same decision only if these other factors, too, are the same. And that is not at all likely. We must take account of individual differences; and in such a complicated matter as this we cannot suppose that nature has been miserly in distributing them.

No matter how scientific criticism may become, then, and no matter how inexorably its scientific aspects are subject to the canons of inductive and deductive logic, it will bring with it no conclusions that impose a uniformity on the way in which a work of art must be observed. It may—indeed, it *does*—rule out certain of these ways, since no one, in the light of knowledge, is content to decide in their favor. But it will not rule out all ways but one. For knowledge influences each critic's decision through the mediation of factors that are peculiarly his own; it guides him but does not constrain him.

x

We have been led to these observations, it will be remembered, by questions about the meaning of certain terms, such as "allegorical," "unified," and "beautiful." Taking these instances of Q_c, we saw that they could presumably be defined by the schema: (D) "This work of art is Q_c" has the same meaning as "This work of art appears Q_s when observed in the proper way." But with regard to the meaning of "proper" in this context we were as yet able to draw only a negative conclusion: that it does not lend itself to a purely naturalistic definition. That suggested, in turn, that criticism involves an element that is other than scientific. We were unwilling to accept this conclusion, however, unless we could locate the other-than-scientific element as it arose in the critic's problem and could show that it does not undermine the possibility of a reflective criticism, in close touch with the sciences. So having first examined the aspects of criticism that clearly are scientific, we concluded that the other-than-scientific element lies not in some knowledge or subject matter that is peculiar to criticism, but simply in the critic's special aim and, more specifically, in his characteristic decision. And we have since considered this decision more closely to see why it requires emphasis.

Our inquiry has not led us, I think it will be agreed, to ignore or underestimate the reflective elements in criticism. Although the critic's decision is not uniquely determined by his knowledge—although he is free to express his own temperament—the fact that he can be guided by knowledge is sufficient to show that his decision need not be capricious. And with this suspicion allayed, we are now in a position to return to the word "proper," in the hope of indicating the other-than-scientific aspect of its meaning in some more positive way.

We must obviously establish a relation between "proper" and the critic's decision. And yet we cannot assign the term a sense that merely *describes* the decision. For in that case it would remain a scientific term (the principle of parsimony excluding, save as a last resort, any subject matter that "transcends" science) and would be open to the objections that we encountered in our earlier efforts to define "proper" (see section 4).

Shall we say, then, that "proper" introduces the beliefs that *guide* the decision? That, too, would make it a scientific term. And it would raise still other difficulties: The beliefs that guide a decision are enormously varied; they are not the same for one work of art as they are for another; and those that one critic considers relevant, for any given work of art, may be considered irrelevant by another critic. So any definition, if it dealt with these matters, would have to recognize a complexity and ambiguity in the meaning of "proper" which—though it might conceivably exist—is scarcely to be accepted, so long as some simpler analysis can be given.[8]

There remains an alternative that we have yet to explore, and one that promises to lead to constructive results. It is possible that "proper"

---

[8] I do not wish, however, positively to exclude this type of definition from aesthetics. When "proper" is allowed to refer to the factors that guide a decision, much the same considerations arise that I have discussed in my *Ethics and Language*, ch. ix and ch. x, where I deal with "the second pattern of analysis." For those familiar with those chapters let me simply say that second-pattern definitions are persuasive, and although persuasive definitions have often an important use, they are not of the sort that can be defended within analysis itself, but lead directly to questions that are normative. When merely analyzing, one can do no more than give "samples" of the many persuasive definitions that are linguistically possible. But for the "first pattern of analysis," which in effect I am about to follow here for "proper," a normatively neutral characterization of meaning, yielding a sense that *could* be used in all typical contexts, becomes possible.

functions less as a *descriptive* term, giving information that bears on the decision, than as an *imperative* or *quasi-imperative* term, directly evincing such a decision or influencing it. This alternative has immediately two points in its favor. In the first place, it is in accord with our observation that "proper" bears upon the critic's decision in some other-than-scientific way. For an imperative, used to influence a decision (in our special sense of the term), is not an expression that is needed in a purely scientific study of the arts. In the second place, it helps us to locate the *normative* element which we found lacking (section 4) in the definitions we have discarded. For a norm exerts an influence, usually of a sort that extends beyond cognition. And exactly the same may be said of an imperative.

Let us begin the analysis, then, in some such fashion as this: (3) The "proper" way of observing a work of art is the way that *is to be* cultivated and maintained. . . . Although this is *only* a beginning—an additional clause being needed to give "proper" a specifically aesthetic meaning—it is at least serviceable in emphasizing the term's imperative force. The latter is preserved by the phrase "is to be," whose meaning will be evident from this example: When *A*, speaking to *B*, says that the task on which they are working "is to be" completed before they attempt anything else, he is not making a prediction about the task, nor is he merely giving an introspective description of his feelings about it. Rather, he is taking steps to *get* the task completed. In the first place, he is building up his own resolve, strengthening his decision. So, as it were, he is addressing an imperative to himself. In the second place, he is influencing *B*'s decision by addressing an imperative to him.

Before continuing let me remark that "is to be" is somewhat harsh and when addressed to another person tends to exert a unilateral influence, whereas "proper" is less harsh, proposing rather than commanding, and often permitting or positively inviting a counterproposal. If I were to remedy this inaccuracy, however, I should have to enter into an elaborate discussion of the *emotive meaning* of "proper" showing that its subleties must be "characterized" rather than defined;[9] and that I cannot develop, even schematically, in the present paper. Nor is it wholly necessary. If the reader will bear in mind that (3) is rough and approximate, he will see, I trust, that it helps to disclose the cognizable but noncognitive element that we have been seeking.

---

[9] See *Ethics and Language*, ch. iii and ch. iv, particularly p. 82.

We must now "test" (3) to make sure that it is correct. That is to say, we must observe how "proper" occurs in familiar contexts and determine whether or not our analysis of its meaning is faithful to common usage.

Suppose that a critic is temporarily *unable* to decide on a way of observing a work of art: he is in a state of conflict, half inclined to accept C_1, which is correlated with Q_{s1}, and half-inclined to accept C_2, which is correlated with Q_{s2}. Under these conditions he will say, in any usual sense of the word, that he cannot make up his mind which way of observing it is "proper." Now is that what we would expect him to say, if we take "proper" as having the quasi-imperative meaning of "is to be cultivated and maintained"? There can be no doubt that it is; hence (3), so far, is "confirmed." In fact our analysis helps us to supply an explanation: The critic withholds the term "proper" because, when about to use its quasi-imperative force to strengthen his decision in one way, he finds that a counterimpulse leads him in another way. He is uncertain not about how to *describe* his conflict, but about the direction in which to *resolve* it. He cannot make up his mind, then, about which sort of "is to be" expression he will address to himself. And for much the same reason he withholds "proper" when speaking to others. Should he assure them that C_1 (with its correlated Q_{s1}) is proper, for instance, he would be *recommending* C_1 to them; and he does not wish to advise others about a decision that he cannot as yet make for himself.[10]

Let us now test definition (3) in a further way. We have seen that it takes account of the element in criticism that is other than scientific; but will it take account of the element that is scientific?

Suppose that our critic has tentatively resolved his conflict: he has decided upon C_1 with its correlated Q_{s1} and has accordingly judged this way of observing the work of art to be "proper." Now he will

---

10 Let me reiterate the following point, even though I may seem to belabor it: The distinguishing feature of "proper" lies not in its exerting an influence, but in exerting an influence that is not immediately *directed to* cognition. *All* words have *some* influence, both on those who use them and on those who hear them. The essentially cognitive term, "true," for instance, influences beliefs. In fact it may be withheld when the speaker has *conflicting* inclinations to believe; for he then wishes to avoid expressing his own beliefs prematurely, and to avoid exerting a premature influence on the beliefs of others. But it is one thing to influence beliefs and another thing to influence the characteristic decision that attends aesthetic interpretation and evaluation; and "proper" remains distinct from any scientific term in that it has the latter function in a direct, quasi-imperative way.

probably not feel secure about this judgment unless he has *reasons* to support it; and can we account for these *reasons* if we take "proper" to be quasi-imperative? There is no difficulty about this, since any sort of imperative can be supported by reasons. When we say, for instance, "Let's schedule the meeting for Wednesday," we may give as a reason for our imperative, "Since there are no other meetings then, we shall have a larger attendance." Here the imperative exerts a direct influence, and the reason supports it by exerting a supplementary but indirect influence—one that is mediated by cognition. That is to say, a belief of the reason is likely to *cause* one to be more willing to do what the imperative recommends.

We can find a simple example of a reason in aesthetics if we return to our quotation from Donne, as given on page 335. We there saw that a critic might decide to read the lines as expressing horror, being guided by the knowledge that any other way of reading it would involve a cultural anachronism. And we can now say much the same thing by using the terms "proper" and "reason." Thus the critic may judge, "One reads the lines *properly* (i.e., in the way they *are to be* read) only when he reacts to them with horror." And he may give as a *reason* for his judgment, "Any other way of reading it would involve a cultural anachronism."

The example clearly shows that our *reasons* introduce nothing new into our study; they simply point once more to the beliefs that *guide* the critic's decision. Hence they immediately restore the scientific aspects of criticism that our quasi-imperative conception of "proper" may at first seem to exclude. And they bear out our previous conclusions: In the first place, the reasons will take on a special organization, which is precisely the organization we have mentioned in section 9 when distinguishing criticism from pure science. In the second place, the reasons will not serve to eliminate the critic's personal sensibilities; for their relation to the quasi-imperative judgment they support (which is the same, in essentials, as the relation between knowledge and the decision that knowledge guides) is causal rather than logical; hence they "guide without constraining."

It will be obvious that the imperative force of "proper" has far less effect, in influencing a decision, than the reasons that accompany it. That does not imply, however, that definition (3) is injudicious in its emphasis, attending to the element that is unimportant and ignoring the elements that are important. For in itself "proper" actually *has* a modest function. If we should encounter a critic who did no more than reiterate that so-and-so is proper, we should feel that we were being advised dogmatically—advised without being illuminated. We should ask him for his reasons, expecting the illumination to come from *them*.

And yet "proper" has a borrowed importance, for it introduces a situation to which the reasons become relevant. Only by recognizing its imperative force, in fact, can we understand why the reasons that accompany it are so varied in content. Only by taking it as noncognitive can we become fully sensitive to the cognitive elements that surround it. The reasons that support an ordinary descriptive statement of physics, for instance, are usually limited to the subject matter of that specialized scientific field and hence are not (relatively speaking) varied in content; whereas the reasons that support an imperative sentence, that potentially involve literally *any* kind of knowledge that may indirectly cause a person to do what the imperative recommends, can be highly varied in content and will fall within no one specialized scientific field.

There are two other tests of definition (3) that deserve attention. The first concerns the "survey of possibilities," which attends the critic's decision and which, at the beginning of section 7, we classified as psychophysics. Will this survey be relevant, if the critic is determining what decision is "proper," in our quasi-imperative sense? The answer is obviously yes; for in using any imperative—in strengthening or influencing *any* decision—one will wish to know about the alternatives that are open. To resolve upon the impossible, or to advise it, is futile; and to resolve on one alternative in ignorance of another, or to advise it, is to run the risk of subsequent regret.

Our final test introduces a somewhat different point. When a critic says, "Observed under conditions that are proper, this work of art seems Q_s," he will normally be unable to enumerate, in scientific terms, just what the conditions of observation are. He will have no doubt that there are such conditions and that they could be enumerated; but the actual enumeration, he will feel, will take him well beyond anything that he has already indicated by the term "proper" itself. He will occasionally have no other explicit knowledge of the conditions of observation than that given by the description, "the conditions that are correlated with Q_s." Now this observation, which holds true when "proper" is used in its ordinary, unself-conscious way, also holds true when the term is used as we have defined it. Its quasi-imperative reference to the conditions of observation does not enumerate them; it leaves that to be done, when necessary, by *other* terms.[11] Let me add that if a critic *does* go on to enumerate the conditions of observation—when he says that C_1, C_2, and C_3 are proper—he is not explaining what he means, as a preliminary to making a judgment. (That is the point on which definitions [1] and [2], which we rejected in section 4, became confused.) He is actually *making* a judgment, in which "proper" has its quasi-imperative force of resolving or recommending. So far, then, we have found several respects in which definition (3) is satisfactory and, save for its excessive harshness, no respect in which it is unsatisfactory.

XI

I have remarked that definition (3) is incomplete—that it requires an added clause if it is to assign "proper" a meaning that is relevant to the special contexts of aesthetics. The definition can readily be completed in this way: (4) The "proper" way of observing a work of art is the way that *is to be* cultivated and maintained—though only by those who wish to observe the work with care and in an attitude of aesthetic absorption. The added clause prevents the imperative force of "is to be" from being too extensive; it shows that "C is proper" recommends C only to certain people under certain circumstances. To those who are content not to appreciate the work of art in question, for instance, and hence do not wish to observe it for aesthetic purposes, the statement does not rocommend C—even though it does, of course, put a vector in that direction which may influence them should they wish to observe the work for aesthetic purposes later on.

The restriction provided is rough; but I doubt that an attempt to improve it would yield interesting results. The need of *some* such restriction will be evident. Concern with the arts, even if it should have no other effects, always takes time, and therefore competes with other activities—with business, politics, and so on. Now when a critic judges that C (correlated with Q_8) is the proper way to observe a work, he is not, obviously, recommending that people cultivate and maintain C

---

11 If I were not deliberately ignoring the possibility of a "second-pattern" analysis of "proper" (see note 8) I should here have to introduce a number of qualifying remarks.

in preference to all other things they might do. He is scarcely in a position to estimate the importance of cultivating C as compared with other activities, for the latter are by no means the same for all people or at all times. So he simplifies his problem, which is difficult at best, by letting others decide as they will about *whether* to observe, for aesthetic purposes, the work of art in question. Or if he does discuss that question he considers it a broader one than any that falls within aesthetic interpretation or evaluation. For the most part he is content to limit his influence to "those who wish" to observe the work for aesthetic purposes, discussing *how* it is to be observed by them. And his interests, of course, are reflected by his central terms.

XII

Let us now return to such terms as "unified$_c$," "sentimental$_c$," and "beautiful$_c$," with which our study began. Since these have been related to "proper" by (D), page 326, and since "proper" has been defined by (4), page 348, we have only to put (D) and (4) together; and the result, for the special case of "unified$_c$" for instance, will be this: (E) "The work of art is unified$_c$" has the same meaning as "The work of art appears unified$_s$ when observed in the way that *is to be* cultivated and maintained—though cultivated and maintained only by those who wish to observe the work with care and in an attitude of aesthetic absorption. Thus "unified$_c$" (and any other Q_c term that is interpretive or evaluative) is disclosed to have a meaning that, in part, is quasi-imperative. If the previous steps in our analysis are correct, we must accept this conclusion as their consequence. But it will be well to "test" definition (E) independently, to make sure there has been no mistake. Let us see whether we can locate the quasi-imperative element in a simple context.

When a work of art seems disunified$_s$ to us, and when a certain critic, A, says that it is actually unified$_c$, we wonder whether or not to change our way of observing it; for his remark induces us (very slightly or somewhat strongly, depending on our respect for A as a critic) to see it as he presumably does, and we can do this only by changing our aesthetic decision. And it is precisely here that the quasi-imperative force of "unified$_c$" becomes manifest. We do not change our aesthetic decision immediately, since we do not want to yield to A's influence without deliberation; nor would we always be *able* to change our decision immediately, even *if* we wanted to. But at least *A*'s influence leads us to take the possibility of changing more seriously—and that, normally, is all that is accomplished by *any* imperative, so long as the imperative has no legal or physical sanction.

If we now go on to discuss the matter with *A*, we may temporarily stop using the term "unified$_c$" and instead make an overt use of "proper" or "is to be" or their near synonym. We may tell *A*, for instance, that he is making "too much" of the work, i.e., more than is *proper*. Or he may tell us that we observe it "too passively," i.e., passively to a degree that *is to be* avoided. These words occur so readily in the discussion that it is hard to believe that they introduce an imperative element for the first time; it is easier to believe that they intensify the imperative element that "unified$_c$" introduced at the beginning—an imperative element that (*E*), then, has been correct in recognizing. And perhaps "unified$_c$" will disclose its imperative force, once again, at the end of the discussion. If we finally accept *A*'s decision as our own (for instance) and if the work then seems unified$_s$ to us, we are likely to say, as *A* does, that it is unified$_c$. Here the word "imperatively" expresses our new decision and reassures *A* in his old one. (Compare this with the overtly imperative expression, "Yes, let's observe it in the way that makes it appear unified$_s$.")

We may "test" (*E*) in this further way: If the definition is faithful to common usage, we should expect the *reasons* for or against the judgment, "The work of art is unified$_c$," to be the same as those we have discussed previously (section 8) in connection with "proper"—reasons causally rather than logically related to the judgment. Now I think they are in fact the same, as will be evident from this further observation: When we at first object, as in the above example, to *A*'s judging that the work of art is unified$_c$, we may give some such *reason* as this: "It can appear unified$_s$ only when observed in a state of mind that is tense and strained. Is that anything which it is proper to cultivate?" To which A may reply: "A certain amount of habituation is required, as for any new work of art. After that, there is no tension or strain." Note that these remarks, which obviously provide instances of the *reasons* that were mentioned in connection with "proper," here appear, and in a quite ordinary context, as *reasons for or against A's interpretive judgment about unity$_c$*.

Definition (*E*) is "confirmed," then, by the way in which "unified$_c$"

is used in ordinary discourse; and the same can be said, *mutatis mutandis,* for the definition of any other Q_c term that follows the same pattern.

Let us note, before proceeding, that in any problem of interpretation or evaluation a judgment of the form, "The work of art is Q_c," will have a central place. Our analysis has emphasized it for that reason. When a critic hesitates to make such a judgment, or when two or more critics make it in different ways, then there is a problem to be resolved. When a critic makes it without hesitation or conflict, or when crtics make it in the same way, then—from *their* point of view, of course, and not from ours if we tacitly diverge from them—the problem is no longer troublesome. We should expect that to be true; for the Q_c judgment introduces, by implication, all of the essential factors of interpretation and evaluation: the work of art, the conditions of observation, the appearances of the work, and the critic's decision as to which conditions of observation (with the appearances correlated with them) are proper. And indirectly, through the reasons that support it, the judgment introduces the *knowledge* that may *guide* the critic's decision.

XIII

Our analysis of the Q_c terms must end at this point, even though it is manifestly incomplete. We can readily see how "beautiful$_c$" and "unified$_c$," for instance, resemble each other in meaning and how they differ from purely factual terms. But how do they *differ from each other* in meaning? We have provided, by implication, this kind of answer: They differ from each other to whatever extent "beautiful$_s$" and "unified$_s$" differ from each other. And the answer, of course, is not sufficient. But a sufficient answer would lead to a study of the Q_s terms; and as previously stated (page 325) that cannot be attempted here. We must be content with having taken a first step in clarifying the interpretive and evaluative terms, even though so many other steps remain to be taken.

In this section and the following one, then, I shall be concerned less with developing or testing the analysis of the Q_c terms than with emphasizing some of its implications; and I shall attempt to free these implications from certain sources of confusion. In particular, I shall say something more about the way in which interpretive and evaluative judgments can be supported by *reasons*.

We have just seen how reasons can be given for the interpretive judgment, "The work of art is unified$_c$"; and we have seen that these reasons are no different from those that support a judgment about what is proper, as discussed in section 8, and hence are intimately related to the knowledge that guides a critic's characteristic decision, as discussed in section 6. The same considerations arise, of course, not only for judgments about unity$_c$ but for all judgments of the form, "The work of art is Q_c," and thus for all interpretive and evaluative judgments. The reasons that support one of these judgments need not be identical, in factual content, with those that support another; but they are all alike in that they are comparable to reasons supporting an imperative: they are related causally rather than logically to the judgments they support and "guide without constraining."

Now in this connection there are two points that deserve further attention: In the first place, the reasons that support Q_c judgments should be more adequately illustrated; for otherwise their variety may be imperfectly evident, with the result that their importance may be underestimated. In the second place, these reasons must be contrasted with supporting statements of a quite different kind—supporting statements that, in a familiar sense, may also be called "reasons" for an interpretive or evaluative judgment and, if left unmentioned, might be confused with the reasons that have previously been discussed.

It will be convenient to begin with the second of these points—which is of interest, let me add, not only for avoiding confusion but also in its own right. We can then return to the first point in section 14.

To prevent ambiguity let us hereafter refer to the reasons that have previously been discussed as "primary reasons," and let us refer to those that are about to be discussed as "secondary reasons."

The nature of the secondary reasons can best be indicated by an example. In criticizing the landscapes of Rubens, Mr. A. C. Barnes[12] finds them "as a rule, inferior to" those of Claude of Lorraine. This is of course an evaluative judgment, "inferior to" having much the same meaning as "less beautiful$_c$ than." And Barnes supports his evaluative judgment with the remark, "because the animation and movement which are intrinsic to Rubens' technique are not adapted to the placidity so often characteristic of landscape." Now in some sense, this latter remark is a "reason" for the former. But note that it is not a primary

---

12 *The Art in Painting* (1937), p. 279.

reason. For a primary reason is always a *factual* statement. Here the reason is not a factual statement but is itself an interpretive judgment —such terms as "animation," "movement," and "placidity" being obvious examples of interpretive Q_c terms. I call it, then, a "secondary reason"; and in general I speak of a "secondary reason" whenever one Q_c judgment is used to support another.

Since the secondary reason in the above example is itself an interpretive judgment, it could be supported by primary reasons in its turn. Barnes provides it with no such support, and his omission is scarcely one that we shall wish to censure. For primary reasons lead to very complicated questions (as we shall see better in the following section), and a practical critic cannot always take time to make them explicit. And perhaps Barnes assumed that the primary reasons would be gratuitous—perhaps he assumed that the conditions of observation under which Rubens' paintings appear to have animation$_g$ and movement$_g$, and under which landscapes appear to have placidity$_g$, are so commonly accepted as *proper* that his own interpretation, concurring with the general one, required no defense. But however that may be, the interpretation given by the secondary reasons *could* have been supported (or attacked, of course) by primary reasons. And should any controversy arise about whether or not the secondary reason gives a correct interpretation of the works in question, it would lead back to the primary reasons, which would be essential in settling the issue, so far as it could be settled. It is on that account that the terms "secondary" and "primary" seem to me to be appropriate.

To explain the *modus operandi* of secondary reasons, when these are viewed in relation to an evaluative judgment that they support, it will first be necessary to make this observation about the Q_g qualities. Between beauty$_g$ and various other Q_g's, of which animation$_g$, movement$_g$, and placidity$_g$ are examples, there is often an intimate relation. Should we have an experience in which the first two of the latter qualities clash$_g$ with the third, we should be likely to have a relatively low degree of beauty$_g$ characterizing the experience. The relation between the Q_g's is contingent and subject to exceptions, but it holds often enough to be of interest. Bearing this in mind, let us continue the above example, at first paying less attention to the Q_g terms than to the quasi-imperative effect introduced by the Q_c terms:

By his initial evaluative judgment, Barnes tends to make us accept, as *proper,* the conditions of observation under which Rubens' land-

scapes seem less beautiful$_s$ than Claude's. But we shall not want to give
assent to his judgment—unless, of course, we are content to set him up
as our ultimate authority in such matters—until we have tried these
conditions of observation ourselves, to make sure that we too consider
them proper. And here we may encounter a difficulty. We may have
very little knowledge about what these conditions are, being able to
describe them, perhaps, only as "the conditions which, for these paintings, will be correlated with the relative degrees of beauty$_s$ that Barnes
has presumably experienced." So our efforts to try out these conditions
may be unsuccessful, since we are unable to locate them. We may accordingly suspend judgment, feeling that we do not want to make a
final decision about what is proper until we have taken these conditions, which elude us, into account. Barnes's secondary reason, however,
may not be attended by this difficulty. His reason, being an interpretive
judgment, will tend to make us accept, as proper, the conditions of
observation under which qualities of animation$_s$, movement$_s$, and
placidity$_s$ are experienced; and we shall again not want to give assent
to it until we have tried these conditions out. But we may now be more
successful in locating the conditions; for in general we have a better
idea as to what we must do—how we must attend to the pictures, en-
couraging these reactions and discouraging those, etc.—when we are
looking for animation$_s$, movement$_s$, and placidity$_s$ than when we are
looking for the highly generic quality of beauty$_s$. With regard to the
interpretation given by the secondary reason, then, we may *not* feel
that we have to suspend judgment.

By putting together the observations of the last two paragraphs, we
can now see why the secondary reason is helpful. I shall consider only
the case in which our reflections might lead us to agree with Barnes—
i.e., lead us to make the same sort of *decision* that he does—without discussing the many ways in which we might be led to disagree.[13] Let us
assume that, having initially suspended judgment on his evaluation,
we later come to accept the interpretation provided by his secondary
reason. We then maintain, as proper, the conditions of observation that
lead us to experience an animation$_s$ and movement$_s$ clashing$_s$ with
placidity$_s$ in the landscapes of Rubens, but not in those Claude. Now
these qualities, as we have seen, are intimately related to beauty$_s$, so
when experiencing them we also experience, let us assume, the relative

---

[13] When people make the same sort of decision, their agreement is analogous, in
important respects to the "agreement in attitude" that I have discussed in *Ethics
and Language*, particularly ch. i.

degrees of beauty$_s$ to which Barnes has implicitly referred. And being confident that the conditions of observation that are proper for interpreting the pictures are also proper for evaluating them, we conclude that the landscapes of Rubens seem less beautiful$_s$ than those of Claude when observed properly—or in other words, that they are less beautiful$_c$. So the secondary reason is instrumental in leading us to accept the evaluative judgment. And it frees us (partially, at least) from the fear of having made an evaluative judgment prematurely; for it helps us to explore certain possible conditions of observation which we might otherwise have been unable to take into account.

Had I space to do so I should say much more about secondary reasons. I should like to give a more complete account of their *modus operandi*, the above account being in several respects incomplete. I should like, moreover, to discuss them in connection with norms.[14] And I should like to show how they affect the meaning of many interpretive terms—explaining how these terms, being so often used in secondary reasons that support evaluations, come to acquire, by association, an evaluative function of their own.[15] But these are matters that I must leave until another time.

Enough has here been said, I trust, to prevent the secondary reasons from being confused with primary reasons and to show that the present analysis can recognize a place for both. And let me especially emphasize this point: the secondary reasons in no way make the primary reasons unnecessary; for, being interpretive judgments, they can be supported by primary reasons in their turn.

XIV

I have said that my discussion of the primary reasons, to which we must now return, is in need of further examples. Occasional examples have been given, of course, dealing with philological or cultural anachronisms, with the comparative permanence of certain moods (see page 336), with the intentions of the artist, and so on. But in addition to

---

14 For an interesting discussion of evaluations, reasons, and norms, see Arnold Isenberg's paper, "Critical Communication," in *Phil. Rev.*, LVIII (1949), 330-344. Isenberg presumably regards the reasons he discusses as factual; but many of his conclusions, including those about the practicability of criticizing without the use of articulate norms, would hold if the reasons were taken, in my own fashion, as "secondary," and hence interpretive and quasi-imperative.

15 In other words, we must recognize "two aspects of their meaning," as already mentioned in passing. I have subsequently ignored the evaluative element in some of my "interpretive" terms, finding it necessary to sacrifice accuracy to simplicity.

these somewhat obvious primary reasons there are others that, in promise, seem to me more interesting. I refer to reasons that point out the *consequences* of that channeling of sensibilities that I have called the critic's "decision"—consequences that bear not merely on subsequent artistic experience but upon various aspects of practical life. But perhaps this suggestion will immediately provoke a question.

It is widely held that beauty$_s$ is experienced only when patterns$_s$, emotions$_s$, and meanings$_s$ are dwelt upon for their own sake, rather than as cues to practical action or theoretical speculation. When appreciating, one dwells upon the "aesthetic surface." It may be asked, then, how the reasons that I have envisaged—reasons that deal expressly with practical consequences—can help but be foreign to aesthetics.

The answer is simply this: It is the task of a critic not merely to dwell upon an aesthetic surface, but to make up his mind, and to help others make up their minds, *which* aesthetic surface is to be dwelt upon. For an aesthetic surface is an experience; and as we have repeatedly seen, a given work of art brings with it not some one experience, but many possibilities of experience, the possibility that is in fact realized depending upon one's aesthetic decision. So if we acknowledge that the contemplation of an aesthetic surface, once selected, involves a nonspeculative, nonpractical state of mind, we need not acknowledge, and in sanity we must wholly deny, that the same state of mind attends the decision governing its selection.

When a critic is making his characteristic decision, how *can* he be nonspeculative and nonpractical? It is true that he can temporarily avoid *certain* practical matters. I have myself remarked (section II) that in interpretation and aesthetic evaluation a critic will address his suggestions to "those who wish" to observe a given work for aesthetic purposes, thereby avoiding the often practical problem of indicating who should or should not, amid competing activities, actually appreciate it. But *other* practical matters are likely to influence the decision even of those who definitely *do* wish to observe the work for aesthetic purposes, and these virtually cannot be ignored.

For example, should a man react to a poem in a way that involves many stock responses, even though the poem permits more subtle reactions—and Mr. I. A. Richards has cited examples of this[16]—we might wish to say that he is approaching it improperly. What primary reasons

---

[16] *Practical Criticism* (1930), particularly pp. 240-242; and *Principles of Literary Criticism* (1924), pp. 202 f.

could we give for our judgment, particularly if his reactions are immediately agreeable to him? We could say what Richards has himself said: the stock responses transfer to practical life, with effects that the man will not welcome. He will then avoid them, should we establish our point, only as a means of avoiding their practical effects, not as unpleasant "surfaces" to dwell upon. But in any case he may be led to a new channeling of his sensibilities and gradually come to dwell upon another sort of surface. So the fact that his decision was *guided by* practical matters does not deprive his experience, when he returns to the poem, of its aesthetic character. Let me add that he is likely, later on, to find stock responses (I refer only to crude ones, of course) unrewarding even to dwell upon; for what is first avoided as a means of escaping certain effects often comes, by a process of conditioning, to be distasteful in itself. If aesthetic experience is different from the experience that attends practical activity, it does not follow that the two are causally unrelated.

Let me take a further example. Camille Bellaigue once wrote of Debussy's *Pelléas and Mélisande,* "Art such as this is unhealthy and harmful. . . . Its hardly perceptible vitality tends to the lowering and the ruin of our existence. It contains germs, not of life and progress, but of decadence and death."[17] To this one might wish to reply, on the basis of observations that time has since made possible, that the fears are groundless, that one can immunize himself to the "unhealthy" aspects of the music and progressively grow sensitive to other aspects that are "healthy." But would such an issue be aside from the point—irrelevant to pure criticism? To say so is to run the risk of making criticism altogether too pure for comfort. One's effort to immunize himself to the "unhealthy" aspects of the music, though practically motivated, is not hostile to aesthetic experience. As in the preceding example, it simply alters one's sensibility; it still permits him, when later appreciating the music, to dwell with aesthetic immediacy upon the new forms and moods that the music then occasions. And in this case we have a further consideration: a man who has practical fears of the music is insistently *prevented* from dwelling on its forms and moods. So if we refuse to discuss his fears and engage only in "pure" criticism, we narrow our considerations in a curious way. In insisting on the demands of aesthetic experience we neglect the factors that make it possible.

---

17 An early criticism, quoted by Edward Lockspeiser in *Debussy* (1936).

So there is no irrelevance in the variety of the practical, primary reasons by which an aesthetic decision may be guided. There is a genuine problem, of course, in establishing the reasons as true—one that is all too genuine. No one can be perfectly sure, for instance, just how much stock responses to poetry actually transfer elsewhere, or just how much one can actually immunize himself to "unhealthy" aspects of music; nor are intuitive convictions an adequate substitute for controlled experiment and intersubjective evidence. But that is only to say that criticism is difficult, and all the more difficult when it ceases to be superficial.

Throughout all history critics have wanted a philosophical basis for their judgments. They have profited little, however, by vast, speculative generalizations, cut off from the sciences and set up in rivalry to them. So perhaps, in their place, critics can find a basis in the form of a more comprehensive, more carefully organized body of empirically verified primary reasons, *guiding* their judgments in the way I have described. Their results, to be sure, will always fall short of finality; for their reasons will be elusive, manifold, never more than probable; and their tastes, which in part will depend on factors *other* than these reasons, will be likely to diverge in this way or that and remain subject to variation. But let us not forget this: these critics will always have a direction in which to travel and a not unreasonable hope that discussion and inquiry, whether it provokes agreement or dissent, will progressively be attended by a greater enlightenment and a richer reward.

Generalization and Evidence

FREDERICK L. WILL

"Philosophical analysis," "analytical philosophy," and so on, like such other broad terms as "liberalism" and "scientific method," mean many different things to different people. Because of the very wide and various usages of these terms it is not possible to define clearly what one means by them in a short definition, nor is it easy in a long one. Fortunately the commission of this paper is not to define analytical method in philosophy but to employ it. It may therefore be sufficient as a preliminary notice of things to come, to specify two of the characteristics of the type of analysis which the paper is intended to illustrate. It is, first, a type which, though its philosophical lineage is long and its relations wide, has been practiced with great concentration and with a special style or manner by some English speaking philosophers during the past two or three decades. And, secondly, it is a type which, though it traces many philosophical problems to linguistic sources and consequently emphasizes throughout the basic importance of clarity and precision of meaning, differs markedly from some of its contemporary relatives in the manner in which it proceeds to deal with philosophical problems and to achieve these desirable ends. It proceeds, not by the invention of wholly new and aseptic languages into which all "real" philosophical problems must somehow be capable of translation without a remainder, but rather by striving to clarify and purify, by whatever means are possible, the philosophical domains of the rich and complex vernacular languages in which these problems have arisen and in which, it has turned out, many of them can also be very fruitfully treated.

Although the function of this philosophical analysis is by no means solely remedial and therapeutic, nowhere has it demonstrated its power more strikingly than in connection with certain persistent and seemingly insoluble philosophical problems which for centuries have seemed to many philosophers to be both unavoidable and at the same time to issue, when broached, inevitably in skepticism concerning the foundations of human knowledge and belief. In dealing with these problems, concerning such characteristic topics as our knowledge of the "external world," or of "other minds," or "our capacity to know statements about the future," analytic method has displayed its effectiveness in clarifying and resolving the perplexities and in allaying the intellectual anxieties which are expressed by those who find themselves forced, they think, "by the evidence," to admit that we can never "really know" the existence of other minds, or of objects external to us, or that inductive conclusions are "never really justified."

Even in its application to these philosophical perplexities analytic method has a two-sided function. To be sure, skeptical pronouncements like the above are false and in some respects ridiculous;[1] and it is a proper and fundamental part of the analytic treatment of the perplexities to expose their falsity and laughability and also to reveal their origins in the confusions, largely of a linguistic character, from which they spring. But this alone is not enough; if one stops there and fails to search also for the insights which these statements of philosophical perplexity typically, though confusedly, express, his understanding of these statements and of the perplexities of which they are signs will be seriously deficient. For there is more behind these philosophical statements or theories, as John Wisdom observed some years ago,[2] than linguistic confusion; there is also some genuine linguistic penetration. An adequate treatment of these statements or theories and of the perplexities of which they are the linguistic signs, must therefore also pay attention to those real differences and similarities, both in the language about knowledge and reality and in the knowledge and reality to which the language refers, which typically

---

[1] In a sometimes bitter way, as the symptoms of a compulsion neurosis are ridiculous.

[2] "Philosophical Perplexity," *Arist. Soc. Proc.*, XXXVII (1936-7), 71-88.

the man in the throes of a skeptical perplexity is striving, though awkwardly and misleadingly, to recognize and deal with.

The following study is intended to illustrate the results which are attained when one applies these modern analytic methods to the kind of arguments which have seemed to so many philosophers to lead irresistibly to inductive skepticism. Two somewhat different but closely congruent lines of argument will be studied. The first of these is the historically important and conveniently brief one concerning "the foundation of all conclusions from experience" presented by Hume in his first *Enquiry*. In this argument the key terms upon which much of the persuasiveness of the reasoning depends and which invite analytic scrutiny are "reasoning," "argument," and "the understanding." Because of the familiarity of philosophers with Hume's ideas upon this point and because also of the increasing familiarity of the analytic approach to them, the main steps in the analysis and the results therewith reached will be set forth in a fairly brief, compact fashion. This brevity will make possible in sections 2 and 3 a closer and more extensive study of a somewhat different line of argument which seems to support conclusions like Hume's but in more modern, less psychological, and more compelling terms. The central difficulty which this line of argument finds in induction concerns the question, as it may be put schematically, how the inductive testing or examining of a set of events, $E_1, E_2 \ldots E_n$ can provide a warrant or basis for belief about the character of another numerically distinct event E_{n+1}. This question is, in the argument, made to appear inductively unanswerable, since to answer it one clearly needs evidence not only about the events E_1 to E_n, but also about E_{n+1}. But E_{n+1}, being an unexamined event, appears to be just the kind of event which the inductive testing or examining, by itself, is incapable of providing evidence about.

In the analysis and criticism of this latter line of reasoning, attention will be concentrated upon the terms "evidence" and "inductive evidence" and the way these are employed in the passage from plausible premises to the skeptical conclusion. Beneath the dissimilarity of terminology in the two types of argument, the analysis will strive to show that there is a basic and close congruence in idea. Both of them feed upon and derive their strength from the same kinds of linguistic or logical confusion, and both of them employ the same basic principles and illustrate the same linguistic predilections concerning what a "reason" or "evidence" for a conclusion may properly be said to be. Finally, and in line with the above general comments upon the positive and negative functions of philosophical analysis, both will be revealed in the light of analysis to be the products and symptoms, not only of philosophical confusion, but of philosophical insight as well. Although as bases for their ostensible skeptical conclusions they must be counted as mischievous paralogisms, these arguments do also at some points contain valuable and salvageable suggestions for the philosophy of inductive knowledge, concerning the character of inductive evidence and the requirements which that evidence must satisfy in order to constitute the grounds of a sound inductive conclusion.

I

As the terms "inductive knowledge" and "inductive belief" are ordinarily understood they are extremely comprehensive, embracing as they do all of our knowledge and belief which is based upon observation and experimental testing, with the possible minute exception of that set of beliefs which, it is argued by some philosophers, can be established by observation or experiment directly, without dependence upon any inferential process requiring evidence beyond that which is alleged to be "immediately given." Concerning so great an expanse of our beliefs or knowledge, and the grounds thereof, an enormous number and great variety of questions can be asked, as can readily be seen in the many available works dealing either with the general theory of knowledge or more particularly with the methods of the sciences and the other developed disciplines in the social studies and the humanities. And not one or a few, but many of these questions have been discovered in centuries of philosophical thought to bear within them the seeds of that sort of puzzlement which eventuates in such extremely broad skeptical conclusions as that inductive inferences are never justified.

Of the many questions which may be raised about inductive inference, some, and those that have engaged the most attention of philosophers, concern the grounds of empirical generalizations. How is it possible by means of inductive evidence to establish or support such generalizations? In order to procure from the many possible topics or queries about the grounds of inductive conclusions one which will be manageable within the limits of this paper, it will be useful, first, to concentrate attention upon those conclusions which have the form of generalizations and, secondly, to consider only those among these generalizations which can be expressed in the simple form "All *A*'s are *B*." Concerning this conventional paradigm of inductive conclusions there is one direct, obvious, and often asked question which still seems to be worth some exploring. This is the question, as it is sometimes put, of the role of positive instances in the support of a generalization, where by "positive instances" is meant objects or events, or reports thereof in the evidence, which are *A*'s and likewise conform to the generalization by having the property *B*. How, or by what right or justification, do sets of positive instances of this kind constitute grounds for the generalization "All *A*'s are *B*"? It must be presumed, of course, that the set of *A*'s which is available as evidence is not marred by an admixture of any established "negative" or refuting instances, that is, *A*'s which are not *B;* otherwise the generalization is false, in this simple, unrevised form, and thus beyond the range of any inductive support. But granting that all the known *A*'s are indeed *B,* by what right does a set of such instances function as a ground for affirming the generalization that all *A*'s, actual and possible, are of this character? Is it by right of the Uniformity of Nature? Or the Pure Concepts of the Understanding? Or the Presuppositions of Experience? Or, as the skeptic has it, in this source of philosophical perplexity, is it by no right whatever?

"Inductive conclusions are never justified." In particular, "Positive instances of the character of *A*'s which are also *B* are never good evidence for the generalization that all *A*'s are *B*." The traditional pattern of argument set by Hume in reasoning to such negative conclusions as these is well known. In inquiring, as he said, concerning the "foundation of all conclusions from experience," which in more recent terminology would be rendered as the "foundation of all inductive conclusions," Hume discovered what appeared to be a serious gap in any such inference between the premises and the conclusion. For in such an inference the premise reports something to this effect: objects of a certain kind have been attended with effects of some specific kind. And the conclusion proceeds to affirm, on this basis, that other objects like this, or, if it is a generalization, *all* objects like this, will be attended with effects of the same kind. And the gap, said Hume, lies in the fact that it is impossible to derive conclusions like this from premises like this by any process of "reasoning," or "argument," or "the understanding."[3] It would be possible by reasoning or argument to pass from premises like this to such conclusions only on the presumption of some further validating premise to the effect *"that instances, of which we have had no experience, must resemble those, of which we have had experience, and that the course of nature continues always uniformly the same,"*[4] or, more simply and in reference just to the future, that "the future will be conformable to the past," and that hence one may put trust in past experience so as to "make it the standard of our future judgment."[5] But the further validating premises of this kind can never be properly substantiated and introduced to inductive inference, said Hume, because they are themselves clearly conclusions about matters of fact or existence and hence can be supported only, if at all, by an inference from experience, that is, an induction. But they cannot be supported in this way because they are the foundations of all such inferences from experience and hence any attempt to establish them by experience would have to presume at the start exactly what it set out to establish, and the attempt then would be patently circular and without force. People do, however, constantly draw inductive conclusions. Since they cannot do this, as the above considerations are intended to show, by any process of reason or argument, they must do it in a nonrational way. And there is a nonrational principle in human nature which, reason failing the task, normally carries one over the gap between premise and conclusion, and the discovery and elucidation of which can bring the inquiry into the principles of experiential inference to a definite, though skeptical, termination. This is the psychological principle of custom or habit; and it is this then, not reason, which is the great guide of human life and experiential belief. And it is in these terms that one can understand Hume's provocative comment that "if we believe, that fire warms, or water refreshes, 'tis only because it costs us too much pain to think otherwise."[6]

If this is so, there is indeed real reason for philosophical perplexity; but is it? Upon this question, and many of the puzzling doubts and anxieties which it expresses, careful philosophical analysis has already

---

[3] E.g., *An Enquiry Concerning Human Understanding*, Sect. IV, Pt. II, Selby-Bigge ed. (1902), pp. 32-39.

[4] *A Treatise of Human Nature*, Bk. I, Pt. III, Sect. VI, Selby-Bigge ed. (1896), p. 89.

[5] *Enquiry*, loc. cit. (Selby-Bigge ed., p. 35).

[6] *Treatise*, Bk. I, Pt. II, Sect. VII (Selby-Bigge ed., p. 270).

demonstrated its capacity to throw much light. It has revealed with special clarity (though the discovery was not altogether new) and in striking terms that to this question, as to many others with which philosophers deal, the answer must be "Yes and No," and, again, "It depends upon what one means." It depends upon the usage or interpretation of several of the crucial terms in which this skeptical account of inductive inference has been put. For if this account, in its talk of "reason," "habit," and so on, is taken to mean that the modern physician has no better grounds for his beliefs concerning the causes and treatment of jaundice than the Italian peasants described by Carlo Levi, who attribute it to exposure to the rainbow, then it is false. It is false that the informed man who believes that water is a better beverage than nitric acid can have no better grounds for believing this than a moth might have for believing that the flame will be more comforting than the air about it, since in both cases, in a way, it would cost each too much pain to think otherwise. Both the physician in his judgments concerning jaundice and the informed man judging the comparative qualities of water and nitric acid can support their judgments with a degree of evidence far superior to that which can be adduced for the other judgments with which they have been favorably compared.

Then why, indeed, is there puzzlement here, why a threatening skepticism to be avoided? Why do arguments like that of Hume seem so often to lead irresistibly to over-all doubts concerning inductive conclusions? One reason is that in another sense Hume is right. In some sense in which these terms "reason" and "habit" can be defined, inductive conclusions can be said to depend upon habit and not upon reason alone. When arguing with the terms in this sense, therefore, Hume can lead himself and his readers convincingly to this conclusion, although, so long as the argument is carefully interpreted and the specific meaning of the terms kept in mind, there is no good ground for any appraisal, skeptical or otherwise, of the merits of any or all inductive inferences.

The basis of the Humean argument that inductive conclusions cannot be derived from their premises by any "argument," process of "reasoning" or of "the understanding" is that these inductive conclusions are not derivable from their premises by a deductive process. This is the proof Hume consistently gives for his pronouncement that conclusions from experience are not to be validated by reason. If "reason" is interpreted in this way to mean just deductive reason, so that those conclusions from empirical premises which can be drawn by a deductive process, and only those, will be called reasonable, then in this sense of the term inductive conclusions are not drawn by reason. On the other hand, there is truly in inductive procedures, and especially clearly in inductive generalization, an aspect of repetitive, uniform experience which bears some analogy with the conditions of the formation of habits. In this way there is in the skeptical argument, complementing the recognition of the genuine difference between deductive and inductive procedures, a recognition also of a genuine analogy, in the aspect of the commonly confirming effect of repetitive experiences, between inductive conclusions and habits. If now, setting out to express these insights, with an eye also to the stir which this apparently paradoxical way of speaking will create in the circles of the learned, one chooses to call by the name "habit" all the other procedures of inference in which in the sciences, the arts, and all the other areas of empirical practice and inquiry, nondeductive conclusions are drawn from empirical premises, then upon this use of terms one will have validated the conclusion that inductive inferences all depend upon "habit" and not upon "reason" alone. And unless one keeps clearly in mind the specific meanings which these terms bear in this conclusion and resists firmly the natural tendency to interpret them in their broader, more normal senses, the conclusion will seem to mark a great skeptical victory.

That it is not a skeptical victory, and not even a battle, follows from the same considerations and with the same interpretation of the terms upon which the argument leading to the conclusion may be accounted a sound one. As an argument calling attention to, and insisting upon, the nondeductive character of inductive inferences, it is a piece of philosophical analysis of merit; for the conclusion is not only sound, but of great importance for the philosophy of knowledge and, through it, for all the other fields of inquiry, philosophical and nonphilosophical, in which a broad understanding of the ways of knowing and of the related question of the adequacy of the rationalist conception of knowledge is of value. Unfortunately what is sound in the conclusion is expressed in a perversely provocative and misleading manner, in linguistic expressions which, unless they are treated with extreme caution, easily and almost irresistibly impose upon one by seeming to convey something much different and more radical than is justified by the grounds upon which they are based.

The Innocent Landman, brought up to have both familiarity and respect for the firmness and supporting qualities of the solid earth, has much to learn from his first encounter with the sea and the novel types of life and activity which characterize its shores and harbors and the vast ocean beyond. Let him be supposed now, with some imaginative license, to be a man of extreme innocence of and lack of preparation for understanding these new types of phenomena of the seaman's life which he is now encountering. He is astonished by the lack of conformity between many of these new experiences and what he has previously known; and, beginning to express both his astonishment and the lack of conformity, he has only the resources of the language with which he was brought up and equipped in the hinterland. So he might be inclined to say concerning the phenomena of floating vessels which he has seen passing in and out of the harbor that there is nothing supporting these vessels upon the surface of the water. And in *his sense* of support there is not. The kind of support he has come to know and recognize in the Landman's life is the kind that houses, trees, and men have, resting with their foundations, bases, or legs upon the solid earth. In this specific sense of "support," floating vessels indeed do not have any support. There are no protuberances extending like stilts from the keels to the bottom; on the contrary, if there were the vessels would no longer be said to be afloat, just as grounded vessels are not said to be afloat again until they have been pried loose from such support on reefs or sandbanks.

Within the limitations of his language, then, the Landman is describing a genuine distinction, but because of these limitations he is describing it unwell, in a way which is readily open to and indeed invites misinterpretation. How easy it is to interpret his statement that floating vessels have no support as saying more than that such vessels are not supported in the way that houses, trees, and standing men are supported! How easily it may be interpreted as saying that nothing at all holds such a vessel up or secures it from sinking! And if that is so, then a vessel may founder at any time. To be sure, though they have no support, vessels do not always, or commonly, sink. They have a remarkable custom or habit of staying on the surface of the water, but, since they really have nothing to support them or hold them up, there is no guarantee that this curious custom may not at any time be spectacularly broken and all such vessels immediately sink. That vessels do sometimes sink, astonishing, discomfiting, and even destroying those who have trusted them to continue their floating careers, is sufficient concrete illustration to lend a realistic color to this diffident interpretation of the affirmation that the vessels have no support. They really do sink; and, having no support, they might all sink! Of course, commerce and water transportation go on, and one must plan for their continuance tomorrow; but, when one considers each vessel setting out into the vast wastes of the ocean with no support whatever to hold it up, how can one help being anxious and concerned?

From the vantage point of our superior knowledge we can see that as an affirmation of the fact that floating objects are not supported by a firm platform, as are houses and standing men, the Landman's expression that floating vessels have no support is, though justified, innocent of any consequences concerning the disposition of such bodies to sink. To say that these vessels have no support is to recognize in this language a genuine distinction; and, having recognized it, one is in a position to investigate the conditions under which vessels and other bodies float well or ill, the conditions of the buoyancy of liquids, the various ways in which seaworthiness is secured in vessels of different types, and many other fundamental related topics. So long as the Landman retains his original way of expressing the above distinction however, it will be difficult for him to communicate the distinction without conveying also to himself as well as others, in speaking of the lack of support of these vessels, connotations of the precariousness of their position as floating objects. This particular difficulty, this particular cause of anxiety and concern about the precariousness of floating bodies, can be greatly reduced by a liberalizing of the language which will permit him to say that floating bodies are different from other supported objects without being forced, by the limitations of his modes of expression, to say this in a way which seem to impugn the safety or reliability of either type of supported object. Such a liberalization will enable him better to discover, to speak about without prejudice, and to understand the novel kinds of phenomena which his introduction to the sea has brought and, in understanding, to realize that, as it might be put in less misleading language, the sea does have its own ways of support, which the Landman's language knew not of.

Similarly, though it is of great value in the philosophy of knowledge to have the sound distinction between inductive and deductive inference recognized and presented with unmistakable emphasis, so long as this distinction is presented in a language bound by rationalist limitations, it is apt to appear, as it did in the Landman's expression, in a misleading way. When the fact that inductive inferences are not deductive is expressed by saying that they are not based upon or justifiable by reason alone, this mode of expression will normally and naturally suggest, unless great care is taken to keep clear constantly the sense in which justification by reason is to be understood, that there is something dubious and unsound about all inductive inference and that scientists and others who put their trust in inductive procedures are all really misled. Here, too, in escaping and securing release from the gratuitous doubts and anxieties thus generated concerning the trustworthiness, or disposition to sink, of all inductive conclusions, a liberalization of the language responsible will be of value, a liberalization having the effect that one will be able to recognize clearly and express the fact that deductive and inductive inferences are different from each other, without impugning or overvaluing the appropriate merits of each. Are inductive inferences ever, sometimes, or always sound? Are they all without support and hence deserving the skeptical doubts of a thoroughly reasonable being, and of all of us insofar as we aspire to be more and more reasonable? There is nothing in the above affirmation of the lack of basis in reason of inductive inferences, in so far as it is soundly established, to indicate either an affirmative or a negative answer to any of these questions. There is nothing to indicate whether or not inductive conclusions do sometimes possess the kind of validity, justification, or support which is appropriate to their function as trustworthy guides for belief and action as these bear upon the past, the present, and the future. One does need constantly, in the conduct of practical affairs as well as of theoretical inquiries, to be able to compare and evaluate the soundness, warrant, or support of inductive inferences. Recognizing, in a fashion analogous to the Landman's, that this warrant or support is different from the kind of support which one learns about in the hinterland of deduction, and freeing oneself from the derogatory and perplexing connotations which the recognition of this distinction within the limitations of the expressions of the language of that hinterland so easily conveys, one is now in a position to speak about without inland prejudice, to investigate, and to come to understand the kinds of support afforded along the coasts, in the harbors, and upon the wide ocean of induction, and, with the understanding of these supports, to improve the design and construction of the inductive vessels which we must all set to float upon it.

II

One aspect of this skeptical reasoning concerning inductive conclusions which will repay further careful consideration here is its striking plausibility and seductiveness. This has already been considered in the preceding analysis of Hume's argument, where it has been pointed out that the logical ground of Hume's alleged discovery of the lack of validity or rationality in inductive inference lay in the fact that the only kind of validity or rationality which he was prepared to recognize in an inference was that of a deductive kind, and, examining inductive inference with such a criterion in hand, he was bound to find it wanting. To be sure, then, inductive inferences present a different kind of support for their conclusions than deductive ones; and to a considerable extent the deceptiveness of Hume's argument consists in its capacity to lead one in the examination of inductions to adopt, without realizing it, a criterion of support which is appropriate and capable of satisfaction only if one is dealing with deductions. But, now, if the misleading persuasiveness of this argument does consist so much in effecting, by a suitable use of such terms as "reason," "validity," and "habit," a mischoice of criteria for inductive inferences, how is it that, as many philosophers from the time of Hume on can testify, an argument embodying this choice can be so overwhelmingly persuasive and deceptive? How can one be so easily and convincingly led to ask of inductive inferences that they satisfy requirements which it follows from their very nature as inductive that they cannot satisfy?

There is much to be said in answer to these questions from various sources which cannot be treated here. On the historical side, for example, there is much to be learned from the development of both the rationalist and empiricist viewpoints in modern philosophy and the acceptance by the most influential of the empiricists, namely Locke and Hume, of a rationalist criterion of knowledge. So striking is this latter fact about the empiricists, and so important is its effect, that its understanding warrants a reversal of the judgment not uncommonly made that Hume's skeptical conclusions show the result of pressing an empiricist theory of knowledge to its logical conclusions. They seem to show rather, as the rudiments of such skepticism, which had already appeared in Book IV of Locke's *Essay* also seem to show, the consequences of tenaciously maintaining and applying a rationalist criterion of knowledge in the vast field of empirical inquiry; and thus they seem to reflect less upon the adequacy of empiricist principles than upon the appropriateness of this vestigial rationalism in a philosophy which was explicitly empiricist in intent.

Illumination of a different and more valuable sort can here be gained from a study of an alternative, supporting argument in which these rationalist preconceptions sometimes express themselves and in which their skeptical consequences are likewise persuasively formulated and communicated. In the argument of Hume considered above, one point which is exploited, though somewhat indirectly, is that in an inductive inference a conclusion is drawn concerning facts other than those described in the premises or evidence. If this were not so, the inference would not be inductive, but deductive. But since it is so, how is it possible, for example, in a generalization based upon instances to infer that because some set of empirically tested or observed *A*'s have the character *B*, all *A*'s whatsoever have this character? It is this general type of question, raised by the skeptical analysis of inductive inference, which constitutes what one recent writer has termed "the tragic puzzle of induction," namely, "the question whether and how any one set of facts furnishes a valid basis for an inference concerning another set of facts."[7] The skeptic is prepared to concede, according to this writer, that if one "were assured of the fundamental principle that what is true of a sample or subclass of any population . . . can be reasonably asserted of the rest of the population" then one would have a valid ground for inductive inference. But, as the skeptic's argument also is intended to show, neither this validating principle of induction, nor any other similar principle, can itself be established by inductive means, because of the inevitable circularity of such a proposed procedure. And since the skeptic further presumes, rightly or wrongly, that these principles are likewise incapable of a priori or demonstrative validation, on this basis the justification of any inductive inference turns out to be an impossible, hopeless project.

The main apparent principle employed in this argument is one so immediately obvious and plausible as to count as a truism. For it is, in one sense at least, truistic and obvious that if one is to be able to infer with good reason and warrant that because some set of empirically tested *A*'s have the character *B*, all *A*'s whatsoever have this

---

[7] Donald Williams, "Induction and the Future," *Mind*, LVII (1948), 227.

character, one must have evidence that whatever other A's there are or may be counted upon to resemble the tested A's in respect to the possession of this character. This much is involved analytically in the idea of inductive evidence as applied to generalizations of this sort. If it is ever possible with good evidence or warrant to conclude from the ascertained character of the tested A's, which are uniformly B, that all the other untested A's likewise are B, it must be that there is good warrant or evidence for holding that in respect to the possession of B the unobserved A's do thus resemble the observed.

A good portion of the plausibility of the skeptical reasoning about induction formulated in these terms derives from its seeming to do no more than draw direct logical consequences of the above incontestable principle. Granted, the argument says in effect, that in inferring from the examined A's to the unexamined ones one needs evidence that the unexamined instances are like the examined ones, this evidence which one needs is precisely the kind of evidence which he cannot have, so long as he restricts himself to what can be ascertained inductively. For after all, just as it is obvious that evidence of the similarity of the unexamined with the examined is indispensable, is it not equally obvious that all the information or evidence which any inductive testing of the A's can provide is information or evidence about the examined A's, and the examined A's only? Granted that in the inductive generalization from some A's to all there is a set of unexamined A's, A's which either simply have not been examined, or which, like possibly future A's, are not available for examination, it is of course just the character of this set of A's which is in question in the induction and which the conclusion is presuming to determine. And it is just this character, likewise, which the inductive testing cannot, and no inductive testing can, provide information or evidence about. On the one hand there are the A's which have been examined and whose possession of the character B has been inductively determined. On the other hand there are the unexamined A's, whose possession of B, like that of the examined A's, is being affirmed in the conclusion. But so long as one restricts himself to evidence which can be got by inductive testing, whether by the testing of A's or any other thing, he will have evidence only about the character of the examined A's or the other examined things, not about the A's which remain unexamined. This is so, and must be so, no matter how long and extensively the inductive testing is pursued. Therefore, so long as the inference is concerned with concluding something beyond the character of the examined things, something about the unexamined *A*'s, so long then the inference will, and necessarily must, go beyond that for which there is inductively available evidence.

It is clear that if one follows an argument of this kind it will lead him to the conclusion that all inductive evidence is defective in principle. And though the reasoning is not put in so bald and simple a manner, but more circuitously and deceptively, it seems likewise clear that the principle of the reasoning is fundamentally the same in the typical skeptical arguments which are alleged to establish the incompetence of inductive evidence to provide a warrant for believing, in any inductive inference, that the *future* instances will be like *present* and *past* ones. This fundamental principle of the reasoning is expressed indirectly in the characteristic thesis concerning inductive inferences from past to future that such inferences would be valid and justified only if one were assured in some way that the future will be like the past and that hence no inductive inference is itself capable of providing this assurance. Thus Bertrand Russell argued that the crucial question whether the future will be like the past "is not to be answered by an argument that starts from [the] past . . . alone."[8] And Hume earlier contended that it is not possible by "any arguments from experience" to "prove this resemblance of the past to the future." For, he said, "Let the course of things be allowed to be hitherto ever so regular; that alone, without some new argument or inference, proves not that, for the future, it will continue so."[9]

If this is a fair representation of the kind of reasoning which is expressed in terms of "futures" and "pasts," "examined" and "unexamined instances," in various typical skeptical arguments concerning inductive inferences, then, just as it is inevitable for such arguments to arrive at the conclusion that these inferences are all infected and vitiated by an irremediable lack of evidence, so it is apparent that, precisely because of the nature of the principles from which this inevitability derives, the conclusion has skeptical force only to the extent that its nature and basis are not clearly understood. Whenever anyone employs the term "evidence" in such a way that evidence derived from the examination of facts is evidence only concerning the nature of *these* facts and never about any other unexamined ones, then it will follow upon this usage that there is no inductive evidence for any generaliza-

---

8 *The Problems of Philosophy* (1912), p. 100.
9 *Enquiry*, Sect. IV, Pt. II (Selby-Bigge ed., p. 38).

tion or other inductive conclusion, for the precise reason that such evidence is a contradiction in terms. Having defined or otherwise fixed the usage of this key term "evidence" in such a way that it can be applied to facts or statements only if the facts or statements are not considered in reference to inductive conclusions and ceases to be applicable the moment they are so considered, one can conclude directly and necessarily that no facts or statements can ever be inductive evidence. That is, so long as they are considered in relation to inductive conclusions which might be based upon them, they cannot properly be called evidence.

Upon such principles one can proceed forthwith to deal sweepingly with all inductive inferences, all the various kinds that have been made and all those that remain possible, and to indict them all, without any attention to the specific methods they involve and the results they achieve, as lacking in evidence and validity. But it is the same principles which enable one to do this so sweepingly, with complete assurance that no inductive method can ever be devised and no inductive evidence procured that will jeopardize the conclusion, which also, when properly understood, rob these allegations of lack of evidence or validity, in so far as they are based upon such reasoning, of any sting. It requires little consideration for one to recognize that if a man defines the term "Republican" in such a way that in his usage it may be applied only to individuals and groups which are dominantly conservative and not liberal, then in this usage it will follow directly and sweepingly that all Republican individuals or groups must be conservative and can never be liberal. In this usage the conclusion follows convincingly enough, but considered as political analysis rather than an exercise in definition it is unimpressive. And it is hard to imagine anyone seriously believing that in such reasoning there is any good basis for judging the conservative or liberal characteristics of Republicans, as that name is employed in political thought and discussion in the United States, for affirming, for example, without attention to the evidence concerning the liberal phases of the history of the Republican Party, or to whatever evidence there may now be of possible future devotion to liberal principles by that group, that no Republican can be a liberal or can fail to be a conservative. And so it is readily apparent that if reasoning on principles of this same kind is what leads ineluctably to the conclusion that no inductive inference is supported by evidence, since the usage of the term "evidence" has been fixed in such a way that it applies to premises and facts only if they are not being employed as bases for inductive conclusions, there is no good basis therein for making any judgment concerning the soundness, trustworthiness, or credibility of any inductive conclusion. For the same reason upon which in this reasoning the conclusion is inescapable that there is no inductive evidence, since, as in the case of "liberal Republican," "evidence" is defined in the language in such a way that "inductive evidence" becomes a contradictory expression incapable of application, there is in the necessary conclusion no implication one way or the other concerning the question whether any inductive conclusion has been drawn by a trustworthy, reliable method, whether it is supported by a sufficient amount of factual information that it would be intelligent to accept rather than to deny it, or even to suspend judgment. Indeed the conclusion follows necessarily precisely because it is determined by the linguistic rules of usage for the expressions involved and hence conveys no such implication.

If a man were to define "water" in such a way that in order for anything to be water it must be a liquid, it would of course follow necessarily in his language that there is no water either in a solid or gaseous form. No sane person would however be induced by such a procedure to deny as illusory all the previous experience and knowledge he had of frozen or gaseous water, from ice cubes to icebergs, from teakettles to steam engines. While he would require no extensive examination of the matter to see the mistake in drawing skeptical conclusions from the reasoning, he might also, upon understanding the reasoning, be interested in why men should on occasion be led to seize upon and hold to such linguistic usages as render these conclusions inevitable. And turning now to the skeptical argument concerning inductive inference which has been under analysis, one finds that one important answer to questions of this kind is not difficult to discern.

Consider again the skeptical argument outlined above. The ground which it advances for holding that one cannot procure evidence of what the future will be by means of an examination of the present and past, or what the character of the unexamined instances is from the character of the examined ones, is that all the information which inductive testing provides is information about the present and past, or the examined, never about the future or the unexamined. Test ever so many A's; test ever so many other things the characteristics of which are relevant to the characteristics of A's; all that the testing tells one is about these examined facts, never about the other, unexamined facts about which the inductive conclusion speaks. Now obviously, whatever kind of inductive procedure one follows, he is restricted in his examining to what is examinable, in his testing to what is testable. And the reports which record the results of his testing or examining will then be reports of the character of the tested or examined facts. Let all this be granted; let it be granted (and how could it be otherwise?) that statements reporting the character of the examined instances or facts are always statements about the examined, and not about the unexamined. Why should this commit one to the further proposition, and it is very much a further one, that because these are reports of tested instances they are *evidence* only of the character of these tested ones and cannot be evidence concerning the untested ones?

The preceding analysis has already provided one answer to this question. It is that one is compelled, on pain of contradiction, in the above argument to say that the character of an examined fact, or a report thereof, is and can be evidence only concerning the character of the examined facts, and never about the character of any unexamined ones; and one is so compelled by the definitions or rules of language which have been adopted for the key term "evidence" and which, once adopted, forbid one to say otherwise. But this answer has in turn suggested a further question of why, in thinking about inductive inference, men can be and so frequently have been led to adopt usages for "evidence" and similar terms from which it follows that no inductive evidence can be affirmed without logical contradiction to exist. To ask, thus, for the reasons why in the above argument an examined instance, or a report thereof, can be evidence only concerning the examined instances, and never concerning the unexamined, and hence never concerning any inductive conclusion, is to ask indirectly, in these different words, for the sources of the preference of those who choose to employ these terms in such a way that the expression "inductive evidence," or the idea of such evidence, is determined to be a contradictory, impossible one.

One fundamental reason which becomes more and more evident as one pries further into the kind of argument in which these linguistic predispositions have their skeptical effect is that a principle which is being employed therein, in the deliberations concerning the unexamined and the examined, is a version of the same fundamental principle which was exposed earlier in this paper in the examination of the allegations that inductive inferences are incapable of justification by reason. They are not capable of justification by "reason," and an argument can be provided to substantiate this allegation, because reason, as applied to inference, is restricted to deduction. When this term is so restricted, it must follow that, since inductive inferences are not deductive, whatever name is given to their bases, it cannot be "reason." Whether these bases are good or bad, sound or unsound, and in what sense of "good" or "sound" any such affirmations can be made, is not decided by any such argument. Whatever their character, since the term "reason" is applicable to inferences only in so far as their basis is presumed to be deductive, no inductive inference is based on reason; in this specific sense none of them is justifiable by reason alone.

So, in reasoning concerning the observed and the unobserved, the examined and the unexamined, and so on, in inductive inferences, and the necessity, if the inference is to be well grounded, that there be evidence that the unexamined conform in some manner with the examined, the fundamental principle of criticism which is at work in the reasoning and, though implicit, appears to be at the root of the assurance that the necessary evidence is not inductively procurable, is that any alleged evidence procurable in this manner is not deductive. Again and again one is told, in reasonings of this kind, that inductive testing is restricted to the examined or past instances, which it obviously is, and that, because of this, inductive testing cannot by itself furnish the evidence, which is necessary for the grounding of the inductive conclusion, that the unexamined or future instances do conform with the tested ones. But why indeed cannot the past or examined instances themselves be, as they are sometimes regarded, evidence concerning the future or unexamined instances and the very character of resemblance with the former ones which is in question? It is because, so it is held, no conclusion concerning the unexamined cases can be drawn from premises which affirm or report solely concerning the character of the examined cases, as all inductively established premises are logically fated to do. But such conclusions have been drawn from such premises for thousands of years in human knowledge and experience and are constantly being drawn in ways which have yielded many valuable, reliable conclusions. What, therefore, does it mean to say that such conclusions cannot be drawn; and why can they not?

The chief clue to an answer to the first question lies in the answer to the second. The crucial reason for the contention that there is in principle an insuperable difficulty in drawing inductive conclusions from inductive premises alone, unsupported by some Principle of Induction, or of the Uniformity of Nature, and the like, is the incontestable fact that the unexamined cases of which the conclusion speaks are other than, numerically different from, the examined cases which are reported in the inductive premises. To say, however, that this fact is an insuperable difficulty in the drawing of inductive conclusions, that inductive premises by themselves, unsupported by some Principle of Induction which alone provides a reason for supposing some resemblance between the examined and the unexamined instances, give one no basis or reason for drawing any inductive conclusion, is implicitly to commit oneself to a very wide but now familiar assumption concerning what is a basis or reason for drawing a conclusion. To say that from such inductive premises alone it is not possible to draw inductive conclusions because of the fundamental fact that these are conclusions about instances which are not included in the class of the examined instances covered by the premises is in effect to adopt a criterion of possible inferences, conclusions, and evidence which is deductive in character and which in this dissimilar context mirrors the same deductivist linguistic presumptions which were revealed earlier in the analysis of the skeptical arguments expressed in terms of "reason" and "understanding," "habit" and "custom."

To be sure, the principle of criticism which is employed here, in accordance with which the only conclusions that are permitted to be drawn from premises are deductive and hence premises are evidence only for conclusions which can be drawn from them by a deductive process, does not appear thus explicitly and baldly in the skeptical argument about examined and unexamined instances, but functions rather as an implicit assumption, as a part of the basic skeleton of the argument. And like skeletal structures generally it is important for its most efficient functioning that it have its effects indirectly and that it remain submerged, not protruding above the surface. A good part of the persuasiveness of the argument employing this presumption consists in the manner in which the skeptical advantages, or disadvantages, are wrung from the principle without the principle itself appearing explicitly in the reasoning and challenging the critical examination which an explicit appearance of such a radical and sweeping principle would normally arouse. There is no doubt that such a principle, once accepted and employed, must make short work of the pretensions of any inductive argument to be supported by evidence, must condemn all inductive arguments of whatever variety, so long as they are not deductive, as equally and completely without evidence. And there is little doubt too that the traditional skeptical arguments about the future and the past, the unexamined and the examined, and the necessity, in reasoning inductively from the examined to the unexamined, of evidence concerning the similarity between these two types of instance or fact, owe much of their charm, persuasiveness, and sweeping effect to their capacity for inducing men, in their philosophizing about inductive inference, although not in their inferring, to accept such a principle for the criticism or evaluating of evidence.

From such a principle it follows directly that since only deductive evidence is genuine evidence, since only deductive conclusions follow from or have any support in their premises, all inductive conclusions, in so far as they are considered in relation to purely inductive evidence, unsupported by any principles that would make them follow deductively from these premises, are, simply because they are inductive and not deductive, without any evidence; the affirmation that there is such evidence has become, by virtue of this principle, a contradictory expression. To recognize this is to recognize that here also in the usages followed in the skeptical arguments concerning the examined and the unexamined are rationalist preconceptions of the type previously revealed in the analysis of the arguments concerning reason and habit, in accordance with which premises are evidence, reasons, or support only for conclusions which can be deduced from them. And in helping to establish that this is so, and in this way helping to dispel the misleading and devastating charm with which these arguments lead to skeptical perplexities about the deficiencies in the grounds of all inductive knowledge, philosophical analysis performs a valuable service, not only to the philosophy of knowledge, but also through it, to human enlightenment generally.

III

It is to be granted, then, as has been stated before, that in any inductive generalization one is restricted to examining the examinable and must hence, when the generalization is made, employ what he has learned in his study of these examined facts as a basis for his affirmation about the unexamined. It is to be granted too that in order for a generalization like this to be warranted there must be evidence, and indeed evidence of a degree sufficient for the circumstances, to permit one to pass from the tested character of the examined to the character of any other unexamined things about which the generalization affirms. If the conclusion, for example, is a generalization of the form "All A's are B," based upon a process of testing for B among various instances of A, this second requirement may be stated as follows: there must be evidence that the untested A's, actual or possible, do resemble the tested A's in respect to the posession of the character B.

According to the preceding analysis a good measure of the persuasiveness of the skeptical reasoning concerning the distinction between the tested and the untested in inductive generalization derives from the fact that it appears deceptively to do no more than draw sound logical conclusions from these two incontestable principles. Granted, it says in effect, that one's inductive testing is always restricted, when the conclusion is drawn, to what has been examined, that the reports of all the tested characters which constitute the inductive premises are reports concerning the character of the examined facts, this means that the inductive premises are information about, are evidence about, only the character of the examined facts, and thus by themselves are in principle incapable, no matter how derived, of furnishing one with evidence concerning any unexamined facts. One needs to know about the unexamined; but all one can learn, if one restricts himself to what there is evidence for, as distinguished from what all human beings in their inductive habits actually proceed to infer, is about the examined. This is the predicament and weakness of all human belief in so far as it rests upon inductive premises alone.

It is generally good practice, before adopting remedies, to make sure that the patient is sick. And the intention of the preceding analysis has been to call into question the peculiar, over-all, deadly malady which has been diagnosed by many philosophical physicians in the body of inductive knowledge and for which, since the time of Kant, they have been prescribing various remedies, some of them, in keeping with the desperate character of the alleged ailment, most extreme and odd. It is of course not to be denied that the patient in question is in many parts and organs not in the best of condition. Some of our inductive knowledge of matters of fact in the sciences, in the social studies and the humanities, and in practical life, suffers a need for improvement which is both great and acute; and there are in many areas serious, difficult problems concerning the proper inductive methods to be followed in achieving this improvement which seem to require for their solution liberal applications of intelligent analysis, effort, and trial. But in the case of this peculiar deadly malady which the patient is said to suffer in all his parts, despite any apparent signs of health and improvement in any of them, it seems that the tragic affirmations of disease and dissolution follow, at least in the diagnoses which have been herein analyzed, only because somehow the physicians have been led to employ an inappropriate criterion of health, a criterion in accordance with which no inductive organ or part can fail to be sick, because the usage of the terms "sick" and "healthy" has been fixed in such a way that "healthy" applies only to inferences and conclusions which are non-inductive, deductive ones. The diagnosis of the over-all weakness of inductive knowledge is a sign, then, not of the over-all deficiency of evidence for inductive conclusions, in all areas of experience and by whatever methods drawn, but of the deficiency of the language in which the grounds of inductive belief have been discussed and reasoned about, in which it is impossible to affirm without contradiction that inductive premises are ever evidence for their conclusions, are ever evidence, not only concerning the character of the examined facts of which they speak, but also concerning unexamined ones.

And now before leaving this analysis of the skeptical reasoning concerning the examined and the unexamined in inductive generalization it seems valuable, as well as congruent with the theme with which this essay began, to observe briefly how, in spite of its misemployment of the two fundamental principles concerning inductive inference, there is nevertheless in this reasoning a sound emphasis upon a very important point concerning inductive evidence which has been insufficiently appreciated. It is a point which is expressed very indirectly and somewhat obtusely in the reasoning, and must be regarded as a by-product or subsidiary intention of it, rather than one of its major intentions. Having now argued at length that the points which are its major intentions are mistaken and vitiated by logical confusion, a notice of this subsidiary one may serve as a helpful supplement to what has been previously said concerning the reasons for the attractiveness and persuasiveness of the reasoning in question and also concerning its merits as an expression of some genuine philosophical discrimination.

What this reasoning, though its skeptical claims be dismissed, may serve as a useful sign of is the fact that, as it is frequently conceived in philosophical reasonings concerning the bases of inductive inference, inductive evidence is restricted in a narrow, artificial fashion, and that as so restricted it is unquestionably deficient for the purposes in relation to which it is appraised. The tendency to view inductive evidence in this mistaken manner has been aided and abetted by the conceptions or language of "positive" and "negative instances," in which much of the analysis of inductive problems has been carried out, and by such typical questions which arise in the analysis, concerning the role of repeated positive instances in strengthening a generalization. What the skeptical reasoning says which is highly pertinent here is that, regardless of how extensive one's evidence is concerning the examined A's in the generalization, one still must have evidence concerning the unexamined ones which will ground the inference that because the examined A's are B, the unexamined ones are B likewise. That is to say, as it is typically put in the skeptical argument, there must *also* be evidence that the unexamined resemble the examined—this in addition to the evidence that the examined A's are uniformly B.

In a way and in an important way, as has already been observed, this is a thoroughly sound contention. In an inductive generalization that all A's are B, based upon an examination of a set of A's, one does need both these things, i.e., evidence that the examined A's are B, and also evidence that the unexamined A's resemble the examined in such a way that the uniform possession of B by the latter may be used as a model for affirming B universally of the A's. Now, if inductive evidence in a case like this is restricted to reports that a set of A's, numerous or few, has been examined and that all the members of the set do have the character B, then it is true that this inductive evidence by itself is deficient for the purpose of establishing the generalization. One does need to know more than this, as the skeptical reasoning so repetitiously, but not pointlessly, emphasizes. One needs evidence that the unexamined resemble the examined in such a way that if the examined A's are uniformly B, the unexamined ones are, or probably are, too. If therefore, one conceives inductive evidence in such a way as to exclude this, since it is indispensable to the soundness of the generalization, the inductive evidence as so conceived will necessarily be incapable of grounding or warranting the generalization. All one would know about, upon such limited evidence, would be the character of the examined A's; he could never affirm with good grounds concerning the unexamined.

The conclusion which the skeptical reasoning proceeds to draw from this sound hypothetical principle is that, *since* inductive evidence is so restricted, a generalization like this is never warranted upon purely inductive evidence. But a different moral which can be drawn by means of the same principle and which, on the basis of the preceding analysis appears to be far sounder, is that, if the restricting of inductive evidence leads one inevitably to the conclusion that generalizations like this, and, indeed, all inductive conclusions, are never warranted by their inductive evidence, then there is something wrong with the view of inductive evidence which this restricting expresses. If in setting out philosophically to understand the procedures and results of inductive generalization, scientific and otherwise, and the discriminations which can be made between sound and unsound inductive conclusions, this restricted conception of what inductive evidence must be fails so signally by leading to the sweeping and frustrating result that no such discriminations can be made and that hence there is no real difference between a hasty or weak inductive conclusion and a well-founded or strong one, then this result by itself, independently of the supporting results which the preceding analysis has now developed, seems to constitute a strong hint concerning the unsuitability of the conception of inductive evidence for these philosophical purposes. And taking this clue and turning then to the examination of inductive generalizations and inferences, as they are carried out and appraised, both in theoretical inquiry and in the conduct of practical affairs, one can begin to appreciate without difficulty how unrealistic it is to conceive of the inductive testing of the A's in the generalization that all A's are B as ascertaining only that the tested A's do or do not have this character.

Let it be admitted, then, that an inductive generalization that all A's are B is never warranted when it is supported only by inductive evidence that this, that, and other objects or events constituting a set of A's are at the same time B.[10] But with this admission should be coupled the reminder that, as inductive experience will testify, if consulted, fortunately in many cases which are the objects of our interest and curiosity, inductive inquiry and evidence is not restricted to the establishment of anything so meager as this. The establishment that there are these A's and that they are B is, to be sure, a typical feature of the testing and establishment of an inductive generalization of this kind.

---

[10] Readers familiar with Peirce will recognize here the main lineaments of what that author called a "Pooh-pooh Argument."

But to think of inductive testing as being limited to the ascertainment of this restricted information, to think of inductive evidence as the kind of information which could be provided by any detecting device capable of recording the proportion of AB's in the class of the examined A's, is to impoverish the conception of inductive evidence and rule out so much of it that doubts concerning its weight, and skepticism concerning its capacity to establish a conclusion, automatically follow.

One way of expressing what is left out of this conception of inductive evidence and what is of cardinal importance is that inductive testing is frequently, and typically in contexts and areas in which inductive methods are highly refined and have an achieved record of great reliability, a highly complex process such as can be engaged in effectively only by intelligent beings. Inductive testing of A's for the possible establishment that all A's are B in the developed sciences and practical arts requires more than sense organs and other instruments of observation; it is by no means a process of gaping at or intuiting A's or other facts, or of merely noting in the A's the presence or absence of the critical character B. On the contrary, the kind of testing of A's which distinguishes expert practice in the developed sciences and other established inductive arts is that in which one studies, examines, and, if he can, manipulates the A's in such a way as to lead them to disclose facts relevant to the occurrence of B which otherwise might not be revealed, and further, if he can, counts and measures those aspects of the situation which promise some illuminating result from the application of these techniques. In a vast variety of ways of manipulating, observing, investigating, measuring, calculating, and deducing, one seeks to discover, not just that a set of A's are B, but anything one can with the means appropriate to the significance and interest of the problem, concerning the characters A and B, the conditions of their occurrence, their variability, the way in which the tested A's have been or may be selected for testing, if selection is possible—in short anything which is relevant in a considerable degree to the question whether the A's which have been examined and found to be B may be regarded in this specific respect as typical of all A's and hence a proper model for the inductive generalization that they are all B.

It is a popular superstition, a kind of conventional pattern of thought and expression about inductive inference in the sciences, that the generalizing which leads to the formulation of laws and other general principles consists of a process of inferring that, because a uniform connection between characters, such as A and B, has manifested itself in all known cases of A, it may be affirmed to hold generally of all cases. Nothing, one is tempted to say, with perhaps pardonable exaggeration, is further from the truth. Naturally, the degree of assurance which is necessary to warrant the acceptance of an inductive conclusion varies from situation to situation in the sciences, as in everyday life, depending upon the importance of the conclusion, the seriousness of the consequences which would follow from a mistake, and other similar circumstances. But, speaking broadly, one of the things which distinguishes the inductive practice in the sciences from the crude *post hoc* inferences, so similar in their effects to those of mere conditioning, custom, or habit, is that in scientific practice, as in enlightened inductive practice generally, a report of such an observed uniformity by itself would not be regarded as a proof, but rather, if it is sufficiently interesting and important, as a sign of a problem. That all the reported A's have been uniformly B does not by itself establish the generalization that all A's are B. It does, however, in the absence of contravening evidence, suggest that they may be, the reported uniformity of the AB's thus constituting, not the end or conclusion of an inquiry, but a condition for beginning one and, by an inductive study of the A's and the character B, determining if possible whether the repeated uniform conjunction of A and B is an expression of a genuine, dependable uniformity in nature or only a striking coincidence.

When, in what circumstances, and in the employment of what methods is there sufficient evidence to warrant the conclusion that there is a genuine uniformity and that all A's are truly B? No attempt has been made in this paper to provide a positive answer to this complex question, which, speaking more accurately, does not even appear to be a question, but rather the form or schema of a question, when phrased so generally, an expression which itself asks nothing but which, when applied more particularly in specific contexts, does ask many important though various things. It has been argued, on the other hand, in the analysis of certain types of skeptical reasoning that this reasoning does not justify the contention that never, under any circumstances, is the inductive evidence sufficient to establish such a conclusion. On the positive side it has been observed that there is in this reasoning a sound and valuable emphasis that in an inductive generalization from the examined to the unexamined there must be evidence, not only concerning the character of the examined instances, but about the unexamined, about the relations between the latter and the former which permit one to infer the character of one from the tested character of the other. The skeptical reasoning concerning the examined and the unexamined does also show rightly that, whatever evidence inductive testing and reports of such testing provide for an inductive generalization, it is not deductive evidence for the generalization and that, consequently if in appraising this evidence one will be satisfied only with evidence of a deductive character, he must inevitably judge it to be deficient. It is by no means an oddity in the history of philosophical illumination and insight that the recognition of these sound philosophical points did not come in the form of an unmixed blessing, but came clothed in a language and buttressed with reasoning which seemed, to many, most persuasively and misleadingly, to be important chiefly because they established something else.

A Note on Probability

JOHN WISDOM

What is probability? In other words how are disputes about probability settled? Some one way, some another. But we want to know what these ways are, how they are connected with each other and with ways of settling disputes which are not about probability but, for example, about entailment.

Some disputes about the probability of q given p are a priori, that is, settleable provided only that one knows the language; others involve claims of fact. For example "Given that he is to be married in the next fortnight from today, Monday, and not on a day next a Sunday, what is the probability that he will be married on a Tuesday?" is an a priori question; but "What expectation of life has a butcher of 50?" is a question of fact. And the question "Given that he is to be married in the next fortnight from today, Monday, and not on a day next a Sunday, what is the probability that he will be married on a Tuesday?" is a question of fact whenever the answer is taken to depend on the frequency of marriages on the several days of the week.

Amongst these questions about probability which are questions of fact, some make a *definite* factual claim which if satisfied enables one to reach by a definite calculation a figure for the probability of q given p; others are concerned with a claim which is enormous and hazy and such that, though if it is satisfied a figure may be reached, this figure is not reached by arithmetical calculation. For example, a definite, limited claim is made by the statement "The expectation of life of a butcher of 50 is 10 years." For it says that there are facts of a certain sort which together with the fact that a man is a butcher of 50 give a probability of $\frac{1}{2}$ to his reaching the age of 60. The facts in question are records of the ages at death of butchers for the last n years and the probability is obtained by counting how many of them in these years, having reached 50, later reached 60 and how many did not. The question what, given the fact that a man is a butcher of 50 and these records, is the probability of his reaching 60 is an a priori question—it is settled by arithmetic.

A large, hazy, factual claim is made by "Liberty Light is a 66-to-1 chance for the Cambridgeshire." This means "There are ascertained facts which together with the fact that Liberty Light is running in the Cambridgeshire give a probability of 1 in 67 of his winning." Here the facts are anything that's relevant—form, pedigree, weight, conformation, whispers, physiology, biochemistry—nothing barred. The figure for the probability is not arrived at by arithmetic. (Of course a book maker may arrive at a figure by a calculation based on the bets that are coming in, like the totalisator does, but we are not considering that case.) Here we cannot complete the *statement* of the relevant facts; but the more nearly we do so, the more nearly a priori is a claim that, in view of these facts and the fact that Liberty Light is a runner, the proper odds to offer against him are 66-to-1.

It is this fact that we cannot state all the evidence and not the fact that the figure for the odds is not reached by calculation which prevents such assertions about probability being perfectly a priori. Given that all Englishmen are perfidious and that Jack is an Englishman the probability that Jack is perfidious is 100 per cent. This is an a priori truth, but the figure is not arrived at by calculation. In this case not only does p entail that the probability of q is what it is; it also entails q. With argument from past experience and present observation to the future, p does not entail q; indeed their connexion is of course contingent. But this leaves necessary the connexion between p, the incompletely stateable past experience plus the incompletely stateable present experience, and the statement "probably q," e.g., "66-to-1 against Liberty Light."

Amongst a priori questions of probability there are those cases where q entails p and the probability depends upon the nature of this entailment and those where it does not. Where q is the proposition that a certain man will reach the age of 60 and *p* the proposition that he is a butcher of 50 plus the actuarial records for the past ten years, *q* does not entail *p*, although *p* entails that *q* has the probability it has. Again where *q* is the proposition "A six *will* be uppermost *in a moment*" and *p* is the proposition that a die *is* falling plus records of, say, all past throws, *q* does not entail *p*. But where *q* is the proposition "A six will be uppermost in a moment" and *p* is the proposition "A die will have fallen in a moment" then *q* entails *p*. In such cases questions as to what probability *p* gives *q* are settled by considering how much *q* overentails *p*. *q* overentails *p* if *q* entails *p*, but *p* does not entail *q*. "This is red and hard" overentails "This is red." *r more* overentials *p* than does *q* if *r* overentails *q* and *q* overentails *r*. Thus "A six" more overentails "Either a six or a five or a four or a three or a two or a one" than does "Either a six or a five" and "Either a six or a five" more overentails "Either a six or a five or a four or a three or a two or a one" than does "Either a six or a five or a four," and so on; "He will be married next Sunday" overentails 7 to 1 "He will be married next week." "He will be married next Sunday or Monday" overentails 7 to 2 "He will be married next week." If we have an understanding as to how we count the alternatives in two propositions such as "A die has fallen" and "A number less than four is uppermost," we can have a rule for calculating a number measuring overentailment. We shall say *q* overentails *p* by *m* to *n* provided *p* is or is equivalent to an alternative proposition with *m* alternatives and *q* is or is equivalent to an alternative proposition made up of *n* of these same alternatives: "*q* overentails *p* by *m* to *n*" means the same as "the probability of *q* given *p* is $\frac{n}{m}$." Just as the peculiar logic of "*p* entails *q*" is brought out by explaining how its truth arises from the way *q* repeats *p*, i.e., by the equation "*p* entails *q*" = "*p* and *q* = *p*," so the peculiar logic of this class of statements of the form "*p* lends probability to *q*" is brought out by saying that in them "*p* lends probability to *q*" means "*p* or *q* = *p*."

It will be noticed that the examples chosen by mathematicians to reach the mode of settling probability claims of the last kind—I mean the examples of dice, balls in bags, etc.—have two features: (1) They incline us to confuse different sorts of probability claim, question, or dispute. (2) Because of this they explain why the mathematicians choose to use the words of their calculus as they do and to count alternatives as they do.

If one says "With a die the probability of a six is 1 in 6," one is right whether one intends this as (a) the tautology "A die has fallen" is over-entailed 6 to 1 by "A six is up" and is comparable to "He will be married next week" gives a probability of 1 in 7 to "He will be married next Tuesday"; or as (b) the statement of fact "In throws with dice to date the proportion of sixes has been 1 in 6"; or as (c) the statement of fact "All facts of nature observed to date give us no reason to expect one side of a die rather than another; that is, combined with the information that a die has fallen one side uppermost, all facts of nature give a probability of 1 in 6 to a six and, given the information that a die is in the air, they give a probability to a six negligibly less than 1 in 6, since though they give us no reason to expect one side of a die rather than another they give the best of reasons for expecting a die now in the air to fall and to fall one side uppermost and not poised on one corner."

Only when we set "With a die the probability of a six is 1 in 6" beside "With a man who is to be married next week the probability of his being married on a Tuesday is 1 in 7" do we realise how "With a die the probability of a six is 1 in 6" may be a tautology but also a summary of experience like "With a goat you can bet your life it'll get out however you fence it in." That there are two interpretations is obvious with "Given that a man is to be married next week the probability of his beeing married on Sunday is 1 in 7." We can easily see why the figure 1 in 7 is given; we can also easily realise that someone might insist on saying that the statement is false because records show that people seldom marry on Sunday. We can easily see how absurd would be a dispute between such a person and one who read off the probability from the number of days which a week is defined as having.

It is now possible to correct and explain the confused sentence I wrote in *Mind:* "A probability claim about the future cannot be a transformation of premises about the present and the past."[1] The statement "The probability of a butcher of 50 living another ten years is $\frac{1}{2}$" is a transformation from the actuarial records; and one who says "This man is a butcher of 50, the records run thus and thus, so the probability that this man will live another ten years is $\frac{1}{2}$" is making a purely deductive move. It follows that what I said was false.

---

[1] LVII (1948), 419.

What I ought to have said was this. "The idea that a claim of the form 'It is probable that such and such will happen' can be a transformation of data about the present and the past *in the way that* 'It is probable that *q*' is a transformation of '*p*' when *q* overentails *p*, is absurd." It is a corollary that the idea that a claim of the form "It is probable that such and such will happen" can be a transformation of premises about the present and the past in the way that "A six will be uppermost is probable to the degree 1 in 6" is a transformation of "A die will be lying with one side uppermost" is absurd. "A die is about to be thrown" or "A die is falling" does not *in this way* give the faintest probability to a six. This is obscured by the fact that the step from "A die is falling" to "A die will be lying with one side uppermost" is so very reasonable in the light of experience. The consequence is that, told that a die will be thrown a thousand times and asked what I will bet against a run of 6 sixes, I pass without notice that I do so from the given premiss to a new one "A die will fall a thousand times with one or other side uppermost and not come down poised on one corner or remain in the air." From the new premiss I arrive at proper odds for a bet by considering the ratio among those things, one or other of which it says will happen, which will give me a win to those that will make me lose—as I might consider whether it is advisable to play with a man who explains that he is about to throw a penny and that if it comes down heads he wins while if it comes down tails I lose.

Another, a different, fact conceals the absurdity of the idea that premises about the present and the past can give probability to a conclusion about the future in the way that has demonstration as a limit, i.e., as "A die will fall" gives probability to "A six will be uppermost." It is the fact that statements which appear to be about the present contain claims about the future. Thus suppose we stand before a house of three storeys and notice three bell buttons. We know that the top-storey bell is connected either with the top button, the middle button, or the lowest button. It seems a deduction in accordance with the ratio formulas that the probability of the top button being the right one, being the one connected with the top storey, is 1 in 3. We press the top button and a bell rings but not on the top storey, so we infer that the bell for the top storey is connected either with the middle button or with the bottom button; and it seems a deduction in accordance with the ratio formulas that the probability that it is connected with the bottom bell is now increased to 1 in 2. We press the middle button and

still the bell on the top storey doesn't ring so it is not connected with
the middle button. We now have premisses which seem to demonstrate
that the bell on the top storey is connected with the bottom button.

But the expression "*x* is connected with *y*" may mean "a wire links *x*
with *y*" and may mean "whenever *x* is pushed *y* rings." This
ambiguity is of no practical importance because experience makes it
so safe a step from the one to the other. But, if we are concerned to
describe the nature of the argument above, it is of great importance.
For if (1) in that argument expressions of the form "*x* is connected
with *y*" are employed in the same sense throughout, then our deductions as to probability are conducted in accordance with the ratio
formulae. But then also either (a) the conclusion means merely that
a wire links the bottom bell with the top storey and says nothing about
what will happen; or (b) the first premiss claims not merely that the
bell on the top storey is linked by a wire to either the top, the middle,
or the bottom button but that it is connected with one of these buttons
in the sense that whenever that button is pressed the bell rings, and
thus makes a concealed claim about the future.

And if (2) in the argument above expressions of the form "*x* is connected with *y*" are not used in the same sense throughout but are first
used to mean "A wire links *x* with *y*," so as to have premisses which
make no claim about the future, and then used to mean "Whenever *x*
is pushed *y* will ring," so as to have a conclusion which predicts the
future, then at that point in the argument where the sense is changed
a step is taken, which, though experience in this instance makes it safe,
is not in accordance with the ratio formulae.

There remain other sorts of probability claim, and one of these I
would like to mention. When we say "The expectation of life of a
butcher of 50 is such and such," we may, as we have said, be making a
claim only about past records, but also we *may* be making a claim not
only about past records but also about future records. In other words
we *may* so use this statement about the butcher that the mortality
among butchers *subsequent* to the statement we make is relevant to it.
If we do we may then say "It *seemed* that the probability was such and
such but in fact it was so-and-so." Thus in spite of Keynes, the Times
Racing Correspondent writes, May 28, 1936, "It seemed then all
Lombard Street to a China orange that Thankerton would win. For he
is by Manna a Derby winner, out of Verdict, the dam of Quashed.
Suddenly when all seemed over Thankerton began to stop."

Here the fatal word "seemed" speaks of the old model for expressing hopes and fears—one of the Fates holds high the balances in which the chances for us and against us lie; but what is in those balances we can never quite see.

Suggestions for Further Reading

I. Anthologies

Ayer, A. J., ed., *Logical Positivism.* Glencoe, Illinois: The Free Press, 1959. Includes a section on "Analytical Philosophy." A very full bibliography lists many writings by the authors of essays in the present collection.

Elton, William, ed., *Aesthetics and Language.* New York: Philosophical Library, Inc., 1954. Essays that "diagnose and clarify some aesthetic confusions" that are held to be "mainly linguistic in origin."

Flew, A. G. N., ed., *Essays on Logic and Language. First and Second Series.* New York: Philosophical Library, Inc., 1951, 1953. The editor provides extensive introductions to these valuable collections of some of the most famous analytical essays of the past two decades.

———, ed., *Essays in Conceptual Analysis.* New York: St. Martins Press, 1956. A sequel to the two previous collections, showing an interesting shift to problems of philosophy of science and metaphysics.

Flew, A. G. N. and Alasdair MacIntyre, eds., *New Essays in Philosophical Theology.* New York: The Macmillan Company, Inc., 1956. Sixteen British philosophers discuss such problems as the existence of God, omnipotence, and the possibility of miracles.

Scheffler, Israel, ed., *Philosophy and Education.* Boston: Allyn and Bacon, Inc., 1958. A notable attempt "to present current philosophical methods in application to educational problems."

Melden, A. I., ed., *Essays in Moral Philosophy.* Seattle: University of Washington Press, 1958. Eight original essays on specific problems in moral philosophy.

II. Historical Background

Passmore, John, *A Hundred Years of Philosophy.* New York: The Macmillan Company, Inc., 1957. A masterly and admirably comprehensive survey.

Urmson, J. O., *Philosophical Analysis: Its Development Between the Two World Wars.* New York: Oxford University Press, 1956. A useful brief account of the influence of "logical atomism" on the work of Russell and the younger Wittgenstein.

Warnock, G. J., *English Philosophy Since 1900.* New York: Oxford University Press, 1958. This book and the next are in the Home University Library series.

Warnock, Mary, *Ethics Since 1900.* New York: Oxford University Press, 1960.

III. Important Contributions to Method

Austin, J. L., *Philosophical Papers*. New York: Oxford University Press, 1961. The author's untimely death was a blow to analytical philosophy. His "A Plea for Excuses," included in this posthumous collection of his published writings, is an excellent defense of linguistic method in philosophy.

Geach, P. T. and Max Black, eds., *Translations from the Philosophical Writings of Gottlob Frege*. New York: Philosophical Library, Inc., 1952. After long and unpardonable neglect, Frege's extraordinary achievements are exerting growing influence on contemporary philosophy.

Moore, G. E., *Philosophical Papers*. New York: The Macmillan Company, Inc., 1959. This posthumous collection contains the famous and very important essay, "A Defence of Common Sense."

Wittgenstein, Ludwig, *The Blue and Brown Books*. New York: Harper & Row, Publishers, 1958. Originally prepared as notes for Wittgenstein's students, they are the best introduction to the work of a man whose influence upon modern philosophy has been profound.

————, *Philosophical Investigations*. New York: The Macmillan Company, Inc., 1953. The masterpiece of a great original thinker.

Notes on the Authors

Note: The following contributors have written numerous papers in such philosophical journals as *Mind, The Philosophical Review, The Proceedings of the Aristotelian Society, Analysis,* etc. Only books are listed below.

ALICE AMBROSE (Mrs. Morris Lazerowitz) (1906—   ), Professor of Philosophy at Smith College. Co-author with Morris Lazerowitz of *Fundamentals of Symbolic Logic* (1948) and *Logic: The Theory of Formal Inference* (1961). Co-editor of *The Journal of Symbolic Logic* since 1952.

G. E. M. ANSCOMBE (Mrs. P. T. Geach) (1919—   ), Research Fellow and Lecturer in Philosophy at Somerville College, Oxford. *Intention* (1957), *An Introduction to Wittgenstein's Tractatus* (1959), *Three Philosophers* (with P. T. Geach) (1961). She has translated Wittgenstein's writings.

A. J. AYER (1910—   ), Wykeham Professor of Philosophy at the University of Oxford. *Language, Truth and Logic* (1936, revised ed. 1946), *The Foundations of Empirical Knowledge* (1940), *Philosophical Essays* (1954), *The Problem of Empirical Knowledge* (1956).

MAX BLACK (1909—   ), Professor of Philosophy at Cornell University. *The Nature of Mathematics* (1933), *Critical Thinking* (1946, revised ed. 1950), *Language and Philosophy* (1949), *Problems of Analysis* (1954), *Models and Metaphors* (1962).

O. K. BOUWSMA (1898—   ), Professor of Philosophy at the University of Nebraska.

RODERICK M. CHISHOLM (1916—   ), Elton Professor of Natural Theology at Brown University. *Perceiving: A Philosophical Study* (1957).

HERBERT FEIGL (1902—   ), Professor of Philosophy at the University of Minnesota and Director, Minnesota Center for Philosophy of Science.

WILLIAM K. FRANKENA (1908—   ), Professor of Philosophy, University of Michigan.

MORRIS LAZEROWITZ (1907—   ), Professor of Philosophy, Smith College. *Fundamentals of Symbolic Logic* (with Alice Ambrose) (1948), *The Structure of Metaphysics* (1955), *Logic: The Theory of Formal Inference* (with Alice Ambrose) (1961).

C. LEWY (1919—   ), Fellow of Trinity College, Cambridge, and Sidgwick Lecturer in Moral Science in the University of Cambridge.

MARGARET MACDONALD, at the time of her death in 1956 was Reader in Philosophy at Bedford College in the University of London. She had been editor of *Analysis* since 1950.

C. A. MACE (1894—   ), Emeritus Professor of Psychology, Birkbeck College, University of London. *The Psychology of Study* (1932), *The Principles of Logic* (1933).

NORMAN MALCOLM (1908—   ), Professor of Philosophy at Cornell University. *Ludwig Wittgenstein: A Memoir* (1958), *Dreaming* (1959).

PAUL MARHENKE (1899–1952), was Professor of Philosophy at the University of California (Berkeley).

GILBERT RYLE (1900—   ), Waynflete Professor of Metaphysical Philosophy in the University of Oxford. *The Concept of Mind* (1949), *Dilemmas* (1954). Editor of *Mind* since 1948.

CHARLES L. STEVENSON (1908—   ), Professor of Philosophy at the University of Michigan. *Ethics and Language* (1944).

FREDERICK L. WILL (1909—   ), Professor of Philosophy, University of Illinois.

JOHN WISDOM (1904—   ), Professor of Philosophy at the University of Cambridge, *Problems of Mind and Matter* (1934), *Other Minds* (1952), *Philosophy and Psycho-Analysis* (1953).

Index of Names

A

Alexander, Samuel, 108
Ambrose, Alice, 394
Aristotle, 47, 87, 107n, 116, 119, 166, 243
Austin, J. L., 395
Ayer, A. J., 2n, 100, 101, 169n, 204, 231, 280, 297-301, 394, 396

B

Bacon, Francis, 108n
Bar-Hillel, Y., 22n
Barnes, A. C., 352-355
Basson, A. H., 63n
Beardsley, M. C., 328n
Beethoven, Ludwig van, 321
Bellaigue, Camille, 357
Bergmann, G., 283n
Berkeley, George, 222, 223
Bernays, P., 14n
Beth, E., 14n
Black, M., 2n, 4n, 106n, 395, 396
Bouwsma, O. K., 106n, 396
Bradley, F. H., 166n
Braithwaite, R. B., 296
Brentano, F., 225, 226
Broad, C. D., 101, 128, 150n, 152, 156n, 162n, 289
Brouwer, L. E. J., 119
Burbage, Richard, 200

C

Campbell, C. A., 7n
Carnap, R., 12n, 22, 231, 236, 237, 238, 250, 275-277, 278, 281, 295
Carritt, E. F., 152n, 156n, 157, 159n, 160, 162n, 163n, 164n
Cézanne, Paul, 200
Chisholm, R. M., 396
Church, Alonzo, 23n
Claude (of Lorraine), 352, 354, 355

C (continued)

Coffey, P., 100n, 102n, 106n, 110n
Collingwood, R. G., 115n, 142
Constable, John, 200
Copilowish, I. M., 23
Croce, B., 96
Cunningham, G. W., 167n

D

Dante, 88
Dawes Hicks, G., 100n, 102n
Debussy, Claude, 357
Dennes, W. R., 140n
Descartes, René, 3, 4, 57, 58, 106n
Dewey, John, 101, 103n, 104n
Dionoges, 74, 75
Donatello, 321
Donne, John, 335, 346
Duhem, P., 120
Duncan-Jones, A. E., 2n

E

Elton, W., 394
Engels, F., 119
Ewing, A. C., 151, 155, 156-160

F

Farrell, B. A., 12n
Feigl, H., 129n, 133n, 147n, 396
Findlay, J., 12n
Flew, A. G. N., 394
Frege, G., 121, 194
Freud, Sigmund, 170

G

Garvin, L., 156n
Geach, P. T., 395
Gibson, James, 179n
Greco, El, 321

399